DATE DUE

JUL 0 9 2007	
GAYLORD	PRINTED IN U.S.A.

CURRENT PERSPECTIVES ON CRIMINAL BEHAVIOR

CONTRIBUTORS

Milton L. Barron

Abraham S. Blumberg

LaMar T. Empey

Gilbert Geis

Erich Goode

Walter B. Miller

Arthur Niederhoffer

Richard Quinney

Edward Sagarin

Thomas S. Szasz

Gus Tyler

Andrew Walker

Marvin E. Wolfgang

CURRENT PERSPECTIVES ON CRIMINAL BEHAVIOR

ORIGINAL ESSAYS ON CRIMINOLOGY

EDITED BY

ABRAHAM S. BLUMBERG

John Jay College, The City University of New York

ALFRED A. KNOPF ✦ NEW YORK

First Edition

987654321

Copyright © 1974 by Alfred A. Knopf, Inc.

Library of Congress Cataloging in Publication Data

Blumberg, Abraham S
  Current perspectives on criminal behavior.

  Bibliography: p.
  1. Crime and criminals—Addresses, essays, lectures. I. Title.
HV6028.B55   364   73-21527
ISBN 0-394-31123-X

Manufactured in the United States of America

Cover design by Lawrence Daniels & Friends, Inc.

PREFACE

Criminology as a discipline is virtually as old as sociology itself. The origins of modern criminology are rooted in the social and philosophical ferment of early-nineteenth-century Europe, at a time when Saint-Simon and Comte established a Positivist sociology that would scientifically reconstruct a society left in turmoil by industrial and political revolution. Positivism refers to the attempt to employ the same scientific methods of investigation that are utilized in the study of the physical world and to apply them to the study of the social world. Much of modern criminology is "positivist" in the sense that it purports to employ scientific methods of observation, classification, and the development of propositions of universal validity with respect to causation of crime, behavior systems, treatment, and so on. Many of the substantive issues and ideological controversies that constitute the subject matter of modern criminology were of concern to social philosophers and political reformers long before sociology came into being as a formal discipline. Plato, Aristotle, St. Thomas Aquinas, Hobbes, Locke, Montesquieu, Rousseau, Blackstone, Bentham, and Hegel are some of the theorists who have had a profound influence on a number of the areas we now consider to be within the province of criminology—the problem of order, crime and its relation to social structure, jurisprudence, alternative systems of social control, and penology.

Interest in these issues was generated by a need to understand the human situation through achieving an ultimate perspective with regard to man and his society. Even the early sociologists (and criminologists) were really trying to get at some very basic philosophical questions regarding man and society, which are basically unanswerable in coldly scientific terms. In retrospect, the end product of efforts to grasp the meaning of man's existence was not always grounded in social or historical reality, and too often failed to transcend personal ideological commitments. Much of modern criminology, however, is built upon the output of such European scholars of the 1830s as Adolphe Quetelet and A. M. Guerry, social statisticians who served as the methodological models for what was to become the Chicago ecological school. The work of numerous Europeans such as Gabriel Tarde, Cesare Lombroso, Enrico Ferri, Reffaelle Garofalo, Charles Goring, and William Bonger, to name only a few, have contributed immeasurably to American criminology. The currently fashionable anomie, opportunity, and labeling theories are in large measure inspired by the work of such figures as Marx and Durkheim. As a consequence, in criminology we are indeed "pygmies standing on the shoulders of giants."

The first department of sociology in the United States was organized at the University of Chicago in 1892. Many of the early sociologists possessed an almost puritanical disdain for cities, often equating urban areas with crime, vice, sin, and "social disorganization." Ironically, the academic excellence and prestige of our Chicago forerunners were established in large measure because of their research in the fields of crime and deviance within the context of an emerging urban sociology. The scholarly energy of the Chicago department, and its criminological orientation, are best exemplified by such works as W. I. Thomas, *The Unadjusted Girl* (1923); Nels Anderson, *The Hobo* (1923); Frederick M. Thrasher, *The Delinquent Gang* (1927); Harvey W. Zorbaugh, *The Gold Coast and the Slum* (1929); Clifford R. Shaw, *Delinquency Areas* (1929) and *The Jack Roller* (1930).

Despite a preeminent intellectual tradition featuring a procession of notable theorists, philosophers, and researchers spanning almost two centuries, criminology remains at best a somewhat nebulous, almost marginal specialty in sociology. Although there has been an infusion of funds in recent years in the fields of crime and delinquency (often under the guise of poverty, community action, or law and order training programs), which has stimulated new research, the prestige of criminology in the hierarchy of the sub-specialities of sociology remains problematic. Fields such as medical sociology, sociological theory, and demography, for example, continue to be accorded greater esteem within the profession. Criminology receives its greatest acceptance among undergraduate students who sense that its subject matter and many of its concerns are central to their lives and possibly to their future careers.

This favorable judgment is often transferred into a harsh assessment of the field upon review of the text materials available. Many students (and their professors) see criminology texts as generally standardized in format, content, and style. This is so to the extent that in almost all of them, approximately one-quarter to one-third of the material is devoted to a bewildering, disconnected variety of crime causation schema and theories. This material is often of marginal value except for its historical interest, or its illustration of some of the idiosyncrasies of our predecessors. Except for some of the relatively recent work, especially of younger criminologists, the traditional textbooks soft-pedal the political and economic processes that are involved in formulating, enacting, administering, and enforcing the criminal law. Another feature of most texts is the ritual obeisance to a specious value-neutral position, which is in reality a value-tainted stance because of the perfunctory acceptance of existing political and social arrangements as an almost immutable set of premises. Further, most texts are oriented toward a consensus-shared values view of society and tend to slight the conflict-coercion model of society.

However, a singular weakness of criminology's intellectual output is its veneration of a species of positivism, which in many instances amounts to no more than a vulgar scientism masquerading as the highly revered ideal of tough-minded quantification, especially in the areas of causation, treatment, and prevention. Science and scientism epitomize the American ethic of efficiency and its cult of pragmatism. Moreover, criminology, not unlike other behavioral disciplines, is caught up in method and often ignores moral and ethical issues. This has often been the case in connection with the enforcement and labeling processes; the criminalization of the weak and disprivileged; or the excesses of the "therapeutic state" (subjection to harmful drugs by way of experimentation, for example), in dealing with homosexuals and other sex offenders, alcoholism and other addictions, the mentally ill, and the very young.

Criminology has been insensitive to the threat to civil liberties found in such enforcement establishment measures as stop and frisk laws, no knock laws, preventive detention, police dossiers, and electronic surveillance. These and other strategies of repression are ostensibly employed in a war against crime, especially in connection with drug sellers and users, or with organized crime. The police state potential of these measures is underscored by the fact that they have been employed for political purposes wholly unrelated to the activities of the criminals for whom they were purportedly designed. In addition, mistaken no knock raids upon the homes of innocent victims in the course of the mindless pursuit of drug caches should alert us to some of the problems posed by these seemingly reasonable police measures that endanger every person's liberty and rights to freedom from intrusion.

The accuracy and reliability of our crime statistics have been further eroded by mounting evidence that our government is itself involved in a variety of criminal activities, including coercion, bribery, forgery, burglary, embezzlement, criminal electronic surveillance, larceny, destruction of evidence, criminal conspiracies to violate the civil rights of private citizens, and misprision of felony. But these crimes committed by our public officials are seldom accounted for by our official data-gathering agencies or crime control systems. The tragedy of the Watergate affair is not simply the constitutional crisis that it represents, but the question it calls forth as to our ultimate capacity to govern honorably in mass society.

This book aims to bring together in systematic fashion the urgent issues and problems that have provoked the most intense interest among criminologists, official policy makers, and students alike, because of their impact on the meaning and quality of life in America today. This work is not designed to be encyclopedic in scope. It is primarily policy- and issues-oriented, often employing a conflict-coercion model of our social system as a framework for analyzing the subject matter of criminology. In a number of instances the authors attempt to identify the group processes that define social reality and provide the basis for the political intervention that culminates in the categorization of behavior patterns as criminal or deviant. Through their research and professional experience, the authors of the individual articles have acquired an expertise in their respective areas of criminology that hopefully may prove as useful to the government policy maker as to the undergraduate student.

My opening article, "Crime and the Social Order," reviews the field through a brief synthesis of the historical, theoretical, and ideological controversies that have characterized criminology from its inception. My intention is to set the stage for the subsequent essays. Simultaneously, I have attempted to fill in some of the interstices between the other articles by dealing with some aspect of their subject matter.

Richard Quinney explores the concept of causality in criminology and questions a number of the assumptions regarding man and society of the discipline of criminology, as well as the criminal law. Utilizing a theoretical framework in the form of six propositions, Quinney attempts to establish the interrelationships between the phenomena that define crime (the laws, courts, police, and so forth) and the circumstances under which crime occurs.

Arthur Niederhoffer's article alerts us to the growing dangers to a free society posed by crime control agents who have moved far beyond the traditional activities formally designated as legitimate, socially acceptable procedures for police and other enforcement agencies. Repressive activities that are employed to achieve laudable goals of crime control have become so routine as to endanger all our other values. The war on crime does not justify the excesses that it produces and the assaults upon constitutional liberty that are perpetrated in its behalf.

Milton Barron examines in some detail the hierarchy of American values and concludes that they tend to produce the very behavior that we condemn as socially destructive—crime and deviance.

The five articles that follow are concerned with some of the crucial behavior systems that are of most general interest. Andrew Walker summarizes and updates the field of professional crime, with some predictions for possible future developments. Gilbert Geis defines the parameters of upperworld crime in historical, economic, and political terms, stressing the inherent methodological difficulties in assessing this phenomenon. Data collection in connection with upperworld crime is a tenuous enterprise at best, given the intervening variables of secrecy, the technology of the paper shredder, and political immunity. Edward Sagarin's article demonstrates the rather extraordinary application of the criminal sanction as it is employed in attempting to regulate the expression of human sexuality. In his explicit approach to a heretofore sensitive topic, Sagarin effectively utilizes case materials to demonstrate the futility and stupidity of demanding universal conformity to some mythical standard of conduct in areas that are often quite beyond the capacity and purposes of the criminal sanction. Erich Goode's essay is a searching summary of the sociological and legal issues posed by the problems of drugs and drug use, and is an important statement in the proliferating literature of this area of criminological inquiry. Gus Tyler documents the development of organized crime in America in terms of an ethnic succession approach—namely, history repeating itself, "playing out old scripts with new actors."

The two articles that follow demonstrate the convergence of trends and developments in three related phenomena—American youth gangs, the culture of violence, and the status problems of children and youth. Walter B. Miller presents an elaborate history, ethnography, and theoretic analysis of the juvenile gang. Relatively little of a precise, systematic nature has appeared on this subject in recent years. But the essay is especially significant now, since the gangs, which never really disappeared, have surfaced again in the media. Marvin E. Wolfgang reviews the problem of violence in American life and its implications for social policy; he concludes with some research recommendations.

The final articles discuss crime and social policy, with specific reference to the problems of criminal responsibility and treatment, and some proposals and prospects for crime control. These prospects offer but slight encouragement that we will achieve our objectives in terms of our present correctional structure. Thomas S. Szasz, who has done much to precipitate an agonizing reappraisal on the part of American psychiatry, critically reiterates the scientific, ethical, legal, and moral implications of the existing framework in which we operate in affirming or denying criminal responsibility. In the concluding article Lamar T. Empey outlines some of the more immediate tasks of criminal justice reform that must be taken in terms of intervention and prevention.

Obviously, any attempt to orchestrate the work of thirteen authors is beset with thorny intellectual problems. Hopefully this work will do more than simply review a field, but will arouse interest in and discussion of the issues. Should that occur, then we will have succeeded in our task, regardless of what judgments are made as to the particular approach of an author. Criminologists may differ vigorously as to the validity of some of the lines of argument developed in these essays, but the work must finally be assessed in terms of its usefulness in stimulating student interest and discussion.

Student and instructor alike will easily see that the thrust of this book is not always as sanguine as other texts that appear to assume that many of our dilemmas can be resolved within the limits of our present social and political structure. On the contrary, our present social system has certain pervasive ambivalences and reservations that impair its ability to provide the requisite measure of social and economic justice needed to deal with the problems of crime. The political and economic orders of our society are made up of powerful vested interests that tend to impose their definitions of social reality upon the rest of us in structuring the nature and limits as well as the solutions to specific problems of crime, deviance, and violence. It is one of our tasks as academics and intellectuals to resist such an imposition of distorted reality, myths, and misconceptions.

CONTENTS

CURRENT PERSPECTIVES ON CRIMINAL BEHAVIOR

I / CRIME AND THE SOCIAL ORDER

ABRAHAM S. BLUMBERG

CRIME AS A TRANSHISTORICAL PROBLEM

History is little more than a record of the crimes, follies, and misfortunes of mankind. The present profound concern with crime and violence is not unprecedented, and historians have assured us that our epoch is neither worse nor better than others in producing riots, corruption, gang warfare, social deviance, genocide, murder, and vigilantism. Early settlers in America engaged in fairly continuous law violation characterized by smuggling and illicit trade in firearms, liquor, and slaves.[1] In addition, the American experience has been characterized by racial, ethnic, religious, and class violence, beginning with Shays' Rebellion in 1787, an armed insurrection by debtor farmers against the merchants, politicians, and lawyers of the Massachusetts seaboard towns who were using the legislature and courts to levy high taxes, foreclose mortgages, and imprison the farmers for debt.

Another recurring phenomenon of class conflict and violence in American history is that of the revolt of an "in-between" class that is oppressed and exploited by a more privileged group from above and threatened by an emerging group from below. Examples of this are the cases of the Whiskey Rebellion of 1791–1794, in which the Scotch-Irish of Pennsylvania were "in-between" the Indians and the wealthy Quakers; the Know-Nothing riots, in which an urban, Protestant proletariat was "in-between" newly arrived Catholics and rich industrialists; and the Draft Riots of 1863, in which Irish Catholic workers were "in-between" blacks who had recently won their freedom and a Protestant aristocracy. Violence has been directed at religious groups such as the Catholics and Mormons. Racial violence, lynching, and related civil disorders, as well as widespread violation of laws involving the civil rights of blacks, and the violation of the prohibition laws and antitrust laws, have all contributed to an overall pattern of lawlessness in America.

However, the perspective of the historian, and attempts by the social sciences, especially criminology, to causally explain the phenomenon of crime, offer small comfort to the typical American, who has great anxiety about crime and lawlessness and crime in the streets. In a 1972 *Life* magazine survey of 43,000 readers approximating the national population distribution, 61 percent of the respondents felt unsafe on the streets of their community. In cities of over 500,000 the percentage of respondents who felt unsafe rose to 80 percent. Ominously, 30 percent indicated that they kept a gun for "self-defense." While admittedly not a scientifically drawn sample, this kind of response underscores the widespread apprehension about crime found in this country. And Emile Durkheim's comment that "crime is normal because a society exempt from it is utterly impossible" will not put at ease those who naively equate America's urban malaise with crime.

Crime waves and crises, as well as public and private hysteria about crime, have precipitated numerous legislative investigations and commissions of inquiry, and have launched anticrime crusades. Crime has become the subject of political campaign oratory, has received substantial media coverage, and has served as the theme of many films, novels, and plays. As culmination to such intense activity and discussion, President Lyndon B. Johnson established the President's Commission on Law Enforcement and Administration of Justice (popularly known as the Crime Commission), thereby effectively converting his "war on poverty" into a "war on crime." As a political tactic, its primary purpose was to defuse the issue of crime in the streets.[2]

A procession of presidential commissions followed, dealing with civil disorders, violence, obscenity and pornography, and marijuana. After a series of elaborate, expensive studies, these commissions made literally hundreds of recommendations, the overall effect of which was superficial changes in the legal and criminal justice system that would do little to create new or alternative political, social, or economic institutional arrangements. Apparently, an important consequence of governing by commission is to postpone any action in making basic changes, but at the same time create the illusion that you are at work on the problems at hand.

According to W. I. Thomas' axiom: "If men define situations as real, they are real in their consequences." Thus, if the "crime problem" is perceived as *the* urgent issue, other issues are relegated to a position of secondary importance in the structuring of our social priorities. In this sense the problem of crime becomes an ideological one in that it serves to conceal or distort the underlying reality of the social damage inflicted by such problems as a permanent inflation, chronic unemployment, the ever-widening gap between those earning high and low incomes, class conflict, a seemingly perpetual housing shortage, and environmental damage. These issues are given a marginal sense of importance.

The measure of our commitment to vital public services is best understood in terms of our federal budgetary allocations. For the fiscal year ending June 30, 1971, federal budgetary outlays totaled $211.6 billion; of this, the sum spent on community development and housing was $3.4 billion; on the protection of national resources, pollution abatement, and flood control, $2.7 billion; on education and manpower training, $8.6 billion.[3] In contrast, the criminal justice system (police, prosecution offices, courts, prisons, correction, probation and parole services), which consumed a combined expenditure by the federal, state, and local governments of $3.5 billion in 1960, received $10.1 billion in 1971, nearly triple the amount.[4]

This vast crime control enterprise, employing approximately 800,000 people, attempts to create the illusion that it is making a permanent contribution to the solution of the crime problem. One example quickly shatters the illusion. The area of penology alone employs about 150,000 persons, with a daily offender population of over 1,200,000, and a budget expenditure in excess of $1 billion annually.[5] Former Attorney General

Ramsey Clark reports that 95 percent of the money spent here is for pure custody. Five percent is spent for "rehabilitation" services!

Although great amounts have been spent on our crime control structure, from 1960 to 1970, crimes against property (burglary, larceny of $50 and over, and auto theft) rose 147 percent, and crimes of violence (murder, forcible rape, robbery, and aggravated assault) rose 126 percent. Nevertheless, the conventional wisdom appears to be that "more is better," in this instance more of the same appears to have been counterproductive.[6]

The vast organizational apparatus that has been created to establish legal norms, and to define, label, process, confine, and resocialize criminals and deviants, has become a powerful vested interest. The members of this system benefit from the existing structure in terms of money, power, and prestige; past definitions of their role and status act to confer upon them enormous social and political power over the rest of us. American traditions and culture support them as the legitimate agents to define right and wrong, justice and injustice, morality and immorality, the ethical and the unethical. They possess legal, administrative, legislative, and economic resources, cultural sanction, as well as access to the media in wielding power and influence in connection with any of the issues in their area of decision making. Finally, they resist and oppose meaningful change that would in any way make their jobs redundant, threaten their job security, or challenge the value and propriety of what they are doing.[7]

Law enforcement and crime control agencies are extremely defensive with regard to the ambit of their control and authority, and are most sensitive to their need to justify their budget requests. For example, as described by Howard S. Becker, the Marijuana Tax Act of 1937, rather than being simply the consequence of a moral crusade and shrewd moral entrepreneurship, was the consequence of a struggle by the Federal Bureau of Narcotics for survival in the hostile environment of the economic depression of the 1930s. During that period, decreasing budgetary appropriations threatened its survival. In order to increase its authority, the bureau sought new policing activities, such as the Marijuana Tax Act, to justify its level of funding and subsequently to increase it.[8] In summary,

. . . *vested interests in deviance may be political, religious, or psychic, rather than economic; in any case, even lacking such specific interests, systems of repressive control tend to foster the growth of an 'industry' geared to the official creation of deviance, with a complex organizational structure which strains toward self-perpetuation. They support a division of labor whose personnel depend for their livelihood on the continued supply of confirmed deviants.*[9]

THEORIES OF CRIME CAUSATION

Kingsley Davis has postulated that all sociologists, irrespective of their particular methodological and intellectual commitments, employ a functionalist approach in their study of society. Insofar as functional analysis assumes that a social system is organized to maintain its equilibrium, and that components in that system perform functions and meet requirements for that system's survival, "it is as broad as sociological analysis itself."[10] However, in the areas of crime and deviance, functional analysis cannot be the equivalent of sociological analysis because functionalists accept highly problematic official crime statistics as the starting point of their theories of crime, deviance, and delinquency.

Our official crime rates represent a somewhat distorted version of reality in that they are skewed in large measure to include the most visible offenses of the most marginal groups in our society—young males, the urban poor, nonwhite minorities, and those most vulnerable politically to control agency processing. Enforcement agencies generally seek out those offenses that are most accessible and manageable in terms of an agency's routine operations, and that are calculated to produce a robust set of figures to justify an agency's budget.

Using official rates, definitions, and conceptions of crime and deviance, functionalists view those aspects of society that promote stability of the system as functional (healthy) and those aspects that promote instability or disorganization as dysfunctional (pathological). This organismic view of society, which embodies a sick-well medical model of the social system, conveniently ignores that fact that the values that determine what is functional or dysfunctional are an end product of power. Becker has stated the problem as follows:

> *The question of what the purpose or goal (function) of a group is and, consequently, what things will help or hinder the achievement of that purpose, is very often a political question . . . it is likewise true that the questions of what rules are to be enforced, what behavior regarded as deviant, and which people labeled as outsiders must also be regarded as political. The functional view of deviance, by ignoring the political aspect of the phenomenon, limits our understanding.*[11]

Enrico Ferri, a pioneer in the field of criminology, postulated in his Law of Criminal Saturation that every society has a natural level of crime dependent on underlying social, historical, ecological, and demographic conditions. The debilitating routine of the production line of a factory[12] and the procedures of a criminal court[13] are replete with "work crimes" and deviant actions that are as essential to these systems as are the norms that supposedly structure their boundaries and govern their operations. All social systems are Janus-faced in that they simultaneously wear two masks—the normative rules and expectations as well as their universal patterned evasions in the form of crime and deviance.

Traditionally, criminologists have stressed causation. They have sought to develop comprehensive theories and typologies for classifying the etiology of criminal and deviant behavior. Emulating the model of the physical sciences, criminology has attempted to generate propositions of universal validity embodying comprehensive explanations of crime, but has failed in this effort. Because it draws so heavily on other disciplines for its perspectives on man, criminology has vacillated between a functionalist view of man as a follower of society's discipline through the internalization of and conformity with shared norms,[14] and a view of man the beast as embodied in Cesare Lombroso's "born criminal."

Despite the development of meaningful evidence that human beings are not inherently evil, and convincing indications that man himself is a product of accident, of biochemical and environmental contingency, fortuitousness, and uncertainty, devoid of any grand scheme or overall divine plan, criminologists continue to pursue causal explanations such as biological determinism in the form of somatotyping and XYY chromosome.

Criminological theory begins with the classical school in the Age of Reason of the late eighteenth century, which remains the bedrock of our criminal laws and their enforcement. The central ideas of the classical school, as embodied in the work of Cesare di Beccaria (1738–1794) and Jeremy Bentham (1748–1832), may be stated in the form of six propositions:

1. Crime involves a moral guilt or responsibility, because men possess free will, and are therefore able to will "right" or "wrong." Crimes should be punished not so much because they endanger the state, but because they endanger and infringe upon the rights of others.
2. The criminal sanction should be used sparingly, and only to prevent overt acts, not to support some vague standard of morality. In other words, crime must be defined in precise, legal terms.
3. The criminal laws should be applied equally to all members of society, regardless of rank, wealth, or class. Subsequently, an exemption from these sanctions was made for "children" and "lunatics."
4. Since man is essentially hedonistic, he seeks pleasure and avoids pain. Thus, a "felicific calculus" was employed, in which the pains and punishment meted out to offenders were to be so severe as to exceed the "pleasures" derived from the violation of the law.
5. Rational men would make a free choice as to whether or not to pursue a particular course of action. Having calculated that the punishment or pain that would be inflicted would be greater than the pleasures or profit that might be derived from the commission of a crime, they would be deterred from committing the offense.
6. The emphasis is on the crime, the deed—not the actor. At all times a presumption of innocence should prevail and strict rules of procedure should be applied so as to protect individuals from harsh and arbitrary actions of the state.

The classical school, in its reformist fervor, was able to influence the American and French revolutions in the firm establishment of the principle that there must be an explicit legal definition of conduct as criminal before it can be punished. These notions are incorporated in the legal maxims *nullum crimen sine lege* (no crime without law) and *nullum poene sine lege* (no punishment without law). The hard-nosed legalistic approach of the classicists, in terms of their emphasis on the free will of the actor and the mechanistic imposition of punishments based on vague concepts of a felicific calculus in order to achieve deterrence, still dominates our contemporary legal system and criminalization processes.

If the classicist notion of "free will" was a somewhat naive conception, then the "hard determinism"[15] of the Positivist school, which viewed man as essentially shaped by biochemical, psychological, and environmental forces, is an equally absurd and simplistic formulation. It reduces man to a kind of biochemical particle whose behavior can be tracked in the equivalent of the physicist's bubble chamber, demeaning his humanity.

Positive criminology rejects legal definitions of crime and the principle of deterrence and dismisses the idea that man possesses reason and free will. Also, it replaces punishment with "scientific treatment" of crime and the criminal. When, in a modern society, the features of punishment and deterrence of classicism are combined with the hard determinism and scientific treatment of Positivism, today's offender, in effect, receives the worst of both worlds. For example, the drug addict is confronted with the sanction of both the criminal and the therapeutic processes—the pains of imprisonment and/or therapy may be imposed by the state.[16] The development of a "therapeutic state" poses a threat in the case of mental illness when connected with criminal behavior. With its emphasis on individualizing offenders, treatment, the indeterminate sentence, and a multitude of psychiatric, psychological, casework, probation, and parole practitioners who are its agents, the therapeutic state of the Positivist school has dominated American criminology.

The work of Cesare Lombroso and his followers emphasized man, the actor in society, as a focus of research in criminology. Lombroso's major propositions about the criminal may be stated as follows:

1. Criminal tendencies are hereditary; criminals are a distinct type who possess such tendencies from birth.
2. Criminals are atavistic, that is, they revert to a more primitive type of man who can be recognized by such stigmata as a protruding jaw, an asymmetrical cranium, scanty beard, flattened nose, low sensitivity to pain, and large outstanding ears.
3. These stigmata enable us to identify the "criminal type."
4. Only under the most favorable conditions can such individuals avoid criminality.

Although Lombroso's conceptualization of the born criminal appears in retrospect to be preposterous, it does reappear in terms of genetic, psychobiological, and psychological theories, which are variations on a bad seed theme. Following the biological and constitutional determinism of Lombroso, later studies ineptly attempted to suggest that criminality was inherited. Among these were studies of identical and fraternal twins, comparison of family trees of prominent and notoriously deviant persons, and the factor of feeblemindedness as an inheritable variable producing criminality.[17] Other studies attempted to link constitutional and biological differences between criminals and noncriminals. The findings of these studies were unreliable and the research methods employed were at best suspect and of dubious validity. In one study Earnest A. Hooton concluded that "the primary cause of crime is biological inferiority,"[18] and in another Kretschmer developed a classification of body types as related to personality types and the incidence of psychosis.[19] However, neither of these studies established any relationship between biological characteristics and crime.

Subsequently, William H. Sheldon attempted to distinguish between criminals and noncriminals on the basis of three somatotypes: *endomorph*, a round, soft, body type; *mesomorph*, a physically active, muscular, body type; and *ectomorph*, a thin, fragile, body type. Sheldon attributed temperamental and psychiatric characteristics to each of these types. For example, the mesomorph was supposedly self-assertive and the ectomorph introverted. He concluded that these body types were inherited and that most of the delinquents he studied were mesomorphs.[20] Sheldon Glueck and Eleanor Glueck, utilizing Sheldon's somatotypes, found that approximately 60 percent of the delinquents they studied were of mesomorphic body build. However, they were reluctant to go as far as Sheldon in linking delinquency with this body type, and concluded that there is no unique delinquent personality, temperament, or physique.[21]

Biological determinism still persists in the hypothesis that the presence of an XYY chromosome in males predisposes them to violently aggressive behavior. However, clinicians, behavioral scientists, and courts have not been inclined to accept the validity of the rather speculative, fragmentary nature of the evidence here. Nonetheless, we can continue to expect periodic attempts to isolate some elusive biological variable to explain the cause of criminal behavior. Research to establish the validity of biological determinism, in part because of its appealing simplicity in resolving the nature-nurture controversy, will still go on.

Psychological-psychiatric determinism substitutes for biological determinism a psychological version of the stigmata or biological defects of the Lombrosian constitutional approach. Its central thesis is that a certain organization of human personality, developed entirely apart from any criminal subculture, predisposes the individual to crime or deviance. The psychoanalytic school of psychiatry illustrates how psychological "stigmata" are substituted for the biological indices. In the theory of the classical Freudianism, man at birth is an amorphous bundle of id impulses and instinctual destructive drives that must be repressed, sublimated, or otherwise properly socialized to enable the individual to live acceptably in society. In short, we are all born criminals, and crime and deviance are simply the antisocial expression of id impulses that have not been properly channeled, subdued, or modified in a socially desirable fashion.

Seymour Halleck develops four ways in which an individual adapts in order to achieve relief from an overwhelming sense of helplessness or hopelessness—*criminality, conformity, activism,* and *mental illness.* The stress that is induced by an individual's unwillingness to accept his powerlessness and perceived oppressions and restrictions pushes him into an extreme form of activism—that of criminality. In essence, the performance of a criminal act is a way of retaining one's "sanity."

Although many psychiatrists and psychologists cling to their neo-Lombrosian approach, research evidence has failed to support these theories. In conclusion, criminals and delinquents do not possess personality characteristics significantly different from the rest of the population, nor do they have greater degrees of psychoses, neuroses, and other disturbances than similarly matched samples of the noncriminal population.[22]

Along with biological determinism and psychological-psychiatric determinism, we have social determinism, which ranges from Marxism and its intellectual offshoots, anomie and opportunity theory, to differential association. According to Marx, crime was a product of the capitalist system of production and its accompanying exploitation; when the political state and a money economy disappeared, men would no longer be alienated, and crime would no longer exist. William A. Bonger, a Dutch sociologist, attributed criminality to the poverty and inequities of the class system which were an integral part of capitalism. Crime would cease to exist when the poverty, personal disorganization, and class distinctions produced by capitalism were eliminated.[23]

Robert K. Merton's anomie theory hangs heavily on the fact that modern urban-industrial societies stress the goals of material acquisition, achievement, and similar symbols of success, while simultaneously providing limited culturally approved institutional means for attaining these goals. Thus, a malintegration exists, that is, a disjunction between the culturally approved goals and the institutionally approved means for attaining them. The result is anomie, which is characterized by a strain that produces ruthless innovation (crime, deviance, delinquency) on the part of those cut off from success through legitimate means.[24]

Anomie theory is further refined by opportunity theory. Whereas anomie theory stresses differential access to goals of success by legitimate, culturally approved means, opportunity theory focuses on the fact that a similar differential access is also true in the relative availability of *illegitimate* means of attaining culturally approved goals. This in part accounts for the variety of deviant and criminal adaptations. The class system structures both the content of learning and the possible opportunities that constitute the differential access to both legitimate and illegitimate means.

There has been some rather trenchant criticism of anomie theory, only some of the major features of which can be included here:

1. Anomie theory assumes that crime and deviance are disproportionately

higher in the lower classes. This tends to ignore the differential handling and class bias of the enforcement and labeling processes.

2. The theory assumes that there is a pervasive, universal meaning as to what constitutes "illegitimate means." However, definitions of crime, deviance, and delinquency vary in both time and place.
3. Anomie theory does not explain the importance of deviant subcultures, group-related crime and deviance such as organized crime, and many forms of delinquent gang behavior.
4. The theory neglects completely the political nature of the crime control agencies that define and label crime and deviance.
5. The theory ignores the process of interaction that produces deviance, and does not deal with reference group pressures and identifications.
6. Finally, anomie theory oversimplifies the complex dynamics and etiology of drug addiction, alcoholism, mental disorder, and suicide.

Edwin H. Sutherland's theory of differential association, modified since its initial elaboration in 1939, is the most ambitious and comprehensive attempt to explain crime and deviance. The core of the theory is based on Gabriel Tarde's "imitation theory": criminal behavior results from the same processes as other forms of social behavior; it is the content of the learning process that is different. All patterns of behavior are learned through imitation, identification, and association with others. Criminality is learned in the course of intimate association and identification with criminal role models. Thus, the content of the learning accounts for the critical difference between the criminal and the noncriminal.[25]

Sutherland's explanation of criminal behavior is stated in the form of nine propositions, modified here for purposes of brevity:

1. Criminal behavior is learned and not inherited.
2. It is learned in interaction with others in a process of verbal communication and gestures.
3. Most of the learning occurs in intimate personal groups rather than through the mass media.
4. The learning includes techniques of committing crimes, as well as the motives, attitudes, and rationalizations involved.
5. Motives and drives are learned from definitions of the legal codes as favorable or unfavorable in terms of adherence to or violation of these codes.
6. A person becomes delinquent (or criminal) because more definitions favorable to violation of law are put forth than definitions unfavorable to violation of law.
7. Differential associations may vary in frequency, duration, priority, and intensity.
8. Learning criminal behavior by association with criminal and anticriminal patterns involves all the mechanisms involved in any other learning process.

9. Although criminal behavior is an expression of general needs and values, it is not explained by those needs and values, since noncriminal behavior is an expression of the same needs and values.

Despite a vast amount of research in differential association and anomie theory, it is virtually impossible to empirically measure the "associations" favorable or unfavorable to law violation. Further, differential association cannot account for the how and why of differential response to similar life situations. It is a closed system, in which the learning process is greatly oversimplified for purposes of making the theory internally logical and consistent.

One part of social determinism suggests that lower-class subcultures and value systems generate varying forms of deviance. Albert K. Cohen sees lower-class children as possessed of a value system that impairs their capacity to compete in a society dominated by middle-class values. The resulting social disabilities produce a "status frustration," generating a reaction formation to middle-class values. Lower-class children substitute values of their own that reverse the middle-class values. As a consequence, short-run hedonism and negativistic vandalism and violence are legitimated as measures of striking back at the larger society that produced their frustrations.[26]

Cohen describes the middle-class values that are supposedly rejected by the lower class: ambition; individual responsibility and self-reliance; achievements and the possession and cultivation of skills; the ability to postpone immediate satisfactions in the interest of achieving long-term goals; rationality, planning, foresight, and budgeting of time; the cultivation of manners, courtesy, patience and self-control, and the inhibition of spontaneity; control of physical aggression and violence; recreation employed in the development of new skills; respect for property and property rights.

There are, of course, a number of paradoxes present in the middle-class ethic, as well as ample evidence that middle-class norms are often shot through with inconsistency, evasion, and compromise. A few examples will illustrate this. Ambition is often augmented with nepotism and similar opportunity structures. The huge American consumer debt indicates that the middle class is not postponing gratification. Many middle-class jobs are dead ends, lack meaning or social utility, and produce deadly boredom. There is a widespread frenetic pursuit of leisure and the orgiastic experience among the middle class, including drugs forbidden to their children. The short-run hedonist of the lower class is the long-term sybarite of the middle and upper classes. Middle-class aggression ranges from threats of loss of love to bureaucratic violence.

The work of Walter B. Miller provides another example of how crime and delinquency are attributed to the tensions engendered by deviant subcultures whose values are said to be in conflict with those of the dominant culture.[27] The major aspects of his theory are embodied in three propositions: 1. The lower class is characterized by distinctive values. 2. These values are markedly different from the middle-class values that buttress the legal codes.

3. As a result, conformity with certain lower-class values will *automatically* define a lower-class person as being in violation of the law.

According to Miller, the focal concerns, values, or preoccupations that predispose the lower class to deviant behavior may be defined in terms of:

1. *Trouble:* a concern with keeping out of trouble rather than any commitment to the legal codes.
2. *Toughness:* a preoccupation with physical prowess, masculinity, and bravery as demonstrated by an absence of sentimentality.
3. *Smartness:* the ability to outsmart or "con" others, and to avoid being victimized in the same manner.
4. *Excitement:* the search for thrills and stimulation to relieve the monotony and tedium of life.
5. *Fate:* the quality of being "lucky" or "jinxed," of feeling you have no control over your life and are subject to forces beyond your control.
6. *Autonomy:* freedom from external constraint and from superordinate authority—independence.

According to Miller, lower-class youth have internalized the focal concerns of their subculture, but the control agents of the middle class enforce a middle-class code. Thus, efforts on the part of lower-class youth to conform to the values of their subculture bring them into conflict with agents of the middle class, and they are defined as delinquents.

Subculture theories and their dominant motifs of negativism, hedonism, fate, revenge, destructiveness, and alienation from the values of the larger society, are in reality inspired by the Nietzschean concept of ressentiment, which is based on the phenomenon of the value judgments of those who have been cheated in life, the weak masses who have been rejected, the disprivileged who desire vengeance. Because they are unable to will power—they will nothing, or at best the unreal world of religion. Max Scheler has defined the concept of ressentiment as a "self-poisoning of the mind . . . The emotions and affects primarily concerned are revenge, hatred, malice, envy, the impulse to detract and spite."[28]

Most American criminology is concerned with crime in working-class subcultures rather than with white-collar and corporate crime. Admittedly, it is easier to penetrate a street gang or the addict subculture than it is to observe a corporate board room or the Pentagon "situation room." As a consequence, we have yet to develop a criminology of what C. Wright Mills called "the higher immorality," commanders of power who constitute the corporate, political, military, and foreign policy elite.[29] Of great interest is the degree to which some of the focal concerns and values thought to be peculiar to delinquent subcultures overlap with values found among the upper-class elite of national security managers. Richard Barnet describes their behavior and world views in the following terms:

One of the first lessons a national security manager learns after a day in the bureaucratic climate of the Pentagon, State Department, White House, or CIA is that toughness is the most highly prized virtue . . . the "hairy chest syndrome." . . . To be "soft," that is, unbelligerent, compassionate, willing to settle for less, or simply repelled by mass homicide, is to be "irresponsible." Bureaucratic machismo is cultivated . . . gutsy . . . a free wheeling generalist. The most important way bureaucratic machismo manifests itself is in attitudes toward violence. . . . To demonstrate toughness, a national security manager must accept the use of violence as routine. Crises in which violence is to be used are treated in the national security bureaucracy as mere extensions of everyday life.[30]

Gresham Sykes and David Matza have described five techniques that delinquents employ to neutralize or even deny their responsibility for delinquent behavior. 1. The denial of personal responsibility. 2. The denial of harm to anyone. 3. The denial that the person injured or wronged is really a victim. 4. The condemnation of the condemners—"Society is much more corrupt than I am." 5. The holding of delinquent group or gang loyalties over loyalty to the norms of an impersonal society—defending one's turf, one's group and its values above the law and society.[31] These techniques of neutralization are used by delinquents of the upper-class elites as well as by members of deviant subcultures. For example, they have tried to explain away war crimes—"I was only following orders"; corporate irresponsibility in endangering consumers of their products—denial of the victim; and political corruption—"Society is more corrupt than I am." Furthermore, in-group loyalties of the corporate, legal, medical, and military professions are highly reminiscent of the Sykes-Matza delinquent group or gang loyalties that are said to supersede loyalty to society's norms and values.

What we are observing is a system of double entry moral bookkeeping. A member of the lower class who is engaged in short-run hedonism character-ized by negativistic acts is characterized as an antisocial thug. On the other hand, members of corporate and government elites, who act in the very framework of autonomy that the delinquent is said to seek and engage in similar behavior on a massive scale, are seen as thoughtful, responsible patriots. Merton has written of a "simple formula of moral alchemy: the same behavior must be differently evaluated according to the person who exhibits it . . . I am firm, Thou are obstinate, He is pigheaded."[32] Thus, from the viewpoint of the middle class: I am daring, You are reckless, He is delinquent. I am restrained, You are obsequious, He is cowardly. I am a realist, You are cynical, He is a paranoid. I am profound, You are polemical, He is pejorative.

Middle-class rationality that is functional for the acquiring of skills and achieving goals is also employed for destruction, exploitation, and the promotion of property values over human values. Moreover, the innumerable daily assaults, thefts, and culpable homicides that are committed by imper-sonal corporate conduct are not crimes that are generally feared by Ameri-cans. These antisocial and often criminal acts are perpetrated via poisoned air and water, adulterated food, dangerous drugs, and defective and shoddily manufactured consumer equipment. The average American's notion of crime is of "street crime"—crimes of violence involving robbery, rape, or burglary.

In summary, subcultural and cultural transmission theories of crime and deviance assign moral and social virtue to the middle and upper classes, while consigning the lower and working classes to high risks of delinquency as a virtual self-fulfilling prophecy.

LABELING THEORY

The Chicago school of sociology, with its latent mistrust of and ambivalence toward cities, perceived of crime and deviance as pathological phenomena consisting of assorted forms of vice and corruption, the consequences of poverty and social disorganization.[33] The functionalist has demolished the conception of crime and deviance as simply the products of individual pathology, and instead revealed the persistence and functionality of these seemingly aberrant behavior patterns in a social system over time. However, with the emergence of *labeling theory,* as developed during the decade of the 1960's by the neo-Chicago school, greater attention has been paid to the political variables in the creation of crime and deviance. Labeling theory recognizes that crime control agencies, in defining, locating, arresting, processing, and treating deviance, often precipitate or aggravate the very behavior society wishes to ameliorate. The core of the labeling approach is that deviance is a quality that is imposed upon individuals by more powerful "others," that it is conferred by audiences who witness the behavior, and that it is a consequence of societal reaction to certain behavior. Whereas the clinical interpretations of crime and deviance have concentrated on the actor, the labeling approach concentrates on the formal and informal law enforcement and control agents and tends to ignore the motives or intentions of the deviant. Overall, then, in the words of Emile Durkheim: ". . .we must not say that an action shocks the common conscience. We do not reprove it because it is a crime, but it is a crime because we reprove it."[34]

As might be expected, labeling theorists have been attacked for ignoring that violations of normative standards of conduct do in fact exist and that they are often voluntary. Their zeal in condemning the one-sided imposition of criminal and deviant labels on those in the lower classes and in emphasizing the villainy of crime control agents has also been criticized. Like the Lombrosian biological determinism, and psychological and social determinism, the labeling approach is a kind of social determinism described as "societal reaction." Whether an act or person is criminal or deviant depends upon whether or not interested publics and/or officials acting in their behalf react to the behavior. The theory does little to explain the phenomena of crime and deviance.

In the main, then, criminologists have emphasized the sources of criminal behavior in individual personality, biography, and biological and constitutional factors; in the stresses, dissonances, impact, and contingencies of social structure; or in combinations of these. For the most part, except for the socialist school and neo-Chicagoans, criminologists have underplayed or almost ignored the political and economic variables as sources of social conflict that contribute to crime or deviance. Criminological theory has, in part, failed to heed C. Wright Mills' insight that "whatever else he may be, man is a social and an historical actor who must be understood, if at all, in close and intricate interplay with social and historical structures."[35] The late George Jackson stated this aspect of the crime problem: "All criminals are victims of the attempt to maintain hierarchy. Any other conclusion denies original innocence, or in effect advances that men are criminals before they are born."[36]

Crime and deviance are simply kinds of social conflict that may arise in a polity along with civil uprisings, social movements, civil war, or traditional party politics. The manner in which the conflict will be defined and perceived will depend upon the amount of fear generated and the dimensions and power (political and economic) of the respective parties locked in conflict. See Table 1.

Table 1. Conflict Situations:[37] Dimensions of the Character and Relations of Parties in Conflict

POPULAR DEFINITION OF THE CONFLICT SITUATION	SIZE AND ORGANIZATION OF PARTY FEARED	ECONOMIC AND POLITICAL POWER OF PARTY FEARED RELATIVE TO THE FEARFUL PARTY	DEGREE TO WHICH THE WELL-ORGANIZED OPPOSING LARGE MINORITY OR MAJORITY FEELS FEARFUL OR THREATENED
Deviance	Individual or small, loosely organized groups	Almost none	Very high
Civil uprising or disorder	Small, loosely organized minority	Relatively low	Very high
Social movement	Sizable, organized minority	Relatively low	Mild
Civil war	Large, well-organized minority	Relatively high or almost equal	Very high
Mainstream party politics in the United States	Large, organized minority	About equal	Mild

DEFINITIONS OF CRIME AND DEVIANCE

Definitions of crime and deviance vary widely depending upon individual world views and methodological commitments, and have generated endless semantic and ideological quarrels. For example, Albert K. Cohen begins his study on deviance with this statement: "The subject of this book is knavery, skulduggery, cheating, unfairness, crime, sneakiness, malingering, cutting corners, immorality, dishonesty, betrayal, graft, corruption, wickedness, and sin—in short, deviance."[38] Other recent evaluations of deviance define it as conduct that exceeds community limits of tolerance. One definition asserts that "individual or group behavior is deviant if it falls within a class of behavior for which there is a probability of negative sanctions subsequent to its detection."[39] Elsewhere it is suggested that "behavior is deviant to the extent that it comes to be viewed as involving a personally discreditable departure from a group's normative expectations and it elicits interpersonal or collective reactions that serve to 'isolate,' 'treat,' 'correct,' or 'punish' individuals engaged in such behavior."[40]

This notion of discovery and sanction leads to the subject of so much controversy: What is a crime? and Who is criminal? The simplest, least equivocal response to these questions is the legalistic one. Criminal statutes or codes legally establish normative standards of conduct with accompanying sanctions for their breach. In order to be constitutionally valid, these codes must be definite and unambiguously clear in providing prescriptions of behavior an individual can adhere to in structuring his conduct. The legalistic response to "Who is a criminal?" would be, "Only those are criminals who have been adjudicated as such by the courts."[41] Although the criminal nature of such penal statutes as Sabbath blue laws, abortion laws, laws forbidding sale of contraceptives, and marijuana laws may not always be agreed upon, violation of these laws are nevertheless crimes.

Criminologists often err in defining crime and deviance in failing to recognize that various institutional settings have to employ rather different intellectual processes for defining and ordering that segment of social reality that is their concern. Thus, as a lawyer defending a client in a criminal case, I would be appalled by any other conception of reality than the strict construction of the meaning of legal norms and their application that is required by common law usage and the due process safeguards of the Constitution. Indeed, my client's very liberty would depend upon it. In fact, prosecutors frequently use a catchall conspiracy charge to avoid the strictures attached to proving a substantive criminal charge, since the charge of conspiracy is sufficiently vague as to almost defy definition.

A lawyer would be very interested in what occurs in police interrogation rooms and street patrol operations. His concern is motivated by his effort to establish whether the minimum standards of due process of law are being met with respect to his client. On the other hand, the criminologist is concerned with much more than the narrow legalistic focus. His scope widens to include the manner in which problematic aspects of police recruitment, training, organization, ideologies, and priorities in field operations affect actual police practices.

A police department's book of rules and the laws of arrest are merely beginning points for the criminologist's inquiry. His greater interests are in how matters affecting the police and their operations have an impact on the social and political structures of communities. A criminologist cannot be bound by the official and conventional definitions of law making, law breaking, and law enforcement. It is the essence of his job that he note and account for the disparities and differences between the official world and the real world as he finds it in his field research.

The Uniform Crime Reports and the penal codes are only a starting point for the criminologist's inquiry. He is not bound by them any more than a study of crime causation could be limited to a study of legislatures, although, in effect, legislatures cause crime through their formal enactments of penal codes. A paradigm of the range of human deviance has been suggested and is given in Table 2.

The freak category of deviance denotes a personal quality beyond the average range of human variation in physical, intellectual, or even moral dimensions. What is critical is the nature of the evaluation that is made of

Table 2. The Nature of Deviance[42]

TYPE OF DEVIANCE	EXAMPLE OF DEVIATION	NATURE OF NORMATIVE ORDER	NATURE OF DEVIATION
Freak	Midget, dwarf, or giant; ugly, fat, or disfigured person; mentally retarded person	Physical, physiological, and intellectual ideals	Aberrant in being
Sinful	Sinner, apostate, heretic, traitor	Religious or secular ideologies	Rejects orthodoxy
Criminal	Murderer, burglar, embezzler, addict	Legal codes	Unlawful in action
Sick	Psychotic, psychoneurotic	Cultural definitions or mental health	Aberrant in action
Alienated	Bum, tramp, suicide, hippie, bohemian	Cultural ends and/or means	Rejects dominant cultural values

the particular peculiarity in question. Some very obese persons are greatly rewarded as entertainers and are popular figures; others are shunned. Some giants are side show creatures; others are richly rewarded athletes. In the case of the freak, a negative evaluation of his particular qualities can have disastrous consequences. Similarly, sick states such as those involving mental illness will be viewed more readily in negative fashion than physical illness. However, certain physical illnesses such as epilepsy and tuberculosis are viewed just as negatively. In the case of mental illness, the individual's role performance is unreliable because of the severe symptoms that may be involved, such as the inability to cope with reality and/or acting-out behavior. [Both the freak and the sick person are victims of what Goffman has called "spoiled identity."]

The sinner, the heretic, and the apostate are variations of forms of transgressor in theocratic societies that find their counterparts in modern urban, secular societies. The sinner is one who now violates doctrinal norms that he has previously accepted. The heretic is one who rejects some or all the values and ideologies of a group; he is seen as more threatening to group solidarity than the sinner. The Apostate is a much more extreme deviant from official dogma who embraces an alien, hostile set of principles. Secular examples are the defector and the former communist, who are seen as "traitors."

Alienation as a form of deviation has received extensive treatment in sociological and philosophical literature. Five major variations of this concept have been put forth. First, in terms of *powerlessness:* the sensed inability of individuals to achieve the goals or outcomes they seek. Second, *meaninglessness:* individuals in their search for meaning are uncertain as to what they should believe. Powerlessness is the inability to *control* outcomes; meaninglessness, to *predict* outcomes. The intellectual is seen as one who can predict outcomes, but is unable to control them because he lacks political power. Third, *anomie:* the breakdown or weakening of normative systems so that actors either are no longer governed by the traditional moral values or are ambivalent toward them. Fourth, *isolation:* the individual feels isolated because of his rejection of or low regard for the dominant values and reward systems of his culture. Fifth, *estrangement:* in the attempt to exploit or use each other instrumentally men become estranged from each other. In time a full circle is made, and individuals become estranged from themselves. Self-alienation promotes groupthink, conformity, and personal insecurity, and emphasizes giving oneself over to appearances.[43]

Crime is a political and social phenomenon. By the standards of legal officialdom, behavior is considered a crime when it is characterized by five elements: 1. There must be an act, either of commission or omission. 2. There must be *mens rea* (evil intent or guilty state of mind). 3. The act must involve the violation of a specific legal norm or code. 4. There must be harm of some kind precipitated by the illegal behavior. 5. There must be a sanction or punishment of some kind imposed for the breach.

According to Turk, there are four major sources for the criminalization of behavior in society. Through the intervention of the legal and political process, normative expectations that measure, identify, detect, and control certain kinds of deviant behavior are imposed. These are moral indignation, legalism, response to threat, and political tactics. People characterized by *moral indignation* can be virtually equated with moral entrepreneurs, fervent reformers who want to help people "for their own good," or simply punitive types. *Legalism* is that portion of our value system that emphasizes rationality—coherence, order, certainty, the quest for rule of law; it focuses on society as an orderly system. *Response to threat* is the social system's inherent need to maintain order and stability and to survive. It is also a manifestation of politically powerful individuals attempting to retain their power, perquisites, and favorable definitions of their superior status. The source of criminalization found in *political tactics* is related to response to threat, in that it involves manipulation of the political apparatus of a society to benefit one group as against another. This source of criminalization reinforces the conflict elements that are inevitably present in defining "crime" and "the criminal," as well as who is to be designated as socially opprobrious or dangerous.[44]

TYPOLOGIES OF CRIME

Criminologists have developed a variety of typologies of crime, depending upon their particular methodological approach. For my purposes, modern crime may be said to exist at seven broad and distinct levels. The most profitable and least risky is *upperworld* crime—the least susceptible to the official enforcement machinery and only rarely represented in the Uniform Crime Reports of the F.B.I. Upperworld crime is carefully planned by wealthy corporations and by members of government. Quite often the participants view the criminal venture simply as shrewd business, calculated to produce a profit or to perform a "service" for the consumer, the voter, or some other constituency. Illustrations of upperworld crime include the "Great Electrical Conspiracy," involving General Electric and Westinghouse among others; the peculation of Billie Sol Estes and the activities of the corporate and federal officials without whose help he could not have succeeded in stealing millions; the activities of Bobby Baker; the frauds and larceny connected with the federal highway program; the corruption of public officials to avoid prosecution; and the cost overruns in military procurement, including the irresponsible production of military equipment, which, if not useless, may be dangerous to the consumer.

The marketing of harmful drugs is a further example of the highly profitable criminal activities that take place at the upperworld level. A particularly shocking case is the history of the marketing of a drug called MER/29, designed to reduce cholesterol levels. The drug manufacturer deliberately lied to the Food and Drug Administration by furnishing false data about the MER/29 studies on rats, monkeys, and dogs. Side effects of this dangerous drug after it had been marketed were found to include loss of hair, vaginal bleeding, cataracts, reduced spermatogenesis, loss of libido, and dermatitis. A deputy commissioner of the FDA conceded in 1962 that in retrospect the drug should not have been marketed. A twelve-count indictment against Richardson-Merrell, Inc., was resolved by a total of $80,000 in fines; and instead of the possible five years in prison and $10,000 fine that each of the individual defendants could have received, each was sentenced to six-months probation! Thus, an interesting feature of upperworld crime is that if the crime is not one of obvious violence, and if the defendants are white gentlemen of good background, their punishments are mild indeed.[45]

An important component of upperworld activities is consumer crime. It includes the social and physical harm inflicted upon the consumers of such products as unsafe automobiles, overpriced or dangerous drugs, and food additives that are carcinogenic. Also within this category are unfair credit, harmful pesticides, auto warranties that offer no protection, industrial pollution, microwave oven radiation, appliances designed to fail that require expensive repairs, household improvement rackets, and faulty heating devices, stoves, power mowers, and washing machines.

The federal government is itself one of the chief polluters of our waterways and the oceans. In addition, FDA standards of tolerance for filth in food astound one. "Filth allowances" in canned and processed foods for such items as rodent excreta, insect fragments, larvae, and rodent hairs are permitted, as long as these are present in allowable quantities. For example, in every eight ounces of chocolate 150 insect fragments and four rodent hairs are permitted; tomato juice is permitted no more than ten fruit fly eggs or two larvae per 100 grams. The frankfurter has become a national scandal as a food characterized by high fat, water, and bacteria content. The average frankfurter is 57 percent water, 26 percent fat, 13 percent protein, and 4 percent "other" ingredients. Also, U.S. Department of Agriculture standards allow the inclusion of esophagi, lips, snouts, ears, and other edible offal in sausage products. In the area of air pollution, one corporation alone, General Motors, is thought to produce over 30 percent of the tonnage of air pollutants.

The *Wall Street Journal* and *Consumer Reports* are often better sources on upperworld criminal activity than the official enforcement agencies such as the F.B.I., the FDA or the Antitrust Division of the Department of Justice. These agencies are quite ineffectual in dealing with the social harm ultimately inflicted by upperworld activities; prosecution of violators at this level is a relatively unusual occurrence.

Related to upperworld crime, especially at the level of the political machine, is *organized* crime. Local political machines, which ordinarily control local police and court officials, afford organized crime the protection it requires in order to function. Its activities cut across state lines and national boundaries and range from legitimate enterprises such as labor unions to illegal activities such as gambling, usury, drugs, pornography, and prostitution. Quite frankly, surmise and conjecture provide most of our knowledge about organized crime. However, we do know that at the moment, the F.B.I. and local enforcement agencies probably have more resources and undercover agents operating in student, black, and peace organizations, on campuses, and in pursuit of drug users than they have invested in studying the area of organized crime.

A major objective of organized criminals is similar to that of upperworld criminals—monopoly control of a particular activity. Despite the myths surrounding the Mafia or Cosa Nostra, organized crime in America is *not* the almost exclusive domain of Italian ethnics. In reality it is much more variegated, and cuts across racial and ethnic lines. Indeed, one might best study organized crime in terms of an ethnic succession theory, with organized crime seen as a ladder of mobility of disprivileged working class and underclass ethnics.

It is noteworthy that where organized crime is not trafficking in forbidden goods and services, it seeks out marginal and relatively undesirable legitimate business activities. Usually, these are ventures with hazardous investment and low profit potential at best. However, when organized crime becomes involved in these enterprises, it subjects them to monopoly control of distribution and price, and thus is able to make them profitable. In this perspective one can see the propensity of organized criminals to become involved in labor racketeering and to infiltrate meat processing and distribution, detergents, baking, fuel oil delivery, garbage collection, window washing, garment trucking and contracting, vending machines, and linen supplies.

The third, fourth, and fifth levels of crime are: violent personal crime, public order crime, and commonplace crime. These overlap to some degree in that there are points of congruence in the severity of societal reaction to the offenses that may be involved, the degree of susceptibility of a particular offense to the official enforcement machinery, and the nature of the social harm that ensues as a result of the behavior.

Violent personal crime refers to the most feared of offenses, such as homicide, assault, and rape. However, the criminal offense that stirs up the greatest degree of public reaction and is virtually equated with crime in the streets is robbery. Nationally the number of robberies from 1960 to 1969 rose 177 percent. Recent research indicates that the number of youth offenders in connection with robbery is somewhat exaggerated because of the greater vulnerability of the young to arrest. Of greater significance is the finding that blacks and members of other underclasses, with their feelings of relative deprivation and their rising expectations, have grown impatient with barriers to their social mobility and will not hesitate to use violent means such as robbery, employing "techniques of neutralization" by way of defense.[46]

In 1970 there were an estimated 15,810 murders committed in the United States. In 52 percent of these cases a handgun was used.[47] From 1960 through 1967, 411 police officers were killed in the course of their duties; in 96 percent of these attacks firearms were used. Of the ten assassination attempts on presidents or presidential candidates, all involved handguns except that on President Kennedy. Despite this, meaningful gun control in America remains a rather remote possibility.

Public order crime covers those categories of crime that are thought to offend the smooth functioning of what is thought to be the normative order of a society. Included here are the so-called victimless crimes of drug addiction, gambling, prostitution, drunkenness, abortion, homosexuality, and such offenses as disorderly conduct and vagrancy.

In victimless crimes there is technically no "victim." Because of the consensual nature and relative secrecy of these criminal transactions, there is no complainant. As a consequence, these offenses often generate illegal behavior and corruption on the part of the police in their zeal to enforce the unenforceable.

These offenders in turn commit much secondary crime in order to obtain the funds to purchase the goods or services made scarce by the enforcement process. Thus, the F.B.I. estimates that about one-third of the robbery, burglary, and larceny offenses during 1970 were drug related. In addition, harsh treatment of heroin users and relentless police action in attempting to deal with heroin use, simply drives the user to other dangerous sources of addiction such as barbiturates which are legally manufactured at the rate of billions of pills a year.

Of the 8,117,700 arrests in 1970, almost one-third of these were alcohol related (1,825,000 for drunkenness, 555,000 for driving while under the influence of alcohol).[48] Nevertheless, control agencies tend to soft pedal alcohol as the *real* addiction problem in America—perhaps because it is a vast industry. Alcohol is said to affect the lives of 9 million persons and to cost $10 billion in lost work time, and an additional $5 billion in health and welfare costs.

In the area of public order crime, enforcement agents make a considerable number of arrests and appear to accomplish the least by way of solutions to problems. In economic terms the rigid law and order approach is counter-productive. For example, in 1970 the New York City police estimated gambling to be a $236 million industry in that city. The department spent $6 million worth of manpower and resources to put it down; and the city spent an additional $2 million in court costs to process the cases, *but the fines collected by way of penalty added up to only $67,000!*[49]

Commonplace crime is the fifth level of crime. It is often the least remunerative and least protected, and is of the sort most readily available to those with a limited range of skills and circumscribed options for action. Crime at this level ranges from shoplifting to gang thefts. It is usually the most visible sort of criminal activity and therefore the most vulnerable to law enforcement. Included in this category are vandalism, auto theft, burglary, check forgery, petty thefts, and acts of fraud.

The "rip off," a commonplace crime, is not the sole province of vandalizing youth gangs of the lower strata. It is also a middle-class activity involving such behavior as students using recycled term papers and cheating on examinations and university professors using their relatives and friends as "consultants" on publicly funded projects. Various occupational crimes that may occur in the course of practicing such professions as law, medicine, dentistry, the military, or in academia have become endemic and quite properly belong in the category of *commonplace* crime. Sutherland's concept of white-collar crime has become highly problematic, if not completely archaic in describing the kinds of activity he contemplated: that of persons favorably situated in the social structure who commit crimes in the course of performing their professional and occupational roles, are relatively invulnerable to arrest, and do not think of themselves as criminals. The collars are no longer simply white, but also blue—and the concept is no longer accurate or particularly descriptive of reality. The rip off is closer to reality, assumes many guises and variations, and is endemic in that it cuts across all class, racial, and ethnic lines.

In pricing products or services, many industries allow for a percentage of theft on the part of their own employees, handlers and shippers, and customers as simply another cost incurred. Various forms of embezzlement, such as padding expense accounts, inventory thefts, kickbacks, and bribes, are seen by many employees as the only way to redress the balance of what they perceive to be inequities in their compensation, and to adjust other possible grievances. In New York City alone bribery is a routine part of the construction industry, amounting to $25 million annually. Contractors, architects, and construction foremen pay off building inspectors, highway department inspectors, policemen, state safety inspectors, agents of the Federal Housing Administration, clerks in a variety of municipal agencies, workers, and union officials.

The rip off assumes other configurations. Worker hostility engendered by the wearisome, mind-shattering routine of assembly line work has resulted in widespread sabotage of products, especially the automobile, as a form of protest against inhumane production conditions.

Another form of rip off in connection with the automobile is the "insurance job." This is often planned and executed by the car owner himself because of some dissatisfaction with mechanical or other defects in his vehicle. Angered owners of cars they consider to be "lemons" will "steal" their own autos by leaving them at points where they will be sure to be stolen, vandalized, or otherwise destroyed. The purpose of this is to collect the insurance money with which to make necessary repairs or to replace the car with which they were unhappy in the first instance.

The most egregious form of the rip off occurs when the state itself lends its aura of legitimacy and political power to effect the theft of lands of a powerless ethnic minority, as in the case of the middle Rio Grande Valley of northern New Mexico. During the period between 1880 and the 1930's, Spanish-Americans lost over 2 million acres of private land and 1.7 million acres of communal land, which had been guaranteed them under the 1848 Treaty of Guadalupe Hidalgo ending the Mexican-American War.[50]

Finally, it is saddest of all that the rip off in its various manifestations has not only become an institutionalized feature of American life, but that official socialization for it begins as early as the primary grades.

A sixth level of crime is *political* crime. Technically, espionage, sedition, and treason are the only political crimes explicitly recognized in our penal statutes. Obviously, other offenses have political overtones and implications (bombings, sabotage, flag desecrations, desertions, selective service violations, assassinations, and so on). But in the main, political crime is best understood in terms of the qualities individuals are thought to possess, rather than the deeds for which they have been condemned (Eugene V. Debs, Alger Hiss, Dr. Benjamin Spock, Daniel and Philip Berrigan).

In many instances the political criminal is not actually prosecuted for the real grievance harbored against him, but for a legalistic substitute; in the case of Alger Hiss, it was for perjury. In a broader sense all crimes may be seen as "political" in that the police, courts, and prisons are but administrative arms of a polity and its political apparatus, and its ideologies as embodied in the criminal laws. But true political crime is generally recognized to have at least these four characteristics:

1. The regime in power seeks to put down those who have led opposition to some aspect of its policies.
2. The arrest and trial of a person or group of persons is used as a warning to others not to engage in similar behavior involving political opposition.
3. Under the guise of prosecuting an individual or group of individuals for some substantive crime, the regime uses the criminal trial as a platform from which to discredit and stigmatize the holders of opposing political views and thereby to label them and their views as socially opprobrious.
4. The trial is an attempt to manage in theatrical fashion the public abasement of the defendant and/or his ideas. The primary objective being to anathematize his political position, rather than to simply convict him of a crime.

The seventh category of criminal activity is professional crime. The traditional definition of a professional criminal is one who derives a substantial portion of his income from illegal activities. He is a "professional" in the sense that he develops a set of skills and has a major commitment to criminal activity as a career. He is in a sense a businessman exchanging information, techniques, and economic opportunities with a circle of associates who are engaged in similar activities.

In the last decade the professional criminal has apparently shifted to become a generalist rather than a specialist in one sort of crime. Certain types of professional crime, such as safecracking, have almost become obsolete. Technology and the computer have threatened other types, such as check forgery. But because of his organizational ties, technical knowledge, and planning, the professional criminal remains relatively immune from the enforcement process when he commits such crimes as arson, hijacking, burglary, theft of securities, homicide, hustling, confidence games, credit card thefts, car thefts, stripping of autos, fencing stolen merchandise, and large-scale selling of drugs. The way of life of the professional criminal has been celebrated in the mass media in the genre of the "big caper" movie.

Table 3. Crime and Societal Reaction[51]

CRIMINAL BEHAVIOR SYSTEM	DEGREE OF VISIBILITY	SOCIETAL REACTION	NATURE OF SOCIETAL REACTION
Violent personal crime	High	High	Fear, strong disapproval, capital punishment, long imprisonment, desire for vengeance
Political crime			Strong disapproval, regarded as threat to society, prison, desire for vengeance
Commonplace crime			Arrest, jail, probation, institutionalization, parole, restitution, fines
Public order crime			Arrest, jail, fines, probation, stigmatization, "treatment," enforced hospitalization
Organized crime			Media clamor, but considerable public toleration; arrest and sentence rare
Professional crime			Most cases "fixed"; secretly admired and even envied, especially for a "big caper"
Upperworld crime	Low	Low	Indifference, monetary penalties, injunction, antitrust consent decree; seen as tough-minded, successful businessmen

In terms of our present perceptions about crime, the order of priorities as reflected by the amount of resources committed, our ideological perspectives, and the level of fear generated, a tentative paradigm of the degree of offense visibility and societal reaction is depicted in Table 3.

CONTROL STRATEGIES

The range of control strategies to deal with the variety of behavior patterns is very wide indeed. I suggest the following as a framework for our existing crime and deviance control system.

THE IMPACT OF SOCIAL CONTROL— A FRAMEWORK FOR ANALYSIS

Types of crime and deviance

1. Primary aberrance. Behavior patterns deemed to be contrary to the basic cultural norms, and therefore thought to be *male in se* (evil in themselves). Such behavior would include homicide, forcible rape, arson, robbery, kidnap, and conduct that outrages us, such as incest and cannibalism.
2. Defined or regulatory deviance. Behavior considered evil because it is forbidden *(mala prohibita)*. These activities generally fall within the domain of public order and morals legislation and include such offenses as gambling, drug abuse, pornography and obscenity, prostitution, homosexuality, traffic violations, and other activities deemed in some way to endanger the community and its interests.
3. Secondary and induced deviance. The additional crime and deviance produced as a result of the social reaction to and the enforcement of laws with respect to behavior indicated in 1. and 2.

Range of Control Strategies

1. No controls.
2. Social pressures of normative reference groups.
3. Religious controls and sanctions.
4. Formal education as socialization for submission to institutional control systems.
5. Market controls: the operations of economic and related market pressures and sanctions as a control device.
6. Treatment and resocialization: medical, psychiatric, and/or psychological conditioning, placement in a mental hospital.
7. Civil sanctions: injunctive relief, reparations, and restitution obtained through the civil courts.
8. Administrative sanctions: use of the state's police power to grant or deny a license in order to gain compliance.
9. Criminal sanctions: fines, imprisonment, release under probation or parole supervision, restitution, stigmatization, hospitalization in a mental institution for the criminally insane.
10. Elimination: life imprisonment, execution, deportation, assassination.

Intensity of Control

1. Absolute prohibition and enforcement.
2. Absolute prohibition and selective enforcement.
3. Prohibition and no enforcement.
4. Absolute freedom of action.

It is submitted that entirely too much has been relegated to the criminal sanction, and that a significant amount of seriously antisocial conduct is either subject to absolute prohibition and selective enforcement or prohibition and no enforcement. Too much administrative time and resources of our criminal process are devoted to areas not appropriately suited to the criminal sanction. The prosecution of these offenses—for example, gambling, vagrancy, drunkenness, disorderly conduct, prostitution, drug usage, and most so-called sex offenses—simply clog the channels of enforcement, relegating more serious conduct to a secondary priority.

Our laws, law enforcement agencies, and courts are in large measure geared to detecting, sorting out, and adjudicating the kinds of crimes and delinquencies most often and most visibly engaged in by the socially marginal strata. Candidates are selected for the adjudication process by well-defined limits imposed by the stratification system. The clients served by our enforcement agencies, criminal courts, and the public mental hospital, prison parole, and other "rehabilitation" systems are overwhelmingly drawn from segments of the lowest socioeconomic stratum.

While it is initially the lower class that bears the brunt of the erosion of the legal system's commitments to safeguard individual liberty, the trend will undoubtedly continue and intensify as the nation's capacity to cope with its problems falters. The mystique of law and order will be increasingly extolled as a panacea. This is best demonstrated by some recent trends and developments in the criminal process. The standard of "probable cause" as a basis for a police search and arrest has in effect been watered down to a lower standard of "reasonable suspicion" by stop-and-frisk laws. Police have now been given statutory and judicial support for what they had been doing anyway when they were fabricating "probable cause." In the frenzied pursuit of drug users and sellers, "no-knock" laws have afforded enforcement agents the privilege of breaking into dwellings under the guise of searching for illicit drugs. Widespread [illegal] bugging and wiretapping have become almost routine. Of interest is that out of 148,000 conversations overheard by federal agents with court permission during 1970, only forty-eight convictions resulted, mostly for gambling.

Rules of arrest, charge, and prosecution are quite meaningless in that they do not reflect the underlying reality of police behavior. Internal stresses and organizational environment contribute more to the nature and quality of police performance than do formal rules and legal etiquette.[52]

In the field of criminology we virtually ignore the vast network of almost unlimited surveillance that constitutes part of our crime control system. However, these activities engage more than 200,000 people in foreign and domestic intelligence; and the aggregate budget is conservatively estimated at approximately $5 billion. Domestic surveillance agencies can create dossiers on almost any person or group.

Upperworld corporate crime and organized crime have received slight attention from surveillance agencies, while a significant amount of manpower has been employed in building often useless files and dossiers on persons who have not and are not about to commit a crime. Indeed, in the field of domestic intelligence, there are, in addition to the F.B.I., twenty-six independent, noncooperating intelligence agencies, whose activities duplicate and frequently trip over each other; for example, Internal Revenue Service, Secret Service, General Accounting Office, Federal Power Commission. Resources and personnel are invested in building, maintaining, and disseminating files and dossiers, many of which contain dated, useless, irrelevant, and often unverified material. Much of this activity is busywork, performed simply to utilize available funds.[53]

In the enforcement and adjudication process today, the intolerably large caseloads of defendants in our criminal justice system encourage police, prosecution, and court personnel to be concerned largely with strategies that lead to a guilty plea. What has emerged is an institutionalized system of justice called "bargain justice," or justice by negotiation, in which 70 to 90 percent of the defendants plead guilty. The system of bargain justice is a contrived, synthetic, and perfunctory substitute for real justice in too many instances. Its routinized, almost mindless procedures and methods lend themselves too readily to favoritism, venality, coercion, and arbitrariness. The system is particularly susceptible to political manipulation. What pass for full, fair, and open hearings are in reality secret, superficial, and hasty negotiation sessions, rarely subject to review.

This system of administering justice has been underscored as a reasonable and proper procedure by the United States Supreme Court. The standard to be employed is whether the plea of guilty represents a voluntary and intelligent choice among the alternative courses open to the defendant.[54] What is conveniently overlooked is the unequal balance of resources and power between a defendant and the state; in the guilty plea process many defendants hardly make a "voluntary" choice. Coercion in all its subtle or savage forms is present in varying degrees at every stage of the proceeding. A more candid evaluation of the situation would undoubtedly find that the bargain system is simply the most efficacious manner of handling the many problems that have been shunted into the criminal process.

A grave problem is posed by the concept of preventive detention. For, how does one predict who will commit a crime that threatens life and limb? The

most serious constitutional shortcoming of the concept of preventive detention is that it seriously compromises any notion of a presumption of
innocence. Our bail laws are in effect an insidious form of preventive
detention, and there are well-organized efforts at the federal and local level to
formalize these procedures, which are ostensibly designed only for dangerous
offenders who are likely to commit crimes while on bail or parole.

Unless there is a major shift in our perceptions of problems and in our
emphases and priorities in our political and economic life, we cannot expect
present rates of violent crime and property offenses to decrease. On the
contrary, it has been suggested that despite the fact that the poor have
increased their share of the gross national product, a significant underclass
will continue to exist well into the 1980s, crowding the deteriorating cities
and spilling over into the suburbs.[55] As the GNP grows, property crimes will
probably increase, and as even more intense rising expectations develop,
crimes of violence in the form of robbery will, if anything, increase as well.

What will be the outcomes of such a direction? The elaboration of welfare
state benefits (health, housing, education), abundant consumerism, and a
meritocracy based on "credentials" are some results. These will be employed
as manipulatory devices, and access to them will be dependent upon the good
behavior of those who can be co-opted by terms set by the larger society and
its politically inspired control agents. What is new in this formulation is that
it will be a more consciously manipulative, managed society consisting of a
complex of warfare-welfare-industrial-communications–law enforcement
bureaucracies that will constitute the neodemocratic centralism of the new
authoritarian state. Hard-fisted, cybernetic control systems of policing,
rehabilitation, resocialization, computerization, preventive detention, and the
like will be reserved for underclass recalcitrants, criminals, unpopular
deviants, and similar uncooperative outcasts.

Obviously, although some of the elements of the foregoing patterns have
begun to manifest themselves, evidence of countertrends exists. For example,
there is mounting criticism from within the correctional system itself that the
present system of prisons and related modes of "rehabilitation" or punishment be abandoned for much more humane alternatives. In addition, the
death penalty as presently constituted has been declared unconstitutional as
cruel and unusual punishment.

TOWARD A MODERN CRIMINOLOGY

In the traditional idea of criminology five major areas are dealt with: (1)
conditions associated with the causes of crime; (2) the development and
interpretation of the criminal law; (3) the law enforcement process; (4) the
formal and informal operations of the criminal justice system; and (5)
penology and its various subsystems of punishment, imprisonment, and
resocialization.[56] However, modern criminology is more than that. Its very

subject matter places it at the heart of social and political ferment. Like its parent discipline, sociology, it is interested in the official and unofficial versions of events, the formal versus the informal power relations of organizational life. It is profoundly committed to going beyond the externals of social structure and the institutionally approved interpretation of events to the conditions it finds to be the operative reality. The criminologist engages in the debunking motif, unmasking men's pretensions. He is willing to accept as valid world views other than his own. While he is not averse to getting his hands dirty with data, at the same time, he must avoid becoming committed to the political or other interests of the group or institution he is studying.

Modern criminology is characterized by at least twelve properties:

1. It does not encapsulate itself within the traditional cul-de-sac of crime causation.
2. It is political: the realities of power and conflict over scarce resources are omnipresent in its assessment of criminological problems.
3. It neither identifies with the control agents nor glorifies the deviants they seek to control. It reveres personal values over property values.
4. It condemns a criminology that serves simply as the instrument of those who would manipulate social norms for their own private purposes or control with more sophisticated means of domination.
5. It is not bound by middle-class values and norms.
6. It is voluntaristic and rejects hard determinism or an "oversocialized conception of man" as pseudoscientific.
7. It views official crime statistics and definitions of crime with great skepticism, and as at best the mere point of beginning of research.[57]
8. It critically evaluates psychiatric, psychological, and social-psychological generalizations of such vague concepts as sociopath, emotional immaturity, weak superego, anomie, social disorganization, maladjustment, and mental illness.
9. It rejects the existing systems of prisons, mental hospitals, "treatment," and "rehabilitation" as unworkable and counterproductive in many instances.
10. Criminologists recognize that they constitute an interest group that seeks access to funds, resources, and official patronage of the very groups they wish to study, and that a price will be exacted for this institutional respectability.[58]
11. As a corollary to point 10., they recognize that they have a vested interest to some degree in existing social arrangements in that they share some of the benefits along with the police, prison, parole, probation, and other crime control functionaries.
12. Criminological research without some degree of partisanship or value bias is almost impossible.[59] But, on the other hand, it is immoral to seek to avoid responsibility for the uses to which the results of one's scientific research is put. The criminologist cannot be a handmaiden to repression and exploitation.

NOTES

1. See William M. Bowsky, "The Medieval Commune and Internal Violence: Police Power and Public Safety in Siena, 1287–1355," *American Historical Review,* 73 (October 1967), pp. 1–17; Herbert Asbury, *The Gangs of New York* (New York: Knopf, 1928); James McCague, *The Second Rebellion: The Story of the New York City Draft Riots of 1863* (New York: Dial, 1968); Hugh D. Graham and Ted R. Gurr, *The History of Violence in America* (New York: Bantam, 1969); Richard Hofstadter and Michael Wallace (eds.), *American Violence* (New York: Vintage, 1971); John J. Tobias, *Urban Crime in Victorian England* (New York: Schocken, 1972).

2. Isidore Silver, "Introduction," *The Challenge of Crime in a Free Society* (New York: Avon, 1968), pp. 17–36.

3. *Your Federal Income Tax, 1972* (Washington, D.C.: U.S. Treasury Department, Internal Revenue Service), p. 161.

4. "Combatting Crime—The Price Goes Up," *U.S. News and World Report,* June 5, 1972, p. 62.

5. President's Commission on Law Enforcement and Administration of Justice, *Task Force Report: Corrections* (Washington, D.C.: U.S. Government Printing Office, 1967), p. 1.

6. James Vorenberg, "The War on Crime: The First Five Years," *Atlantic Monthly* (May 1972), pp. 63–69.

7. Paul B. Horton and Gerald R. Leslie, *The Sociology of Social Problems,* 4th ed. (New York: Appleton-Century-Crofts, 1970), pp. 88–93.

8. Donald T. Dickson, "Bureaucracy and Morality: An Organizational Perspective on a Moral Crusade," *Social Problems,* 16 (Fall 1968), pp. 143–156.

9. Elliot P. Currie, "Crimes Without Criminals: Witchcraft and Its Control in Renaissance Europe," *Law and Society Review,* 3 (August 1968), p. 31; see also Walter D. Connor, "The Manufacture of Deviance: The Case of the Soviet Purge, 1936–1938," *American Sociological Review,* 37 (August 1972), pp. 403–413.

10. Kingsley Davis, "The Myth of Functional Analysis as a Special Method in Sociology and Anthropology," *American Sociological Review,* 24 (December 1959), p. 758.

11. Howard S. Becker, *Outsiders: Studies in the Sociology of Deviance* (New York: Free Press, 1963), p. 7.

12. Joseph Bensman and Israel Gerver, "Crime and Punishment in the Factory: The Function of Deviancy in Maintaining the Social System," *American Sociological Review,* 28 (August 1963), pp. 588–598.

13. Abraham S. Blumberg, *Criminal Justice* (Chicago: Quadrangle, 1970), pp. 83–86.

14. Dennis H. Wrong, "The Oversocialized Conception of Man in Modern Sociology," *American Sociological Review,* 26 (April 1961), pp. 183–193.

15. David Matza, *Delinquency and Drift* (New York: Wiley, 1964), pp. 5–12.

16. See Nicholas N. Kittrie, *The Right to Be Different: Deviance and Enforced Therapy* (Baltimore: Johns Hopkins Press, 1971).

17. Edwin H. Sutherland and Donald R. Cressey, *Criminology,* 8th ed. (Philadelphia: Lippincott, 1970), pp. 112–118.

18. Earnest A. Hooton, *Crime and the Man* (Cambridge, Mass.: Harvard University Press, 1939), p. 130.

19. Ernst Kretschmer, *Physique and Character* (London: Kegan Paul, Trench, Trubner, 1936).

20. William H. Sheldon, *The Varieties of Delinquent Youth* (New York: Harper, 1949).

21. Sheldon Glueck and Eleanor Glueck, *Unraveling Juvenile Delinquency* (New York: Commonwealth Fund, 1950), p. 221.

22. Karl F. Schuessler and Donald R. Cressey, "Personality Characteristics of Criminals," *American Journal of Sociology,* 55 (March 1950), pp. 476–484; Arthur P. Volkman, "A Matched Group Personality Comparison of Delinquent and Nondelinquent Juveniles," *Social Problems,* 6 (Winter 1959), pp. 238–245.

23. William A. Bonger, *Criminality and Economic Conditions* (Boston: Little, Brown, 1916).

24. Robert K. Merton, "Social Structure and Anomie" and "Continuities in the Theory of Social Structure and Anomie," in *Social Theory and Social Structure* (New York: Free Press, 1968), pp. 185–248.

25. Gabriel Tarde, *Penal Philosophy* (Boston: Little Brown, 1912).

26. Albert K. Cohen, *Delinquent Boys: The Culture of the Gang* (Chicago: Free Press, 1955).

27. Walter B. Miller, "Lower Class Culture as a Generating Milieu of Gang Delinquency," *Journal of Social Issues*, 14 (April 1958), pp. 5–19.

28. John R. Staude, *Max Scheler: An Intellectual Portrait* (New York: Free Press, 1967), p. 37.

29. C. Wright Mills, *The Power Elite* (New York: Oxford University Press, 1957), p. 361.

30. Richard Barnet, "The Game of Nations," *Harpers*, 243 (November 1971), pp. 53–59. The article is drawn from his book, *Roots of War* (New York: Atheneum, 1972).

31. Gresham Sykes and David Matza, "Techniques of Neutralization: A Theory of Delinquency," *American Sociological Review*, 22 (December 1957), pp. 664–670.

32. Merton, *op. cit.*, p. 482.

33. David Matza, *Becoming Deviant* (Englewood Cliffs, N.J.: Prentice-Hall, 1969), pp. 30–37, 71–73, 94–95.

34. Emile Durkheim, *The Division of Labor in Society* (New York: Free Press, 1964), p. 81.

35. C. Wright Mills, *The Sociological Imagination* (New York: Oxford University Press, 1959), p. 158.

36. Tad Szulc, "George Jackson Radicalizes the Brothers in Soledad and San Quentin," *New York Times Magazine*, August 1, 1971, p. 10.

37. John Lofland, *Deviance and Identity* (Englewood Cliffs, N.J.: Prentice-Hall, 1969), p. 15.

38. Albert K. Cohen, *Deviance and Control* (Englewood Cliffs, N.J.: Prentice-Hall, 1966), p. 1.

39. Donald J. Black and Albert J. Reiss, Jr., "Police Control of Juveniles," *American Sociological Review*, 35 (February 1970), p. 63.

40. Edwin M. Schur, *Labeling Deviant Behavior* (New York: Harper & Row, 1971), pp. 24–25.

41. Paul W. Tappan, "Who Is the Criminal?" *American Sociological Review*, 12 (February 1947), pp. 96–102.

42. Simon Dinitz, Russell R. Dynes, and Alfred C. Clarke, *Deviance: Studies in the Process of Stigmatization and Societal Reaction* (New York: Oxford University Press, 1969), pp. 13–18.

43. Melvin Seeman, "On the Meaning of Alienation," *American Sociological Review*, 24 (December 1959), pp. 783–791; see also Milovan Djilas, "On Alienation," *Encounter*, 36 (May 1971), pp. 8–15.

44. Austin T. Turk, *Legal Sanctioning and Social Control*, National Institute of Mental Health (Washington, D.C.: U.S. Government Printing Office, 1972), pp. 10–18.

45. Robert L. Heilbroner, *et al.*, *In the Name of Profit: Profiles in Corporate Irresponsibility* (Garden City, N.Y.: Doubleday, 1972), pp. 106–127.

46. John E. Conklin, *Robbery and the Criminal Justice System* (Philadelphia: Lippincott, 1972), pp. 10–38.

47. *Crime in the United States: Uniform Crime Reports, 1970* (Washington, D.C.: Department of Justice), pp. 7–8.

48. *Ibid.*, p. 119.

49. *New York Post*, November 5, 1971.

50. Clark S. Knowlton, "Violence in New Mexico: A Sociological Perspective," *California Law Review*, 58 (October 1970), pp. 1054–1084.

51. Adapted from Marshall B. Clinard and Richard Quinney (eds.), *Criminal Behavior Systems: A Typology* (New York: Holt, Rinehart & Winston, 1967), pp. 14–18.

52. See Arthur Niederhoffer, *Behind the Shield* (Garden City, N.Y.: Doubleday, 1967); Jerome H.

Skolnick, *Justice Without Trial* (New York: Wiley, 1966); Albert J. Reiss, Jr., *The Police and the Public* (New Haven, Conn.: Yale University Press, 1971); Paul Chevigny, *Cops and Rebels* (New York: Pantheon, 1972); James Q. Wilson, *Varieties of Police Behavior* (New York: Atheneum, 1971).

53. Victor S. Navasky, *Kennedy Justice* (New York: Atheneum, 1971), pp. 50–51; Thomas Powers, "The Government Is Watching," *Atlantic*, 230 (October 1972), pp. 51–63.

54. *Brady v. United States*, 397 U.S. 742 (1970); *Parker v. North Carolina*, 397 U.S. 790 (1970).

55. Lee Rainwater, "Post-1984 America," *Society*, 9 (February 1972), pp. 18–27.

56. Herbert A. Bloch and Gilbert Geis, *Man, Crime, and Society* (New York: Random House, 1970), p. 52.

57. Yale Kamisar, "How to Use, Abuse—and Fight Back with—Crime Statistics," *Oklahoma Law Review*, 25 (May 1972), pp. 239–258.

58. See Alvin W. Gouldner, "The Sociologist as Partisan: Sociology and the Welfare State," *American Sociologist*, 3 (May 1968), pp. 103–116.

59. Howard S. Becker, "Whose Side Are We On?" *Social Problems*, 14 (Winter 1967), pp. 239–247.

2 / THE SOCIAL REALITY OF CRIME

RICHARD QUINNEY

The history of criminology is filled with a multitude of "theories of crime." The beginning criminology student is thus likely to be overwhelmed by the number and variety of theories. One might well ask: If there are so many theories, and such disparity between them, do we really know anything about crime? What is the truth?

The great complexity of theoretical criminology is inevitable given the many different ways of approaching any phenomenon. Crime has therefore been explained in many diverse ways, according to different aspects of the phenomenon. Hence, there are theories that focus on the legal structure of crime; on the other hand there are theories aimed at either the individual offender or the social behavior of the criminal. And within each of these approaches, there are many different theories to explain the particular phenomena.

But the principal reason for the complexity of criminology is the fact that theories emerge from a wide and diverse range of underlying assumptions and modes of thought. It is according to these more pervasive concerns that criminology has developed. Criminological theory ultimately rests on metaphysical and political considerations. In the end it is this deeper structure that gives criminology its importance. The theories of crime that emerge have consequences for the kind of society we create.

THEORETICAL ASSUMPTIONS IN THE STUDY OF CRIME

All scientific enterprises are based on the faith that there is a knowable order in the universe. Science is thus a tautology: order is assumed and that assumption leads to the discovery of order. Furthermore, science has traditionally assumed a special kind of order: a *causal order*. The principle of causality has served as a foundation for all the sciences. Causality has been both a methodological device and a substantive theory of reality. Until fairly recent times the concept went unquestioned.

The objective of most of the theoretical explanation in criminology has been to find the "causes of crime." The search for the causes of crime continues to be a principal concern of criminologists.[1] All such efforts assume that phenomena can be divided into units, or variables, and that the variables can then be causally linked. The study of criminal behavior, for the most part, is devoted to establishing that an "A is the cause of B," B being crime and A being a social phenomenon, preferably some kind of pathology.

Modern thought in the philosophy of science, however, tends to either dispense with the concept of causation or use it with qualified meaning. In the physical sciences the concept of causation has lost much of its utility. What is occurring is a revision in the conception of the natural world and the relation of the observer to it. The basic challenge of modern physics to the principle of causality is in the idea that the very act of observing has an influence on that which is being observed.[2] Since causal statements depend upon a knowledge of the present state of a phenomenon in order to calculate the future state of another phenomenon, skepticism regarding the scientist's ability to objectively observe the present state of affairs casts doubt on the application of the law of causality.

The implication of modern philosphy is the rejection of the idea that science is a "copy of reality." Even that which many of us regard as real, such as atoms, are the *constructs* of the scientist. A philosopher of science expresses the important idea that reality is a construction rather than the perception of the observer:

Percepts are based on first person sense experience, while constructs are creations of our intellect. In my opinion there is no doubt that atoms, molecules, electrons belong to a theoretical conceptual reality created by our intellect and thus are constructs. It is doubtful, however, whether they are also percepts, belonging to the perceptual reality.[3]

The same may be true of causality: Causality is a construct that has been used by the scientist in an attempt to understand the world he or she experiences.

A danger that the social scientist must guard against in a reading of modern science is the temptation to imitate completely the scientific model of the physical sciences. There has been the tendency in the social sciences to copy the philosophical assumptions of the physical sciences as well as their particular methods and techniques. But how, then, is the concept of causation to be used in the social sciences, particularly in criminology? In addition to recognizing that causation is initially a construct, we must make a distinction between the physical world and the social world. The basic differences and the corresponding methods of investigation have been described by Alfred Schutz in the following way:

The world of nature, as explored by the natural scientist, does not "mean" anything to molecules, atoms, and electrons. But the observational field of the social scientist—social reality—has a specific meaning and relevance structure for the human beings living, acting, and thinking within it. By a series of common-sense constructs they have pre-selected and pre-interpreted this world which they experience as the reality of their daily lives. It is these thought objects of theirs which determine their behavior by motivating it. The thought objects constructed by the social scientist, in order to grasp this social reality, have to be founded upon the thought objects constructed by the common-sense thinking of men, living their daily life within their social world. Thus, the constructs of the social sciences are, so to speak, constructs of the second degree, that is, constructs of the constructs made by the actors on the social scene, whose behavior the social scientist has to observe and explain in accordance with the procedural rules of his science.[4]

Following this reasoning, it is important to make a distinction in the social sciences between *methodological causation* and *social causation.* This is essentially the approach MacIver took in his argument that the phenomena with which the social sciences deal exhibit a special kind of substantive causal process, different in significant respects from the causation of phenomena in the physical world.[5] Since social causation is a distinctive kind of causation, he continued, the methodology of the social sciences should be developed accordingly. MacIver maintained that there are a number of distinct levels of causal analysis. The social scientist, he insists, is concerned with the socio-psychological nexus of phenomena. The phenomena of interest to the sociologist are those arising out of the individual and collective "dynamic assessments." Since human beings are immersed in their strivings, purposes, and goals, the assessment of behavior by man must be a basic part of causal analysis. Man himself, as a conscious social being, is the agent of causation and, according to MacIver, must be so considered in the study of social behavior.

A similar argument has been advanced by Sorokin in an attempt to liberate sociology from the concepts and methods of the physical sciences.[6] After distinguishing between several forms of interconnections between socio-cultural phenomena, Sorokin concludes that most empirically grounded socio-cultural systems are bound together as causal-meaningful unities. Hence, for Sorokin and MacIver, as well as for some other social scientists, social causation may be conceived of as a special form of causation, one that combines methodological causation with substantive causation because of the nature of the social world that human beings construct.

Once realizing that the concept of causation must have a special meaning in the social sciences, *alternatives* to causal explanation can be considered. Causal explanation is only one form of explanation and cannot be equated with explanation in general.[7] Certainly when causal analysis is not appropriate for either methodological or substantive purposes, other forms of explanation should be used. Many of the important contributions in sociology have been presented in other than causal form, as empirical generalizations, classifications, statistical descriptions, probabilities, and developmental stages. Generally social scientists have been interested in social structure, the functioning of systems and their parts, regularities of behavior, patterns, and processes. All of these concerns have been pursued for the most part without the aid of cause-and-effect reasoning. It is obvious that there would be a science of human social behavior without the notion of causality.

Another explanatory approach available to criminology as an alternative to causative reasoning is the approach known as *existential phenomenology.* This approach takes human consciousness and its intended meanings as the proper locus for an understanding of social behavior. Drawing from the works of several scholars, Edward Tiryakian observes that "existential phenomenology applied to sociology seeks the *roots* of social existence."[8] Such an approach, a "sociology in depth" as Gurvitch has phrased it, attempts to get at the dynamic complexity of social reality not arrived at by the traditional scientific concepts and methods. Gurvitch has suggested that the surface of the readily observable may be penetrated through the analysis of various depth levels, ranging from the ecological surface to the collective mentality.[9] Existential phenomenology has the promise of providing a method and a body of concepts for the substantive analysis of the wholeness of social phenomena and the processes by which social phenomena become, change, and possibly disintegrate all in respect to man's subjective awareness of his own and others' actions.

There is one other form of explanation that is qualitatively different from all the rest. Rather than attempting merely to describe the existing order, the purpose is to understand what *is* in terms of what *could be.*[10] This involves a *dialectical* form of thought, which allows us to examine all the contradictions in social existence. In being able to *critically* understand existing conditions, we can suggest ways of thinking and acting that will allow for a new existence.

Thus in the development of a critical Marxian explanation of crime the notion of causality can be dispensed with. Our concern, instead, is with the encounter between the objective world and our imagination in understanding it. The concept of causation (whether as substance or method) tends to obscure the true meaning of crime in American society. By eliminating the concept of crime from our explanation, we cease to reify the meaning of crime. The purpose of our theory, then, is to provide the ideas for correct thought and action. Only with a critical theory are we able to adequately understand crime in American society.

THE SOCIAL REALITY OF CRIME

Much of what we have been discussing thus far in theoretical criminology can be summarized in the form of a theory of the *social reality of crime.* The world of crime is conceived of as a social construction, whereby definitions of crime (primarily through the criminal law) are established and subsequently related to the behavior patterns and actions of the members of society. The theory of the social reality of crime integrates the diversity of theoretical criminology into a theory of crime. The following propositions constitute the basis of this theory.[11]

THE OFFICIAL DEFINITION OF CRIME: *Crime is a legal definition of human conduct that is created by agents of the dominant class in a capitalist* society.* The essential

---

*Editor's Note: It is suggested that Professor Quinney's formulation is equally applicable to social systems other than capitalism, in which interest group conflicts emerge because of differential access to political power and the unequal distribution of economic perquisites and privileges.

starting point in the theory is a definition of crime, which itself is based on the legal definition. Crime, as *officially* determined, is a *definition* of behavior that is conferred on some persons by those in power. Agents of the law (such as legislators, police, prosecutors, and judges), as representatives of the ruling class in capitalist society, are responsible for the formulation and administration of criminal law. Persons and behaviors, therefore, become criminal because of the *formulation* and *application* of these definitions of crime.

Crime, according to the first proposition of the social reality of crime, then, is not inherent in behavior, but is rather a judgment made by some about the actions and characteristics of others. This proposition allows us to focus upon the formulation and administration of the criminal law in relation to the behaviors that become defined as criminal in a capitalist society. Crime is seen as a result of the class-dynamic processes that culminate in the defining of persons and behaviors as criminal. It follows, then, that the greater the number of definitions of crime, formulated and applied, the greater the amount of crime.

THE FORMULATION OF DEFINITIONS OF CRIME: *Definitions of crime are composed of behaviors that conflict with the class interests of the dominant economic class.* Definitions of crime are formulated according to the interests of the dominant class that has the power to translate its particular interests into public policy. According to a Marxist analysis, the class interests that are ultimately incorporated into the criminal law are those treasured by the dominant class in capitalist society.[12] Furthermore, definitions of crime in a society change with changes in the interests of the dominant class. In other words, those who have the ability to have their class interests represented in public policy regulate the formulation of definitions of crime.

The formulation of definitions of crime is one of the most obvious manifestations of *class conflict* in society. The formulation of criminal law, including legislative statutes, administrative rulings, and judicial decisions, allows the ruling class to protect and perpetuate its own interests. Definitions of crime exist, therefore, because of class struggle. Through the formulation of definitions of crime the dominant economic class is able to control the behavior of persons in the subordinate class. It follows that the greater the class struggle, the greater the probability that the ruling class will formulate definitions of crime.

The interests of the ruling class are reflected not only in the content of the definitions of crime and the kinds of penal sanctions attached to the definitions, but also in the *legal policies* regarding the handling of those defined as criminals. Hence, procedural rules are created for the enforcement and administration of the criminal law. Policies are also established in respect to programs for the treatment and punishment of the criminally defined and programs for the control and prevention of crime. In all cases, whether in regard to the initial definitions of crime or the subsequent procedures, correctional and penal programs, or policies of crime control and prevention, the class that has the dominant power is the class that regulates the behavior of those without power.[13]

Finally, since law is formulated within the context of the class structure of capitalist society, it follows that law changes with modifications in that structure. New and shifting demands require new laws. When the class interests that underlie a criminal law are no longer relevant to those in power, the law will be reinterpreted or altered in order to incorporate the dominant class interests. Hence, the probability that definitions of crime will be formulated is increased by such factors as (1) changing social structure, (2) emerging class interests, and (3) increasing concern with the protection of class interests. The social history of law can thus be written in terms of changes in the class structure of capitalist society.

THE APPLICATION OF DEFINITIONS OF CRIME: *Definitions of crime are applied by the class that has the power to shape the enforcement and administration of criminal law.* The interests of the dominant class intervene in all the stages in which definitions of crime are created. Since class interests cannot be effectively protected through the mere formulation of criminal law, there must be enforcement and administration of the law. The interests of the powerful, therefore, also operate in the *application* of the definitions of crime. Consequently, as Vold has argued, crime is "political behavior and the criminal becomes in fact a member of a 'minority group' without sufficient public support to dominate the control of the police power of the state."[14] Those whose interests conflict with the interests represented in the law must either change their behavior or possibly find it defined as criminal.

The probability that definitions of crime will be applied varies according to the extent to which the behaviors of the powerless conflict with the interests of those in power. Law enforcement efforts and judicial activity are likely to be increased when the interests of the dominant class are being threatened. Fluctuations and variations in applying definitions of crime reflect shifts in class relations.

Obviously, the criminal law is not applied directly by the dominant class. Rather, the actual enforcement and administration of the law are delegated to authorized *legal agents*. These authorities, nevertheless, represent the interests of the dominant economic class. In fact, the legal agents' security of office is dependent upon their ability to represent ruling class interests.

Because of the physical separation of the groups responsible for the creation of the definitions of crime from the groups delegated the authority to enforce and administer law, local conditions affect the actual application of definitions.[15] In particular, communities vary from one another in their expectations of law enforcement and the administration of justice. The application of definitions is also influenced by the visibility of offenses in a community and by the norms in respect to the reporting of possible violations by the public. And especially important in the enforcement and administration of the criminal law are the occupational organization and ideology of the legal agents.[16] Thus the probability that definitions of crime will be applied is influenced by such community and organizational factors as (1) community expectations of law enforcement and administration, (2) the visibility and public reporting of offenses, and (3) the occupational organization, ideology, and actions of the legal agents delegated the authority to enforce and administer criminal law. On the basis of such factors, the dominant interests of society are implemented in the application of definitions of crime.

The probability that these definitions will be applied in specific situations is dependent upon the actions of the legal agents who have been given the authority to enforce and administer the law. In the final analysis, the application of a definition of crime is a matter of evaluation on the part of persons charged with the authority to enforce and administer the law. As Turk has argued, in the course of "criminalization," a criminal label may be affixed to persons because of real or fancied attributes: "Indeed, a person is evaluated, either favorably or unfavorably, not because he *does* something, or even because he *is* something, but because others react to their perceptions of him as offensive or inoffensive."[17] Evaluation by the definers is affected by the way in which the suspect handles the situation, but ultimately the evaluations and subsequent decisions of the legal agents are the crucial factors in determining the criminality of human acts. Hence, the more legal agents evaluate behaviors and persons as worthy of definitions of crime, the greater the probability that definitions of crime will be applied.

THE DEVELOPMENT OF BEHAVIOR PATTERNS IN RELATION TO DEFINITIONS OF CRIME: *Behavior patterns are structured in relation to definitions of crime, and within this context persons engage in actions that have relative probabilities of being defined as criminal.* Although the substance of behavior varies, all behaviors are similar in that they represent behavior patterns within the society. Therefore, all persons—whether they create definitions of crime or are the objects of these definitions—act in reference to *normative systems* learned in relative social and cultural settings.[18] Since it is not the quality of the behavior but the action taken against the behavior that gives it the character of criminality, that which is defined as criminal is relative to the behavior patterns of the class that formulates and applies definitions. Consequently, persons whose behavior patterns are not represented in the formulation and application of the definitions of crime are more likely to act in ways that will be defined as criminal than those in the class that formulate and apply the definitions.

Once behavior patterns become established with some degree of regularity within the different segments of society, individuals are provided with a framework for the creation of *personal action patterns.* These action patterns continually develop for each person as he moves from one life experience to another. It is the development of certain action patterns that gives the behavior of persons an individual substance in relation to the definitions of crime.

People construct their own patterns of action in participating with others. It follows, then, that the probability that persons will develop action patterns that have a high potential of being defined as criminal is dependent upon the relative substance of (1) structured opportunities, (2) learning experiences, (3) interpersonal associations and identifications, and (4) self-conceptions. Throughout the course of experiences, each person creates a conception of self as a human social being. Thus prepared, persons behave in terms of the anticipated consequences of their actions.[19]

In the course of the shared experiences of the definers of crime and the criminally defined, personal-action patterns develop among the latter as a consequence of being so defined. After such persons have had continued experience in being defined as criminal, they learn to manipulate the application of criminal definitions.[20]

Furthermore, those who have been defined as criminal begin to conceive of themselves as criminal. As they adjust to the definitions imposed upon them, they learn to play the role of the criminal.[21] As a result of the reactions of others, therefore, persons may develop personal-action patterns that increase the likelihood of their being defined as criminal in the future. That is, increased experience with definitions of crime increases the probability of the development of actions that may be subsequently defined as criminal.

Thus both the definers of crime and the criminally defined are involved in reciprocal action patterns. The personal-action patterns of both the definers and the defined are shaped by the interrelation of their common, continued, and interrelated experiences. The fate of each is bound to that of the other.

THE CONSTRUCTION OF CONCEPTIONS OF CRIME: *Conceptions of crime are constructed and diffused in the course of communication.* The social world is a construction: persons with the help of others create the world in which they live. Social reality is thus the world that people create. The construction of this reality is related to the kind of knowledge they develop, the ideas they are exposed to, the manner in which they select information to fit the world they are in the process of shaping, and the manner in which they interpret these conceptions.[22] People behave in reference to the *social meanings* they attach to their experiences.

Among the conceptions that develop in a society are those relating to what people regard as crime. Whenever the concept of crime exists, conceptions of the nature of crime also exist. Images develop concerning the relevance of crime, the characteristics of the offender, the appropriate reaction to crime, and the relation of crime to the social order.[23] These conceptions are constructed through the process of communication. In fact, the construction of conceptions of crime is dependent upon the portrayal of crime in all personal and mass communication. Through such means, conceptions of what is criminal are diffused throughout a society.

One of the most concrete ways in which conceptions of crime are formed and transmitted is through official investigations of crime. The President's Commission on Law Enforcement and Administration of Justice is the best contemporary example of the role of the state in shaping conceptions of crime.[24] Not only do we as citizens have a greater awareness of crime today because of the activities of the President's Commission, but official policy regarding crime has been established in a crime bill (the Omnibus Crime Control and Safe Streets Act of 1968). The crime bill, which itself was a reaction to the growing fears of class conflict in American society, creates an image of the severity of the crime problem and, in the course of so doing, negates some of our basic constitutional guarantees in the name of crime control. Our current social reality of crime has thus been shaped by the communication of the ideas and interests of the ruling class.

Consequently, the conceptions that are most critical in the actual formulation and application of the definitions of crime are those held by the dominant class. These are the conceptions of crime that are certain to become incorporated into the social reality of crime. Furthermore, the more the dominant class is concerned about crime, the greater the probability that definitions of crime will be created and that behavior patterns will develop in opposition to the definitions. The formulation of definitions of crime, the application of the definitions, and the development of behavior patterns in relation to the definitions are thus joined in full circle by the construction of conceptions of crime.

CONSTRUCTION OF THE SOCIAL REALITY OF CRIME: *The social reality of crime is constructed by the formulation and application of definitions of crime, the development of behavior patterns in relation to these definitions, and the construction of conceptions of crime.* The first five propositions can be collected into a final composite proposition. The theory of the social reality of crime, accordingly, postulates the creation of a series of phenomena that increase the probability of crime in a capitalist society. The result, in holistic terms, is the construction of the social reality of crime.

Since the first proposition of the theory is a definition and the sixth proposition is a composite, the body of the theory consists of the four middle propositions. These propositions form a model of the social reality of crime. The model, as diagramed below, relates the proposition units into a theoretical system. Each proposition unit is related to the others. The theory is thus

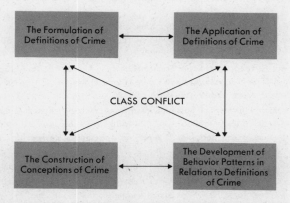

Figure 1 Model of the Social Reality of Crime

in the form of a system of interacting developmental propositions. The phenomena denoted in the propositions and their interrelations culminate in what is regarded as the amount and character of crime at any given time—that is, in the social reality of crime.

The theory of the social reality of crime as I have formulated it is inspired by a change that is occurring in our view of the world. This change, which is pervading all levels of society, pertains to the world that we all construct and, at the same time, pretend to separate ourselves from in our human experiences. For the study of crime, a revision in thought has directed attention to the criminal process: all relevant phenomena contribute to the process of creating definitions of crime, the development of the behaviors of those who are involved in criminal-defining situations, and the construction of conceptions of crime. The result is the social reality of crime that is constantly being constructed in society.

NOTES

1. Critical discussions of causal explanation, however, are found in Hermanus Bianchi, *Position and Subject Matter of Criminology* (Amsterdam: North-Holland, 1956); David Matza, *Delinquency and Drift* (New York: John Wiley & Sons, 1964); Walter C. Reckless, *The Crime Problem* (New York: Appleton-Century-Crofts, 1967); Richard Quinney, *The Problem of Crime* (New York: Dodd, Mead, 1970).

2. Mario Bunge, *Causality: The Place of the Causal Principle in Modern Science* (New York: The World Publishing Co., 1963); Percy W. Bridgman, *Reflections of a Physicist* (New York: Philosophical Library, 1950); Werner Heisenburg, *Physics and Philosophy: The Revolution in Modern Science* (New York: Harper & Row, 1958); Stephen Toulmin, *The Philosophy of Science* (New York: Harper & Row, 1960).

3. Alfred Stern, "Science and the Philosopher," in Paul C. Obler and Herman H. Estrin (eds.), *The New Scientist: Essays in the Methods and Values of Modern Science* (Garden City, New York: Doubleday, 1962), p. 300.

4. Alfred Schutz, "Concept and Theory Formation in the Social Sciences," in Maurice Natanson (ed.), *Philosophy of the Social Sciences* (New York: Random House, 1963), p. 242.

5. Robert M. MacIver, *Social Causation* (New York: Harper & Row, 1964, originally published in 1942).

6. Pitirim A. Sorokin, *Sociocultural Causality, Time and Space* (Durham: Duke University Press, 1943). Also see Sorokin, *Sociological Theories of Today* (New York: Harper & Row, 1966), pp. 17–31.

7. See Robert Brown, *Explanation in Social Science* (Chicago: Aldine, 1963); Abraham Kaplan, *The Conduct of Inquiry* (San Francisco, Chandler, 1964); and Ernest Nagel, *The Structure of Science* (New York: Harcourt, Brace and World, 1961).

8. Edward A. Tiryakian, "Existential Phenomenology and the Sociological Tradition," *American Sociological Review* 39 (October 1965), pp. 674–688. Also see James L. Heap and Philip A. Roth, "On Phenomenological Sociology," *American Sociological Review* 38 (June, 1973), pp. 354–367.

9. George Gurvitch, *The Spectrum of Social Time* (Dordrechecht, Holland: D. Reidel, 1964).

10. Richard Quinney, "A Transcendental Way of Knowing," in Nicholas M. Regush (ed.), *Visibles and Invisibles: A Primer for a New Sociological Imagination* (Boston: Little, Brown and Company, 1973), pp. 168–177.

11. This is a revision of the theory of the social reality of crime as originally presented in Richard Quinney, *The Social Reality of Crime*, pp. 15–25.

12. Richard Quinney, "Crime Control in Capitalist Society: A Critical Philosophy of Legal Order," *Issues in Criminology*, 8 (Spring 1973), pp. 75–99.

13. Considerable support for this proposition is found in William J. Chambliss and Robert B. Seidman, *Law, Order, and Power* (Reading, Mass.: Addison-Wesley Publishing Co., 1971). Also see George Rusche and Otto Kirchheimer, *Punishment and Social Structure* (New York: Columbia University Press, 1939).

14. George B. Vold, *Theoretical Criminology* (New York: Oxford University Press, 1958), p. 202. Also see Irving Louis Horowitz and Martin Liebowitz, "Social Deviance and Political Marginality: Toward a Redefinition of the Relation Between Sociology and Politics," *Social Problems* 15 (Winter 1968), pp. 280–296.

15. See Michael Banton, *The Policeman and the Community* (London: Tavistock, 1964); Egon Bittner, "The Police on Skid-Row: A Study of Peace Keeping," *American Sociological Review* 32 (October 1967), pp. 699–715; John P. Clark, "Isolation of the Police: A Comparison of the British and American Situations," *Journal of Criminal Law, Criminology and Police Science* 56 (September 1965), pp. 307–319; Nathan Goldman, *The Differential Selection of Juvenile Offenders for Court Appearance* (New York: National Council on Crime and Delinquency, 1963); James Q. Wilson, *Varieties of Police Behavior: The Management of Law and Order in Eight Communities* (Cambridge, Mass.: Harvard University Press, 1968).

16. Abraham S. Blumberg, *Criminal Justice* (Chicago: Quadrangle Books, 1967); David J. Bordua and Albert J. Reiss, Jr., "Command, Control and Charisma: Reflection on Police Bureaucracy," *American Journal of Sociology* 72 (July 1966), pp. 68–76; Aaron V. Cicourel, *The Social Organization of Juvenile Justice* (New York: John Wiley & Sons, 1968); Arthur Niederhoffer, *Behind the Shield: The Police in Urban Society* (Garden City, N.Y.: Doubleday, 1967); Jerome H. Skolnick, *Justice Without Trial* (New York: John Wiley & Sons, 1966); Arthur L. Stinchcombe, "Institutions of Privacy in the Determination of Police Administrative Practice," *American Journal of Sociology* 69 (September 1963), pp. 150–160; David Sudnow, "Normal Crimes: Sociological Features of the Penal Code in a Public Defender Office," *Social Problems* 12 (Winter 1965), pp. 255–276; William A. Westley, "Violence and the Police," *American Journal of Sociology* 59 (July 1953), pp. 34–41; Arthur Lewis Wood, *Criminal Lawyer* (New Haven: College & University Press, 1967).

17. Austin T. Turk, "Conflict and Criminality," *American Sociological Review* 31 (June 1966), p. 34. For research on the evaluation of suspects by policemen, see Irving Piliavin and Scott Briar, "Police Encounters with Juveniles," *American Journal of Sociology* 70 (September 1964), pp. 206–214.

18. Assumed within the theory of the social reality of crime is Sutherland's theory of differential association. See Edwin H. Sutherland, *Principles of Criminology*, 4th ed. (Philadelphia: J. B. Lippincott, 1947). An analysis of the differential association theory is found in Melvin L. De Fleur and Richard Quinney, "A Reformulation of Sutherland's Differential Association Theory and a Strategy for Empirical Verification," *Journal of Research in Crime and Delinquency* 3 (January 1966), pp. 1–22.

19. On the operant nature of criminally defined behavior, see Robert L. Burgess and Ronald L. Akers, "A Differential Association-Reinforcement Theory of Criminal Behavior," *Social Problems* 14 (Fall 1966), pp. 128–147; C. Ray Jeffery, "Criminal Behavior and Learning Theory," *Journal of Criminal Law, Criminology and Police Science* 56 (September 1965), pp. 294–300.

20. A discussion of the part the person plays in manipulating the deviant-defining situation is found in Judith Lorber, "Deviance as Performance: The Case of Illness," *Social Problems* 14 (Winter 1967), pp. 302–310.

21. Edwin M. Lemert, *Human Deviance, Social Problems, and Social Control* (Englewood Cliffs, N.J.: Prentice-Hall, 1964), pp. 40–64; Edwin M. Lemert, *Social Pathology* (New York: McGraw-Hill, 1951), pp. 3–98. A related and earlier discussion is in Frank Tannenbaum, *Crime and the Community* (New York: Columbia University Press, 1938), pp. 3–81.

22. See Peter L. Berger and Thomas Luckmann, *The Social Construction of Reality* (Garden City, N.Y.: Doubleday, 1966). Relevant research on the dissemination of information is discussed in Everett M. Rogers, *Diffusion of Innovations* (New York: The Free Press, 1962).

23. See Alexander L. Clark and Jack P. Gibbs, "Social Control: A Reformulation," *Social Problems* 12 (Spring 1965), pp. 398–415; Thomas E. Dow, Jr., "The Role of Identification in Conditioning Public Attitude Toward the Offender," *Journal of Criminal Law, Criminology and Police Science* 58 (March 1967), pp. 75–79; William P. Lentz, "Social Status and Attitudes Toward Delinquency Control," *Journal of Research in Crime and Delinquency* 3 (July 1966), pp. 147–154; Jennie McIntyre, "Public Attitudes Toward Crime and Law Enforcement," *Annals of the American Academy of Political and Social Science* 374 (November 1967), pp. 34–46; Anastassios D. Mylonas and Walter C. Reckless, "Prisoners' Attitudes Toward Law and Legal Institutions," *Journal of Criminal Law, Criminology and Police Science* 54 (December 1963), pp. 479–484; Elizabeth A. Rooney and Don C. Gibbons, "Social Reactions to 'Crimes Without Victims,' " *Social Problems* 13 (Spring 1966), pp. 400–410.

24. President's Commission on Law Enforcement and Administration of Justice, *The Challenge of Crime in a Free Society* (Washington, D.C.: United States Government Printing Office, 1967).

3/ CRIMINAL JUSTICE BY DOSSIER: LAW ENFORCEMENT, LABELING, AND LIBERTY

ARTHUR NIEDERHOFFER

Crime in the streets has escalated into one of the nation's most persistent and troublesome issues. In near desperation the country has turned to the police, whose legal responsibility and professional credo it is to prevent and control crime. Since by tradition and ideology police officers identify themselves as crime fighters and regard themselves as the most important component of the criminal justice system, they have responded to this mandate with enthusiasm, proclaiming that if they were given proper financial and public support, they would stop crime and create a climate of law and order once more. Law enforcement has thus seized the occasion to advance itself occupationally, financially, and politically.

Unfortunately, crime has continued to increase year after year. The generally accepted standard of the number of arrests made was the only evidence the police could marshal as a measure of their efficiency in crime fighting. Thus, policemen are hungry for arrests, especially felon arrests, since they represent the moment of truth.

Arrest—which places the stigma of criminal on an individual—is the culmination of a systematic labeling process. The importance of the police function in this process is expressed by Austin T. Turk:

. . . .*criminality is not a biological, psychological or even behavioral phenomenon, but a social status defined by the way in which an individual is perceived, evaluated, and treated by legal authorities. Legal, extra-legal, and illegal criteria are used by those who enforce legal norms in determining whether and in what ways individuals are punishable.*[1]

The labeling process begins with suspicion, and ordinarily the suspect is known only to the police or some other investigatory agency, not to the public. Because the investigation is clandestine, enforcement of the few nebulous constitutional protections that do exist is very difficult. An individual may become a suspect for the flimsiest of reasons—the dossier with his name on it may be the result of false information, guilt by association, rumor, or, what is even more frightening, the personal aberration or whim of the investigator. The person under investigation may be thrust into a Kafkaesque situation that can destroy him. And in this epoch of electronic criminal justice in which the number of potential suspects will multiply astronomically, we are all in danger of becoming K's.

In general, a law enforcement officer can make a legal arrest for a serious crime when it is committed in his presence or when he has probable cause to believe that the person under suspicion committed it. During the subsequent procedure of preparing the case for presentation in court, the hypothesis on the part of the police that the prisoner is connected with the crime is confirmed—from the desk lieutenant to the investigating detective; from the witnesses to the judge at the preliminary hearing; and, finally, from the district attorney and the grand jury itself. As the case progresses, the officer's emotional involvement and near certainty of the defendant's guilt grows. Generally the other members of the criminal justice system who are familiar with this process silently agree with the imputation of guilt. Later, in the courtroom, a clash of opposing legal forces occurs. Under our adversary system of justice, at the start of the trial the *prima facie* probability of guilt that was so laboriously constructed collides with the contradictory and equally powerful legal presumption of the defendant's innocence.

THE PRESUMPTION OF INNOCENCE

The clearest delineation of the presumption of innocence is in the judge's charge to the jury, toward the end of a criminal trial, to guide it in its deliberations:

Every defendant in a criminal case is presumed to be innocent. This presumption of innocence remains with the defendant throughout the trial unless and until he is proven guilty beyond a reasonable doubt.[2]

In its study draft, the National Commission on Reform of Federal Criminal Laws explains the import of the presumption:

The fact that [an accused] has been arrested, confined or indicted for, or otherwise charged with, the offense gives rise to no inference of guilt at his trial.[3]

The power of the presumption of innocence rises and falls with the spirit of the times. In the early decades of the nineteenth century, Rufus Choate, the illustrious New England lawyer, placed a halo over it, declaring that it is "as irresistible as the heavens till overcome; that it hovers over the prisoner as a guardian angel throughout the trial."[4] A more current view classified it as the most fundamental canon of criminal law.[5] Any veneer of romanticism lingering about this concept was stripped away by the coldly logical analysis of John H. Wigmore, the voice of authority on legal evidence:

The presumption of innocence is in truth merely another form of expression for a part of the accepted rule for the burden of proof in criminal cases, i.e., the rule that it is for the prosecution to adduce evidence . . . and to produce persuasion beyond a reasonable doubt. . .[6]

Although rules of evidence are essentially consistent with the presumption of innocence, this consistency does not extend to the agents and practitioners who make the criminal justice system work—namely, the police, the prosecutor, the presiding judge, and even the defense attorney, as the plea bargaining process has shown. Yet everyone concerned with the trial is supposed to act as if he did believe in the innocence of the accused. In actuality, it is a fiction, and in the minds of most practitioners in the field of criminal justice there is a real presumption of guilt or complicity. In some this creates a compulsion, in others a predisposition, to label a suspect a criminal. Let us examine this more fully.

THE POLICE AND THE LABELING PROCESS

Hostility toward the police is often increased by the secret quality of their decision to stop a citizen and question him, to frisk, arrest, or ignore a suspect. They have a wide gray area of discretion. Studies have documented the fact that these low-visibility decisions are often the result of stereotyping, class and racial bias, personality problems, and, finally, organizational pressures. Professor Yale Kamisar of the University of Michigan adds weight to this indictment by comparing the police investigator to a wild beast stalking its prey:

In the "gatehouse" of American criminal procedure—through which most defendants journey and beyond which many never get—the enemy of the state [the accused] is a depersonalized "subject" to be "sized up" and subjected to "interrogation tactics and techniques most appropriate to the occasion"; he is game to be stalked and cornered. Here ideals are checked at the door, "realities" faced, and the prestige of law enforcement vindicated.[7]

Despite their sensitivity to criticism, with an almost instantaneous resort to denial and attack, the police until recently have been rather ineffectual in convincing the "opposition" of their purity.

Under the Warren court, in a series of decisions from Mapp in 1961 to Miranda in 1966, many due process rights were extended from federal to state jurisdiction and gradually covered all phases of the process of criminal justice, from first contact with the police until the defendant was released from prison. Ostensibly, the Supreme Court was curtailing the autonomy of the police in their private domain of investigation.

Thus, in order to circumvent this civil libertarian trend, law enforcement strategically wielded its political power to persuade legislatures to pass enabling statutes nullifying Supreme Court decisions. Police associations utilized pressure groups, voting blocs, and powerful lobbyists to guarantee success even though they considered the legislatures—as representatives of middle-class interests—to be willing to cooperate and solve the crime problem "the easy way" by passing more laws.

Searches, seizures, and arrests under these new laws raised a variety of legal questions that had not yet been adjudicated. And on appeals, the Supreme Court reluctantly validated the new stop-and-frisk procedures and went so far as to grant legal blessing to a much broader standard of police discretion than ever before—reasonable suspicion in place of probable cause.

A perfect example of the cooperation between police and legislatures is the aftermath of the landmark Mapp case of 1961. For nearly fifty years before Mapp, there were two different philosophies of law, one for federal law enforcement agencies such as the F. B. I. and another for the municipal police. Federal police officials had to observe the Fourth Amendment guarantee against unreasonable searches and seizures. Therefore, only evidence that they obtained in accordance with legal procedures could be admitted in court. But at the local level no such protection existed. The rules of evidence were held to be merely procedural, not substantive and not covered by the Fourth Amendment. Thus city police could with impunity obtain evidence wrongfully without warrants and by other illegal means. This evidence was admissible in court. The Mapp case reversed this time-honored police practice. The Supreme Court said clearly:

We hold that all evidence obtained by searches and seizures in violation of the Constitution is, by that same authority, inadmissible in a state court.[8]

Many states were forced by this decision to add to their codes of criminal procedure an exclusionary rule declaring illegally obtained evidence inadmissible upon the motion of the defendant. The decision shocked the police who, via the mass media and through more subtle political maneuvers, pressured the legislatures to help them recoup their position. The legislatures responded willingly.

In 1962 the constitutional convention in Michigan circumvented Mapp by ruling that the search-and-seizure provisions of the Constitution shall not be construed to bar the admission into evidence of drugs, explosives, and dangerous weapons seized by a peace officer.[9] Other states revised their laws on arrests, searches, and seizures to remove the stigma of illegality from the evidence seized. Illinois and New York granted to the prosecution the right to appeal from lower-court orders suppressing evidence whose seizure contravened Mapp.[10]

The Warren court continued its liberal policy and extended the rights of defendants even beyond Mapp. The decision in *Miranda v. Arizona* (1966) was particularly irritating to the police. Miranda required the police to give a clear warning to a suspect at the start of a custodial police interrogation that he had a right to remain silent and that he had a right to counsel.

President Nixon and Attorney General Mitchell were no less vociferous than the police in demanding legislative action. Repeatedly, the President called for preventive detention of dangerous defendants. And the Attorney General recommended passage of a law that would permit fingerprints, medical tests, and identification lineups of suspects even before they were charged with a crime.[11] Congress responded to the appeal with even more enthusiasm than the state legislatures and passed such a cornucopia of tough criminal laws in the Omnibus Crime Control and Safe Streets Act (June 19,

1968) and the District of Columbia Crime Bill (July 29, 1970) that the President and Attorney General were positively embarrassed. What would happen if they used these new procedures to their fullest extent, and crime still increased? As a result, federal law enforcement agencies have been slow to take advantage of the provisions of these laws permitting preventive detention, increased electronic surveillance, or rules that allow confessions to be admitted in evidence even when they would be inadmissible under the Miranda doctrine.[12]

Unquestionably, the political atmosphere has become more repressive and less concerned with the protection of civil liberties. Its most obvious manifestations are the government's attempted censorship and threatened injunction against the mass media, increased surveillance of private citizens, and the decisions of the Burger court that have curtailed the rights of the defendants in criminal cases. The most significant change may be the extension of police discretionary power arising from the substitution by the courts of an amorphous concept of reasonable suspicion for the long-established standard of probable cause in police searches and seizures.

In this connection, it is instructive to review the reasoning of the New York State Court of Appeals in the Peters case, one of a series of convictions in which the police obtained the incriminating evidence while operating under the doctrine of reasonable suspicion.

The phrase reasonable suspicion provides a defined standard and is, in fact, no less endowed with an objective meaning than is the phrase probable cause. . . . By requiring the reasonable suspicion of a police officer, the statute incorporates the experienced police officer's intuitive knowledge and appraisal of the appearances of criminal activity. His evaluation of the various factors involved ensures a protective, as well as definitive standard.[13]

These decisions were later affirmed by the United States Supreme Court.

What could be more threatening to our constitutional right of privacy and freedom from unreasonable search and seizure than a legal principle that encourages the extended use of a policeman's "intuitive knowledge and appraisal of the appearances of criminal activity"? Harold D. Lasswell states the problem definitively: The political man (i.e., the policeman) displaces his private motives onto public objects (i.e., the citizens) and rationalizes his actions in terms of the public interest.[14]

The inherent danger is that the selection of those public objects depends upon the idiosyncrasies of petty bureaucrats subject to all the sources of misperception, prejudgment, and bias recognized by every one of the behavioral sciences. And when police propose to rely on their intuitive appraisal of the appearances of criminal activity, then they will be particularly prone to these human errors.

The paradox is that, despite personal differences in education, ethnic background, and race, the occupation molds the policeman in its own image. For all practical purposes, he becomes in time very nearly the typical

American sharing the lower-middle-class world view.[15] The natural scapegoats of that ideology are the blacks, the poor, the radicals, and the nonconformist youth. It is these groups who are most likely to be defined by the police as "symbolic assailants."[16] Acts of militancy committed by groups like the Black Panthers and the frequent ambushes upon the police in large cities transform the symbolic assailant into a "probable attacker" in the minds of policemen. Consequently, the police are very likely to label as suspicious anyone who might possibly fit into this category.

THE POLICE AND THE COURT

Believing deeply in the culpability of the arrested person, the arresting officer and the department he represents want the courts to certify that label of the defendant's criminality.

Detectives and plainclothesmen make many arrests necessitating court appearances and are soon sophisticated in trial procedure. However, to the average patrolman, the court is foreign territory: he does not know its rules, its etiquette, its definitions of fact and truth, and its power relations. This is in strong contrast to the street he patrols, where he knows all the laws and regulations and can manipulate and transpose them at will. Here the public defers to his authority—he has the power to interrogate, to accuse, and to order.

In court his role is reversed and he has little power. He is subordinate to the district attorney and the judge. Court protocol provokes the policeman, since he must submit to cross-examination and at the same time must be deferential to the defense attorney. Without knowledge of the intricacies of court procedure and testimony, he can easily be trapped. Limited to a yes-or-no answer when he is on the stand, he is often frustrated because he cannot convey verbally to the judge and jury the whole story that would prove the charge. Finally, instead of a presumption of guilt, it is a presumption of the defendant's innocence that dominates the trial.

The police, therefore, are naturally disposed to mistrust the courts, and although F. B. I. annual crime reports show year after year that 65 to 70 percent of criminal cases brought to the courts end in conviction, the police are sure that many cases are fixed, and that courts are coddling criminals with their leniency.[17] Struggling as it is, the court system naturally resents these charges.

THE POLICE ON THE DEFENSIVE: THE LABELER LABELED

In the tightly controlled territory of the court the police officer does not feel free to counterattack. But what happens when there is no restriction on his freedom to respond? How does he react when he is stigmatized as pig, racist, lawbreaker, grafter, paranoid, or murderer? Does he follow the sage advice to keep cool that has been drummed into his head by police instructors?

Two instinctive response patterns are common. The first is to deny the allegation, which tends to be taken as a slur on the entire profession. The denial is thus an appeal to solidarity among men who, notwithstanding their enormous power, conceive of themselves as a minority group unfairly attacked from all sides. The second reaction is to attack the attacker by means of exaggerated accusations embellished with veiled allusions to subversive conspiracies to undermine the country and weaken the police.

Occasionally, a persistent insult produces in the police a chain reaction so explosive that it defies classification. During the Democratic National Convention in Chicago in the summer of 1968, the notorious clash between police and demonstrators was escalated, if not initiated, because the crowd constantly taunted the police with the epithet "Pig."

It is difficult to understand why the police, with all their power and freedom from accountability, are so sensitive to public criticism, especially when they themselves are more cynical and critical about their job and their organization than any outsider could be.[18] Moreover, police department policy and training attempt to turn out an officer who will remain impervious to insults and name-calling.

Why is this commendable conditioning rejected in action? To all intents and purposes the policeman has a dual citizenship. In times of stress he identifies himself as a loyal citizen of the world of law enforcement—a special nation with its own institutions, codes, laws, rituals, values, and life-style. It has the most advanced communication system so that news and rumor are immediately and universally available. For the shibboleth "My country right or wrong," substitute "My police force right or wrong." Thus, policemen's excessive sensitivity becomes a form of patriotism or nationalism. And, as in any strong nation, most law enforcement officers share the same general world view. If the officer resists embracing this outlook, he incurs suspicion.

THE PROFESSIONAL POLICE OFFICERS' DEFENSE

Predictably, the dramatic expansion of law enforcement courses and criminal justice programs in universities all over the country will bring forth educated policemen-philosophers who will be able to present a new defense of the police role. Already, one can discern the new "police science" emerging. One of its representatives is Sergeant Joseph Wambaugh of the Los Angeles Police Department, the author of the best seller *The New Centurions*. Wambaugh makes a spirited defense of "The Militant Bluecoats"—professional college-oriented policemen who write books and articles and take to the picket lines to demand better working conditions.[19]

It is possible, too, that in time the police will make a statement defining themselves as professionals doing the same type of job that behavioral scientists perform so proudly. Moreover, this position will probably give rise to the same kinds of unavoidable ethical questions.

The police have been charged with employing a different standard of justice for blacks and whites, or lower class and middle class. The gist of the allegation is that, instead of sufficiently protecting the ghetto dwellers from crime, they harass black people, especially the youth, by constant "stop and frisk" procedures. As a defense, a police spokesman can call attention to the acts of the state legislatures and the Supreme Court in lowering the standard for a legal "stop and frisk" from probable cause to reasonable suspicion. These acts confirmed the legality and encouraged the expansion of the use of police intuition and discretion in street investigations.

In addition, the police advocate can call forth three further defenses. The first is that the greatest pressure on the police to prevent crime in the ghetto comes from the residents themselves. Secondly, serious crime in the inner city has become almost the monopoly of youthful black criminals, who prey upon their own community far more than they do upon the white neighborhoods. In the third place, experienced policemen develop an "instinct" for recognizing potential wrongdoers and are generally careful in exercising their special skill. It is not only the police themselves who make the claim; the Supreme Court in several recent decisions has almost as a matter of judicial notice accepted the existence of this skill.[20]

To summarize the police defenses: the policy established by the highest court in the land, the statutes passed by the state legislatures, the demand of the community itself, and the police officer's training and experience, all converge to justify law enforcement's special concern with black youth.

A second pivotal postulate of the critique of the police is that they lack tolerance and understanding of lower-class and minority groups. It is held, therefore, that the police ought to be intimately acquainted with the social and behavioral sciences.

Well-educated professional police may find in this criticism ammunition both to defend their system and at the same time to mount a subtle attack upon the academic community. Although they may well admit that perceptions are often untrustworthy and are judgments distorted concerning societies and groups whose mores differ radically from those of the observer, they may at the same time contend that the police are adhering to the principle of cultural relativism. According to this principle, one should develop a sense of tolerance and even respect for the customs and values of the "strange" culture.

The police argue too that since both law enforcement and the social sciences are involved in the search for knowledge about human behavior, then, ultimately, they have a common scientific goal—prediction and control. In addition, they employ somewhat similar methodologies. Thus, if social scientists are allowed to vindicate their techniques by arguing that they are advancing the frontiers of knowledge and science, then the police must be granted the same license, since their function of protecting life and preserving peace is equally valuable to society.

In fact, the police defender may now assert that social scientists have often trespassed beyond freedom and dignity and have been guilty of the same unethical practices that they are quick to condemn in the police. Moreover, if we are to believe the sociologist Edward A. Shils, the police may have more license than the social scientists for these dubious tactics. Shils has criticized sociologists for using them, but apparently he excuses the police, because

there are situations in which such unadmitted observations are necessary, e.g., in the pursuit of criminals, spies, etc. Their necessity on behalf of the social order does not diminish their morally objectionable character, it simply outweighs it.[21]

Another serious indictment against the police is that their actions have alienated the black community and the militant college youth. The police protagonist may admit that there is a degree of alienation, but will deny that the police themselves are in any way responsible for that condition. In fact, he may proclaim it as further evidence of the similarity between law enforcement and sociology. No less an authority than Alvin Gouldner has come to the conclusion that sociology has lost the confidence of blacks and college militants. They view the sociologist as something of an exploiter and a hypocrite, and sociology as no more than "an ideology discolored by a pervasive conservative bias in the service of the status quo."[22] How often policemen have heard this same diatribe directed at them! Table 1 compares some objectionable data-collecting methods frequently used by sociologists and the police.

NEW DEVELOPMENTS IN POLICE WORK

In an age of amazing technological progress, law enforcement has lagged fifty years behind the times. A policeman who patrolled a beat in a large city in 1930 could easily take his post in 1973, without too much retraining. Why is this so? Is it conservative ideology, bureaucratic stagnation, fear of the courts, or lack of money? In all likelihood, it is a combination of these.

An opportunity to remedy the situation came through the Law Enforcement Assistance Act of 1965. In a special message on crime to the 89th Congress, President Johnson stressed the urgent need for improved methods of law enforcement and crime prevention. "Crime in the streets" had been an important campaign issue. The act authorized the Attorney General and the Department of Justice to award grants of money to improve law enforcement and criminal justice and to prevent crime. It represented a radical shift from the traditional laissez-faire philosophy of criminal justice to a policy delegating to a federal agency caretaker powers over our decentralized law enforcement agencies. Even though the bill contained halfhearted references to all of criminal justice, it was obviously an action program geared heavily toward law enforcement, with only token recognition of the needs of the other parts of the system.

Table 1. Sociological Methods versus Police Tactics

SOCIOLOGY	POLICE
1. "In pure research it is quite common to obtain informants or subjects by promising them a return of some sort, either . . . or a pecuniary reward."*	1. Police obtain informants by promising them a return of some sort or a pecuniary reward.
2. "Several kinds of deception have been frequently practiced by social scientists. For instance, in a field investigation a sociologist may become a participant observer, passing as a gardener, a truck driver, or a factory operative. In such a role he is able to get the confidence of others and to obtain valuable information . . . that would not be available if he were known to be a researcher."	2. Police in their field investigations also become participant observers and pass as gardeners, truck drivers, and factory workers. In such roles they are able to obtain valuable information that would not be available if they were known to be police officers.
3. "In experimental situations an accomplice may be introduced into a group to play a role that has been carefully fixed by the investigator."	3. In important cases the police may infiltrate a group and play a role that has been carefully fixed by the investigator.
4. "The giving of false information . . . This may occur when a researcher wants to foster distrust among the members of a group."	4. Police often give false information to one or more members of a group they are keeping under surveillance to foster distrust among members so that one may "come" to the police.

*The matter in the left-hand column is quoted from Robert C. Angell, "The Ethical Problems of Applied Sociology" in Paul F. Lazarsfeld, William H. Sewell, and Harold L. Wilensky (eds.) The Uses of Sociology (New York: Basic Books, 1967), p. 735. The matter in the right-hand column is a statement of common police practices paraphrasing the left side.

In accordance with the new law, the Office of Law Enforcement Assistance was established within the Department of Justice. During its three years of existence, OLEA awarded more than $20 million to support 359 projects, almost two-thirds of which went to law enforcement, especially for education or training and operations improvement. Corrections received about 15 percent and criminal justice, primarily the courts, was awarded only 8 percent. In all probability, any worthwhile project with scientific and technological applications submitted by a police department would have been approved by OLEA.

One of the largest grants went to the Institute of Defense Analyses, Arlington, Virginia. It amounted to $498,000, ten times the average award, and extended from May 1966 to January 1967. It funded a comprehensive study of the potential application of science and technology to law enforcement and criminal justice. And the grantee did produce a detailed blueprint.

The bill provided the opportunity for law enforcement to come of age, to utilize the technology developed by industry. However, the few OLEA projects that could be classified under the heading of science and technology were of little value. The one significant exception, which more than compensated for the failure of the other projects, was the introduction of the electronic computer into key law enforcement departments across the country.

THE COMPUTER, LAW ENFORCEMENT, AND LABELING

Computers and the personnel required to operate and service them are so expensive that few police departments dependent on state and municipal financing could afford them. Without federal aid, law enforcement would still be compiling its records by hand. In 1968 the newly created Law Enforcement Assistance Administration (LEAA), with vast resources, superseded OLEA. And again, although theoretically the agency funds were earmarked for the entire system of criminal justice, in practice about two-thirds of the money was awarded to law enforcement. LEAA carried forward substantially the same policies, including a number of computer projects.

By 1971 there was hardly one among the hundred largest law enforcement agencies without computer services. The F.B.I. National Crime Information Center (NCIC), the most ambitious of approximately twenty computer projects, had received almost $800,000 from OLEA, and its computer network now covers the fifty states and Canada. Not to be outdone by its predecessor, LEAA awarded $600,000 to six states in fiscal 1969 for Project SEARCH— System for Electronic Analysis and Retrieval of Criminal Histories. In fiscal 1970 the participating states numbered fifteen; LEAA distributed $830,000 to them. On December 10, 1970, the project was transferred from the jurisdiction of LEAA to the F.B.I. That such a massive addition to the data banks of the F.B.I. NCIC might threaten American's freedom and privacy must have been in Attorney General Mitchell's mind, because neither he nor F.B.I Director Hoover ever issued a public announcement of the transfer. Nor was it mentioned when LEAA on December 16, 1970, granted an additional $1.5 million to Project SEARCH.[23]

An LEAA survey disclosed that more than thirty states and Washington, D.C. were in the process of developing computerized law enforcement systems. It reported that computerized information systems were "one of the most dynamic areas in law enforcement and criminal justice." Most of the 1970 state plans contained requests for funds for computerized information systems.[24] And in all states the anticipated need for the computer revolved about law enforcement and the goal of establishing an interface with NCIC. In contrast to law enforcement's past resistance to science, the police eagerly accepted the computer.

Some of the current computer applications to law enforcement are:

1. An auto license plate scanner that checks cars at a toll booth and searches an information file to ascertain if the car is wanted or has been stolen.
2. A personal appearance file that produces a picture to conform to a witness's description of a wanted criminal.
3. A computer technique of classifying fingerprints and comparing them with the fingerprint file. (At present an expert is still needed to classify fingerprints before they can be compared with the computerized data bank.)
4. A method of predicting crime. (Several police departments have been working at this, but so far the results have been disappointing.)
5. A computer method of predicting volume of police calls, so that men and cars can be allocated properly. (The St. Louis, Missouri, Police Department developed a successful computer program that could do this over a three-week period.)
6. The computerization of the management function—personnel, payrolls, performance records, and so on.
7. Storage and retrieval of information that will help the police in their daily work. This last is the most obvious use of computers in law enforcement. There are four main categories of data files: (a) criminal histories; (b) wanted persons; (c) autos, stolen or wanted, registrations, and traffic violations; and (d) property, stolen or wanted, including firearms.

The computer was a technological breakthrough of enormous potential for detectives in their efforts to solve cases. To appreciate the implications of this development, it will be helpful to review the traditional investigative methods followed by detectives. It is axiomatic in police circles that "A detective is only as good as his information." The surest solution is an informer. The next best resource is good witnesses. After these reveal all they can in response to questions, they are taken to headquarters and shown the rogues' gallery, where they may spot someone who looks like the perpetrator. Or they may give a description of the suspect that provides the detective with some lead to pursue.

The third technique is to develop clues left at the scene of the crime. The detective goes to the *modus operandi* file to determine if he can recognize techniques of a particular criminal or criminals. Utilizing the clues, he narrows down the search to a type or class of criminal.

The last method is the most demanding. Ringing doorbells and asking residents in the vicinity of the crime whether they heard or saw anything unusual is a tedious investigative routine, which causes detectives to assert that "legwork is more important than headwork." As a final step, a review is made of all persons known to have committed similar crimes. Ultimately, this procedure may yield enough evidence for an arrest, or possibly for a search warrant or wiretapping order.

It is hardly surprising that the modern detective using traditional methods is disillusioned by a high failure rate and enthusiastically embraces the computer system. With it, he can search thousands of records in seconds. In minutes the computer will print out a list of suspects who have committed crimes similar in detail to the one under investigation.

But these notable qualities of the computer—speed and miniaturization of data—which so dazzled law enforcement, have a double edge. Although for decades the police and other regulatory agencies have been steadily amassing information and compiling dossiers on "persons of interest" (the euphemism for suspects), except for fingerprint identification in criminal records, most of the other records systems were not useful in law enforcement. Files were bulky, lost and misplaced, deteriorated with age, and almost impossible to arrange for speedy access except by name. And unless the record existed in the local jurisdiction where the search took place, there was little hope of finding the specific card or entry. Cooperation among jurisdictions was minimal. Now, with the advent of the computer, all that has changed. Interfaces and terminals across the country make a mountain of data potentially available to any law enforcement officer requesting it.

The other side of computer technology is that it constitutes a threat to democracy—to privacy and freedom to dissent. Inevitably, computerized information systems will place everyone in America from the age of fourteen to seventy into the category of possible suspect. And there is no statute of limitations on tapes, disks, and memory banks; they can be held thirty, forty, and fifty years, or in perpetuity. Moreover, not only state and federal law enforcement agencies, but also the Pentagon, the Army, the Navy, and the Air Force, have gathered data on millions of citizens. They, too, are interested in "troublemakers." The C.I.A. and the State Department have their computerized card files. The Civil Service Commission has millions of names listed in its security files. And how many other governmental agencies are quietly amassing their own computer banks of data on "persons of interest"? In addition, the federal agencies intermesh with private agencies and organizations that collect information on credit risks, peace demonstrators, welfare recipients, radicals, liberals, intellectuals, and writers and speakers critical of the government's policies.

It is disheartening to contemplate that every "person of interest" may now be shadowed from birth to grave by a web of computers. With computers as masters, we are a nation in which the citizens are under control and under suspicion. In fact, a campaign is under way to assign a "universal identifier" code number to each person in America, so that any scrap of information collected anytime and anyplace can be easily assembled.

The invasion of privacy by computers did not become a matter for serious public concern until the mid-sixties.[25] In 1964 about eighty police departments had their own computers. Two years later one-third of all police departments surveyed had incorporated computers into their regular operations.[26] Today almost all important police forces have computers.

The computer threat is a grave social problem, and one that is part of a split in our nation along ideological grounds. To a supporter of the hard line in criminal justice, the drive by law enforcement agencies to compile complete computerized dossiers on everyone is acceptable. They tend to ask, as policemen students attending college often do, "Why should any law-abiding citizen feel threatened when the government or the police collect information about his personal life?" The liberals, by contrast, view this situation as the embodiment of 1984 or the second coming of the era of Senator Joseph McCarthy.

In a series of speeches in early 1950, McCarthy ominously waved a paper alleged to contain a list of 205 (then 81, and finally 57) Communists holding government positions. The source of the information was reputed to be files supplied by the State Department. In testimony before the Tydings Committee in the Senate, McCarthy ranted:

I am not making charges. I am giving the committee information of individuals who appear by all the rules of common sense as being very bad security risks.[27]

Armed with a few incomplete dossiers, McCarthy terrorized the nation's leaders, demolished reputations, and devastated countless lives.

What would happen today if someone like Senator McCarthy could produce, not a spurious piece of paper, but an awe-inspiring computer printout of thousands or perhaps millions of names of people singled out as security risks because they had taken part in a demonstration against the Vietnam War? What would result if he arbitrarily demanded that they be dismissed immediately from their jobs in government or universities? The computer and all its ramifications just discussed constitute an electronic straitjacket, constraining freedom of thought and restricting even politically neutral activity, let alone dissent.

Furthermore, the typical victim of computer accusations is virtually helpless. He may never be able to pinpoint or prove the source of error in the computer record that damns him. And the very features of the computer that induce a paralysis of will in its victims generate in the minds of its masters a peculiar faith in its infallibility that nurtures bureaucratic arrogance.

Ironically, policemen themselves have grown accustomed to living under a dossier dictatorship. In the larger departments, members of the force, especially those in the lower ranks, are covered by complete records transcribed to computer cards or tape. Into their files go every innuendo, scandal, and crackpot complaint. Wild accusations are zealously followed up by internal affairs investigators as though they constituted a *prima facie* case. Policemen fear that these often fantastic charges are transmitted into secret code marks entered upon their dossiers, which will prevent future promotion or will contaminate the fairness of later, unrelated investigations. But the ideology of law enforcement is deeply etched in the minds of the police; their subservience to traditional bureaucratic procedures is almost obsessional. Consequently, if the control of the data banks of national criminal justice remains in their hands, as it does now, ironically the same law enforcement officials who were themselves formerly protesting victims of a dossier dictatorship will use the identical tactics against the public they are sworn to protect. This is the ultimate perversion of bureaucracy.

What, if any, is the recourse for victims of mistakes or abuses of the system? Dean Abraham S. Goldstein of the Yale University Law School and Columbia University Law Professor Alan F. Westin independently developed similar positions on the right of privacy. Goldstein asserted pessimistically that the law provides no magic formula for controlling computers, dossiers, or their dissemination.[28] And even more forebodingly, Westin warned that, despite any safeguards, computer systems can be corrupted from within or penetrated from outside.[29] In their final assessments, however, both became more sanguine and concluded that more protection can be implanted in the new computer system than in the old manual records systems. For example, the computer could be programmed to erase an individual's criminal record after a certain period of good conduct. Professor Arthur R. Miller of the University of Michigan Law School, on the other hand, is grim in his predictions. In his appearance before the Senate Subcommittee on Constitutional Rights he contended that we are on the path to a dossier dictatorship:

Americans are scrutinized, measured, counted, and interrogated by more government agencies, law enforcement officials, social scientists, and polltakers than at any time in our history.

There are no effective restraints on the national government's information activities and no one has undertaken to insure that individuals are protected against the misuse of the burgeoning data banks.[30]

And with the relentless monopoly that law enforcement agencies exert over their computer systems, and their fierce resistance to any diminution of power, Miller's dismal portrait of rampant surveillance becomes a realistic one.

Extending their authority even further, the police have insisted upon access to computer files assembled by other agencies. The Census Bureau, almost alone, has resisted this pressure, affirming that even the most routine data such as age, citizenship, and marital status remain inviolate in its own archives.

There is a growing feeling of dread that privacy and freedom to dissent in America are threatened as never before by the secret accumulation of an infinite electronic reservoir of data. What heightens the threat is the inadequacy of the protective measures taken or proposed thus far. What are the recommendations advanced by authorities on the subject?

PROPOSALS FOR THE CONTROL OF COMPUTER DOSSIERS

1. Electronic controls built into the computer programs.
2. Remedial legislation providing for criminal penalties, civil actions, and injunctions for improper conduct in collecting, storing, or disseminating information.
3. Careful selection, education, licensing, and supervision of professional information keepers. A code of ethics and self-restraint would be the protective mechanisms.
4. A regulatory agency.
5. Ombudsmen.
6. A federal privacy law requiring notification to the individual that a record exists, when its contents have been divulged to another agency, and permitting inspection, correction, and rebuttal.
7. Sabotage and the forcible destruction of the data banks.

EVALUATION OF THE PROPOSALS

The first recommendation, for built-in controls, is naive, since controls are no better than the people who exercise them. Loyalty to the organization, the rewards for bureaucratic efficiency, and devotion to the awesome electronic instrument are likely to conquer any vague responsibility to the anonymous "person of interest" whose fate is at stake.

Legislation will be no more successful than built-in controls in curbing abuses. Ostensibly the servant of the law, law enforcement is nearly always its master. Laws already in existence did not prevent detectives in the New York City Police Department from selling confidential information from secret files to banks, private detective agencies, and other commercial companies.[31] There is no reason to anticipate that other police departments will obey the laws more scrupulously. Yet former F. B. I. director J. Edgar Hoover was satisfied that the law plus F. B. I. security procedures would be adequate to prevent any misuse or abuse of computerized records of a confidential nature. Here is his message on the subject:

Speculation, on the part of some, that the computerization of criminal history will lead to the wholesale misuse of such data is completely unfounded. Detailed security procedures have been established throughout the NCIC to insure that criminal information is used only for those purposes approved by law. Under Federal statute, the F.B.I. is authorized to exchange criminal identification, crime, and other records with "authorized officials of the Federal Government, the States, cities, and penal and other institutions."[32]

It is not easy to accept uncritically Hoover's assurance that no misuse of criminal history will occur because the F. B. I. has established procedures under the law. In fact, the F. B. I. has already been involved in an incident where an ordinary prudent man would say that the F. B. I. misused a criminal history. In October 1970 an assault charge against a defendant in a Washington, D.C., court was dropped by the prosecutor because the arrest was obviously an error. Soon after, at the request of the defendant, the Washington, D.C., police department destroyed the arrest records, the mug shots, and the fingerprints. However, in accordance with standard operating procedure, it had already forwarded copies of the records and the fingerprints to the central office of the F. B. I. Following its usual procedures, the F. B. I. refused outright to invalidate or destroy this criminal history, although the case was unfounded. The judge of the General Sessions Court scheduled a hearing to determine whether the F. B. I. had the right to hold the records or should destroy them. Immediately, the F. B. I. filed a petition in the Federal District Court to remove the proceeding from the jurisdiction of the original court and judge.[33]

This incident dramatizes the ease with which a dossier can be compiled on an individual and the lack of recourse he has when he tries to expunge a wrongfully compiled record. The F. B. I. managed to avoid limitations that might be placed upon data banks, using the theory that once the Washington, D.C., police sent the record to them, it became F. B. I. property, and the defendant in the case had no legal standing in asking for its return or destruction. The F. B. I.'s resistance to any supervision by the courts of its power over criminal records or dossiers proves that when a law enforcement system becomes so powerful as to be immune to court supervision, civil and constitutional rights and liberties are truly in peril.

Related strategies support the master plan to fend off any controls over law enforcement. The advisory committee to the F. B. I. NCIC, composed of forty prominent law enforcement officials carefully selected by the F. B. I., passed a strong resolution advocating that the law enforcement agencies maintain control over the NCIC operation because its confidentiality needed guaranteed protection.[34] The New York City Police Department made it a regular practice to forward to the welfare authorities, the courts, and the schools duplicates of its confidential juvenile records containing unsubstantiated, and possibly incriminating, information about children aged seven to sixteen.[35] And the secrecy and confidentiality of these records were guaranteed by law, not merely by some committee's resolution.

Law enforcement has already defeated other attempts to establish external controls over its operation. The police in various cities have co-opted or, where necessary, routed civilian review boards and ombudsmen. No similar supervisory agency is likely to survive for long, because law enforcement, more powerful now than ever before, will demolish it in the name of law and order.

Despite its vulnerability, a civilian-controlled regulatory agency that will act as an information ombudsman representing the people seems the most feasible means of protection, at least as a stopgap measure. It would be responsible for inquiries into the gathering and transmittal of information by law enforcement agencies. Although such an agency is a sensible proposal, it can readily lose all effectiveness if it succumbs to police pressure and becomes the representative of power it was supposed to regulate.

On the subject of safeguards for the individual, the Department of Justice took an unusual approach. Assistant Attorney General William H. Rehnquist announced that the Department would oppose any legislation that would impair the government's power to gather information about American citizens because there was no need for such controls. The rationale was that self-discipline on the part of the executive branch would constitute the necessary protection against the abuse of information gathering.[36]

In contrast to the Department of Justice, Director Robert R. J. Gallati of the New York State Identification and Intelligence System (NYSIIS) has had the foresight and courage to admit the potential danger to privacy and freedom presented by the gigantic computer data bank that serves as the central clearing house of criminal histories in New York State. He recruited Professor Alan F. Westin to devise methods for the protection of constitutional rights and has made frequent appearances before committees to call attention to the necessity of establishing safeguards in computer information systems. Gallati's testimony before a Senate subcommittee contrasted with the dire warnings of other witnesses. He maintained that computer systems "are essential for the administration of criminal justice and can be operated with adequate security against unreasonable invasion of individual privacy."[37]

To underscore his contention, Gallati outlined the specific protections that had been incorporated into his computer installation. NYSIIS has protected privacy by limiting the number of users, restricting the type of information programmed, forbidding unauthorized disclosure, and permitting individuals to see the files and make corrections. In addition, the system's personnel are carefully trained and closely disciplined; extensive security precautions have been taken; and the entire program is subject to annual review. And finally, as a compassionate "fail-safe" device, NYSIIS has adopted a "forgiveness principle." This means that the only records entered in the computer files are those of individuals who are potentially recidivists.

Unfortunately, despite the laudable effort of the NYSIIS plan to protect civil rights, its ultimate effectiveness in this direction is disputable, as its weak links discussed below will indicate.

1. *Limitation of Users.* Every criminal justice agency in New York State (now numbering 3,600) has access to NYSIIS. And since New York State is a participant in Project SEARCH with interfaces to the NCIC of the F.B.I., an uncontrollable multiplication of users will result.

2. *Restriction of Information to Be Entered.* Currently, any restriction on the kind or amount of information in the NYSIIS must be interpreted as a matter of expediency, not principle. Although "debugging"—that is, narrowing the focus of the entries—has been accomplished, the economics of the million-dollar facility will demand that it be used to its fullest potential. And NYSIIS will undoubtedly include extensive data on "persons of interest" and even on

k.p.c., "known police characters" (any person who has been the subject of a field interrogation), before long.

3. *Permission to Examine and Correct the Dossier.* Obviously, such examination will be the prerogative of those with the money and power to protect their interests. For the average person, without knowledge of NYSIIS and its records, the privilege to examine and correct would at best be a nominal one.

4. *Training and Discipline of Personnel.* A wide variety of bureaucratic, ideological, and personal pressures generate leaks that training and discipline cannot overcome.

5. *Extensive Security Provisions.* The theft from an F. B. I. office in Pennsylvania, of secret reports of the surveillance of suspected militants and radicals, and their distribution to the mass media for publication, indicates that even the F. B. I., with its almost paranoid insistence upon top security, failed. Can NYSIIS do better?

6. *Annual Review.* If an individual is determined to search a computer record and divulge the information privately, can an annual review hope to uncover a trace of an extra printout or visual display from which the disclosure was derived?

7. *Forgiveness Principle.* This policy is humanitarian, but dangerously unscientific and misleading. In fact, there are innumerable situations in which names totally unconnected to the probability of recidivism will be entered on NYSIIS files. In deciding whether an individual will repeat a crime, what new criteria will NYSIIS advance? How will the forgiveness principle operate?

Of all the alternatives suggested to protect our society from the chilling effect of computerized data banks, the most obvious and hopeful, as already mentioned, is to remove control from the government and law enforcement, and delegate it to a civilian regulatory agency that would act as an ombudsman for the public interest. However, under a government that can bend the Supreme Court to its political ideology, can a board guarding such valuable information escape the same manipulation? When even Congress and presidents have lacked either the power or the courage to oppose the F. B. I., can we expect strong independence from the new agency?

A political regime that advertises law and order as its primary domestic goal very nearly guarantees that every year the number of arrests will increase and that computer data banks will necessarily expand. To stop the increase in crime, the criminal histories will become the means of labeling, investigating, and controlling criminals and, in addition to these, possible dissenters. There will be not a reduction but a proliferation of centralized computer data banks.

The joining of technology and bureaucracy will necessarily result in a national system of interlocking computer data banks. A technological development of this magnitude that meshes so exactly with the requirements of our bureaucratic society generates too much momentum to be denied. Congress cannot be expected to provide safeguards, for although it is divided, it is basically sympathetic to the concept of stronger governmental controls over the people. But if law enforcement remains in control of these information networks, the prophecy of 1984 will have been consummated years before its predicted advent.

NOTES

1. *Criminality and the Legal Order* (Chicago: Rand McNally, 1969), p. 25.

2. *Criminal Jury Instructions for the District of Columbia*, no. 6 (1966).

3. *Study Draft of a New Criminal Code* (Washington, D.C.: U. S. Government Printing Office, 1970), p. 3.

4. John H. Wigmore, *Wigmore on Evidence*, 3rd ed., (Boston: Little, Brown, 1940), vol. 9, p. 408.

5. *Barrett v. United States*, 322 F. 2d 292 (1963).

6. Wigmore, *op. cit.*, p. 407.

7. "Equal Justice in the Gatehouses and Mansions of American Criminal Procedure," in Yale Kamisar, Fred E. Inbau, and Thurman Arnold, *Criminal Justice in Our Time* (Charlottesville: University Press of Virginia, 1965), p. 20.

8. *Mapp v. Ohio*, 367 U.S. 643 (1961). In this case the police in Cleveland, Ohio, illegally entered a boarding house over the protest of the owner.

9. Fred E. Inbau and Claude R. Sowle, *Criminal Justice: Cases and Comments*, 2nd ed. (Brooklyn, N. Y.: Foundation Press, 1964 p. 702.

10. *Ibid.*, pp. 776-777.

11. *New York Times*, March 10, 1970, p. 1.

12. *Miranda v. Arizona*, 384 U.S. 436 (1966).

13. *People v. Peters*, 18 N.Y. 2d 238 (1966), later affirmed by the U. S. Supreme Court in *Peters v. New York*, 392 U.S. 41 (1968).

14. *Psychopathology and Politics* (New York: Viking, 1960), pp. 75-77.

15. For data supporting the thesis that the police belong to the middle rather than to the lower middle class, see Nelson A. Watson and James W. Sterling, *Police and Their Opinions* (Washington, D.C.: International Association of Chiefs of Police, 1969), pp. 105-119.

16. Jerome H. Skolnick, *Justice Without Trial* (New York: Wiley, 1967), pp. 45-48.

17. In New York City, at least, the police point of view may be correct and the F.B.I. data misleading. See *New York Times*, March 14, 1971, p. 1.

18. See Arthur Niederhoffer, *Behind the Shield* (Garden City, N.Y.: Doubleday, 1967).

19. See *New York Times*, March 13, 1971, p. 29.

20. *Terry v. Ohio* 392 U.S. 1 (1968) and *Peters v. New York*, 392 U.S. 41 (1968).

21. "Social Inquiry and the Autonomy of the Individual," in Daniel Lerner (ed.), *The Human Meaning of the Social Sciences* (New York: World Publishing Co., 1959), p. 155.

22. Alvin W. Gouldner, *The Coming Crisis of Western Sociology* (New York: Basic Books, 1970), p. 9.

23. *NCCD News*, 48 (November–December), 1969, p. 4. See also, Tom Wicker, "The Goat and the Cabbage Patch," *New York Times*, March 11, 1971, p. 39.

24. *LEAA 1970* (Washington, D.C.: U.S. Government Printing Office, 1970), pp. 38, 76–79. See also *New York Times*, November 30, 1971, p. 30.

25. Alan F. Westin, *Privacy and Freedom* (New York: Atheneum, 1967), p. 299.

26. *Ibid.*, p. 305.

27. Richard H. Rovere, *Senator Joe McCarthy* (New York: World Publishing Co., 1960), pp. 149–150.

28. Abraham S. Goldstein, "Legal Control of the Dossier," in Stanton Wheeler (ed.), *On Record: Files and Dossiers in American Life* (New York: Russell Sage Foundation, 1969), p. 443.

29. Westin, *Privacy and Freedom*, op. cit., p. 324.

30. See *New York Times*, February 24, 1971, p. 24.

31. *New York Times*, June 19, 1970, p. 13. See also, *New York Times*, January 27, 1971, p. 41.

32. *F.B.I. Law Enforcement Bulletin*, 40 (November 1971). See *New York Times*, November 30, 1971, p. 30.

33. *NCCD News*, 50 (January–February 1971), p. 5.

34. See Department of Justice, *OLEA Final Reports of Projects*, 66–100, 68–41, and 67–21 (1966–68).

35. *NCCD News*, 49 (November–December 1970), p. 16.

36. *New York Times*, March 10, 1971, p. 1.

37. *New York Times*, March 11, 1971, p. 26.

4 / THE CRIMINOGENIC SOCIETY: SOCIAL VALUES AND DEVIANCE

MILTON L. BARRON

What sociological truth can one find in the current slogans that crime and its overlapping problem of violence are "as American as cherry pie" and that "we get the crime (or violence) we deserve"? How valid is the theory that ours is a criminogenic, a crime-generating, culture and society? The relationship of American culture and society—especially of the organization and hierarchy of values in American society—to the problems of crime and delinquency needs to be explored. The question we must try to answer is whether any, if not all, of the legal norm-violating behavior and so-called deviant behavior we claim to deplore is actually a normal and consistent product of our way of life.

THEORY OF A CRIMINOGENIC SOCIETY AND CULTURE

An increasingly vociferous and articulate school of thought in the American social sciences in general, and in criminology in particular, subscribes to the point of view that the etiology—the investigation of the causes—of social problems such as crime and delinquency has failed to provide us with satisfactory answers because it has overlooked the proper frame of reference for study and analysis: American society itself. For the most part, etiology has probed only segments and the "outer crust," so to speak, whereas the impelling forces making for delinquency and crime actually inhere deeply and pervasively in the culture and structure of American society. This interpretation calls for a different perspective, one that seeks explanations for legal norm-violating behavior elsewhere than in the narrow confines of genes, personality, family, peer group, community ecology, or media of communication. Instead of placing heavy stress on the alleged deviance marking not only the behavior but also the underlying personality and values of the offender, the criminogenic approach argues that the criminal and delinquent values are far less deviant than commonly portrayed. Many of these values are actually closely akin to those held by the entire society. This may help explain, on the one hand, the large amount of unrecorded crime and delinquency and, on the other, the occurrence of legal norm-violating behavior throughout the whole class structure.[1] In developing their violent gangs, for example, boys really cannot go beyond their experiences and their observation of the activities of their families and other elders. Their codes and chosen life-styles must be studied with reference to the codes and life-styles they encounter in the communities where they live.

Culture molds and shapes behavior, giving direction to what most people will do most of the time. If part of our culture is criminogenic, then many people will engage in delinquency and crime. In other words, in a competitive society organized around profit, people will murder for profit. When a competitive society moves toward large-scale production, people will also move toward large-scale murder.

The theory of a criminogenic society and culture is not without its detractors. Some see it as an avenue of escape from more rigorous etiological thinking. This, of course, may be true of any frustrated search for concise answers that leads to ambiguous, evasively holistic and vague substitute answers. Whether or not the charge is justified in this instance, the student must eventually decide for himself. Others have been seriously reluctant to adopt the theory because, as they maintain, under the guise of moral detachment it actually imputes moral blame on a reified combination of individuals—all of us, or "society." Some see it as an insidious plot by revolutionaries and radicals to attack and undermine our way of life in order to overthrow it eventually, substituting in its place a Communist dictatorship. And still others disparage the theory as carrying the deterministic premises of the social sciences to a point of absurdity: the point where human beings are mechanistically conceived to be irresponsible, passive products of their social and cultural environment. To these critics the theory is as intolerable as its biologically and geographically deterministic precursors in nineteenth-century thought. Do we make society, or does society make us? The answer probably is that both propositions in the question are partly true. One does not exclude the other. The theory of a criminogenic society and culture is neither condemnatory nor unduly deterministic. It merely commits us to the implications of our sociological premises: that society and culture contribute more than any other forces to making us think, feel, and behave as legal norm-violators just as they do in all other roles we may play in life.

PREDECESSORS AND VARIANTS OF THE CRIMINOGENIC THEORY

The first to use the specific concept of a criminogenic culture and to develop it in the context of an etiological theory was Donald R. Taft, a University of Illinois criminologist, in 1942.[2] However, he was by no means the first to theorize that societies experience the kinds and scope of crime and delinquency that their own values and social structure provoke. The theory was implicit, for instance, in the works, written in the late nineteenth century, of the great French sociologist Emile Durkheim, especially in his use of the concept of anomie in relation to urban, industrial, and mobile conditions. To him, suicide, crime, and other social problems were consequences of anomie, both in its original Greek-rooted connotation of social anarchy and in its later connotation of deregulation and normlessness.[3] In *The Rules of Sociological Method,* he said of crime that "there is no phenomenon that presents more indisputably all the symptoms of normality, since it appears closely connected with the conditions of all social life."

Making cross-cultural or comparative studies, cultural anthropologists have also gained criminogenic insights, sometimes with special reference to the greater delinquency- or crime-inducing aspects of some cultures and societies as compared with others. In her classic account of socialization processes during adolescence in Samoa, Margaret Mead[4] contrasted the absence of "storm and stress" among Samoan girls with the deeply troubled personality and delinquent behavior so common among their American counterparts, explaining this contrast in terms of the "general casualness" and lack of cultural contradictions in the whole Samoan society:

For Samoa is a place where no one plays for very high stakes, no one pays very high prices, no one suffers for his convictions or fights to the death for special ends. Disagreements between parent and child are settled by the child's moving across the street, between a man and his village by the man's removal to the next village, between a husband and his wife's seducer by a few fine mats. Neither poverty nor great disasters threaten the people to make them hold their lives dearly and tremble for continued existence. No implacable gods, swift to anger and strong to punish, disturb the even tenor of their days. Wars and cannibalism are long since passed away and now the greatest cause for tears, short of death itself, is a journey of a relative to another island. No one is hurried along in life or punished harshly for slowness of development. In this casual attitude towards life, in this avoidance of conflict, of poignant situations, Samoa contrasts strongly with America. Our young people are faced by a series of different groups which believe different things and advocate different practices. Because our civilization is woven of so many diverse strands, the ideas which any one group accepts will be found to contain numerous contradictions. . . . The presence of many strongly held and contradictory points of view and the enormous influence of individuals in the lives of their children in our country play into each other's hands in producing situations fraught with emotion and pain. . .

The variant form of the criminogenic theory that concentrates on the problem of juvenile delinquency rather than on adult crime appeared in a few published works beginning in the 1950's.[5] Indeed, the annual conference of the Institute of Juvenile Court Judges held in Pittsburgh in 1955 was organized around the theme "The Troubled Juvenile in a Delinquent Society." But the pioneering application of the theory that American society is a delinquent-producing society was by John Bartlow Martin, a distinguished crime journalist, in his study of a highly publicized, "irrational" murder by several young boys in Ann Arbor, Michigan, early in the decade.[6] His conclusion was as follows:

We are all involved in this. Roadside signboards, radio and television commercials, newspaper and magazine advertisements urge people to drive fast and to drink. Well, the revolution is over now. These are its children. . . . We declared inhibition wicked; in warfare we dislocated our population; we leveled classes; we abandoned decorum and broke the Prohibition law and made a cult of sex and sadism. . . . Since 1900 America has been remade. Societies do not necessarily get better or worse; but they do change. Sometimes new controls do not arise to replace ones thrown off; sometimes enlightenment overthrows old taboos but erects falser idols in their places. Just as a psychotic is merely a human being in whom the normal balance has been disturbed, so is a delinquent society merely a distortion of all society, exaggerating its lawlessness and jettisoning its controls. [*Italics mine.*]

Another important variant of the criminogenic theory has been the effort to explain the obviously related but somewhat more comprehensive and nebulous phenomena of "corruption" and "immorality" in the same societal and cultural frames of reference. In the same year that Martin introduced us to the concept of a delinquent society, the sociologist and criminologist Marshall Clinard[7] was analyzing that election year's (1952) Republican charges of corruption against the incumbent Democratic administration by noting, first of all, that "political corruption, crime, immorality, athletic scandals, the current disorders of our society, cannot be diagnosed as independent, isolated phenomena." All, he claimed, are common consequences of a general social disruption in the ways we live and work and think together as human beings. There is in our society a current pattern of dishonesty, illegal advantage, loss of integrity, and moral indifference. The pervasive pattern of dishonesty and corruption is underscored one generation later in connection with the now famous Watergate affair that involved, among other crimes, the burglary and illegal electronic surveillance of the Democratic national headquarters in 1972. Responsibility for the planning and funding of the burglary, recruitment of the burglars, and the subsequent efforts to conceal their crimes, apparently reached into the White House itself. It is unfortunate, Clinard pointed out, that the problem of corruption is so often identified exclusively with politics and politicians. Actually it has no such specific connection. The state of affairs is much more general and serious, for not only can politics and government be corrupt but also business, labor, the professions, and even the general public.

To C. Wright Mills,[8] who was addressing himself to the same problem in the same year, corruption was merely one aspect of a more general immorality, a "structural immorality" in our society:

Think of it this way. When a handful of men do not have jobs and do not seek work, we may look for the causes in their immediate situation and character. But when 12,000,000 men are unemployed, then we cannot believe that all of them suddenly "got lazy" and turned out to be "no good." Economists call this "structural unemployment," meaning, for one thing, that the men involved cannot themselves control their job chances. I think many of the problems of white-collar crime and relaxed public morality, of high-priced vice and fading personal integrity, are problems of structural immorality.

SOCIETY, CULTURE, AND VALUES

What are the criminogenic characteristics of American society and culture? The culture of every society comprises learned and socially shared symbols to which conventionalized significations are assigned. These symbols each stand for objects, concepts, images, social processes or norms, and social objectives or goals of varying degrees of concreteness and abstraction. Most important of all, for the purpose of this discussion, are social values. These refer to cultural symbols which have become meaningful to members of the society from the point of view of the two criteria of truth and worthiness. The social values of a society are so meaningful to members of that society that they accept them largely without the demand for proof and without any serious skepticism. Williams defines social values as "those conceptions of desirable states of affairs that are utilized in selective conduct as criteria for preference or choice or as justifications for proposed or actual behavior." They are closely related to social norms, which are more specific or concrete; values are the criteria by which norms themselves may be judged.[9] One may add that they are likewise the criteria by which goals are chosen.

The qualities of values include a conceptual element and an affective, or emotional, charge.[10] Jessie Bernard has suggested[11] that one may test what is and what is not a social value by imagining a person being elected to office on a platform advocating a specific program. If there is no hesitation in imagining that the candidate could be elected with such a program, then the program unquestionably contains values held by the society. If, on the other hand, there is doubt, then the program conflicts with the voters' values. In most American communities, it would, for instance, be impossible to elect a person to office on a program advocating more poverty, disease and ill health, aggressive war, ignorance, and illiteracy. American values can also be deduced or abstracted from Fourth of July orations, Sunday sermons, and commencement addresses. In short, a second test of values is their triteness. They are taken for granted.

Up to this point, the reference has been to "official" values. These are the values that are verbally respected by most adult members of the society and that are formally and systematically indoctrinated in the young as an integral part of the socialization process by parents, the school, the church, and character-building agencies like the Boy Scouts and Girl Scouts. In their famous sociological study of Middletown, the Lynds identified hard work, honesty, kindness, friendliness, and considerateness as some of the official values in a typical American community of the 1920's and 1930's.[12] They are found in the sacred documents of American society, and many of them appear in the criminal law and the laws defining juvenile delinquency. For example, a careful examination of virtually any state law on delinquency would bring out such values as the inviolability of private property, subservience to parents, guardians, teachers, and other authoritative adults, linguistic discretion, and economic and financial integrity.

But one must also reckon with "unofficial" values. These are informally and unsystematically inculcated in the young during the process of socialization. Theoretically they are very significant with regard to crime and delinquency. In Middletown the Lynds identified them as the values that cluster around "forcefulness," "enterprise," "shrewdness," and "power," the qualities particularly important in gaining competitive advantage in a business-oriented culture.[13] Merton maintains that people learn them first as children observing the daily behavior and listening to the casual conversation of their parents and other adults.[14] They detect them and incorporate them in their own value system even though the values are originally only implicit in adult communication and behavior. The best evidence for this, according to Merton, can be found in the language patterns of the child, especially when persistent grammatical errors occur in such patterns. An error such as "goodest" instead of "best" indicates that the child has detected the implicit paradigms or models for the inflection of adjectives. Analogously, people are probably involved from childhood onward in detecting and incorporating implicit paradigms or models of cultural evaluation even when they may conflict with the explicit, official admonitions, advice, and evaluations they receive from others.

Implicit, unofficial values seem at first glance to be related to crime and delinquency more directly than explicit, official values in terms of actually encouraging if not motivating legal norm-violating behavior. One cannot fail to note, however, that the following American values, which may foster such violations, in fact include both official and unofficial ones.

Success

In American culture, success is undoubtedly one of the supreme objects of desire and emulation, more so perhaps than in any other culture of the Western world. As Williams sees it, American culture is geared to active mastery rather than passive acceptance; hence a low tolerance of frustration, the refusal to accept ascetic renunciation, the positive encouragement of desire, the stress on power, and the approval of ego-assertion.[15] No one can claim that success is exclusively an American value, but in a society characterized by extraordinary mobility and the absence of rigidly fixed classes, success occupies high priority among American goal-values. "Winning isn't everything," said the late eminent professional football coach Vince Lombardi, "it is the only thing."

American culture places a high value upon upward gradients. We ask how fast a baby is growing, how much a schoolchild is improving, how a person is "going up in the world." We give rewards not so much for achievements as for increasing achievement. We value the distance "from log cabin to White House" because it represents a long upward gradient. The credo of success in America, it may be said, includes the conviction that, since success begets success, the appearance of success may bring actual success. The result is that individual Americans admit failure only with the greatest reluctance. Like the father in the well-known play *Death of a Salesman,* a man feels obliged to bluster and give an appearance of prosperity, no matter how hollow it is. Not only is it difficult for Americans to admit to others that they are merely "getting along," but it is increasingly difficult for them to feel that life is worthwhile unless income and position are constantly being bettered.[16]

More than any other people, Americans have traditionally been taught to believe in the Protestant ethic, namely, that hard work and thrift bring success. But as American society has developed, the possibility for upward gradients has diminished. And since millions of normal and useful Americans do not have the energy, intelligence, and opportunity to earn more than a limited amount of recognition and income, feelings of frustration and despondency are rife. When people come to the realization that they cannot attain success by conventional hard work and thrift, many are apt to turn to delinquency and crime, despite fear of punitive sanctions and a preference for achieving the symbols of success legitimately.

In societies where the general level of consumption is considerably lower than in American society, delinquency and crime rates are also likely to be far lower because, for one thing, the level of success to which the majority aspire is not remote from the one they are likely to reach. Individual aspirations and expectations seldom go beyond the achievement level of the parents. In American society, on the other hand, both parents and children usually expect subsequent generations to aspire to and achieve higher levels of success than the previous generations.[17] In his study of American character and behavior patterns, Bradford Smith[18] examined the dynamics of the value of success, observing the trend from the rugged individualism of pioneer days to the contemporary yearning, manifested in some subcultures, for approval, social adjustment, and happiness in security. Even so, he noted, success remains the goal of most Americans, not necessarily in the form of material rewards, but in the form of recognition of some sort, preferably measurable. The emphasis on success and achievement, coupled as it is with a desire to be loved and admired, leads to a critical dilemma of personality, according to Smith. To succeed one must be aggressive; to be loved or at least liked, one must be easygoing and friendly.

Status and Power Ascendance

Americans are said to live in a "pressure" culture in which the question is, "How far can I get?" Inasmuch as the answer is usually thought of in terms, not only of success and failure, but also of social status, the struggle for higher status may be discerned even in the earliest years of childhood. The school experience, for example, has become meaningful to many children as a struggle for grades—the symbols of position or status in relation to other schoolchildren. Outside the classroom, one writer[19] has the following vivid recollection of the struggle for status and power in his own ghetto-bound boyhood and its behavioral consequences for himself and others:

The battle for status was the chief determinant of our lives. Status came from skill in fighting and in such key games as punchball and basketball, but also from a certain indefinable quality of personality, the gift of making others accept and conform to one's style of behavior. Even fighting was not so simple an affair as it seemed on the surface, and success in fighting was not altogether a matter of sheer physical skill. The question of who could fight whom was constantly on our minds, and hardly a day went by without someone trying to put some newly conceived opinion of himself to the test. The boys at the very top were more or less unchallenged. Those at the very bottom were likewise immune so long as they accepted the humiliations and insults which were their daily lot. But for a boy lodged precariously in the middle ranks, life was a tornado of fists and faces, the faces he was out to damage on his way up or the fists that were hammering him down to the nightmarish, infra-human realm. . .

That status consciousness and the struggle for higher status as they are expressed in social class are preoccupations of American adolescents as well as adults can easily be documented in the findings of Hollingshead's penetrating study of the teen-agers of a midwestern community.[20] One veteran social worker's conclusion concerning the relationship between status-striving and delinquency and crime was that three basic factors underlying American social structure lead constantly to legal norm-violating behavior: (a) inequality in status, (b) competition in school, on the playground, in the community, and for a living, and (c) aggressive individualism.[21]

Pertinent here is what Jules Henry has identified as the "technological drivenness" of American culture.[22] In traditional societies, the significance of culture patterns typically derives from their role in satisfying relatively fixed human needs. In American society, however, Henry detects the continual manufacture of new needs in order to sustain the culture. Hence the crucial role played by advertising in the maintenance of American culture. Capable of producing more than they themselves can consume, and until recently barred by fear and ideology from tapping the vast markets of the Communist-dominated societies, Americans are prodded toward orgies of consumption, required to keep industry running and the population employed. Heroic feats of consumption, however, require the destruction of traditional Protestant "impulse controls" and the accompanying values of parsimony, asceticism, and restraint. With an infinitude of wants and no ceiling on the accumulation of property, with an industrial economy that restricts most employees to dreary routine work, Americans are offered as compensation for their drivenness an even higher level of consumption and the culture of fun as "an escape from the spiritual Andersonville in which technological drivenness has imprisoned us." Culture is against man, claims Henry, in the sense that the otherwise efficient social organization of affluence actually starves people emotionally. American institutions not only celebrate but actively support the drive to achievement, accumulation, profit, competition, and mobility. The gentler values of identity, kindness, and generosity tend to be banished from the institutional structures. The great exception is the family, which, as the sole source of emotional relief and a sense of identity for the individual, bears such a burden in an environment dedicated to impersonality and anonymity that it frequently breaks down.

Pecuniary and Material Wealth

Money and material wealth are American values so closely related to success, status, and power ascendance that it would seem unnecessary to consider them separately. Much of success and status-striving, however, have been transformed into monetary and materialistic terms. It is often not what a person is that matters, but rather what he has. The more he has, the greater must be his effort to demonstrate to others how much he has; the less he has, the greater must be his effort to accumulate—if not by legitimate methods, then possibly by illegal ones.

In large measure, then, money and material goods have been consecrated as values in themselves. The ideology of pecuniary success, according to many sociologists, best characterizes the basic motivation that spurs Americans to action and provides them with a sense of significance in their lives. The dollar is dominant, if not almighty, so that the desirability of having it and spending it often leads to minimal regard for its source, even when other values such as honesty are thereby sacrificed. The extent to which material values are enmeshed in the lives of offenders is roughly indicated by the high proportion of known offenses against property that are concerned with the illegal acquisition and possession of money and other wealth.

Resistance to Authority

Whatever one prefers to call it—independence, individuality, nonconformity, or freedom—there is in American culture a value that pivots around resistance to authority. In his study of the "lunatic fringe," Gerald W. Johnson, for example, vigorously and convincingly challenges the theory that Americans are basically conformists.[23] We never were, he insists; we are not now; we will not be, unless, of course, conformity is seen in such acts as turning on light when one goes into one's own house at night, eating at least once a day, lighting the tobacco end of filtered cigarettes, and so on.

Americans tend to resist rules and regulations. In contrast to the Hindus, for instance, who are fascinated by rules and red tape, Americans prefer to be free from the control of too many societal norms. They have never tired of exalting "rugged individualism." One consistent end result is a high incidence of nonconformity as manifested in the extreme end of its spectrum: delinquency and crime. Some historians trace American resistance to authority back to Plymouth Colony, the Boston Tea Party, the Whiskey Rebellion, the Abolition Movement, the industrial robber barons, straight down to the contemporary phenomena of gangsterism, racketeering, and organized crime. Others, like Frederick Jackson Turner,[24] have seen its origin specifically in the frontier, a moving line in American history marked by an imbalanced sex ratio and weakness in such institutions as family, church, and government, which were unable to play their traditional roles of inhibiting nonconformity. Attracting the adventurous, norm-violating young male to begin with, frontier life, subject to boredom and disputes, encouraged heavy drinking, gambling, fighting, and killing. Today, except in Alaska, little is left of the frontier in the sense of a continuous land mass through which the American people can move and which is theirs to develop. But to those who follow the frontier interpretation of the American way of life as outlined by Turner, the frontier, in a psychological and cultural sense, still operates in such characteristic American values as the resistance to authority.

Complete subservience to authority in the form of literal observance of all laws and other social norms is actually subject to ridicule in American society, on both juvenile and adult levels—the current appeal for "law and order" notwithstanding. What is found contemptible and absurd in overconformity is typified by the well-known cartoon character Caspar Milquetoast. Long ago James Tufts[25] suggested that it has become a virtually religious and patriotic duty among Americans to resist restraints upon free adventuring. The hostility shared by many Americans against police personnel—witness the longstanding negative connotation of the term "cop" and the recent use of the even more blatantly pejorative "pig"—is largely an expression of resistance to authority. The same is true of many of the attacks on concentration of political power and against centralization of government functions and controls.

Toughness

Another American value significant in the etiology of crimes and delinquencies that are offenses against persons tends to appear especially in the personality makeup of the male. That value is "toughness," the facade of hypermasculinity. "Boys in all the lower-class New York neighborhoods took pride in their toughness," recalled Poster of his boyhood, "but in Brownsville, somehow, we worked at it full time."[26] In a similar autobiographical account, John Knight[27] remembered that in his early childhood years

the sissy taunt was engraved in the air wherever I turned in Middletown: clothes might be too neat; attractive, bright colors in sport shirts or bathing trunks could bring it on. One might pay too much attention to girls or perhaps be seen escorting them from school. Carrying a violin case through the neighborhood of the gashouse toughs was almost suicidal. I can remember begging Mother to ask the violin teacher to give me lessons at home, and during music practice periods I closed all the windows, even in summertime. It was dangerous to approve of literature, especially poetry, or to join the dramatics and arts clubs.

Knight draws the following general conclusion about the implications of the "sissy complex":

An individual dominated by an intense masculine drive has such a great compulsion to "be a man" that he possesses little objectivity. . . . We American males spend an inordinate amount of time on baseball, gambling, and convivial evenings with male companions. Our national sissy complex prevents impressionable children and young adults from considering music, painting, sculpture or the dance as desirable careers or even acceptable hobbies.

Although there is undoubtedly a social-class differential in this respect, in most strata of American society intense pressure is placed upon males from their earliest years regarding the necessity of "fighting back" and "not being a sissy." Boys are generally taught to use physical violence when the occasion calls for it, as in self-defense. They are apt to be ridiculed for any display of sensitivity. Even when the family does not communicate the desirability of toughness, the boy will nevertheless acquire the value from other cultural sources. American culture is permeated with the unavoidability of violence in interpersonal relations. Movies carry this theme to such a degree that many children and adults no longer consider a performance satisfying unless it includes several violent deaths. Violence is celebrated in crime and gangster programs on the radio and television, as well as in countless magazines, cartoons, and comic strips, generally in the context of superhuman and therefore dehumanized achievements. Business and the unions have been known to condone violence implicitly or explicitly, setting themselves against anything that does not "pay off" in the toughest terms.

Dupery

In his own struggle for power and success, the legendary American showman P. T. Barnum provided many of his fellow Americans with a supporting slogan in the achievement of these goals: "There's a sucker born every minute." The truth and worth of these words and of others such as "Do others in before they do you in" and "Everything is a racket" have made an unofficial value of dupery. The significance of dupery in relation to delinquency and crime is theoretically far greater than most Americans are willing to concede.

Dupery seems to operate in situations where an official value or "publicly accepted norm" such as honesty is covertly violated on a large scale, with the tacit acceptance or even approval of the society or group, at least as long as the violations are concealed. Dupery in such a case is an alternative norm that is being observed, and expresses a different cultural value from that of the ideal, official norm that is being evaded.

One of the most convincing investigations of the extent of dupery in commercial life was a nationwide study carried out after the Second World War by a man-and-woman team who tested garages, radio repair shops, and watch repair shops, employing a simple experimental technique.[28] Before driving into the garages, they merely disconnected a coil wire. Of the 347 garages visited, 129 noted the trouble at once, honestly informed the investigators, and either charged them nothing or only a nominal fee. The others, 63 percent of the total sample, treated the investigators as dupes, overcharging them, lying, inserting unnecessary parts, or charging them for work not done, for new parts not needed, and for parts not installed.

For the purpose of testing the radio repair shops, the investigators loosened a tube or disconnected a wire in a new radio. Of the 304 shops visited throughout the country, 109 honestly identified the trouble, corrected it, and either made no charge or merely a token charge. The remaining shops, a clear majority of the sample, tried to cheat the investigators by selling them tubes, batteries, and service that the radio set did not need, or by charging them for new parts that were not inserted. In some cases the shops even removed good parts from the radio and added them to the supply on their shelves, at the same time substituting inferior equipment.

The most honest were the watch repairmen. The test here was made by loosening the little screw that fastens the winding wheel in the watch. Of the 462 watch repairmen investigated throughout the nation, only 49 percent lied, overcharged, gave false diagnoses, or suggested expensive and unnecessary repairs. A bare majority, 51 percent, were honest, only 8 of them charging anything at all.

Other Criminogenic Characteristics

The values described above do not comprise the full range of criminogenic social and cultural forces in American life. Criminologists[29] are convinced that the following features of the American way of life also have much to do with crime and delinquency.

AMERICAN CULTURE IS DYNAMIC. Change, fluidity in norms, which characterizes all Western urban and industrial societies and particularly American society, is bound to weaken the sense of a difference between right and wrong behavior, to create a feeling that the two are relative. In other, non-Western societies where change is slow—almost imperceptible in some cases—and the norms have become firmly fixed in tradition, there is less proneness to norm-violating behavior.

The newest conceptualization of the implications of culture dynamics for behavior is Alvin Toffler's "future shock."[30] Just as anthropologists introduced the concept "culture shock" into social science terminology to refer to the bewildering experience of man exposed to a radically different culture through space, or horizontally, so sociologists now apply "future shock" to the shattering stress and disorientation induced by too much change in the dimension of time, or vertically. Future shock, according to Toffler, arises from the superimposition of a new culture on an old one. It is culture shock in one's own society. But its impact is far more detrimental psychologically and sociologically. Most Peace Corps representatives, and even cultural anthropologists themselves, have the comforting knowledge that the culture they left behind will be there for them upon their return. The victim of future shock, on the other hand, does not. Take an individual out of his own culture in time and set him down suddenly in a culture with a sharply different set of cues and different conceptions of work, love, religion, and sex. If you then cut him off from any hope of retreat to a more familiar cultural landscape, the dislocation he will suffer will be doubly severe. Moreover, if this new culture is itself in constant turmoil, and if its values are incessantly changing, the sense of disorientation will be still further intensified. Given few clues as to what kind of behavior is rational under the radically new circumstances, the victim may well become a hazard to himself and to others. Now imagine, stresses Toffler, not merely an individual but an entire society, an entire generation—including its weakest, least intelligent, and most irrational members—suddenly catapulted into this new world. The result must be mass disorientation, or future shock on a grand scale. Change is avalanching upon the heads of Americans, and most of them are grotesquely unprepared to cope with it.

AMERICAN CULTURE OFFERS ALTERNATIVE AND CONFLICTING VALUES AND NORMS. A society as dynamic and complex as American society finds that such alternatives to the "right" way of behavior as delinquent or criminal acts, as the law defines them, are not necessarily the "wrong" ways in the subcultures of its various groups. In a sense, American society is a mosaic of ethnic, economic, regional, and other substructures whose conceptions of conformity and norm-violating behavior are frequently in conflict with the legal definitions as well as with each other. Unlike Americans, people in many other parts of the world have had for centuries a clear image of themselves and of the cultural expectations to which their roles should conform. Obviously a society that cannot give a person a clear and coherent notion of himself, from childhood onward, and that cannot tell him with reasonable assurance what things are true, worthy, and of good repute, cannot be a society in which a stable and abiding order prevails between people and within them.

It is not difficult, therefore, writes Anthony Lewis,[31] to discern the real reasons for the severe anomie in American society, primarily among its young, in the seventh decade of the twentieth century:

They are brought up on the creed of possession, sold hard by the advertising message that goods are happiness. But they soon find that possessions do not assure human satisfaction. They know beauty; they have read about it. But they likely live in an esthetically arid suburb, and all around them they see the most beautiful of countries wantonly destroyed for reasons of private greed. Their nation is the richest in history, but they see that it allows its poor to go hungry and its cities to decay, that its tax system encourages life on expense accounts and favors personal consumption over urgent social needs. They see that the United States cannot bring itself to do as well as relatively impoverished Britain in providing a decent system of medical care; they read about large numbers of American doctors, the most prosperous anywhere, fiddling their tax returns. They hear much about law and order, but they know that corruption is widespread among American politicians and law enforcement officers. They are told that violence is evil, but they know that guns can be bought and sold in the United States as in no other civilized land. And they observe the President of the United States photographed happily with union leaders—some with criminal records—whose members have just made news by beating up young people opposed to the Vietnam war. They have dinned into them from childhood the appeal of sensuality, assured that this cigarette or that car or deodorant will bring them sexual success. They see on every hand evidence of their elders' exploitation and commercialization of sex. Yet their own possibly naive efforts to express sexual feelings in an open, easy way are met by moralizing outcry and repression. Those among them who have tried marijuana are lectured, on inadequate facts, about the potential danger; some are sent to jail. But they see billions spent, legally, to promote the use of the proven narcotic killers, alcohol and tobacco. . . . It is the values of American life and the hypocrisy that make the young so uneasy. . . .

SOCIAL RELATIONSHIPS IN AMERICAN SOCIETY HAVE BECOME INCREASINGLY IMPERSONAL. The shift of American society from predominantly rural to urban community structures has meant, among other things, the decline of face-to-face relations as a form of social control and the rise of impersonal relations. The human environment is being reduced to a series of fleeting contacts with strangers and near strangers. Social relationships tend to become more shallow and dehumanized. It is the general consensus among sociologists that this transition from primary to secondary groups, or "lonely crowds," in mass society has encouraged delinquency and crime. City life does not provide the restraints on social behavior formerly built into the rural social structure.

A MULTIGROUP SOCIETY FOSTERS A DUALITY OF LOYALTY AND ETHICS. An interesting hypothesis proposed by Taft and others is that ethnic and other subgroups in American society tend to retain such intense feelings of ethnocentrism that they hold one code of ethics in their relations with the ingroup and a quite different code in their relations with the outgroup. Raping an outgroup female is defined differently from raping an ingroup female, and the sanctions applied are quite different too. Members of a religious group who would not tolerate the desecration of their own church buildings and cemeteries may feel justified in tolerating the desecration of buildings and cemeteries belonging to another group.

Finally, a representative of the new generation of criminogenic theorists,[32] Edwin Schur, has urged that American society is a criminal society not only because certain values emphasized in American culture help generate crime, but also because of American inequality (i.e., widespread poverty and lack of economic opportunity), involvement in mass violence abroad, and the tendency to overlegislate and thereby create unnecessary crime. As Schur put it, "Often our criminalizing of a problem leads to a good deal of secondary crime."

LIMITATIONS OF THE CRIMINOGENIC THEORY

Despite its cogency, the theory that American society and culture are criminogenic is by no means immune from criticism. In the first place, not even its most enthusiastic advocates could claim that all members of the society are equally immersed in delinquent and criminal behavior. What accounts for the differential involvement of Americans in crime and delinquency? Which conditional variables attenuate, and which exacerbate, criminogenic forces?

Secondly, how valid is the assumption implicit in the criminogenic theory that the curvilinear ascent of crime through time reflects the evolution of American society from a relatively stable and quiescent agrarian order to the present metropolitan disarray? Central to this assumption appears to be "a pervasive strain of agrarian suspicion and mistrust of the sinister city," or what may be called a kind of intellectual antiurbanism.[33]

What is perhaps the greatest weakness of all is not inherently a part of the theory but rather a characteristic of many of those who apply it, namely, a lack of epidemiological perspective on criminogenic societies in terms of both time and place. The social scientist who fails to see American society and culture with sophistication in both historical and cross-cultural contexts encourages the misuse of the criminogenic theory. When misused, that theory reinforces American self-hatred and lowers morale. It becomes part of that peculiar American malaise that may be called "negative narcissism." It is important to recognize, first of all, that American scientific research on social problems such as delinquency and crime is more statistically detailed and descriptively prolific than that of any other society. Furthermore, it must be stressed that American social scientists, with the exception of the cultural anthropologists, have been inordinately parochial in defining their spheres of study. Analyzing American society and its problems without cross-cultural comparisons, sociologists and the other behavioral scientists have given us a distorted picture of the world's spatial and societal distribution of crime, scandals, vice, and immorality. America appears to have a larger share of these problems than is actually the case. Also important in creating an exaggerated picture of a problem-ridden American society are the American mass communication media. They are second to none in reaching a nation-wide audience and in the freedom to exercise the fine art of muckraking. The media must have advertisers, and advertisements depend on the assurance of a mass audience. To insure such audiences, news needs to be entertaining, and what is more entertaining than crime and corruption? We are indebted to Lincoln Steffens, one of the most respected American crime journalists and muckrakers, for providing an insider's view of the manner in which some mass media find it profitable to manipulate and enlarge news on crime. As he wrote in his famous autobiography, many so-called American crime waves are fabricated in order to enliven an otherwise dull month with newsworthy events and thus stimulate circulation.

But probably the leading reason for the unwarrantedly dim view Americans take of themselves with regard to crime, delinquency, and deviant behavior in general is that they lack historical and horizontal perspective. What little they know of history in general and American history in particular comes down to a naive glorification of the past, a nostalgic apotheosis of a golden age. Their knowledge of other contemporary peoples is no better and, one could easily argue, worse.

The very concept of corruption contains a built-in notion that the present fares badly by comparison with the past; "corrupt," to one dictionary, "implies a loss of original soundness, integrity or purity." Yet history refutes the view that crime, delinquency, and corruption are peculiar only of our own time and society.

Consider the following quotation: "I see no hope for the future of our people if they are to be dependent upon the frivolous youth of today, for certainly all youth are reckless beyond words. . . . When I was a boy, we were taught to be discreet and respectful of our elders, but the present youth are exceedingly wise and impatient of restraint." The Greek poet Hesiod wrote these all-too-familiar words of despair almost three thousand years ago. There may be small comfort in the knowledge that anxiety concerning delinquent behavior already plagued adults nine hundred years before Christ. But historical perspective of this sort does help toward a more realistic appraisal of the problems of legal norm-violating behavior in the present era.

Consider the eighteenth century, a period idealized by Americans more than any other because it saw the birth of the nation and gave the new society its founding fathers, many of its sacred documents, and many of its lasting symbols. Yet the Age of Reason, so called, was anything but free of crime and corruption. Much can be learned from the works of the great English painter and engraver William Hogarth (1697–1764), an unusually perceptive social observer. The London Hogarth saw was even more delinquent and criminogenic than many of our modern urban metropolitan communities. Crimes were frequent and brutal in his day, and so were the punishments that were meted out. Flogging was universal for children as well as adults. Conditions in prisons, orphanages, asylums, and hospitals were appalling by today's standards. But all this merely reflected the culture of Hogarth's time. The amusements of most males included such sports as prizefighting, cockfighting, and bull baiting. Disputes were generally settled by hand-to-hand fighting, and drunkenness was common in all social classes. London was unsafe after dark. On the filthy, cobbled streets of the city, thieves, drunkards, and prostitutes roamed virtually unchecked by the ill-paid watchmen.

All periods of American history contributed their share of crime and corruption, but the best documented are the late nineteenth and early twentieth centuries. In the preface of his best-known work on American fortunes, Gustavus Myers wrote:

I had come across some documentary facts which severely shattered the inculcated conception that, with an exception here and there, the great fortunes were unquestionably the result of thrift and sagacious ability. . . . Up to and at that time the fashion of romanticizing and eulogizing the careers of men of great wealth was fixed in the publishing world. Volumes had been issued presenting the magnates as marvels of achievement and as models for emulation by American youth. [34]

The criminal machinations of the nineteenth-century robber barons were described by other American historians, notably Charles and Mary Beard.[35] Of the grandfather of one successful candidate for the governorship of New York State, the Beards recorded that "with remorseless precision, devices of doubtful legality and questionable morality, including espionage and intimidation, were used to compel merchants" to sell his oil product. The father of the unsuccessful candidate for office in the same gubernatorial race employed indefensible financial methods. He was denounced for looting, and at least one United States Senator declared that he should have been sentenced to prison. What probably saved him from this fate was his generous contributions to the political coffers.

As for crime, delinquency, and corruption at the present time outside the United States, there are virtually daily indications of hooliganism, prostitution, political and moral scandals, teen-age vandalism, and other illegal activities in all parts of the world. A penetrating insight was offered by an outstanding contemporary American criminologist upon her return from Germany after a year in that country as a Fulbright Lecturer.[36] In the ordinary American's view, according to Mabel Elliott, Germans are among the most law-abiding of all peoples because they are allegedly indoctrinated and trained from birth to obey the law whoever is in power. But, she notes,

my experience lecturing on American crime problems at the University of Bonn convinced me that Americans have accepted an exaggerated conception of our lawlessness which has unfortunately spread to other countries. Certain crimes are actually much more prevalent in Germany than the United States. For example, there is much more petty thieving in Germany than in America. Every American I knew in Germany had some difficulty with thefts. Several times I had money stolen while I laid it (in American fashion) on the counter to pay the bill. Germans, themselves, know better than this and clutch the money until the cashier takes it from their hands. But Germans also commit many petty thefts against their own people. . . . We regard furniture as relatively safe from theft, whereas such thefts are common in Europe. . . . Political corruption, though seldom punished, is likewise admittedly common although not so often publicized. We, on the other hand, tend to ventilate the peccadilloes of congressmen and cabinet members [without inhibition].

CONCLUSION

We have indicated that crime and delinquency in American society are pervasive phenomena calling for the equally pervasive etiology that ours is a criminogenic culture and society. But we have tempered the impact of the theory somewhat by pointing to the irrefutable facts of widespread crime and corruption in other times and places. Of course, their existence in American society cannot be condoned merely because they are not peculiar to it at the present time. Nonetheless, before vigorous and effective measures can be taken to correct, control, and prevent American delinquency and crime, the badly skewed conception that they are uniquely contemporary and American needs to be modified by the exercise of a realistic perspective.

NOTES

1. David Matza and Gresham M. Sykes, "Juvenile Delinquency and Subterranean Values," *American Sociological Review*, 26 (October 1961), p. 712.
2. Donald R. Taft, *Criminology* (New York: Macmillan, 1942; 3rd. ed., 1956).
3. See Durkheim's *Suicide* (1897; Eng. ed., Free Press, 1951) and *The Rules of Sociological Method* (1895; Eng. ed., Free Press, 1938).
4. Margaret Mead, *Coming of Age in Samoa* (New York: Morrow, 1928). See especially chap. 13, "Our Educational Problems in the Light of Samoan Contrasts."
5. Milton L. Barron, *The Juvenile in Delinquent Society* (New York: Knopf, 1954); Don J. Hager, "This Delinquent Society," *Congress Weekly*, May 9, 1955, pp. 12–13.
6. John Bartlow Martin, *Why Did They Kill?* (New York: Ballantine, 1952), pp. 128–129.
7. Marshall B. Clinard, "Corruption Runs Far Deeper than Politics," *New York Times Magazine*, August 10, 1952.
8. C. Wright Mills, "A Diagnosis of Our Moral Uneasiness," *New York Times Magazine*, November 23, 1952.
9. Robin M. Williams, Jr., *American Society*, 3rd ed. (New York: Knopf, 1970), p. 442.
10. *Ibid.*, p. 440.
11. Jessie Bernard, *American Community Behavior* (New York: Dryden, 1949), p. 73.
12. Robert S. and Helen M. Lynd, *Middletown in Transition* (New York: Harcourt, Brace, 1937), pp. 403–419.
13. *Ibid.*, pp. 423–424.
14. Robert K. Merton, "Social Structure and Anomie," *Social Theory and Social Structure* (Chicago: Free Press, 1949), pp. 147–148.
15. Williams, *op. cit.*, pp. 501–502.
16. Morris Opler, "Living Patterns in the U.S.A.," *Patterns for Modern Living* (Chicago: Delphian Society, 1950), p. 567.
17. Nathaniel Cantor, "Crime—a Political Problem," *Ideas for Action*, I (1946), p. 51.
18. Bradford Smith, *Why We Behave like Americans* (Philadelphia: Lippincott, 1957).
19. William Poster, " 'Twas a Dark Night in Brownsville," *Commentary*, 9 (May 1950), p. 464.
20. August B. Hollingshead, *Elmtown's Youth: The Impact of Social Classes on Adolescents* (New York: Wiley, 1949).
21. Louise McGuire, "Social-Work Basis for Prevention and Treatment of Delinquency and Crime: Community Factors," *Proceedings of the National Conference of Social Work*, 1936, pp. 579–589.
22. Jules Henry, *Culture Against Man* (New York: Random House, 1963).
23. Gerald W. Johnson, *The Lunatic Fringe* (Philadelphia: Lippincott, 1957).
24. Frederick Jackson Turner, "The Significance of the Frontier in American History" [1893], in Henry Steele Commager (ed.), *Living Ideas in America* (New York: Harper, 1951), pp. 73–80.
25. James Hayden Tufts, *America's Social Morality* (New York: Holt, 1933), pp. 220–221.
26. Poster, *op. cit.*, p. 459.
27. John Knight, *The Story of My Psychoanalysis* (New York: McGraw-Hill, 1950).
28. A summary of the investigation appears in John R. Ellingston, *Protecting Our Children from Criminal Careers* (New York: Prentice-Hall, 1948), pp. 20–22.
29. See Taft, *op. cit.*, pp. 229–237.
30. Alvin Toffler, *Future Shock* (New York: Random House, 1970).
31. Anthony Lewis, "Dear Mr. Vice President," *New York Times*, September 26, 1970.
32. Edwin M. Schur, *Our Criminal Society: The Social and Legal Sources of Crime in America* (Englewood Cliffs, N.J.: Prentice-Hall, 1969), pp. 12, 16–21.

33. Hugh Davis Graham and Ted Robert Gurr (eds.), *Violence in America* (New York: New American Library, 1969), p. 441.

34. Gustavus Myers, *History of the Great American Fortunes* (New York: Modern Library, 1936).

35. Charles A. Beard and Mary R. Beard, *The Rise of American Civilization* (New York: Macmillan, 1927), II, p. 185.

36. Mabel A. Elliott, "Perspective on the American Crime Problem," *Social Problems,* 5 (Winter 1957–1958), pp. 184–193.

5/ SOCIOLOGY AND PROFESSIONAL CRIME

ANDREW WALKER

"What shall I be when I grow up? A doctor? A lawyer? A robber? Yes, maybe a robber like Robin Hood. Or maybe a pirate and people will be afraid of me and I'll live on an island with my gold."

There are thousands of ways of making a living. This article is about one way: professional crime. Some people owe their livelihood to the tendency of the human body to malfunction periodically; some people make a living guiding other people through the intricacies of our legal system; and some people make their living taking advantage of opportunities in ways the laws prohibit.

There is nothing new about crime as a profession. In fact, what is notoriously the world's oldest profession is (and always has been) illegal. From earliest times, highwaymen, robber barons, pirates, and hired killers have played their part in the human comedy along with butchers, bakers, and candlestick makers.

And yet professional crime has a kind of fascination for the public at large and a special attraction for sociologists. The notable concern of American sociologists with crime is an outgrowth of their concern with social problems. In the early 1900's, when American sociology was in its infancy, most sociologists, conscious of the tremendous social upheaval the country was undergoing, recorded and analyzed the emerging urban character of American society.[1] Social problems have preoccupied American sociologists ever since, and an extensive literature on deviance has accumulated. And of all social problems, the one that has aroused the keenest sociological interest is crime.

Over the last three-quarters of a century, crime as a social problem has been broken down into a number of types: juvenile delinquency, white-collar crime, professional crime, and so on. Each of these types has acquired its own school of sociologists. To understand the sociology of professional crime, therefore, we must examine the major works in this field.

At first, that would appear to be a laborious task, since nearly all criminologists include a discussion of professional crime in their textbooks. On closer inspection, however, we find very few sociologists or criminologists who have actually done field studies on professional crime. In fact, most discussions of professional crime are based either on an occasional book by a reformed criminal, a social worker, or some other person telling about "crime as I saw (or lived) it," or on the fieldwork of a handful of sociologists who have attempted a systematic investigation of the nature of professional crime.[2] The work of these few social scientists contains the source material on which other criminologists have drawn.

Before looking at these works, however, we should briefly consider what is meant by the terms "professional crime" and "professional criminal." At first glance, it seems reasonable to assume that professional crime is simply crime that is committed by professionals, and that professional criminals are persons who make their livelihood from illegal practices. But over the years these terms have come to acquire more qualified meanings.

If we were to lump together all the people who make the major part of their living from illegal activities, we would have an extremely heterogeneous group. Included would be the usual assortment of thieves, con men, and dope pushers, as well as many politicians, judges, lawyers, businessmen, file clerks, and even teachers and an occasional psychologist. In order to arrive at a slightly more homogeneous group, sociologists have broken the category of occupational criminals into three major groups:

1. *Organized criminals,* who are members of large-scale criminal syndicates that have a hierarchy of authority and stable organization.
2. *White-collar criminals,* who engage in criminal activities as part of an otherwise legitimate occupation.
3. *Professional criminals,* who have chosen an illegal occupation and work at it continuously.

Most criminologists would agree that a professional criminal has the following characteristics: he makes the major portion of his income from activities that violate the law; he does not use a legitimate occupation for illegal ends; although his activities might fit into a larger structure, he is for the most part free to determine the scope of his own activities. Beyond this, the various sociologists we shall examine put forward other criteria—for example, recognition by other professionals or identification with a criminal subculture. To understand each man's work and to make comparisons, we must be sensitive to the nuances of his definition, for one theorist may be deliberately more narrow in his scope than another.

As to the term "professional crime," it has come to imply the whole situation in which the professional criminal operates, rather than simply the crime of a professional criminal. Thus an analysis of professional crime has come to include the roles of the criminal, of the agents of control, and of the victim, as well as all the other factors instrumental in giving the crime its particular form. Once again, different writers have used broader or narrower definitions.

Although there are numerous definitional intricacies in the contemporary sociology of professional crime, they can best be presented in the context of the work in which they were originally introduced. Let us turn, then, to the work of the sociologists who have most significantly influenced current thought: Edwin Sutherland, whose writings span the thirties and forties; David Maurer, who wrote in the forties and fifties; Edwin Lemert, who wrote in the fifties; and a group of sociologists headed by Leroy Gould, who investigated professional crime in the mid-sixties.

EDWIN SUTHERLAND

Edwin Sutherland stands out in the history of criminology for giving both form and substance to the positivist approach to deviant behavior. When Sutherland first turned to criminological work, he found the object of study—crime—to include an extremely heterogeneous range of behaviors. In order to make some sense of the confusion, he broke crime into a theoretically finite series of homogeneous units called "behavior systems." The notion of a behavior system is similar to the more recent sociological concepts of "subculture" and "reference group." Unlike these later concepts, however, Sutherland's conception of a behavior system referred neither to a disembodied set of ideas nor simply to a group of people. Instead,

The behavior system of crime may be described by its three principal characteristics. First, a behavior system in crime is not merely an aggregation of individual criminal acts. It is an integrated unit, which includes, in addition to the individual acts, the codes, traditions, esprit de corps, social relationships among the direct participants, and indirect participation of many other persons. It is thus essentially a group way of life. . . . Second, the behavior which occurs in a behavior system is not unique to any particular individual. It is common behavior. Third, while common and joint participation in the system is the essential characteristic of a behavior system, it can frequently be defined by the feeling of identification of those who participate in it. If the participants feel that they belong together for this purpose, they do belong together.[3]

Sutherland's concept of behavior systems influenced all his work and much subsequent criminological research.[4] In his introduction to the autobiography of a professional thief, Sutherland says:

The hypothesis may well be taken that professional thieves constitute a group which has the characteristics of other groups and that these group characteristics are in no sense pathological. Also, the hypothesis may be taken that tutelage by professional thieves and recognition as a professional thief are essential and universal elements, in the definition, genesis, and continued behavior of the professional thief. No one is a professional thief unless he is recognized as such by other professional thieves.[5]

Although Sutherland speaks in terms of hypotheses to be proven empirically, these hypotheses are, in fact, definitions, which underlie all of his work. For example, of a man who gains his entire livelihood through petty theft, but who never associates with other thieves and is, indeed, unknown to them, Sutherland would undoubtedly say that he is *not* a professional thief, by virtue of the fact that he does not participate in the behavior system of professional thieves.

Now, using the concept of behavior systems has the great advantage of shifting the object of study from the individual criminal to the social group or subculture of crime. In this way, the entire structure and process of criminal activities lie open to analysis. But in focusing on behavior systems, Sutherland necessarily restricted his analysis to those criminals who were associated with behavior systems. When behavior systems or subcultures including all criminals can be isolated, then the technique is extremely powerful. But when those criminals who are excluded from analysis through definitional fiat end up in a theoretical limbo, then the technique becomes a means of focusing attention on those criminals whose behavior makes sense while ignoring the rest. To a certain extent, Sutherland's work suffers from this flaw. Several classes of legal offenders, especially those who tend to operate alone or are not associated with any particular type of crime, are never given theoretical consideration.

Now, the behavior system of professional theft includes a variety of techniques for separating people from their valuables without the use of force. For example, pickpocketing, confidence games, and shoplifting are some forms of professional theft. In his analysis Sutherland found that "the essential characteristics of the profession of theft . . . are technical skills, status, consensus, differential association and organization."[6] Although these characteristics are closely interrelated, they can be discussed separately.

Technical Skills

The technical skills of professional theft include all the knowledge the thief has about how to steal profitably and safely. As Sutherland's thief put it, " . . . every act is carefully planned. The selection of spots, securing of the property, making a getaway, disposing of the stolen property, and fixing cases in which he may be pinched (arrested) are all carefully planned."[7] One of Sutherland's main points is that, for the professional, nothing is left to chance. The professional thief makes it his business to know all the conditions and contingencies of any criminal act and to be prepared to deal with circumstances that will or could arise. Furthermore, the professional uses knowledge (technique) to make his living rather than force.

Because the techniques used by professionals are specific responses to the problems of specific types of theft, and since professionals engage only in those types of theft at which they are proficient, Sutherland concluded that professionals "tend to specialize on a relatively small number of rackets that are related to one another."[8] That is, con men play con games, pickpockets stick to picking pockets, and so on. But, Sutherland hastened to add, owing to the "generality of some of the techniques of crime" and the fluidity of "underworld contacts," the professional thief often finds himself in rackets not dear to his heart (much like a criminal lawyer who helps write wills occasionally, or a criminologist who teaches an occasional course in formal organizations). In other words, within the behavior system professionals think of themselves as specialists and in fact generally operate within their specialty, but the underworld is sufficiently loose for professionals to pick up work in other rackets if they want or need to.

Status

Status, for Sutherland, is the respect accorded a professional on the basis of his membership in the "society of thieves." Although we might expect the term to imply respect only in the eyes of other criminals, Sutherland explicitly expanded the reference to include the police, court officials, political bosses, newspapers, and others. Sutherland cites numerous instances where the guardians of public morality have accorded professional thieves special treatment and respect. While some of this special treatment might be attributed to the constant flow of money from robbers to cops, much of Sutherland's data shows that the guardians of public morality seem to have a respect for "an honorable thief" that goes beyond the fix.

Members of the profession purport to feel strongly the obligations of their status. They are contemptuous of amateur thieves and feel no ties with them. Furthermore, they experience the need to "act like a professional" in order to maintain their position of respect, be it in the eyes of other professional criminals or noncriminals. In sum, Sutherland contends that the behavior system is accorded respect by others, and that members feel pride in membership.

Consensus

Professional thieves share an elaborate set of ideas that define the nature of their world and their proper place in it. Just as doctors assimilate a set of ideas defining their relationship with patients, with auxiliary personnel, with the government, and so on, so professional thieves acquire a common conception of the world in which they spend their lives and tend to react similarly to their victims, to cops, to money, and to other important elements of their world.

This consensus includes a shared "code of thieves" and an *esprit de corps* that provides the individual thief with the emotional support he needs to be a social outcast. According to Sutherland, there is a hierarchy of rules binding professional thieves, from "Thou shalt not squeal" at the top to "Thou shalt not be late" toward the bottom. While admitting that violations are not infrequent, he concluded that most of the rules are embedded in a felt need for collective self-protection and hence that compliance is usually in the thief's best interest.

Adherence to the rules is motivated not only by self-interest but also by an emotional dependence of the thief on his peers. It is interesting that, even though the professional thief is a skilled member of a high-status group providing him with a set of values that "neutralize" the dominant social mores,[9] "nowhere in America, probably, is a criminal so completely immersed in a group that he does not feel his position as an enemy of the larger society."[10] It is only in the company of his peers that this sense of "outsideness" is mitigated. The strain of isolation produces in him both another pressure to comply with the thieves' moral code and an *esprit de corps* that helps him face out the negative opinions of the dominant society. In support of this conclusion, Sutherland observed that when isolated from the company of other thieves (as in prison), the professional thief experiences considerable apprehension over his identity. However, "once he is back in his group, he assumes the bravado attitudes of the other thieves, his shuddering ceases, and everything seems to be all right."[11] Once again we are reminded of the social character of professional theft. Stripped of social support, the professional thief cannot maintain the attitudes necessary to pursue his livelihood.

Differential Association

Differential association, implicit in the very definition of professional theft as a behavior system, became a central element in Sutherland's whole criminological doctrine. Although he built an axiomatic theory of developing criminal behavior on the notion of differential association,[12] in this specific context he was using a more restricted meaning. By "association" Sutherland meant "meaningful relations," and by "differential" he meant "grouped." His point was that professional thieves form a social unit unto themselves. They live together, work together, and sleep together. But differential association is not solely a characteristic of criminal groups. All subjectively meaningful groupings, whether of doctors, lawyers, merchants, or hippies, maintain certain boundaries between themselves and the larger society. For professional thieves, these boundaries are somewhat stronger than for most, for two reasons. First, the larger society has no desire to intermingle with habitual criminals and hence shuns the thief who might wish to mingle. And second, because of the hazardous and secretive nature of their profession, thieves maintain their isolation from legitimate society for self-protection.

Differential association is basic to Sutherland's entire conception of professional thieves. For him, professional thieves are not just a set of people who have the same occupation; they are a *group* of people who interact, who behave more or less the way their culture says they should behave, and who actively share and pass along this culture.

Although Sutherland was emphatic about the differential association of thieves, he warns that "it would be a decided mistake to think of professional thieves as absolutely segregated from the rest of society."[13] The professional thief is continually in contact with the rest of society, both his victims and his sources of help when he gets caught. In addition, he lives in the midst of the dominant order. That is, he reads newspapers, watches ball games, and sees the new styles in store windows the way anyone else does.

This qualification of differential association is important, because Sutherland has been criticized for attempting to isolate the thief from legitimate society. On the contrary, he realized that the thief is in close contact with the rest of society. In fact, the thief is as much a part of our society as the doctor. Only a moralist would equate being outside the law with being outside society.

Organization

An important characteristic of professional crime is organization. By organization, however, Sutherland did not mean a hierarchical structure, but rather a system that contains established channels for the exchange of information, goods, and assistance. Since there is no central coordinating body, the organization of professional crime derives from its culture and the individual thief's dependence on it. Thus the professional thief is part of a well-organized group, even though he is always "his own man."

Analysis of these five characteristics of the behavior system of professional crime is only part of Sutherland's contribution to the sociology of professional crime. His greatness lay in his ability to break away from three strong traditions in writing about crime and criminals: journalistic sensationalism, moralism, and individualism. Sutherland regarded the professional criminal (be he thief, gambler, burglar, or whatever) as a member of a group which has a set of internal processes and external relations similar in form, if not in content, to other social groups.

DAVID MAURER

After Sutherland's work on professional crime, sociological interest in the field declined, in part because of increased interest in white-collar crime and juvenile delinquency in the years during and immediately following World War II. Nevertheless, during that period David Maurer published two important books on professional crime: *The Big Con*[14] in 1940, and *Whiz Mob*[15] in 1955, as well as several journal articles.[16] Maurer is not a sociologist but a linguist, and he called his work "an experiment in what might be called the social structure of language."[17] By whatever name, it provides an extremely rich empirical account of professional crime, as well as important theoretical contributions to its understanding.

Maurer's definition of the professional criminal is extremely similar to Sutherland's:

The professional criminal works at crime as a business, he makes his living by it; he is recognized and accepted by other professionals in his class as a professional; he knows and uses the argot or semisecret language of the profession; he subscribes to the code of behavior long established for professionals in his group; he has status and is known within a considerable circle of other professionals; he adopts certain attitudes towards other criminals, the law, the sucker, society in general; he feels no shame for his acts against the dominant culture, and seldom if ever "reforms." He is, in short, a member of the parasitic subculture. [Italics in original.][18]

Thus for Maurer the critical element in distinguishing the professional criminal is identity with a parasitic subculture—which is wholly consistent with Sutherland's notions of behavior systems and differential association. Unfortunately, Maurer did not develop the concept "subculture," except to say that it "designate[s] parasitic criminal groups with a way of living which differs from that of the dominant culture."[19] In other words, the idea of "groupness" is central to Maurer's conception of subculture, much as it was central to Sutherland's idea of behavior systems. Once again, we find the idea of professional crime intimately linked to the idea of real, subjectively meaningful groups complete with social structures, mores, attitudes, and values common to all the members of the group.

Perhaps even more than Sutherland, Maurer stressed the "concept that professional crime is primarily a social phenomenon and only secondarily an individual event" and, further, "the discovery that the criminal cannot be studied intelligently separate from his social matrix."[20] In place of individualistic, psychiatric accounts of criminal behavior, he proposed the "common sense grounding of everyday behavior" as the proper starting point for understanding the behavior in question.

Although his work covered many aspects of professional crime, one of his most important contributions concerned the internal structure of the subculture of crime. He observed that the underworld is made up of a "cluster of subcultures," corresponding to categories recognized and labeled by professional criminals themselves:

The first [category] constitutes the heavy rackets, comprising those criminals who use violence or the threat of violence in order to operate. . . .
The second is the grift, which includes all the infinity of rackets which utilize the skilled hand or the sharp wit, or both. . . .
Third, there are the lone wolves, who are professionals, but who operate predominately alone, without the support of a mob. . . .
Last, there are those who might be called quasi-criminals, this label being mine . . . includes prostitutes, underworld narcotic addicts . . . etc.[21]

Within each category, individual professionals are located on a status scale more or less specific to the particular racket. Within the grift, for instance, pickpockets have a status scale that runs between the "class cannon" at the upper end to "riffraff" at the lower end. An individual's place on this scale is not simply a function of his technical prowess; it represents, rather, a complex interplay of his ability, his "character, reliability, and reputation for integrity," as well as other factors.

The working unit of most professional criminals is the "mob," and it is in his analysis of mobs that Maurer's real contribution lies. A mob is neither a permanent group nor a group pulled together for a specific set of acts. It might be characterized as a "group in flux." Membership tends to be stable, but members may drop out at will, or may be jailed, and are replaced with other individuals from the racket. Members must be loyal to the mob, but this loyalty is business-based and independent of whatever personal bonds might prevail between members.

Maurer particularly studied pickpocket mobs. Within the profession of pickpockets, the mobs are classified by the professionals themselves according to a variety of criteria.[22] The first distinction they make is between "road mobs" and "locals." The road mob is constantly on the move, working a race in Louisville, then a convention in Chicago, then the World Series in Pittsburgh, and so on. Locals, on the other hand, prefer the stability of one location, with some sort of permanent arrangement with the local police.

In addition to personal status, mobs also have status as units. Thus a group of class cannons make up a class mob, while the riffraff form "makeshift" or "junker" mobs. This classification is fairly self-explanatory, but it is interesting to note that within a mob most members are of roughly the same status.

Mobs can also be differentiated according to social or ethnic identification. Accordingly, distinction is made, for instance, between "jig mobs," "mocky jew mobs," "spic mobs," and "old country mobs." Although mobs may be classified by some ethnic characteristic, they are not necessarily strictly segregated by ethnicity. Many Jewish professionals work with gentile mobs and sometimes an "old country" pickpocket fills in with a native American mob. Still, mobs do acquire an ethnic character in the eyes of other professionals and tend to maintain that character.

Finally, mobs have preferred places of work. For instance, a "third-rail mob" is one that works the subways, and "jug mobs" work banks. It would appear that this sort of specialization is decreasing, but Maurer's evidence on this point is scanty.

Thus within a particular racket there are numerous ways of going about business, and groups tend to be classified according to their style. The examples above are from pickpocket mobs, but similar classifications are used in the confidence racket. Here mobs are classified according to whether they play the short con or the big con, and also by the kind of con they prefer: the "payoff," the "wire," the "rag," or whatever.[23] But all these classifications must be seen as preferences, not as unqualified and permanent types. A short-con man might fill in with a big-con store, a road mob might have to spend two or three months in the same town waiting for trial, a mob that generally runs the wire might find a mark who is perfectly set up for a payoff trick.

Turning to the internal workings of the mobs, Maurer found them comprised of subgroups playing very specialized roles. The success of the mobs depends as much on integration of the separate roles as on the technical proficiency of the individual thieves. To illustrate, let us follow his analysis of a pickpocket (whiz) mob, which is perhaps the simplest case, since there are only two major roles: the "tool" and the "stall." The tool is the person who actually extracts the mark's wallet. After selecting the mark and locating his wallet, the tool signals his stalls, who maneuver the mark into proper position for the tool to remove his wallet. Once the stalls have done this (completely unobtrusively), they also see to it that the mark's attention is not on his money for the brief instant that the tool needs to remove the wallet. At this crucial instant, the tool extracts the wallet, while the stalls are holding the mark in position and concealing the act from passers-by. Once the wallet is theirs, the stalls either take the wallet and melt into the crowd, or maneuver the mark so that he cannot see or follow the retreating tool.

In this example, we have seen a simple yet devastating division of labor that requires split-second timing.[24] A mob generally consists of one tool and from one to three stalls. As part of the division of labor, however, one of the stalls usually acts as the "steer" or "folder" man, that is, as the mob's road manager. While the tool is the director of every particular act of theft, the steer man is in charge of the mob's itinerary and knows where to work once they get to the city of their choice, where to set up the fix, where other mobs are operating, and so forth. While his role is not manifest in the act of theft, it is one of the most crucial in the whole mob.[25]

Two factors limiting division of labor in a whiz mob are the need for mobility and inconspicuousness. In the big con, both these restrictions are neutralized, and the division of labor and specialization of tasks increase markedly. This is because the big con is generally organized around a "store," which appears to be a legitimate business establishment but is staffed entirely by confidence men. Instead of working the mark on the street, the con men bring him to the store to be "beaten." The two basic roles in the confidence game are the "inside man" and the "roper." It is the roper's task to find the mark and bring him to the inside man (usually at the store) and in the meantime feed him spurious information that the inside man will embroider on to gain his confidence. The inside man then suggests how the mark can beat the store through some illegal device. The mark puts up his money, only to find that the scheme does not work. Since the store, not the inside man, has his money, the mark cannot complain that he has been swindled and is simply left frustrated.

Although we can explain the big con in terms only of the roper, the inside man, and the store, there are really a number of other roles in the game. The store must have a manager (who directs the store), and be staffed by shills (who play cashiers, teletype operators, other customers, and so on). Also, there must be "tailers" to keep the mark under surveillance, and "fixers" to forestall any legal action. All told, a big store might have upward of one hundred grifters on its payroll.[26]

In its microscopic detail, Maurer's work is unsurpassed in the literature of professional crime. Without forcing his analysis, he demonstrated the extent to which the successful grifter is part of an organization whose goal and routine are the separation of the mark and his money in the safest possible way. And yet Maurer never fell into the trap of transforming his mobs into monoliths. While his thieves occasionally seem to possess almost superhuman manual and intellectual dexterity, Maurer nonetheless achieved a delicate descriptive balance between the thief as an element in a subculture and the thief as a person whose job is robbing other people's money.

EDWIN LEMERT

By the early 1950's the "behavior system-differential association" theory of professional crime was fairly well established in the sociological literature. To be sure, it sometimes came under attack by psychiatrically oriented writers on one side and legalistic writers on the other. But because it maintained, in Sutherland's phrase, that "professional [crime] is a group-way of life," it appealed to sociologists, who had little difficulty in parrying attacks from various quarters.

At about that time, however, Edwin Lemert wrote several papers that drew attention to a different aspect of professional crime. The first paper, concerning the "naive check forger," dealt with "persons who have had no previous criminal record and no previous contact and interaction with delinquents and criminals."[27] In explaining how a criminally unsophisticated person comes to commit check forgery, Lemert tried to show that

naive check forgery arises at a critical point in a process of social isolation, out of certain types of social situations, and is made possible by the closure or constriction of behavior alternatives subjectively held as available to the forger.[28]

In other words, the act of forgery can and does result from a complex of situational and personal factors that have nothing to do with any professional behavior system. Such findings did not present any real problem to the established theory, since both Sutherland's and Maurer's professionals scornfully recognized the existence of "hit-and-run" amateurs, but the way was opened for Lemert's later treatment of "systematic" check forgers.

In his next paper,[29] Lemert challenged the established behavior system-differential association theory through an innocent-looking flanking movement. He used a sample of systematic check forgers to verify Sutherland's hypotheses about professional thieves. Now, Lemert never explicitly equated "systematic" with "professional." Instead, he used the term "systematic" to connote that

they (1) thought of themselves as check men; (2) had worked out or regularly employed a special technique of passing checks; and (3) had more or less organized their lives around the exigencies or imperatives of living by means of fraudulent checks.[30]

Even though Lemert never claimed that his sample consisted of professionals, he compared their attributes with those of professional thieves. His findings did not correspond to Sutherland's. Instead, he found the systematic check forgers to be isolated criminals: "they avoid not only cooperative crime but also any other kinds of association with criminals."[31] They tended to be very emotionally involved in their crimes, tended to work impulsively with only minimal planning, and relied on commonsense knowledge of check passing rather than highly evolved technical skills. In addition, unlike both Sutherland and Maurer, Lemert found no evidence that the forgers used the fix to insure their occupational safety.

Faced with these discrepancies between the behavior system-differential association theory of professional crime and his own results, Lemert went on to hypothesize that the everyday situations in which checks are used have changed radically over the past hundred years, and that the kind of criminal response to the conditions has changed correspondingly. Thus with increasing use by the police and merchants' protective agencies (Pinkerton, for example) or rapid-communication systems, check-writing machines, and informant systems, the viability of forgery gangs decreased, while at the same time the drastic increase in the use of personal and payroll checks made the situation extremely tempting for solitary criminals.

Having established a fundamental distinction between his "systematic forgers" and Sutherland's professional thieves, Lemert then went on in a later paper[32] to explore the implications of the "game" for the individual forger's psyche. Three elements of the systematic forger's life-style seemed important in determining his psychological adjustment: pseudonymity, mobility, and seclusiveness. Lemert explored each of these situational exigencies and their psychological ramifications.

Pseudonymity refers to the forger's need for continually assuming new social roles in order to ply his trade. At one store he may present himself as a college professor in a strange town, at the bank he may be a real-estate agent from out of town, while later on he becomes a businessman in town for the convention. In each case, the forger must overlay his "real" identity with some transient role. The point is that slowly, but inevitably, the real identity deteriorates.

The forger's mobility is a direct result of the necessity to prey upon resident businessmen. When he has "made his spread," all the worthless checks are in one locale, and it is imperative that he be someplace else by the time (relatively short) the crime is discovered. This forced mobility has the dual effect of denying the forger a territorial identification and of making all relationships with other people transitory.

Finally, seclusiveness closes off the possibility of social support. Since forgers feel that very little protects them from the long arm of the law, they tend to reject all but the most superficial social relations. For obvious reasons, they are disbarred from any close ties with legitimate society, and with "suspicion and distrust marking their relationships with one another,"[33] they have nowhere to turn.

An unavoidable conclusion seems to be that the more successfully the forger plays his roles the greater becomes his anxiety. The more checks he has outstanding the greater is his perception of the danger of arrest, and hence the greater his necessity to move on and devise new identities which conceal his previous behavior.[34]

Thus, as the forger continues his work, his anxiety constantly increases, while his self-identity deteriorates. At some point (usually within a year or two), the whole game becomes too much, and the forger surrenders, either literally or symbolically, to the police. It is extremely important in understanding Lemert's argument to realize that the eventual surrender is the resolution of an identity problem, not a moral problem. That is, Lemert explicitly rejects the hypothesis that his forgers surrender because of "guilty consciences." It is through isolation, the undermining of identity, and geographical transience that the forger comes to prefer the stable, if negative, identity of a convict to that of a forger.

Although the scope of Lemert's work on professional crime is narrow, it signaled an important theoretical shift. Yet Lemert never directly challenged the behavior system–differential association theory of professional crime. In his textbook,[35] for example, he adopted Sutherland's theory with only minor alterations. Then in his later articles he was scrupulous in maintaining a distinction between his systematic criminals and the general class of professional criminals. He states, for instance, that "although it is possible to describe these forgeries as systematic, it is questionable whether more than a small portion can be subsumed as professional under the more general classification of professional theft."[36] And again, systematic check forgery "is neither the same nor the equivalent of professional crime, for it lacks social organization, occupational orientation, careful planning, common rules, a code of behavior, and a special language."[37] Sutherland, moreover, recognized that isolated criminals are subject to the kinds of pressures Lemert discussed in his last paper.[38]

Thus the impact of Lemert's work did not lie in its direct contradiction of the established theory; there was no explicit conflict. What Lemert did was to shift attention away from the successful criminal, firmly entrenched in the criminal subculture, and to focus on the marginal or unsuccessful criminal. While Sutherland's and Maurer's role models were class cannons and big-con operators, Lemert's subjects were crooks who developed stomach ulcers and spent much time in prison. To be sure, the established theory recognized that there are professionals who "don't make it," but that observation seemed to get lost among the stories of successful thieves. Thanks to Lemert's work, sociology had to confront the fact that many people who make a living from crime have a miserable time doing it, and that even outside the law some people are so situated that they "make it" while others do not.

LEROY GOULD

Following Lemert's articles, little work was done on professional crime until 1966.[39] Then, under the auspices of the President's Commission on Law Enforcement and the Administration of Justice, a group of sociologists headed by Leroy Gould undertook an investigation of professional crime. Their report is probably the most up-to-date assessment of professional crime available today.[40]

Rather than simply verify or refute the classical model of professional crime, they chose to start anew with a broad definition of professional criminals as

individuals whose major source of income is from criminal pursuits and who spend a majority of their working time in illegal enterprises, [excluding] regular members of crime syndicates or . . . people who engage in illegal activities as part of an otherwise legal profession.[41]

Equipped with this definition, the researchers first contacted the law enforcement agencies in several cities, explored the working knowledge those agencies had of professional criminals and their crimes, and finally interviewed numerous professional criminals, both in jail and on the streets. As might be expected, this broadened definition and a "shotgun" field strategy gave the group access to a range of professional criminals and professional crimes greatly exceeding that of *any* previous empirical study. For instance, such widely diverse crafts as auto theft, burglary, business fraud, abortion, credit-card theft, arson, murder, cartage theft, and check forgery all came under their definition of professional crime. And the criminals ranged from those who owned homes in the suburbs to those who would have to borrow money to buy a gun for their next job.

In describing such a wide range of people and life-styles, the Gould group had to reject explicitly a number of classical hypotheses. Taking a fresh approach, they built much of their report around the idea of "hustling." When researchers asked professional criminals what they did (in order to determine their criminal specialty), "over and over . . . they would answer 'I hustle.' " Now, "hustling," which summarizes a criminal's predatory activities, is an extremely intuitive concept:

To "hustle" is to be persistently on the lookout for an opportunity to make an illegal buck. A criminal "on the hustle" will do pretty much whatever is required; he will consider whatever comes up.[42]

Hustling does not necessarily mean simply looking for someone to rob. It means moving around bars and making connections, contacting other professionals to see "what's up," reading the papers to see if there are any opportunities, contacting fences to see if any special orders have been placed, and so on. To hustle is to use every bit of knowledge about crime and criminals, and the "straight" world and "straight" people, in order to make money, with no holds barred.

If the idea of hustling is accepted as fundamental to a life of professional crime, it should be obvious that a hustler requires versatility. He must be able to commit a burglary, pass forged checks, work confidence games, and "boost" from a department store—possibly all on the same day. In Gould's view, the professional criminal is in business to cash in on opportunities, and "if one specializes too narrowly, he is likely to miss too many opportunities."[43]

This view of specialization requires several qualifications, however. First, the data collected by the Gould group seem to indicate that the more successful a criminal is, the more he can afford to specialize. There is always a certain amount of risk in any criminal act, and the greater the financial stability of a criminal, the more selective he can be in choosing his jobs to minimize risk. But even the most successful professional will accept jobs outside his specialty if the price is high enough to outweigh the risks.

Another factor that encourages specialization is preference. Almost all professionals have a preferred activity in which they are most comfortable. All other things being equal, a professional would always engage in that activity. But the point is that all other things are seldom equal; the check man, for instance, simply cannot afford to pass up the camera in the back seat of an unlocked car. Thus, in the same way that a sociologist might prefer to teach only courses in criminology but is often forced to accept consulting jobs and a more diverse course load, the professional criminal must often forgo his preferences to take advantage of the opportunities presented to him.

This view of professional crime presents serious challenges to the traditional model of the structure of the criminal subculture. Whereas Sutherland and Maurer identified the mob as the organizing unit of association, the Gould study found the job to be more important in determining associations. For example, an individual criminal may decide to burglarize a warehouse at the waterfront. To do so he enlists the aid of a man (or organization) that can supply a truck, perhaps two or three burly assistants, and someone with a weapon to overpower the guard and stand watch. After the crime, this gang will disband, although if they are successful, they might reassemble to try again, but the chances of their forming a stable mob are slight. Hence Gould concluded that "present-day relationships between professional criminals . . . are not structured by strong on-going group relationships, but are structured primarily by the crimes that professional criminals commit."[44] Although Gould was emphatic about the transient character of most criminal associations, he remarked that stable relationships do sometimes exist, even though they are "the exception rather than the rule and are more likely to be found among the more successful professional criminals."[45]

If the relationships between criminals tend to be highly transient, there are nonetheless two classes of people with whom the professional criminal must have fairly stable relations: the fence and the "juice man" (loan shark). The Gould group took pains to investigate the role that these entrepreneurs play in the maintenance of professional crime.

Whenever a professional has stolen goods (as opposed to negotiable instruments), he must either sell them directly to the public, which is sometimes done, or sell them to a fence, who in turn distributes them to the public. It does the thief no good to have hijacked $20,000 worth of cigarettes if he cannot convert them into cash. Thus every professional must have intimate knowledge of the means of disposal. Just as professional crime appears to be ubiquitous, so do fencing operations, but their extent varies considerably, from operations geared to distributing extremely large quantities to the bartender of the local pub, who might sell a couple of cameras a week. Indeed, numerous respectable businessmen buy large quantities of stolen goods, for those "special deals" beloved of customers. Often professional thieves work out quasi-stable relations with a particular fence. For instance, a dealer in automobile parts might be "serviced" by a number of car strippers who supply him with parts his customers have ordered. But thieves do not appear to be tied to any one fence, and if they think they can do better elsewhere, they are always free to move on.

As a source of ready cash, the juice man, too, is very important in the professional criminal's life, for several reasons. First, many jobs require an initial investment which the solitary criminal cannot afford. Trucks may have to be rented, expensive clothes bought, expenses met while planning a job, or a whole gang might need transportation to the site of the operation. Thus the juice man is an important element in the execution of many operations.

But it is in his dealings with the legal system that the professional criminal has the greatest need for the juice man. As anyone who has ever, rightly or wrongly, been processed by the American legal system knows, the price of freedom is usually high. As soon as a professional criminal is arrested—and most are at some point—he becomes involved in a very costly cycle. He must immediately pay a bail bondsman and hire a lawyer. Since he needs that money on the spot, he usually depletes his cash reserves and turns to a juice man. In order to pay the incredibly high interest rates, he must intensify his criminal activities and engage in more high-risk crimes. Thus the probability of a second arrest increases. When he is caught again, his bail is set higher and his lawyer demands more money. Through appeals, additional bonds, and rising interest rates, the thief is forced into continuing his criminal career at an ever-accelerating pace until a conviction is final or he cops a negotiated guilty plea and goes to prison. During that period his lawyer, the bail bondsman, and the loan shark play a crucial part in his life and manage to extract a tremendous amount of money from him.

Having found that the juice man is an important factor in structuring the professional criminal's operations, the Gould group were led to consider the entire law enforcement system and its effect on the structure of professional crime. Although they uncovered almost no evidence of a systematic "fix" operating in the cities studied, they found that all levels of control agents, from the police through the district attorney to the courts, "engage in some practices that seem to work to the advantage of professional criminals."[46] In contrast to Sutherland and Maurer, the Gould group were not scornful of our machinery for law enforcement, but recognized, rather, that many aspects of that machinery could be exploited by the criminal in preserving his freedom.

Two aspects of police organization tend to favor the professional criminal: a strategy of complaint orientation and specialization of function. The police typically move into action after a specific crime has been committed. A uniformed patrolman fills out a report, which makes its way to a specialized detective unit (burglary squad, auto-theft detail, and so on, which assigns a detective team to investigate. By the time this team is put on the case, there is little they can do but question the victim and any witnesses the victim can provide, and then use their personal informant system to see if they can get a line on the responsible criminals. If these maneuvers are unsuccessful (which they usually are where professional criminals are concerned), all that the detectives can do is put the case in the records. Then, sometime later when they have caught a criminal in a similar act, they may be able to use these records to tie him to a number of previous crimes.

This approach impairs the detectives' ability to control professional crime in several ways. First, the activity of any one professional criminal for a given day might come to the robbery, fraud, forgery, and narcotics details, but because each detail gets only one case, the detectives miss the larger picture and fail to connect the man with the pattern. Second, although a given detective might suspect that a professional criminal is working in a certain area, he is more or less tied down by the cases he is given, and unless he can relate his suspicions to those cases, he cannot pursue his man. Third, some detective on another detail might easily solve the case (supposing, say, he knew what criminals were in the area of the crime), but because there is very little communication between details the detective with the answers might never get together with the detective that has the case. And fourth, several detectives may be pursuing the same criminal in ignorance of each other, with the effect of interfering in each other's work.

In these and a number of other ways, the police have not adopted the most effective stance for eliminating professional crime. The Gould group noted, however, that there are sound organizational and legal reasons for some of the police's shortcomings, and further that, were the police to adopt maximally effective measures, the price to the public, in terms of money and civil liberties, might be too high.[47]

The office of the district attorney offers the professional thief other opportunities for escape. Both time and other resources being limited, the D.A. (or more likely his assistants) often has to compromise with the criminal. The best-known form of compromise is plea bargaining, a process whereby the defendant forgoes all the legal maneuvers he could employ and pleads guilty to some charge, in return for which the prosecutor recommends that he receive a lighter sentence than that ordinarily imposed for the crime.[48]

The district attorney is sometimes also hampered by the "client-centered" orientation of American law enforcement. Thus "a large proportion of offenses involving property loss, for example, cannot be prosecuted because the victims prefer to accept compensation rather than pursue prosecution."[49] In some cities prosecutors are willing to hold informal hearings in which the victim and the offender get together to see if restitution is a possible solution to the legal problem. Although such procedures clearly impede their ability to control professional crime, district attorneys are very sensitive to the need for victim cooperation in prosecution. Where such cooperation is unavailable, some form of victim compensation is the best they can provide.

The courts, too, contribute to the structure of professional crime, for example by setting high bonds and then letting the criminal go free, and by cooperating with prosecutors in the plea bargaining. In addition, the ease with which the professional criminal can obtain continuances and appeals helps keep him operating for several years after arrest. In a way, then, the courts practically guarantee that the criminal will continue his career for some time after arrest. The result is an increase in the amount of crime in the society and a lowering of police morale.

In expanding their report to deal with the agents of control as well as criminals, the Gould group were following a classic criminological tradition. Their intention was not to moralize, but simply to describe those factors which contribute most to the structure of professional crime. Within the ranks of professional crime they found much variation, but a common concern with and adaptation to the methods of law enforcement. Their report might be faulted for emphasizing those aspects of law enforcement that can be worked to the criminal's benefit, but it is valuable as a pioneering attempt to integrate in-depth data on both law enforcement and criminal patterns.

In the long run, perhaps the greatest contribution of the Gould group was to provide a totally fresh picture of professional crime. Their work has many provocative implications. For instance, it appears that a single attribute—success—characterizes the entire subculture of professional criminals and that many of the earlier observations of Sutherland and Maurer are relevant only to the most successful thieves. Concepts of organization and specialization seem to lose much of their applicability when we deal with the run-of-the-mill thief. In addition, by considering the role of the fence and, more generally, that of consumer pressure, the Gould group at least touched upon an important dimension of professional crime never even considered by classical theory.

The work of the Gould group did not settle any arguments, nor did it offer criminology a new framework for the analysis of professional crime. It did, however, cast a new light on the orderly professional world of crime that criminologists have come to accept.

SOCIOLOGY OF PROFESSIONAL CRIME: TODAY AND TOMORROW

Each of the studies we have examined has contributed to contemporary knowledge of professional crime, and together they account for a substantial proportion of the data our theorists have to draw upon. Suffering from some of the same omissions, these studies both corroborate and contradict each other. To a certain extent, the contradictions relate to the basic question: What is a professional criminal? If we accept Sutherland's proposition that membership in a tightly meshed subculture characterized by a language, codes of behavior, and stable specialized roles is the essential attribute of a professional criminal, then we must exclude by definition much of Lemert's and Gould's research and say that no findings to date rebut the model presented by Sutherland and Maurer. But this stratagem leaves us with two other questions: What are we to do with Lemert's and Gould's data? And are there any "real" professional criminals left? The second question is empirical. In 1966, according to the Gould group, there were probably not many criminals left who satisfied Sutherland's definition. Even Sutherland and

Maurer conceded that the number of professionals was declining by the 1930's.

To extend the first question, a theoretical one: Should we develop a new concept that would take into account the criminals studied by Lemert and Gould? Possibly we should take over Lemert's own term "systematic." But such a strategy would ignore the tantalizing similarities between "systematic" and "professional." In fact, if Gould's data are correct, it might be possible for a person to shift back and forth between the status of systematic and professional criminal, depending on the extent to which he was operating within the context of a specific behavior system.

It seems much more reasonable to accept the broadened definition utilized by both Lemert and the Gould group. This would not preclude further study of the "real" professional criminals, but open up a wider range of criminal behavior to analysis. In fact, we might adopt the hypothesis that as a criminal's success increases, his participation and identification in behavior systems similar to those described by Sutherland and Maurer also increase. If this hypothesis should prove to be empirically true, then many of the disparities between the Sutherland-Maurer and the Lemert-Gould findings would reduce to mere differences in information sources. Sutherland described his informant as "near the top of the profession,"[50] while Maurer's primary sources of information were class cannons, who tended to be quite successful. On the other hand, Lemert's check forgers were almost all in prison when he interviewed them (which means that at least in the short run they were failures), and the informants of Gould's group tended to be persons known to the police or available in the prisons.

Accepting the narrow Sutherland-Maurer definition would have the effect of drastically limiting empirical scope. Accepting the alternative definition set forth at the beginning of this paper—that a professional criminal is one who has chosen an illegal occupation and works at it continuously—means accepting the need for considerable field research. Any broad conception of professional crime must include a number of elements that have not yet received sufficient empirical study.

For instance, it has become clear that criminologists are largely ignorant of most kinds of professional crime. To be sure, fine studies exist of pickpocketing, confidence games, shoplifting, and circus grifting, and some preliminary work has been done on check forgery and various forms of theft (cartage, banks, and so on). Still, next to nothing is known about such diverse crimes as credit-card fraud, arson, the heavy rackets (those employing violence or threats of violence), narcotics, pornography, and fencing. These are all areas in which professional criminals practice, but they have never received any criminological scrutiny.

Another area that needs immediate attention is the distribution of stolen goods. As the Gould group discovered, fences and other distributional mechanisms are not simply passive outlets for the fruits of crime, but instead are active agents in determining what kinds of goods will be stolen, and in what quantities. For some purposes, it seems useful to see professional crime as situated in a "marketplace" context, in which laws of supply and demand help explain large-scale property transfers.[51] Clearly, the use of this model must be restricted by a number of other, noneconomic factors, but in general the question of distribution has been completely ignored and the market model is one way of approaching the problem.

The need will also be felt for additional work on careers in crime. Of course, both Sutherland and Maurer explored at length the career of typical professional thieves, from apprenticeship and "turning out" to the decision to "pack it in" and move into a semilegitimate occupation. But their descriptions pertain to the acquisition and use of highly technical skills, and are not always applicable to the run-of-the-mill hustler. The Gould study suggested that one kind of typical crime career involves movement from small-time theft to narcotics dealing, to big-time theft, to loan sharking, but these data also indicate that a number of other career patterns could be observed. Since it would likewise appear that the intervention of the law enforcement apparatus at different times can have vastly different effects on the individual's career, comparative studies might be undertaken to determine the effects of early versus late apprehension. To avoid overgeneralization, any such career studies must be made in the context of a more complete understanding of the overall structure of professional crime. It is reasonable to assume, for instance, that people who start boosting from stores when they are thirteen years old would have a completely different type of career from people who start stripping cars when they get a job in an automotive-parts store. Noncriminal factors, such as education and family status, might also affect career.

Finally, a considerable amount of work remains to be done on mechanisms of social control and their effects on the structure of professional crime. Previous studies have dealt with some of these relationships, but there has been almost no attempt to develop a comprehensive approach. In addition to studies of the police, the prosecuting attorneys, and the courts, research is needed on the various private concerns that guard the goods which attract professional criminals. Included here would be department store detectives, private protection companies such as Pinkerton, and even the computerized systems that credit-card companies utilize.[52] Since the professional criminal generally takes advantage of the weakest spot in any protective system—be it public or private—an intimate knowledge of the strengths and weaknesses of all our protective systems is essential to understanding the overall structure of professional crime.

It goes without saying that serious study of the relations between protective systems and professional crime is something other than simplistic muckraking of police practices that "permit" crime to flourish. It must focus on the ways in which information is gathered, disseminated, and then acted upon by both control agencies and professional criminals; it must consider the resources each side can muster in dealing with the other and the liabilities brought into any encounter; and it must come to grips with the multiplicity of goals that each side must somehow reconcile. This kind of research is, of course, much more difficult than the usual criminological work, but without it we are left with common sense as our sole tool.

We could continue on this theme: the need for further research is the stuff of sociological litany. At some point, however, we must inquire into the prognosis of the sociology of professional crime. And it seems that the fate of this branch of sociology is closely tied in with the fate of the currently debated "labeling theory" in the sociology of deviance. Whatever the merits of labeling theory, there is little interest at present in its application to professional crime. It is a theory of deviance primarily concerned with the way in which social meaning is ascribed to behavior. The theory holds that deviance is not inherent in any kind of behavior, but is an offered, argued, and then agreed-on judgment of that behavior. Labeling theorists pursue the relation between a world that cannot exist without meaning and meaning that cannot exist without a world. Because ambiguity is important to the theory, it is easy to see why professional crime is of little interest: its meaning is not particularly hard to agree on. For instance, the criminal planning to hijack a truckload of cigarettes, the driver who tacitly cooperates (for a fee), the company, and the investigating policemen are all in substantial agreement as to the meaning of the behavior: it is a cartage theft.

And so professional crime lies in a kind of sociological limbo. Undeniably significant data have been collected, and there is a whole theoretical apparatus—behavior systems-differential association—that can be invoked whenever criminologists are called upon to comment on professional crime. That the entire theory of professional crime is in need of reformulation and reinvestigation is of concern only to a few criminologists who have followed the empirical findings of the past twenty years and who are not seduced by the new horizons opened by labeling theory. Unless those criminologists can get support for the kind of research needed, it appears that, given the indifference of most sociologists of deviance, the sociology of professional crime is fated to stay in limbo until new theoretical interest stirs.

FUTURE TRENDS IN PROFESSIONAL CRIME

Like most other patterns of social organization, professional crime is constantly changing—responding to new pressures and opportunities. This is not to say that many of the old patterns will not persist; on the contrary, as long as people can make money safely by given techniques (murphy games, fencing stolen goods, or whatever), those techniques will endure. But professional crime of any sort is necessarily embedded in a complex set of conditions, which include the normal structure of business transactions, public attitudes toward the criminal and his victims, prevailing police and court practices, and the market for stolen or contraband goods. Taken together, these factors (and many more) constitute a system, and a change in one element will produce changes in the others, including the type and volume of professional crime. The Gould group found, for instance, that an elaborate apparatus for smuggling black-market cigarettes into New York State was fully operational within a month after the state levied a tax on cigarettes sufficiently high to make cigarette smuggling and bootlegging worth the risk. Before the dramatic increase in cigarette taxes, this form of bootlegging was almost unknown.

In order to predict the future of professional crime with any confidence, we would have to integrate data on all the factors that constitute the relevant social system. Clearly, such a degree of data management is far beyond the scope of contemporary criminology, but we can select a few factors and estimate what effect they will have in the near future.

The Expansion of Credit Systems

Since colonial times, media of fiscal exchange have been slowly but constantly changing. At different periods and in different places, material goods, precious stones and metals, government-backed currencies, bank drafts, personal dispositions, and even human lives have taken their place as instruments for the exchange of value. To the extent that a given medium has value at any particular time, professional criminals have found ways of exploiting weaknesses in the system utilizing that medium. When credit-exchange systems change, professional crime changes to accommodate the new system.

Today professional criminals are developing new techniques for taking advantage of the greatly expanded use of personal checks and credit cards. Fifty or seventy-five years ago a pickpocket, stickup man, or prostitute could steal a wallet and expect to find up to several hundred dollars in it if the victim was chosen with care. The money could be pocketed, the wallet dropped, and the crime was complete. Today it is increasingly rare to find much cash in a wallet, but that wallet may contain up to six or seven credit cards. The thief, then, has to convert the cards into either cash or goods, that is, either sell the cards or use them himself. To use them safely himself, he must learn at least the rudimentary principles of credit-card systems (which is not very difficult, especially if he can get a credit card of his own to practice with). If he adopts this strategy, however, he must engage in two distinct criminal activities: the original theft and subsequent credit-card fraud. While he has greatly increased his criminal liabilities, he has also greatly enhanced his returns, since each credit card can provide him with up to several thousand dollars' worth of goods and services (which he can turn around and sell), as opposed to the one or two hundred dollars in cash that was the best he could hope for from a single wallet before credit cards became popular.

The alternative to using the cards himself is to sell them to a credit-card specialist or a middleman. In this case, there is some risk, because someone else knows that he committed the original theft, but the danger of exposure is minimal. Actually this second option is much safer, since the crime of passing on a stolen credit card to another criminal does not involve the same degree of risk as using the card, but the profit is correspondingly smaller: the black-market value of a hot credit card is usually between fifty and one hundred dollars.

The extension of credit systems has ramifications that go well beyond the organization of theft. A wide range of professional crimes, from safecracking to confidence games, have had to accommodate to an increased reliance on credit systems in legitimate society. It is getting harder and harder to extract large sums of cash, while at the same time it has become easier to steal or manipulate instruments, such as credit cards and personal checks, that can be negotiated. The potential profit is greater—hence there are probably more people willing to engage in credit crimes than previously—but increased technical and organizational resources are necessary to realize that profit. Since the credit-card industry is still expanding at a tremendous rate, it seems reasonable to expect that systems exploiting this form of exchange will be increasingly important to the operation of much professional crime within the foreseeable future.

Drugs

There is little doubt that the late 1960's and early 1970's saw a vast increase in the illicit use of drugs in the United States.[53] That increase, although its magnitude is hard to assess, will almost certainly have an impact on the immediate future of professional crime in many of its facets. For our purposes, we can consider the following: personnel, markets, and diversion of law enforcement resources.

Changes in the personnel of professional crime are probably related to increases in the number of people addicted to the opiates. Whereas normal consumption of most illicit drugs (marijuana, barbiturates, speed, for example) can easily be supported through legitimate income, the cost of an average opiate habit is sufficiently high (at least ten to fifteen dollars a day) to be extremely difficult to support by legitimate means. Hence most addicts at some point in their careers turn to some form of professional crime.[54] It follows that as the absolute number of addicts increases (which it probably did in the late 1960's), the number of potential criminals also increases. But does this mean that the absolute number of criminals will increase by the same number? Probably not, for if we assume that property crime obeys the fundamental economic laws, then the actual amount of goods stolen will be a dual function of the demand for these stolen goods and of the number of thieves and their willingness to steal. Since demand curves are generally well established, the total amount of goods stolen will change only if thieves are willing to sell at lower prices. But as the black-market price for stolen goods drops, not all thieves will necessarily be willing to take the same risks for decreased profits. Thus some will drop out of the "labor force." Given the nature of addiction to opiates, it may be assumed that most addicts are willing to take more risks for lower profits than nonaddicted thieves. Consequently addicts, in joining the labor force and driving down the market value of stolen goods, may well displace other thieves from their occupation.

The absolute number of thieves would therefore remain roughly constant, but the percentage of addict-thieves would increase.[55]

As criminals, addicts tend toward the kind of low skill–high versatility hustling Gould noted in his professional crime study: shoplifting, theft, check and credit-card forgery, and prostitution. So it would seem that, barring a major breakthrough in the treatment of opiate addiction, or a radical change in the moral and legal posture society has adopted vis-à-vis the drug user, a large number of street hustlers will probably still be active in the foreseeable future. In other words, there will be no drastic change in the trends noted by Gould: highly versatile, individualistic criminals hustling for a buck will continue to account for the majority of all professional criminals. While it is probable that professional crime will develop sophisticated new techniques for acquiring money and goods, there will remain a pool of addicts who will maintain the traditions of street hustling.

The second impact of drugs on professional crime is in the area of a stabilized black market. Whereas the black market for drugs was relatively small a decade ago, today billions of dollars' worth of drugs are illegally marketed annually. Strictly in terms of dollar value, then, we can probably say that the marketing of illicit drugs has become an increasingly important sector of professional crime. It is almost certain that much of the distribution is in the hands of well-organized syndicates, but not all. According to our scanty information, most marijuana is imported and distributed by free-lance criminals; barbiturates fall outside the scope of syndicated operations, at least after the initial diversion from legal channels; and even considerable amounts of heroin and cocaine are distributed by free-lancers. The reason is plain: considerably more money is to be made now from illegal sale of drugs than was the case even ten years ago. Since drug sales are not closely tied in with other traditional forms of professional crime, such as hijacking or confidence games, this increased importance of sales will probably not drastically alter the overall structure of professional crime. But it will provide more jobs for a specific class of professional criminal. Of course, not all illegal drugs are distributed by professional criminals; all kinds of people, from diplomats to college students, are involved in the distribution of illegal drugs. Still, many persons make the bulk of their income from drug sales. And if prevailing rates and patterns of drug use continue, the role of the professional dealer should be assured.

The third aspect of the impact of the drug explosion on professional crime is the diversion of law enforcement resources. This topic, however, leads us into the entire system of priorities in the administration of justice.

Law Enforcement Priorities

The entire apparatus for the administration of justice in America is currently under considerable strain. There is such a multitude of statutes in force today that their complete enforcement is beyond the scope of any acceptable enforcement system.[56] Even under a regime of partial enforcement, the dockets of many courts are logjammed; prosecuting and defense attorneys' offices are overburdened; and the police cannot possibly arrest all known offenders.[57] Under these conditions, it is not surprising that all levels of the legal system have been obliged to set priorities for allocating manpower resources. The priorities of the police, prosecuting attorneys, and courts are not necessarily consistent, but taken together they shape the flow of cases through the legal system. Hence one factor in the prevalence of any particular type of criminal activity is the resources allocated to control that activity. It would be extremely difficult, if not impossible, to determine the overall hierarchy of legal system priorities in America at any given time, but the probability is that professional crime does not occupy a high place on any list of pressing national problems. Routine maintenance of order mobilizes a large part of the legal system's resources;[58] according to F.B.I. statistics, the drug explosion accounts for a 765 percent increase in narcotics arrests between 1960 and 1971;[59] and "political" cases are taking an increasing share of the courts' time and manpower. With these priorities, it does not appear that professional crime is under any severe pressure from the legal system.

Moreover, the overburdening of the legal system opens it to exploitation by professional criminals. Most successful professionals are aware of the inadequacies of our system of law enforcement and take advantage of all of them. They know where the police are the weakest, what kinds of cases prosecutors will not handle, how to "con" a harried judge, and how to keep understaffed probation or parole offices out of their lives. Most law enforcement personnel concede that the successful apprehension and judicial processing of professional criminals is a difficult matter under even ideal conditions, and conditions today are far from ideal. Unless changes are made, it is hard to foresee any decrease in the incidence of crime by professionals.

Future Trends Reconsidered

It should be obvious that professional crime is an integral part of society, and thus subject to a myriad of influences. We have suggested a few of the more relevant ones, but about future developments we can only speculate. Perhaps an economic boom will remove all but the most hard-core criminals from the streets; perhaps political repression will increase to the point where professionals cannot benefit from the civil liberties guaranteed by the Constitution; perhaps the technology of financial transactions will be developed to the point where it is impossible to transfer negotiable instruments illegally. None of these possibilities are very likely, but it must be emphasized that all professional crime is dependent on the patterns of legitimate society; whenever those patterns change, the nature of professional crime also changes.

Predicting the future directions of professional crime is the same as predicting the future of American society. Given the changes that are currently taking place in the political, legal, economic, and technological sectors of our society, it is difficult to say what either society or professional crime will look like even ten years from now.

NOTES

1. George Lundberg et al. (eds.), Trends in American Sociology (New York: Harper & Row, 1929). See also David Matza, Becoming Deviant (Englewood Cliffs, N. J.: Prentice-Hall, 1969).

2. Ned Polsky, Hustlers, Beats and Others (New York: Free Press, 1965), chap. 5.

3. Edwin Sutherland and Donald Cressey, Principles of Criminology (6th ed.; Philadelphia: Lippincott, 1960), pp. 238-239.

4. See Marshall Clinard and Richard Quinney, Criminal Behavior Systems: A Typology (New York: Holt, Rinehart & Winston, 1967), chap. 1.

5. Chic Conwell, The Professional Thief, annotated and interpreted by Edwin Sutherland (Chicago: University of Chicago Press, 1937), p. vi.

6. Ibid., p. 197.

7. Ibid., p. 3.

8. Ibid., p. 199.

9. See Gresham Sykes and David Matza, "Techniques of Neutralization: A Theory of Delinquency," American Journal of Sociology, 22 (December 1957), pp. 664–670.

10. Conwell, op. cit., p. 205.

11. Ibid.

12. Edwin Sutherland, Principles of Criminology (3rd ed.; Philadelphia: Lippincott, 1939), chap. 3.

13. Conwell, op. cit., p. 207.

14. David Maurer, The Big Con: A Story of the Confidence Man and the Confidence Game (Indianapolis: Bobbs-Merrill, 1940).

15. David Maurer, Whiz Mob: A Correlation of the Technical Argot of Pickpockets with Their Behavior Pattern (2nd ed.; New Haven, Conn.: College and University Press, 1964).

16. David Maurer, "The Argot of Check Forgery," American Speech, 16 (1964), pp. 243–250.

17. Maurer, Whiz Mob, op. cit., p. 4.

18. Ibid., pp. 9–10.

19. Ibid., p. 6.

20. Ibid., p. 14.

21. Ibid., pp. 30–31.

22. Ibid., chap. 6.

23. Maurer, Big Con, op. cit., chaps. 3, 8.

24. For a complete description of the act of theft, see Maurer, Whiz Mob, op. cit., chap. 5.

25. Ibid., p. 67.

26. Maurer, Big con, op. cit., chaps. 3, 5.

27. Edwin Lemert, "An Isolation and Closure Theory of Naive Check Forgery," Journal of Criminal Law, Criminology and Police Science, 44 (September 1953), pp. 296–307. Reprinted in Edwin Lemert, Human Deviance, Social Problems, and Social Control (Englewood Cliffs, N.J.: Prentice-Hall, 1967).

28. Lemert, Human Deviance, op. cit., p. 101.

29. Edwin Lemert, "The Behavior of the Systematic Check Forger," Social Problems, 6 (Fall 1958), pp. 141–148. Reprinted in Lemert, Human Deviance, op. cit., pp. 109–118.

30. Lemert, Human Deviance, op. cit., p. 109.

31. Ibid., p. 112.

32. Edwin Lemert, "Role Enactment, Self, and Identity in the Systematic Check Forger," in Lemert, *Human Deviance, op. cit.*, pp. 119–134.

33. *Ibid.*, p. 112.

34. *Ibid.*, p. 124.

35. Edwin Lemert, *Social Pathology* (New York: McGraw-Hill, 1951).

36. Lemert, *Human Deviance, op. cit.*, p. 110.

37. *Ibid.*, p. 121.

38. Conwell, *op. cit.*, pp. 204–205.

39. One important exception was Mary O. Cameron, *The Booster and the Snitch: Department Store Shoplifting* (New York: Free Press, 1964).

40. Leroy Gould, Egon Bittner, Sheldon Messinger, Kris Kovak, Fred Powledge, and Sol Chaneles, "Crime as a Profession," U. S. Department of Justice, 1966.

41. *Ibid.*, p. 10.

42. *Ibid.*, p. 25.

43. *Ibid.*, p. 27.

44. *Ibid.*, p. 34.

45. *Ibid.*, p. 33.

46. *Ibid.*, p. 75.

47. *Ibid.*, p. 87.

48. See A. Alschuler, "The Prosecutor's Role in Plea Bargaining," *University of Chicago Law Review,* 36 (1968), pp. 50–112.

49. Gould *et al., op. cit.*, p. 76.

50. Conwell, *Professional Thief, op. cit.*, p. v.

51. See Leroy Gould, "Changing Structure of Property Crime in an Affluent Society," *Social Problems*, 48 (September 1969), pp. 50–60.

52. See Elihu Blotnick, "How to Counterfeit Credit Cards and Get Away with It: The Confessions of a Plastic Man," *Scanlan's Monthly*, 1 (June 1970), pp. 21–28.

53. See Laurie Richards and Eleanor Carroll, "Illicit Drug Use and Addiction in the United States," *Public Health Reports*, 85 (December 1970), pp. 1035–1041 and Max Singer, "The Vitality of Mythical Numbers," *Public Interest* 23 (Spring 1971), pp. 3–9.

54. Patrick Hughes *et al.* "The Social Structure of a Heroin Copping Community," *American Journal of Psychiatry*, 128, November 1971, pp. 43–50.

55. See Leroy Gould, "Crime and the Addict—Beyond Common Sense," in James Inciardi and Carl Chambers (eds.), *Drugs and the Criminal Justice System* (London: Sage Publications, 1973).

56. Norval Morris and Gordon Hawkins, *The Honest Politician's Guide to Crime Control* (Chicago: University of Chicago Press, 1970), especially chap. 2.

57. Task Force on the Administration of Justice, *Task Force Report: The Courts* (Washington, D.C.: U.S. Government Printing Office, 1967), *passim;* Joseph Goldstein, "Police Discretion Not to Invoke the Criminal Process: Low-Visibility Decisions in the Administration of Justice," in Abraham Goldstein and Joseph Goldstein (eds.), *Crime, Law and Society* (New York: Free Press, 1971), pp. 145–172, especially p. 151.

58. Steven Ging and S. Steven Rosenfeld, *The Quality of Justice in the Lower Criminal Courts in Metropolitan Boston* (Boston: Lawyers' Committee for Civil Rights Under Law, 1970), p. 15.

59. U.S. Department of Justice, *Uniform Crime Reports: 1971* (Washington, D.C.: U.S. Government Printing Office, 1972), p. 118.

6/ UPPERWORLD CRIME

GILBERT GEIS

Upperworld crime provides clues to a wide range of issues important to the understanding of criminal behavior and of the relationship of such behavior to the social system in which it occurs. The study of upperworld crime is revealing in many ways:

1. Upperworld crime challenges the more banal kinds of explanations of criminal activity. To say that poverty "causes" crime, for instance, fails utterly to account for widespread lawbreaking by persons who are extraordinarily affluent.

2. Upperworld crime indicates the distribution of power in our society. An examination of statute books shows what kinds of occupational acts of the wealthy have come to be included within the criminal codes and which go unproscribed. The enactment of laws curbing the activities of certain classes of persons demonstrates that, at least for a time, other persons with other interests had the power to prevail legislatively.

3. Upperworld crime portrays the manner in which power is exercised in our society. A review of upperworld violations and the manner in which they are prosecuted and punished tells who is able to control what in American society and the extent to which such control is effective.

4. Upperworld crime indicates the degree of hypocrisy present in a society. It is hypocrisy when, for instance, fraud among the lower classes is viewed with distaste and punished by law, while upper-class deception is countenanced and dismissed as nothing more malevolent than "shrewd business practice." Hypocrisy may be seen as leverage by means of which the society can be forced toward congruence between its verbal commitments and its actual conduct.[1]

5. Upperworld crime illustrates changes in social and business life. Thus the old-time grocer, weighing merchandise by hand and dealing on a personal, daily basis with his customers, may have had less inclination and less opportunity to mislead and defraud. Today's supermarkets, engaged essentially in the rental of shelf space to commodity manufacturers, epitomize growing commercial impersonality and its consequences for the emergence of a new form of upperworld crime, that involving consumer fraud.

6. Upperworld crime furnishes materials helpful for an understanding of changes in social values. For example, as reviews of legislative enactments show, a "right to life" doctrine is emerging in the United States. Laws demanding that foods be uncontaminated and that pollution be controlled reflect a belief that man should be accorded every reasonable opportunity to remain alive and healthy until cut down by uncontrollable forces. In the future, new forms of upperworld crime may be declared, if support grows for enunciation of the right of each human being to achieve his full potential, as such potential comes to be defined.

There are, besides these, many other phenomena associated with an investigation of upperworld crime—or, as Edwin H. Sutherland called it in his 1939 presidential address to the American Sociological Society, "white-collar crime."[2] We can, through the study of upperworld crime, see the use of rationalization by "respectable" persons as they struggle to maintain their self-esteem in the face of attempts to label them as criminals. We can watch responses in suburbia as other "respectable" citizens strike a posture of self-righteous indignation over the disclosed depredations of their neighbors. We can also examine the impact of the traditional processes of criminal justice on the upperworld offender and determine, among other things, how constitutional guarantees won by the rapist and the robber are used by the corporate-class criminal conspirator. We can, in addition, consider the impact of punishment, especially incarceration, upon the upper-class violator who is accustomed to think of prisons as places where "bad" people, and certainly none such as himself, are deposited for safekeeping.

The following sections will deal first with the problems of defining upperworld crime and then with attitudes toward it in various periods of history. Later sections will consider the social consequences of upperworld crime, its investigation by reform groups, its handling by the system of criminal justice, and, finally, the influence of the study of upperworld crime on the study of crime in general.

DEFINING UPPERWORLD CRIME

Difficulties in delineating with precision the realm of upperworld crime are a function of the problem of defining adequately the two components of this designation—"upperworld" and "crime." We must therefore try to indicate when an act might reasonably be regarded as a crime and then attempt to draw some boundaries that will set off the upperworld from the rest of the world.

When Is a Crime a Crime?

It needs to be noted, initially, that it is perfectly reasonable to provide any definition that one chooses for either of the two terms, so long as what is being discussed is clearly specified. The goal, however, ought to be a definitional state of grace that will move others to exploration of the same concept; otherwise, one is apt to be engaged in an idiosyncratic and dead-end enterprise. It is possible, for example, to maintain that the rate of infant mortality in the United States is so shocking (as indeed it is, with this country as far back as thirteenth in international statistics) that every member of the medical profession must stand convicted of criminal negligence. Such a position, I would maintain, makes fine polemics, but rather bad social science.

For one thing, there is no law against inadequate diffusion of medical services. For another, it would be impossible to demonstrate that all doctors have acted with the intent to violate the standards of criminal law—or, for that matter, any other reasonable set of standards designed to punish those responsible for the death of so many infants before their first birthday. There is a further difficulty. If all doctors can be regarded as criminal because of the infant mortality rate, then presumably all citizens, by the same stroke of semantic justice, could have been said to be criminal because of the Vietnam War, or because of some equivalent event whose perpetration offends us. If the concept of crime is going to have any discriminatory and analytical strength, it will have to be tied more firmly to a set of delimited criteria.

I would maintain that the label "upperworld criminal" ought to be confined to persons who commit acts in violation of criminal statutes, that is, statutes designated by lawmakers as criminal and providing for fines, terms of imprisonment, or similar disabling penalties. I would reject the overdelicate stipulation of Paul Tappan that to be an upperworld criminal a person must be *convicted* of such violations.[3] It seems unreasonable to maintain that an unapprehended armed robber or an undiscovered antitrust violator, for instance, is not a criminal. Under such rules, only the more unlucky or the more inept fit the category, rather than all those who have engaged in the stipulated behavior. Tappan's concern, of course, was that the opprobrium of the social epithet "criminal" not be lightly or loosely attached to persons innocent of any violation of the criminal law. This concern, certainly an important one, can be met, however, by seeing to it that unconvicted criminals are so designated, with the clear stipulation that they may not be legally guilty of the offense alleged against them. It should also be noted, in turn, that convicted criminals might not in fact legally be guilty of the offense for which judgment was pronounced against them.

This kind of dictum, however, addresses but one phase of the definitional dilemma. What about upperworld acts which could be prosecuted as criminal violations but which are handled by other adjudicatory and punitive methods? The issue here is intricate, and some resolution might again be obtained by reference to the procedures employed with more traditional kinds of offenses. It seems clear, for instance, that Al Capone might reasonably have been regarded as a person performing acts classifiable under the heading of organized crime. Yet Capone's major criminal conviction was not for extortion or for murder, both acts that it seems highly likely he committed, but for income tax violations.[4] This, too, was, of course, a criminal conviction. But suppose Capone had been dealt with instead under civil law. I would argue that he still might reasonably have been considered a key member of a group engaging in the patterned form of behavior known as organized crime, and that his activities in organized crime consisted variously of extortion, murder, and, indeed, income tax evasion.

In the same manner, upperworld offenders who are handled, because of administrative decisions, by means other than criminal statutes—though such statues might have been employed—can be regarded as upperworld criminals. It is true, of course, that the administrative decisions are neither whimsical nor haphazard (though, on occasion, they may be both), but represent, rather, the considered judgment of the relevant government agency regarding the character of the offense and the offender and a variety of other factors. The basis for such judgment, however, should be part of the criminologist's analytical material, and it seems perfectly proper to second-guess the administrators. After all, such second-guessing is routine among administrators themselves. Shifts in internal power, and changes in the coloration of political leadership, can mean the sudden movement of cases from criminal to civil categories as well as their total elimination from court or administrative agency calendars. For the criminologist, the caveat should be this: "Such an act, being considered part of the category of upperworld crime fits the definition of criminal activity in the statutes. The act apparently was not so prosecuted because . . ." The "because" might be that the person in authority, finding the action under review negligible, decided that justice would be better served by ignoring the matter, just as the officer on the street corner may decide to ignore behaviors that violate the laws defining juvenile delinquency.[5] Perhaps the explanation is more invidious, and based on political, social, or economic favoritism. But since the law exists, I think we may reasonably classify the person violating it as an upperworld criminal, though we should look further to determine why in fact he was not officially so classified. We could also attempt to differentiate between those who are acted against officially and those who are treated more benignly. In such a manner, we may gain insight into the wellsprings of power and decision making which lie at the heart of the criminal justice system and which should be at the core of criminological study.

What may we say, then, about acts not outlawed by criminal statutes, but seemingly harmful to individuals and/or the social system, acts that are engaged in deliberately (perhaps even diabolically) by members of the upperworld who are aware of the detrimental consequences of their behavior? Acts such as—the selection depends upon one's political and social viewpoints—writing advertising copy for cigarettes, manufacturing automobiles with built-in obsolescence, mercilessly harassing one's wife or husband, or endlessly haranguing one's children? Or, perhaps, administering examinations to college classes which cause "irreparable" damage to the self-esteem of students?

It seems to me that we will slip into definitional quicksand if we include such behaviors—on such grounds—as part of the realm of upperworld crime. For one thing—and a very important thing—the perpetrators of the acts cannot be aware of official definitions of their behavior as criminal (since no such definitions exist), and therefore cannot bring to the acts that state of mind legally required for most (though, it should be said, not for all) criminal acts. For another thing, there seems little chance of achieving agreement among investigators regarding the kinds of acts which ought to be included in such amorphous categories as infliction of "social injury" or "personal harm." It may be of great concern to the sociologist and to the political scientist to determine why particular acts are not included in the criminal statutes despite an inherent element of harm. But it must be remembered that the reasons for such omissions are multifarious; for instance, certain acts universally regarded as vile and reprehensible may not fall under criminal law for the one reason that the criminal law is not seen as an effective weapon for dealing with such acts.

It may be observed, in this connection, that no law lies against failure to warn a blind man that he is about to walk off a cliff, even if the onlooker can easily do so without any risk to his own safety (he would be liable if he were related to the blind man, had an agreement to protect him, or had previously undertaken to forewarn him against danger). We might want to know what components of the power system, what elements of the democratic ethos, and, indeed, what requirements of criminal justice procedure have led to the exclusion of behavior such as this from the criminal law. And we might want to determine what interests appear to be served by allowing high infant mortality rates, deficient automobiles, and detrimental advertising to exist beyond the concern of criminal statutes. This would appear to be about as far as the boundaries of criminal law might legitimately be extended. For the criminologist probing these limits the danger is strong that he will be neither an adequate social scientist nor, it follows, a responsible citizen, if he is not excruciatingly clear as to just what he is about and what criteria he is using to select his material and to reach his conclusions.

The criminologist may, of course, if he chooses, insist that car manufacturers ought to be considered upperworld criminals because of their failure to go beyond their legal responsibility in adopting safety precautions. Or he may maintain that legislators *ought* to be regarded as upperworld criminals for their failure to proscribe various car manufacturing techniques. But the criminologist taking such a line should not be surprised if others, for their part, regard him as one who *ought* to be called an upperworld criminal for his failure to stay within the bounds of fair comment and to observe fundamental due process principles, even though his accusations no more violate the criminal law than do the acts of those he is using as object lessons.

The heart of definitional problems such as these lies in the fact that criminology, by its very name, deals with behaviors which, once they are included in its realm, brand their perpetrators with a label carrying derogatory connotations. The aim of social justice would seem to be to see to it that all persons performing similarly objectionable acts share equivalently in the label. The pinning of the label, however, is a function of the power system of the society, and criminology, by accepting the official labels in part (though not necessarily altogether), reinforces such labels. A partial saving grace is that power in the United States, however ill-distributed, is a multifaceted phenomenon. No group has an unqualified monopoly on its exercise; otherwise there would be no such thing as upperworld crime in the legal sense of the term.

What Part of the World Is the Upperworld?

The term "upperworld crime" obviously constitutes a counterpart to "underworld crime," and this differentiates it from the designation "white-collar crime" employed by Sutherland in his pioneering work. For Sutherland, white-collar crime was defined "approximately" as "a crime committed by a person of respectability and high social status in the course of his occupation,"[6] a definition posing a number of analytical problems. Consider, for example, the crimes of two corporate managers, one respected, the other not (say the second is a former organized-crime boss, now gone righteous, but still far from country-club material). Both might commit the same offense in the course of their occupation—perhaps an antitrust violation. One of the violators would presumably satisfy Sutherland's regarding his credentials as a bona fide white-collar criminal; the second, lacking respectability, would not. Thus it is neither the act nor the particular statute which has been violated that is the reference point for classification, but rather the social position of the actor. It seems to me, in this regard, unrewarding to differentiate between, say, income tax violators in the more respectable segments of society and income tax violators in the less respectable segments of the society; it is, indeed, odd to do so if, as could happen, both groups cheated for similar amounts on their returns.

Nor is Sutherland any more helpful in later elaborations on the definition of "white-collar." One such attempt appears in an early footnote in his monograph *White Collar Crime,*[7] in which he observes, ". . .[t]he term 'white collar' is used here to refer principally to business managers and executives, in the sense in which it was used by a president of General Motors who wrote *An Autobiography of a White Collar Worker.*"[8] But, only a year before, Sutherland had said: "The term white-collar is used in the sense in which it was used by President Sloan of General Motors, who wrote a book entitled *The Autobiography of a White Collar Worker.* The term is used more generally to refer to the wage-earning class, which wears good clothes at work, such as clerks in stores."[9]

Indeed, Sutherland's most extensive discussion of his concept of white-collar crime is, as has been observed, a "model of obfuscation":[10]

Perhaps it should be repeated that "white-collar" (upper) and "lower" classes merely designate persons of high- and low-socioeconomic status. Income and amount of money involved in the crime are not the sole criteria. Many persons of "low" socioeconomic status are "white-collar" criminals in the sense that they are well-dressed, well-educated, and have high incomes; but "white-collar" as used in this paper means "respected," "socially accepted and approved," "looked up to." Some people in this class may not be well-dressed or well-educated or have high incomes, although the "upper" classes usually exceed the "lower" classes in these respects, as well as in social status.[11]

The semantic waters are now so muddy that it seems better to move upstream from Sutherland rather than attempt a purification project. In this article, the term "upperworld" is meant as no more than a very rough contrast to "underworld." It points at a group of people engaged in a variety of acts contrary to the law; in this sense, the term is used as a publicist or a muckraker would use it. It is employed to call attention to a wide range of lawbreaking that usually escapes public attention and indignation and to persuade that offenses such as advertising fraud, antitrust violation, and water pollution ought to be attended to seriously, and that their perpetrators ought to suffer the public indignity of the label "criminal" and to benefit or suffer from whatever action appears necessary and reasonable to bring them within the ranks of the law-abiding.

Most fundamentally, in respect to upperworld crime, we are interested in various *offenses*, regardless of the persons who commit them. These offenses are very various, but most are committed by persons who, because of their position in the social structure, have been able to obtain specialized kinds of occupational slots and/or skills essential for the commission of these offenses. Thus anybody with the physiological capacity can commit murder, but only a limited number of persons are in a position to violate the antitrust laws. Dentists and carpenters, Rotary Club members and ministers, as well as the unemployed, can (and sometimes do) commit forcible rape, but to violate the statute forbidding pollution of navigable waters with factory refuse it is necessary to have some decision-making position within a factory.

To repeat, the term "upperworld" is not a scientific criminological designation, but rather a label designed to call attention to the violation of a variety of criminal statutes by persons who at the moment are generally not considered, in connection with such violations, to be the "usual" kind of underworld and/or psychologically aberrant offenders. Such persons often possess a number of qualities that differentiate them from violators of other statutes, just as burglars tend in some ways to be different from murderers. But we lack sufficient information to discern a persistent patterning among them; and we have yet to uncover an interlocking array of circumstances of sufficient homogeneity to merit a separate criminological nomenclature that will embrace these upperworld offenders and their offenses. Nor do we really have enough useful information about individual kinds of upperworld offenses. Someday, however, we will undoubtedly be able to devote major criminological attention to polluters and to misrepresenters in the same manner that we now attend to offenders such as rapists and arsonists. We should likewise soon be able to formulate patterns for what might be called "occupational crime" or "economic crime," patterns that will provide us with the same kinds of insight as the study of entities such as professional crime and organized crime.

UPPERWORLD CRIME IN HISTORY

Behavior duplicating in form and spirit what would now be regarded as upperworld crime can be found throughout recorded history. Nonetheless, it must be remembered that a large number of offenses currently prominent in the inventory of upperworld crime could not have come into existence until the appearance of social arrangements permitting their performance; corporate crime, for example, could obviously not occur until the emergence of the corporation as a business form.

Testimony from biblical times and from the preindustrial period supports the view that upperworld crime was not persistently regarded as a significant social ailment, although there were intermittent pleas for reform and occasional diatribes against the irresponsible employment of power. It is true, as Tocqueville pointed out, that disruptions of the social order are apt to occur not when things are at their worst, but when they are in the process of change for the better.[12] It is then that people come to appreciate the potential gains they may achieve and to become restive about the extent and the speed of change. With a rigid class system and strong authoritarian rule, persons on the lower rungs of the social order were powerless to insist that they be treated fairly and decently. Slaves lacked the prerogatives to press for justice and peasants lacked leverage to gain protection from predators. As Leys has noted, "Institutions are geared for well-organized complaint by people who have bargaining power; they are not responsive to unlettered misery."[13]

The triumph of laissez-faire capitalism in the nineteenth century saw the entrenchment of doctrines establishing the supremacy of property rights. It is notable that writers of this period employ terms from the criminal law to defend what they regard as the right of capitalists to make unchecked use of their holdings. Thus Lord Gainford wrote that it was nothing other than "sheer robbery" to limit the profit on coal mines,[14] and Lord Hugh Cecil, in a book on conservatism, insisted that whether or not private property was employed mischievously, society could not interfere with it because to do so would be "theft."[15]

The attitude which prevailed at this time, and which continues today, though to a lesser extent, has been described by R. H. Tawney:

The secret of industrialism's triumph is obvious. . . . It concentrates attention upon the right of those who possess or can acquire power to make the fullest use of it for their own self-advancement. By fixing men's minds, not upon the discharge of social obligations, which restricts their energy . . . but upon the exercise of the right to pursue their own self-interest, it offers unlimited scope for the acquisition of riches, and therefore gives free play to one of the most powerful of human instincts. To the strong it promises unfettered freedom for the exercise of their strength; to the weak the hope that they too one day may be strong. Before the eyes of both it suspends a golden prize, which not all can attain, but for which each may strive, the enchanting vision of infinite expansion. It assures men that there are no ends other than their ends, no law other than their desires, no limit other than that which they think advisable. . . . It relieves communities of the necessity of discriminating . . . between enterprise and avarice, energy and unscrupulous greed, property which is legitimate and property which is theft . . . because it treats all economic activities as standing upon the same level, and suggests that excess or defect, waste or superfluity, require no conscious effort of social will to avert them.[16]

In the 1920's, however, the tide began to turn slightly, following a crusade against the more glaring abuses of big business by the muckrakers, a fervent and articulate group of writers including Ida Tarbell,[17] Lincoln Steffens,[18] and in the realm of fiction, Frank Norris,[19] Upton Sinclair,[20] and Sinclair Lewis.[21] In addition, early work in American sociology was animated by a reformist zeal born of a conviction that the nascent social science held the answers to the world's most pressing moral and legal problems.[22]

Muckraking, the antecedent of later studies of white-collar crime and upperworld crime, had begun as a coherent enterprise about 1902, though its aims had received their major statement before the turn of the century in two books that penetrated deeply into American awareness: Lord Bryce's *The American Commonwealth* (1888) and Henry Demarest Lloyd's *Wealth Against Commonwealth* (1894). Well-documented findings of corruption in American politics and business underlay Bryce's conclusion that democracy in America, then just a dozen years past its centennial, had not altered human traits and conditions that foster upperworld crime. Bryce entered the following items on the debit side for American democracy:

(1) It has often been wasteful and unusually extravagant; (2) It has not produced great contentment; (3) It has done little to improve international relations and ensure peace, has not diminished class selfishness, has not fostered a cosmopolitan humanitarianism nor mitigated the dislikes of men of a different color; (4) It has not extinguished corruption and the malign influences wealth can exert upon government; (5) It has not enlisted in the services of the State a sufficient number of the most honest and capable citizens.[23]

Nonetheless, Bryce's conclusion was generous: "[Democracy] has, taken all in all, given better practical results than either the Rule of One Man or the Rule of a Class, for it has at least extinguished many of the evils by which they were effaced."[24]

Secure, like Bryce, in his own privileged status, Lloyd lashed out at the predators he saw throughout the commercial and political structure of American society. Typical was the following accusation:

In an incredible number of the necessaries and luxuries of life, from meat to tombstones, some inner circle of the "fittest" has sought, and very often obtained the sweet power which Judge Barrett found the sugar trust had: It "can close every refinery at will, close some and open others, limit the purchases of raw material, artificially limit the production of raw sugar, enhance the price to enrich themselves and their associates at public expense, and depress the price when necessary to crush out and impoverish a foolhardy rival."[25]

The control of political life by corporate enterprise came in for scathing denunciation by Lloyd. The Standard Oil Company, he noted sarcastically, "has done everything with the Pennsylvania legislature except to refine it."[26]

During the first decade of the twentieth century, the muckrakers assiduously and effectively plowed the fields laid out by Bryce and Lloyd. A certain irresponsibility, however, and a tendency to sensationalism for its own sake earned the label given to them by President Theodore Roosevelt, who recalled the man in Bunyan's *Pilgrim's Progress* who could "look no way but downward, with a muckrake in his hands; who was offered a celestial crown for his muckrake, but who would neither look up nor regard the crown he was offered, but continued to rake to himself the filth on the floor."[27] But the muckraking movement clearly left its mark. Roosevelt himself voiced a plaint often echoed today in writings about upperworld crime; though the roster of offenses may differ, the essential problem is the same:

Swindling in stocks, corrupting legislatures, making fortunes by the inflation of securities, by wrecking railroads, by destroying competitors by rebates—these forms of wrong-doing in the capitalist, are far more infamous than any ordinary form of embezzlement or forgery; yet it is a matter of extreme difficulty to secure punishment of the men most guilty of them, most responsible for them.[28]

SUTHERLAND AND WHITE-COLLAR CRIME

The ethos of the muckrakers did not penetrate into the mainstream of criminological study until 1939, when Edwin H. Sutherland spoke on white-collar crime before the American Sociological Society. True, some earlier work had been done by, among others, Edward A. Ross[29] and Albert Morris,[30] and Sutherland himself had begun research on white-collar crime some fifteen years earlier. His textbook, *Criminology,* the first edition of which appeared in 1924, provides clues to the thrust of his later work on commercial fraud and upper-class lawbreaking. In this book he questioned legal distinctions between criminal and civil cases based on whether the injury involved was a public or an individual one. "In recent years this historical differentiation is questioned by many people," Sutherland wrote, "because it is sociologically unsound to make such an opposition between the individual and the public."[31] He continued on this theme:

If a tort (that is, a violation of civil law) injures an individual, it injures the public to some extent. Some torts do more injury to the public than some crimes. Most crimes and most torts injure some particular individual more than other individuals. But it is not necessary that a particular individual be injured either by a tort or a crime, for there are torts, known as "penal actions," in which any individual whatever who will bring suit may recover for injuries done to the community, and there are crimes, such as treason, that need not cause special injury to one individual more than to another.[32]

Finally, though he granted that "in a way" the point might be "exaggerated," Sutherland was not loath to quote George Bernard Shaw on the contrast—one that has often been underscored since—between upperworld and traditional kinds of criminals:

The thief who is in prison is not necessarily more dishonest than his fellows at large, but mostly one who, through ignorance or stupidity, steals in a way that is not customary. He snatches a loaf from the baker's counter and is promptly run into gaol. Another man snatches bread from the table of hundreds of widows and orphans and similar credulous souls who do not know the ways of company promoters; and, as likely as not, he is run into Parliament.[33]

In his 1939 address, Sutherland explicitly denied that he was interested in muckraking or in "reforming anything except criminology," a patently disingenuous disclaimer, and as much as anything an attempt to forestall accusations that he lacked a "scientific" attitude toward his material.

The "robber barons" of the latter half of the nineteenth century were upperworld criminals, Sutherland noted, "as almost everyone now agrees."[34] White-collar crime, he added, "is found in every occupation, as can be discovered readily in casual conversation with a representative of an occupation by asking him what crooked practices are found in his occupation." Business and professional white-collar crime was said to consist principally of violations of delegated or implied trust, and much of it could be reduced to two categories: misrepresentation of asset values and duplicity in the manipulation of power. "The first," Sutherland asserted, "is approximately the same as fraud or swindling; the second is similar to the double-cross."

Ultimately, the major distinction between lower-class and upperworld criminality lay for Sutherland "in the implementation of the criminal laws which apply to them," and he saw this difference in implementation as due chiefly to the "disparity in social position of the two kinds of offenders." White-collar criminality, Sutherland maintained, flourishes at points where powerful business and professional men come into contact with persons who are weak; in this respect, "it is similar to stealing candy from a baby."[35] The power that Sutherland saw might be documented for more recent times by noting that in the mid-sixties General Motors employed more than 600,000 people, a figure exceeding the combined payrolls of the state governments of New York, California, Illinois, Pennsylvania, Texas, and Ohio, and that the annual sales of Standard Oil of New Jersey were over $10 billion, more than the total tax collections of Wisconsin, Connecticut, Massachusetts, and the six states mentioned previously.[36]

In his later treatise, *White Collar Crime,* published in 1949, Sutherland argued that modern industry was nothing more than "private collectivism" and that it was "undermining our traditional institutions." The first 163 pages describe, with thinly veiled disapprobation, the roster of offenses committed by corporations. Public utility companies under private ownership are singled out for closest scrutiny, on the ground that, since they are vested with public interest, they have "unusual rights and duties." Examining their performance, Sutherland could only echo a remark of Franklin D. Roosevelt's: "Nothing more atrocious in the way of thievery inside the law has ever been successfully attempted against the American public."[37]

Sutherland, however, took exception to the phrase "inside the law," insisting that the public utilities had directly violated the law, even though criminal justice agencies had chosen to ignore their behavior. Among the reasons for failure of the governmental agencies to act, Sutherland saw a campaign of organized public utility propaganda designed to develop favorable public sentiment. "Perhaps no group except the Nazis have paid so much attention to indoctrinating the youth of the land with ideas favorable to a special interest," he noted, "and it is doubtful whether even the Nazis were less bound by considerations of honesty in their propaganda."[38]

CONSEQUENCES OF UPPERWORLD CRIME

In spite of the prod supplied by Sutherland's pioneering work, upperworld crime remains a relatively neglected area of criminological investigation. One reason appears to be that criminological research is conducted primarily by sociologists, who tend to have sparse training in economics (in contrast to, for instance, psychology) and hence find the intricacies of upperworld business manipulations difficult to comprehend. In more recent years, however, with the growing politicalization of sociology, upperworld crime has come in for greater attention, as sociologists have been more willing to attack entrenched interests and to buttress their attacks with studies of criminal activity by such interests. In particular, attention is now being paid to the consequences of upperworld crime, among them: (1) financial costs; (2) social costs, including ghetto distress, political turmoil, and public cynicism; and (3) spin-off costs, for example, the rationalization of their crimes by lower-class offenders, who say that unpunished lawbreaking is endemic in the upper classes.

Financial Costs of Upperworld Crime

Estimating the cost of any type of crime is a hazardous undertaking. For one thing, it is difficult to decide what kinds of items shall be included and what kinds omitted from the balance sheet. For another, there are factors such as emotional harm and pain and suffering that do not readily translate into financial terms.

The early estimate by Sutherland that the financial cost of upperworld crime is probably several times as great as the cost of all crimes customarily regarded as the "crime problem" in the United States is probably as accurate as any guess is apt to be. Sutherland pointed out that an officer of a chain grocery store embezzled $600,000 in one year, or six times more than the losses that chain suffered during the year from burglaries and robberies. The persons designated by the F.B.I. as public enemies 1 to 6 during 1938, Sutherland calculated, had netted $130,000 by burglary and robbery, while the sum stolen by Ivar Krueger, a stock manipulator, was believed to be $25,000,000, or nearly two hundred times as much.[39]

In regard to another type of upperworld crime, it has recently been suggested by Dr. L. F. Saylor, director of public health in California, that medical quackery[40] kills more persons than all crimes of violence taken together. Saylor believes that people in his state spend more than $200 million a year on quack drugs, devices, cosmetics, and food fads.[41] Nationally, it is estimated that the public is mulcted of $2 billion a year by persons "treating" ailments with useless mechanical devices and by other fraudulent practices.[42] In the tax field, indications are that some $350 billion in taxable income goes unreported each year in the United States, an omission that costs the national treasury $4 to $5 billion annually,[43] and a loss that falls as surely on honest taxpayers as if the money had been stolen from them by a pickpocket or purse snatcher. Nearly $4 billion in dividends and interest paid to Americans likewise fails to appear on tax returns.[44] Similar kinds of upperworld offenses of commission and omission can be cited from a variety of sources.

Further Costs of Upperworld Crime

There are far subtler social costs of upperworld crime, however, than those calculable in terms of dollars and cents. British historian Arnold J. Toynbee, for instance, has asserted that modern advertising (at least some of which undoubtedly violates criminal statutes) represents a greater threat to Western civilization than Communism. Modern advertising, Toynbee insists, has forced Americans to waste ability, time, and resources in obtaining goods "we should never have dreamed of wanting if left to ourselves."[45]

It is an illustration of the power of advertising that national brands of aspirin, an item where one brand is basically the same as another, are able to sell at considerably higher prices than local products only because, as Donald Turner, chief of the antitrust division of the Department of Justice, has noted, "producers have convinced a large number of consumers that their product is different."[46] Undertaking a more overt kind of deception, the advertising agency for the Libby-Owens-Ford Glass Company in 1960 attempted to illustrate the difference between the company's safety plate glass and sheet glass by filming television commercials "through an open or rolled down automobile window" instead of through the advertiser's product.[47] As David Maurer concluded after a study of confidence men, the practices of this elite cadre of professional crime "differ more in degree than in kind from those employed by more legitimate forms of business.[48]

To control advertising, as demanded by a growing reaction against upperworld excess, the federal government now requires advertisers to provide proof of product claims. The need for such a requirement was pointed out by Ralph Nader and an associate, who mentioned that only three out of fifty-eight companies had chosen to respond to a request for documentation of advertising claims, such as that made by Ralston Purina that "good" dogs had selected their product "six to one in a recent test."[49]

In a more general sense, the consequences of upperworld crime are suggested by an assistant United States district attorney in the fraud division: "People should be able to trust one another and they should know that laws designed to punish those who abuse trust are being enforced effectively"; otherwise, "everything starts falling apart."[50] A similar view has recently been put forward by the former attorney general Ramsey Clark:

White-collar crime is the most corrosive of all crimes. The trusted prove untrustworthy; the advantaged, dishonest. It shows the capability of people with better opportunities for creating a decent life for themselves to take property belonging to others. As no other crime, it questions our moral fiber.[51]

Upperworld crime may also create anger among persons who find themselves deprived of what they regard as the essentials of decent living, while all about them they hear reports of dishonesty and exploitation by those in positions of power. The National Commission on the Causes and Prevention of Violence, in its report, spoke of a pervasive suspicion among the poor that "personal greed and corruption are prevalent among even the highest public officials."[52] United States Senator Warren Magnuson has insisted that it is such kinds of discontent that underlie ghetto riots. "It seems undeniable," he observed, "that the scandalous gouging of minority groups by dishonest merchants and salesmen contributes to a potentially explosive situation in every ghetto in America and is one of the discontents leading to riots."[53] Explicit reference to upperworld crime as an explanation of the roots of social protest appeared in a 1970 resolution of a Philadelphia meeting involving some 5,000 persons, including members of the Black Panther Party,[54] the Women's Movement, and the Gay Liberation Movement, allegedly convened to demand a rewriting of the American Constitution. As reported by the *New York Times,* "The convention delegates said that the American economic system was composed of 'bandits' who stole from the people."[55]

That cynicism may also be a product of upperworld crime is suggested in the report of the President's Commission on Law Enforcement and Administration of Justice:

Most people pay little heed to crimes of this sort when they worry about "crime in America," because these crimes do not, as a rule, offer an immediate, recognizable threat to personal safety. However, it is possible to argue that, in one sense, those crimes are the most threatening of all . . . because of their corrosive effect on the moral standards by which American business is conducted.[56]

C. Wright Mills has made the same point, by noting the casual way in which Americans react to upperworld crime:

Many of the problems of "white-collar" crime and of relaxed public morality, of high-priced vice and of fading personal integrity, are problems of structural *immorality. They are not merely the problem of the small character twisted by the bad milieu. And many people are at least vaguely aware that this is so. As news of higher immoralities breaks, they often say, "Well, another one got caught today," thereby implying that the cases disclosed are not odd events involving occasional characters but symptoms of widespread conditions. There is good probative evidence that they are right.*[57]

The imperceptive attitudes often connected with upperworld crime are rather strikingly revealed in remarks attributed to two persons in positions of power in the United States. The first was the political boss Carmine DeSapio, who was charged with soliciting bribes from Con Edison when the electric company requested permission to build a new transmission line on an aqueduct right-of-way owned by New York City. A city commissioner had held up Con Edison's contract while DeSapio suggested to the company that unless he was paid off the permit would not be forthcoming. As DeSapio left the courtroom during his bribery trial, a newspaper reporter mentioned to him the planting of bombs that was then plaguing New York. "It's terrible," said this upperworld criminal. "I don't know what's happening to the city."[58] Equally revealing is the remark of the chairman of the Business Council when told that a bill imposing new safety standards on automobiles had passed the Senate by a vote of 76 to 0. "This country is on a safety kick," the chairman said. "It is a fad, on the order of the Hula Hoop. We are going through a cycle of overemphasis on safety."[59]

A term used by Al Capone sums up the underworld view of upperworld criminal activities. They are, Capone said, "the legitimate rackets."[60] An articulate explanation of how one professional thief views upperworld "rackets" is found in the comments of Robert Allerton:

Take the case of a jeweler. He's a business man, and he's in the game to make money. O.K., so I'm a business man too, and I'm also out to make money. We just use different methods. The jeweler makes a profit—and often a very big profit—out of what he sells. On top of that he fiddles the income tax and the purchase tax, and even the customs duty if he can get away with it. That's considered all right by him and others like him, and if he makes enough to buy himself a big house and a posh car everyone looks up to him as a clever fellow, a shrewd business man. But how's he got his money? By rooking people, taking advantage of soft young couples getting engaged to sell them a more expensive ring than they can afford, and fiddling the authorities whenever he can. But at least he didn't steal it. Well, what's in a name? Tell me exactly where the line is between thieving and "shrewd business" and I might believe it. What's more, the jeweler can insure himself against people like me going and pinching his stock. But I can't insure against the police nicking me. The Law's on one side only, the side of the pretenders, that's all.[61]

CONSUMERISM: THE WORK OF NADER'S RAIDERS

At least two factors, sometimes present in combination, can be recognized in the social malaise generated by upperworld crime: (1) moral outrage over the violation by others of fundamental principles of human decency; and (2) jealousy that others are commanding more of the wherewithal of the society. Little research has been conducted on the processes by which certain upperworld behaviors come to be labeled as criminal or deviant while other behaviors remain beyond the definitional process.[62] Nor has research been directed toward the kinds of social climates in which attention tends to be paid to upperworld crime. It is possible that such concern goes in cycles, recurring from time to time when things get badly out of hand, then abating until a later crisis arises. Or, perhaps, affluence and leisure are directly related to the growth of social concern with exploitative behavior on the part of socially entrenched persons. Certainly, an element of security from decimating reprisal must be present before reform movements can make headway.

Whatever its source, concern with upperworld crime seems to be at a relatively high point in the United States today. It is undoubtedly epitomized by the work of Ralph Nader, head of the Center for the Study of Responsive Law, a group known in the vernacular as Nader's Raiders. "The real challenge," one of Nader's associates has said while trying to describe the group's work, "is going into a courtroom against a corporation and having the establishment's own judge come down on your side and say the other guy is wrong. That does more to shake up the corporate structure than destroying some buildings."[63]

Investigation by a Nader study group of the work of the Food and Drug Administration (F.D.A.) demonstrates how the Raiders come to grips with upperworld offenses. They rely primarily on (1) research; (2) use of legal processes; and (3) publicity. The legal process is employed, among other methods, to make certain that the investigators are given access to relevant materials. Research undergirds their case, and publicity hits at the upperworld's special sensitivity to spotlighted notoriety.[64]

The Nader teams work on the premise that industry will take advantage of virtually any opportunity to exploit the consuming public, and will desist from such exploitation only when forced to do so by governmental organizations goaded into action by the pressure of public opinion. The focus of the Nader work, therefore, has been documentation of the failure of federal and state regulatory agencies to control practices which Congress gave them the power to regulate.

The Nader survey of the F.D.A., for instance, begins with an overview of the food industry, which, according to Nader, has become concentrated into "fewer and fewer corporate hands," with the following result:

The competition, such as it is, has focused heavily on massive promotional expenditures (between 16 and 18 percent of gross revenues), on brand-name identification, wasteful nonprice competition, and other marketing expenses that do not provide added value for the consumer but simply increase food prices. In addition, the food companies have one of the tiniest research budgets (for nutrition and food quality) of any United States industry.[65]

The probe into the work of the F.D.A., conducted largely by college students and recent graduates, found that, rather than launch campaigns against major firms that routinely break the law, the F.D.A. pursues small and inconsequential violators, so as to give the appearance of activity with a record of successful prosecution, while allowing major depredators to proceed unmolested. Even when successful, as in the following case, the F.D.A. is hampered by an archaic penalty structure:

In 1958 the FDA became involved in a complicated legal battle with the Caltec Citrus Company after having staked out the company's warehouse and observed sugar, vitamin C, and other substances not allowed in pure orange juice being carried in a back door. It was *estimated that the watering and adulterating practices of the company cost consumers $1 million in lost value—$1 million of pure company profits. The outcome of the case . . . was a total fine of $6,000 and a suspended sentence for the violators. A man who could return $1 million on a $6,000 investment would be considered brilliant in any business circle.*[66]

Nonetheless, the Nader team was not convinced that it was limited enforcement power that primarily hamstrung the F.D.A.; if the F.D.A. allowed the public to be bilked, the cause was its own apathy and indifference. "As long as the FDA believes that the food industry wishes to provide the safest, highest-quality food possible to the American people," the team concluded, "no amount of legislation, manpower, or money will turn the agency into an effective food regulator." The Nader group found the F.D.A.'s faith in industrial self-regulation "ludicrous, if not tragic." The food industry, it insisted, "has vigorously set about its task of making profits." Therefore it was time that the F.D.A. set about "*its* assigned task of insuring that profits made by the food industry are not the result of fraud, deception, adulteration, or misbranding." Otherwise, the public interest will continue to be mauled by the food industry's "callousness, ignorance, and greed."[67]

The resemblance of upperworld crime to the most destructive kinds of traditional crime is underscored by Nader in the following broadside on air pollution:

The efflux from motor vehicles, plants, and incinerators of sulfur oxides, hydrocarbons, carbon monoxide, oxides of nitrogen, particulates, and many more contaminants amounts to compulsory consumption of violence by most Americans. There is no full escape from such violent ingestions, for breathing is required. This damage, perpetuated increasingly in direct violation of local, state, and federal law, shatters people's health and safety but still escapes inclusion in the crime statistics. "Smogging" a city or town has taken on the proportions of a massive crime wave, yet federal and state statistical compilations of crime pay attention to "muggers" and ignore "smoggers." . . . In testament to the power of corporations and their retained attorneys, enforcement scarcely exists. Violators are openly flouting the laws and an Administration allegedly dedicated to law and order sits on its duties.[68]

The difficulty with enforcement of air pollution laws undoubtedly has something to do with the fact that "most of the state boards primarily responsible for cleaning up the nation's air and water are markedly weighted with representatives of the principal sources of pollution."[69]

In large measure thanks to Nader and his associates, the number of acts defined as upperworld crime has grown dramatically in recent years. Nader's book *Unsafe at Any Speed*,[70] developed from a third-year paper written while he was a student at the Harvard Law School, was instrumental in bringing about passage of the National Traffic and Motor Vehicle Safety Act of 1966. In 1967 national legislation was passed to insure that the states come up to federal meat inspection standards, so that the public might be protected from so-called 4-D meat—meat derived from dead, dying, disabled, or diseased animals. Testimony by federal meat inspectors told of packing plants where "abscessed beef and pork livers and parasitic infected livers were mixed with edible products" and where meat was dragged across floors on which there were vermin droppings.[71] The Fair Packaging and Labeling Act went into effect in mid-1968, and by the following year it was reported that, among other things, the number of different kinds of packages for toothpaste had been reduced from fifty-seven to five and of peanut butter from twenty-nine to twelve.[72] The Truth in Lending Act, signed into law in May 1968, saw the almost immediate inclusion on customer statements of the interest rates being charged. In addition, many acts long dormant on statute books are being used now to regulate practices detrimental to the quality of life. Thus, in February 1970, eleven Illinois companies were charged under the 1899 Refuse Act with dumping waste materials into navigable waters.[73] Similar attacks against polluters are being mounted by municipal governments, which make use of their power to define new forms of upperworld crime. Thus, at the end of 1970, a news magazine carried the following report:

Reacting to charges that leaded gasolines are a prime source of air pollution, the Buffalo city council has adopted the nation's first anti-lead ordinance. Starting next September, all service stations in the city must have at least one pump for low-leaded gas. . . . The goal by Jan. 1, 1980: no leaded gas in Buffalo. Meanwhile, Akron has ordered a ban on the sale of detergents containing phosphates by June 30, 1972. Offenders will be slapped with fines ranging from $100 to $300 and jail sentences up to a maximum of six months.[74]

UPPERWORLD CRIME AND THE CRIMINAL JUSTICE SYSTEM

One of the difficulties that the criminal justice system in the United States faces in dealing with upperworld offenders is that there is a price on justice, that, to some extent, justice can be bought. The wealthier the defendant, the more apt he is to command resources permitting him to bring about a judicial conclusion favorable to his interests. As Solon noted very long ago, " . . . laws are like cobwebs, for if any trifling or powerless thing fell into them, they held it fast; while if it were somewhat weightier, it broke through them and was off."[75]

"Justice delayed is justice denied," a federal attorney is quoted as saying in regard to what seemed an endlessly postponed trial of an affluent upperworld criminal. "That's what they say about the junkies, but not about these guys."[76] In court, the upperworld offender is able to present a bland appearance that helps shield him against the more severe sentence that might be given to a disreputable-appearing defendant. With regard to variations in sentencing based on financial position, Stuart Nagel has noted:

The reasons for the economic class sentencing disparities, holding crime and prior record constant, are due possibly to the quality of legal representation that the indigent receive and probably to the appearance that an indigent defendant presents before a middle-class judge or probation officer. In other words, there may be some class-biased attitudes present among judicial personnel.[77]

Another consideration, of course, is that upperworld criminals do not represent great recidivistic threats. If they are embezzlers, for instance, they are not again likely to gain positions of financial trust for further defalcations. Besides, they are apt to be older persons, whose attorneys tell the court that two years in the penitentiary—given the background and sensitivity of their client—would be equivalent to a death sentence. Difficulties involved in prosecuting upperworld criminals are indicated in the following statement by a United States attorney:

People who are victimized by white-collar criminals are embarrassed. Very often they feel stupid afterwards and don't want to get involved because of their business reputations. . . . Even when we get the witnesses, sometimes we decide not to prosecute. Unless the offense is outrageous, there's a danger that the criminal will receive a light sentence. Some judges just don't consider such a person a serious threat to society. We're afraid that when a light sentence does come down other white-collar criminals will be encouraged to forge ahead.[78]

Even when imprisoned, upperworld offenders are apt to be sent to the cozier kinds of institutions, those in which security is minimum, since they are not considered escape threats. Thus, for a federal offense, the upperworld criminal is likely to go to the penitentiary at Lewisburg, Pennsylvania, the traditional offender to the penitentiary at Lorton, Virginia. The difference? "I'd much rather serve two years at Lewisburg," says a federal prosecutor, "than two months at Lorton."[79]

The irony of disproportionately lighter sentences for upperworld crime lies in the fact that upperworld offenders seem to be a good deal more responsive to tougher penalties than their underworld counterparts. It might be noted that the antitrust conspirators in the notorious 1960 heavy electrical equipment case, six of whom were given thirty-day jail sentences, refused to have their families visit them, presumably out of embarrassment.[80] With more at stake, upperworld offenders are obviously more sensitive to the degradation involved in penal incarceration.

For this reason, tough sentences against discovered upperworld criminals would seem to be particularly effective deterrents to potential offenders. "The imposition of jail sentences," the President's Commission on Law Enforcement and Administration of Justice noted in regard to upperworld crime, "may be the only way adequately to symbolize society's condemnation of the behavior in question. . . . And jail may be the only sanction available which will serve as an adequate deterrent."[81] The same point was made earlier and more colorfully by the sociologist Edward A. Ross: "Never will the brakes of law grip those slippery wheels until prison doors yawn for the convicted officers of lawless corporations."[82] These views are corroborated by the experience of the director of the fraud division of the Department of Justice:

No one in direct contact with the living reality of business conduct in the United States is unaware of the effect the imprisonment of seven high officials in the Electrical Machinery Industry in 1960 had on the conspiratorial price fixing in many areas of our economy; similar sentences in a few cases each decade would almost completely cleanse our economy of the cancer of collusive price fixing and the mere prospect of such sentences is itself the strongest available deterrent to such activities. [83]

However, to argue that these indications of the deterrent value of prison terms justify "unreasonable" sentences for upperworld offenders is like arguing that the more sensitive rapist ought to be given a longer sentence than the callous one because he seems more likely to be responsive to the aim of reform through incarceration. But it is noteworthy that the social response that might be most effective with upperworld offenders and offenses is the one least employed.

There would also appear to be an urgent need, if upperworld offenses are to be subject to the same obloquy as the more traditional kinds of violations, for the public to redefine upperworld offenses and offenders in terms of stronger abhorrence. A lesson might be learned in this connection from a policy followed in Leningrad during the merciless siege of that city in the Second World War. Women would take captured German pilots through the ruins to show them what their bombing had wrought, thus impressing upon them a definition of their behavior very likely foreign to their habits of thought.[84]

CRIMINOLOGY OF UPPERWORLD CRIME

The study of upperworld crime has been the precursor of the contemporary swing of criminology toward more penetrating investigation of the political processes by which certain behaviors become defined as criminal. Studies of offenders such as robbers and rapists were apt to concentrate on individual psyches and to reflect what Schur saw in criminology as "a general disdain of political, economic, and historical considerations."[85] If attention was paid in the past to social conditions seemingly associated with offenses of violence, for instance, it likely did not extend much further than tongue-clucking over the deadening effect of slum existence upon human compassion. To define rape as a socially dictated drive for emotional success and robbery as an attack upon capitalistic strongholds seemed more poetic and polemical than the methodology of objective social science inquiry could tolerate.

Upperworld crime, however, could not very readily be analyzed in terms of its participants and their psychological experiences. For one thing, the upperworld offender, not being imprisoned or otherwise readily accessible, was unavailable for direct investigation. Thus such data as his I.Q. and his responses to items on an investigator's inventory were lacking. In addition, the usual psychiatric explanations for traditional crime are patently inappropriate for upperworld offenses. As Sutherland noted, General Motors does not have an inferiority complex, United States Steel does not suffer from an unresolved Oedipal problem, and the Du Ponts do not desire to return to the womb.[86]

Partly out of necessity, therefore, explanations for upperworld crime focused on the value system of the society and upon the processes through which certain kinds of behavior come to be singled out for attention by the system of criminal justice. This line of inquiry led to a reexamination of social values and to a repudiation of the common, and rather banal, causal explanations of criminal activity. In addition, as Cressey has observed, attention to upperworld crime led to an insistence that explanations be sought regarding the failure of the society to take note of it.[87] The absence of tabulations of upperworld crime in the F.B.I.'s *Uniform Crime Reports* is characteristic.[88] To date, upperworld crime remains ineptly defined, inadequately investigated, and inexpertly assessed in regard to causality and consequences. But in large part because of its failure to fit readily into earlier molds of definition and explanation, attention to upperworld crime has rejuvenated the entire study of criminal behavior.

NOTES

1. See Gunnar M. Myrdal, *An American Dilemma* (New York: Harper, 1944).

2. Edwin H. Sutherland, "White-Collar Criminality," *American Sociological Review*, 5 (February 1940), pp. 1–12.

3. Paul W. Tappan, "Who Is the Criminal?" *American Sociological Review*, 12 (February 1947), pp. 96–102

4. See Alson J. Smith, *Syndicate City* (Chicago: Regnery, 1954); John Roeburt, *Al Capone* (New York: Pyramid, 1959).

5. Nathan Goldman, *The Differential Selection of Juvenile Offenders for Court Appearance* (New York: National Research and Information Center, National Council on Crime and Delinquency, 1963), pp. 17–22.

6. Edwin H. Sutherland, *White Collar Crime* (New York: Dryden, 1949).

7. *Ibid.*, p. 9.

8. The book, miscited by the usually meticulous Sutherland, is: Alfred P. Sloan and Boyden Sparks, *Adventures of a White-Collar Man* (New York: Doubleday, 1941).

9. Edwin H. Sutherland, "Crime of Corporations," in Albert Cohen, Alfred Lindesmith, and Karl Schuessler, *The Sutherland Papers* (Bloomington: Indiana University Press, 1956).

10. Virginia S. Lewis, "A Theoretical Critique of the White-Collar Crime Concept," unpublished master's essay, California State College, Los Angeles, 1970, p. 6.

11. Sutherland, "White-Collar Criminality," *op. cit.*, p. 4.

12. Alexis de Tocqueville, *The Old Regime and the French Revolution*, trans. Stuart Gilbert (Garden City, N.Y.: Doubleday, 1955), pp. 176–177.

13. Wayne A. R. Leys, "Ethics in American Business and Government: The Confused Issues," *The Annals*, 378 (July 1968), pp. 34–44.

14. R. H. Tawney, *The Acquisitive Society* (New York: Harcourt, Brace, 1920), p. 26.

15. Tawney, *op. cit.*, p. 23.

16. Tawney, *op. cit.*, pp. 30–31.

17. Ida M. Tarbell, *The History of the Standard Oil Company* (New York: Macmillan, 1904).

18. Lincoln Steffens, *The Shame of the Cities* (New York: McClure, Phillips, 1904).

19. Frank Norris, *The Pit* (New York: Doubleday & Page, 1903); Norris, *The Octopus* (New York: Doubleday & Page, 1901).

20. Upton Sinclair, *The Jungle* (New York: Doubleday & Page, 1906).

21. Sinclair Lewis, *Main Street* (New York: Harcourt, Brace, 1920); Lewis, *Babbitt* (New York: Harcourt, Brace, 1922).

22. See, for example, Lester F. Ward, *Applied Sociology* (Boston: Ginn, 1906), pp. 338–339; Edward A. Ross, *Sin and Society* (Boston: Houghton Mifflin, 1907).

23. James Bryce, *Modern Democracies* (London: Macmillan, 1923), I, pp. 616–617.

24. *Ibid.*, p. 617.

25. Henry D. Lloyd, *Wealth Against Commonwealth* (New York: Harper, 1894), p. 4. The jurist was George C. Barrett of the New York Supreme Court, the case People v. North River Sugar Refining Co., *N. Y. Supplement*, 3 (January 9, 1889), p. 413.

26. Lloyd, op. cit., p. 315.

27. John Bunyan, *The Pilgrim's Progress* [1678] (New York: Revell, 1903), p. 207.

28. Theodore Roosevelt, *The Roosevelt Policy* (New York: Current Literature Publishing Co., 1908), II, p. 687.

29. Ross, op. cit.

30. Albert Morris, *Criminology* (New York: Longmans, Green, 1935), pp. 153–158.

31. Edwin H. Sutherland, *Criminology* (Philadelphia: Lippincott, 1924), p. 17.

32. *Ibid.*, pp. 17–18.

33. Quoted in Sutherland, *Criminology*, op. cit., p. 25.

34. For a comparison between the "corruption of the robber baron days" and present-day "hanky-panky," see James Reston, "Washington: The Supreme Court and the Universities," *New York Times*, May 18, 1969.

35. Sutherland, "White-Collar Criminality," op. cit., passim.

36. Andrew Hacker, "A Country Called Corporate America," *New York Times Magazine*, July 3, 1966, pp. 8ff.

37. Sutherland, *White Collar Crime*, op. cit., p. 208.

38. *Ibid.*, p. 210.

39. Sutherland, "White-Collar Criminality," op. cit., pp. 4–5. On Krueger see Allen Churchill, *The Incredible Ivar Krueger* (New York: Holt, Rinehart & Winston, 1957).

40. See also Julian B. Roebuck and Robert B. Hunter, "Medical Quackery as Deviant Behavior," *Criminology*, 8 (May 1970), pp. 46–62 and James H. Young, *The Medical Messiahs* (Princeton, N.J.: Princeton University Press, 1967).

41. *Los Angeles Times*, September 4, 1970.

42. *New York Times*, August 20, 1967.

43. Philip M. Stern, *The Great Treasury Raid* (New York: Random House, 1964), p. 162.

44. *Ibid.*, p. 166.

45. *United Press International*, June 11, 1961.

46. *New York Times*, February 8, 1967.

47. *Associated Press*, March 1, 1960.

48. David W. Maurer, *The Big Con* (New York: Pocket Books, 1949), p. 150. See also Edwin M. Schur, "Sociological Analysis of Confidence Swindling," *Journal of Criminal Law, Criminology, and Police Science*, 48 (September-October 1957), pp. 296–304.

49. *Wall Street Journal*, December 14, 1970.

50. Quoted in Harvey Katz, "The White Collar Criminal," *Washingtonian Magazine*, 5 (May 1970), p. 65.

51. Ramsey Clark, *Crime in America* (New York: Simon & Schuster, 1970), p. 38.

52. National Commission on the Causes and Prevention of Violence, *To Establish Justice, to Insure Domestic Tranquility* (New York: Bantam, 1970), p. 36.

53. Warren G. Magnuson and Jean Carper, *The Dark Side of the Marketplace* (Englewood Cliffs, N.J.: Prentice-Hall, 1968), pp. 57–58.

54. It is worth noting Ralph Nader's remark: "If you want to talk about violence, don't talk of the Black Panthers. Talk of General Motors." Quoted in "White-Collar Crime," *Barron's*, March 30, 1970, p. 10.

55. *New York Times*, September 8, 1970.

56. President's Commission on Law Enforcement and Administration of Justice, *The Challenge of Crime in a Free Society* (Washington, D.C.,: U.S. Government Printing Office, 1967), pp. 4–5.

57. C. Wright Mills, *The Power Elite* (New York: Oxford University Press, 1956), pp. 343–344.

58. Peter Maas, "A Classic Case of Corruption," *New York*, March 16, 1970, p. 28.

59. Quoted in *New York Times Book Review*, January 18, 1970, p. 10.

60. Quoted in Sutherland, "White-Collar Criminality," *op. cit.*, p. 3

61. Tony Parker and Robert Allerton, *The Courage of His Convictions* (New York: Norton, 1962), pp. 98–99.

62. See Howard S. Becker, *Outsiders: Studies in the Sociology of Deviance* (New York: Free Press, 1963), pp. 147–163.

63. James S. Turner, quoted in *Wall Street Journal*, November 19, 1970.

64. See, generally, Francis E. Rourke, "Law Enforcement Through Publicity," *University of Chicago Law Review*, 24 (Winter 1967), pp. 225–255.

65. Ralph Nader, "Foreword," to James S. Turner, *The Chemical Feast* (New York: Grossman, 1970), p. vii.

66. Turner, *Chemical Feast*, *op. cit.*, p. 63.

67. *Ibid.*, pp. 85–86.

68. Ralph Nader, "Foreword," to John C. Esposito, *The Vanishing Air* (New York: Grossman, 1970), p. viii.

69. Gladwin Hill in *New York Times*, December 7, 1970.

70. Ralph Nader, *Unsafe at Any Speed* (New York: Grossman, 1965).

71. Stephen Kota, quoted in *New York Times*, November 9, 1967.

72. *New York Times*, March 9, 1969.

73. *Wall Street Journal*, February 10, 1970.

74. *Time*, December 21, 1970.

75. Diogenes Laertius, *Lives of Eminent Philosophers*, trans. R. D. Hicks (Cambridge, Mass.: Harvard University Press, 1959), I, p. 59. Solon's words, slightly paraphrased, find their way into the mouth of Daniel Drew, "a pious old fraud," in Sutherland's *White Collar Crime*, *op. cit.*, p. 47.

76. *Washington Post*, November 2, 1969. For an overview see Herbert Edelhertz, *The Nature, Impact and Prosecution of White-Collar Crime* (Washington, D.C.: Law Enforcement Assistance Administration, U.S. Department of Justice, May 1970).

77. Stuart S. Nagel, "Disparities in Sentencing Procedure," *UCLA Law Review*, 14 (August 1967), p. 1283.

78. Ralph Ogden, quoted in Katz, *op. cit.*, p. 62.

79. *Ibid.*, p. 64

80. Gilbert Geis, "The Heavy Electrical Equipment Antitrust Cases of 1961," in Marshall B. Clinard and Richard Quinney (eds.), *Criminal Behavior Systems: A Typology* (New York: Holt, Rinehart & Winston, 1967), p. 142.

81. President's Commission on Law Enforcement and Administration of Justice, *Crime and Its Impact—An Assessment* (Washington, D.C.: U.S. Government Printing Office, 1967), p. 105.

82. Ross, *op. cit.*, p. 123.

83. Gordon B. Spivak, "Antitrust Enforcement in the United States: A Primer," *Connecticut Bar Journal*, 37 (September 1963), p. 382.

84. Harrison E. Salisbury, *900 Days: The Siege of Leningrad* (New York, Avon, 1969), p. 445.

85. Edwin M. Schur, "Theory, Planning, and Pathology," *Social Problems*, 6 (Winter 1958–1959), p. 227.

86. Sutherland, "Crime of Corporations," *op. cit.*, p. 96.

87. Donald R. Cressey, "Foreword," to Sutherland, *White Collar Crime*, *op. cit.*, p. xii.

88. Harry M. Shulman, "The Measurement of Crime in the United States," *Journal of Criminal Law, Criminology, and Police Science*, 57 (December 1966), pp. 483–492.

7/ SEXUAL CRIMINALITY

EDWARD SAGARIN

Almost from the birth of criminology, sex crimes attracted attention, although usually sex criminals were treated by scholars in separate studies, and not as part of the corpus of knowledge being accumulated about crime and criminality. As criminology shifted its attention to slums and economic hardships, to poverty and social degradation, sexual criminality fell out of fashion as a field of study. The psychiatrists continued to focus attention on such persons as ran afoul of the law because of their sex acts, but early American textbooks in criminology almost ignored the area of sexuality. Descriptions of "degrading" and "unspeakable" matters were considered unfit subject matter for college students.

However, times have changed.

A TYPOLOGY OF SEX CRIMES

For a serious study of sexual criminality, it would appear desirable to make some broad classifications of offenses, rather than depend upon a listing of violations as defined in penal law. In order of ascending social importance, I suggest:

1. Acts in violation of the law, but not condemned by the society, which is inclined to ignore the legal violation.
2. Acts widely deplored within the society, but usually considered private matters outside the proper scope of penal law.
3. Acts widely disapproved, which it is generally felt should be discouraged without being labeled criminal, because they are nuisances or medical problems.
4. Acts felt to be intolerable and regarded by the society as crimes.

This typology does not have clear-cut boundaries. Violations of the law seen as criminal by one social class or ethnic group are tolerated by another, and even approved by a third. Many offenses seem to be on the borderline between nuisances and outrageous conduct.

Culturally Accepted Legal Violations

The oft-repeated "If it's sex, it's illegal," calls attention to America's highly restrictive sex codes. At various times and places, noncoital sex between husband and wife, such as oral-genital relations, or voluntary intercourse between two unmarried adults of different sexes (generally called fornication), has been illegal. But although laws against the so-called unnatural acts between men and women continue to exist in many states, they have been repealed in others, and in still others have been interpreted by courts in such a manner as to relieve most participants of the onus of illegality. Several states continue to define as illegal adult heterosexual consensual relations, in private, when the two persons are unmarried, but the courts have interpreted the penal code to refer only to such open cohabitation as constitutes a flouting of the law and an effort to shock the morals of the community.

Although their potential for harm may have been exaggerated, laws of this sort are not harmless.[1] For example, restrictive sex laws can be used against those who violate the interracial sexual taboos, against political opponents, and against welfare recipients and job applicants.

It has been argued that the laws against fornication, oral-genital heterosexual relations, and similar acts foster blackmail on the one hand and contempt for law on the other. Without suggesting that these anachronistic penal laws should be retained, I doubt if they have either effect. Most people committing such acts would be surprised to learn that they are illegal, but would hardly feel stricken by the revelation. As for blackmail, it is difficult to imagine how a person could be threatened by fear of exposure of an act that meets so little community disapproval, despite the law. Nevertheless, there is no reason to continue to illegalize voluntary fornication and adult consensual extracoital activities, when these activities are performed in private and do not offend other standards of community morality.

Deplored by Many, Prosecuted But Rarely

Some socially disapproved sexual behavior is seldom subject to prosecution. Adultery is an example. In addition, to some people, behavior that should be disapproved but not treated as criminal might include prostitution, homosexuality, transvestism, transsexualism, furtive sex in semipublic places, and group sex (orgies, gang bangs, and other types), all because they are individual or consensual. It seems to me that these are more than private, if undesirable, practices; they are in some instances nuisances, in many instances have potential for secondary criminality, and in others (prostitution possibly excepted) are the result of serious psychological disturbances.

Nuisances, Annoyances, and Crimes Without Victims

This category deals with "crimes without victims."[2] Within it, the outstanding examples are consensual adult homosexuality and prostitution. Public transvestism, voyeurism and exhibitionism, sex with a dead body or with an animal, seem to be best handled as psychiatric disturbances, even if the acts themselves remain illegal.

The exhibitionist is sometimes confused with the child molester, because a certain amount of adult-child sexuality consists only of the adult's exposing himself in the presence of the child. The act itself can be studied in either context. A true case of career voyeurism or career exhibitionism that violates the norms of the community is more of a nuisance to the victim or the community than a threat in the usual criminal sense, and is probably best handled by a combination of legal and psychiatric processes.

Acts Beyond the Limits of Social Toleration

Finally, there are those acts that constitute crimes and that seem to require legal action, whether or not the perpetrator is emotionally disturbed. The most obvious example of such acts is forcible (or violent) rape. Probably the only other act that is almost universally condemned is adult-child sexuality. And some rare and exotic acts, such as indubitably obscene behavior in public, also arouse general condemnation. These acts might be interpreted as exhibitionism; more frequently, however, they involve sex in a semipublic place.

The following sections will discuss in greater detail forcible rape, adult-child sexuality (generally called child molestation), homosexuality, and prostitution. The discussion of homosexuality will be confined to consenting adult nonprostitutive relations; where homosexual acts constitute violent rape, prostitution, or child molestation, they are handled in these categories.

SEX AND THE UNWILLING PARTNER

He laid there for about 20 minutes and Cheyenne came over to the kid's bed and pulled his pants down and got on top of him and raped him again. When he got done Horse did it again and then about four or five others got on him. While one of the guys was on him, raping him, Horse came over and said, "Open your mouth and suck on this and don't bite it." He then put his penis in his mouth and made him suck on it. The kid was hollering that he was gagging and Horse stated, "You better not bite it or I will kick your teeth out."[3]

As Kingsley Davis points out, every society must set up norms for the regulation of sexual conduct.[4] The first and most pervasive such norm in Western society is that sexuality must be by mutual consent: the partners must be willing. Violent rape incites great outrage in our society. The anger is surpassed only when the victim is a child or a member of the oppressor group in an interracial situation.

In 1969 there were an estimated 36,470 cases of forcible rape in the United States.[5] This figure includes "assaults to rape," but not statutory rape without the use of force, and is limited to the heterosexual act in which the woman is victimized. Of the more than 35,000 attempts to commit rape, over two-thirds were completed. If all females in the United States are included, regardless of age, the crime rate for rape becomes approximately 35 per 100,000 *females,* which can be called the "risk of victimization." This means that one female out of approximately 2,850 was raped in America during 1969, a rate of victimization that rose for certain age groups (particularly sixteen to thirty) and some racial groups (particularly blacks).

During the decade of the 1960s, the number of reported offenses somewhat more than doubled. This figure, however, probably exceeds the actual increase, because the reporting of rapes increased. However, according to the Uniform Crime Reports, rape is "probably the most underreported crime" of all serious crimes.[6] The main source of error has been the general reluctance of the victim to report the act. Overreporting also occurs, because of apprehension, pregnancy, or spite, if not plain perjury. It might be thought that the two would balance each other out, but this is pure conjecture. It is more likely that the underreporting has had a much greater effect in distortion of rape statistics. However, the question is complicated by instances where the woman aroused the man, then strongly resisted, only to be overcome. It is of interest that on a national average, according to the F.B.I., "18 percent of all forcible rapes reported to police [in 1968] were determined by investigation to be unfounded."[7]

As will already be clear, the definition of rape offers several difficulties. First, the concept should be separated from "statutory rape," in which force and violence were not used to effect sexual intercourse, but "consent" was not legally given because the person was under age. Sexuality of this type, such as child molestation, is best studied as a separate phenomenon.

A greater difficulty in the discussion of this crime has to do with the amount of resistance that a woman must put up for the act to be called "rape." Rape implies resistance; the "victim" should not be a willing party to the events leading up to it. But how can the difference between coy acquiescence and diminished resistance due to fear be determined?

This is not to suggest that the girl necking with her pickup or with her regular date, *even if she has had intercourse with him before*, does not have the right to be protected from violence when her plans for the continuation of the interaction do not coincide with his. She has, and both morality and law should offer her that protection. But the male, when judged, should not be viewed in the same light as one who rapes a totally unwilling, unresponsive, uninviting, and uncooperating woman, possibly a stranger.

Forcible rape is a crime solved with a fair degree of frequency, although for 1969, 56 percent of all reported cases were officially declared solved, compared to 55 percent in 1968 and 64 percent in 1965.[8] Forcible rape arouses sufficient indignation to bring all the resources of law enforcement into play, except when the victim is black; and the relatively high percentage of young perpetrators is likewise a factor in assisting in clearance by arrest.

Most of those arrested are under the age of twenty-five, with many between the ages of seventeen and twenty. From descriptions offered by the victims in cases that remain unsolved, youths are believed to be the perpetrators of the act in the majority of the unsolved as well as the solved cases. However, the age factor may be misleading; what one may be dealing with here is the high percentage of forcible rapists who are unmarried.

Most rapes occur in situations in which perpetrator and victim are of the same racial group. This may be only a matter of proximity, for large cities have relatively few highly integrated residential areas. This is not to say that interracial rape is a fiction, but merely that a folklore and mythology surround it. In the South particularly, the black as rapist of the white woman was a specter probably deliberately invoked to give institutional support to segregation, oppression, and lynching.[9] The fact is that the black man is offered little opportunity for rape of the white woman; is frightened by the severity of the punishment that faces him, if apprehended, at the hands of mobs, police, courts, and juries; and, since the rise of the black nationalist movement, often sees interracial sexuality as a betrayal of the black woman and the black cause. Opportunity for the white to rape a black woman has likewise diminished. At one time he had little to fear in the way of prosecution, and the generally slighting attitudes toward both blacks and women encouraged his viewing the possession of the black woman as his "right." But attitudes have been changing, and so has the likelihood of prosecution, for the civil rights movement has compelled white officials and white juries to bring the white rapist to justice.

Part of the mythology surrounding the rape of a white woman by a black man may be rooted in the fantasy needs of whites, who have long believed (as have other race-oppressor groups) in the "sexual superiority" of the oppressed, to whom they attribute the powers of the savage and the beast. According to this myth, black men are genitally bigger, more powerful, and more capable; they are what has been jeeringly called sexual athletes. The white man's fantasy of a black man taking a white woman by force gives him a vicarious thrill.

That interracial rape—of a white woman by a black man—is more severely punished than intraracial rape is dramatically illustrated by data offered by Haywood Burns, national director of the National Conference of Black Lawyers:

National Prison Statistics shows that of the 19 jurisdictions that have executed men for rape since 1930, almost one-third of them—six states—have executed only blacks. There have been some years in which everyone who was executed for rape in this country was black. Detailed state-by-state analysis has shown that the discrepancy in death sentences for rape is related to the race of the victim.

Blacks raping blacks is apparently less serious than whites raping whites, and certainly less serious than whites raping blacks. But the black man today convicted of raping a white woman can be as certain of receiving the harshest treatment as was a Kansas black convicted of an interracial sex crime in 1855.[10]

Along the same lines, Hartung has pointed out that from 1909 to 1950 there were 809 rape convictions of white men in a group of Southern states, and not one man had been executed; whereas, during the same period, 54 Negroes were executed for rape, not to mention the many lynchings.[11]

In addition, Burns reports that of the 285 convicted men, 133 were white, 152 were black; of the victims, 209 were white, 76 were black. Of the rapes, 193 were intraracial, 92 were interracial. However, these figures are misleading; it should be borne in mind that rapists of blacks (whether the criminal is white or black) are prosecuted and convicted far less frequently than those of whites. Fuller information on this subject is offered by Amir, who made a study of all rapes reported in Philadelphia for the years 1958 and 1960.[12] During this time, there were 646 reported cases.

Amir found that rape is mainly an intraracial event (black against black, 76.9 percent; white against white, 16.2 percent; white against black, 2.6 percent; black against white, 4.2 percent), but the potential for victimization of the black woman in Philadelphia during these years was twelve times as great as that for the white. The relatively high incidence of rape among blacks, in a context of lesser social sanctions against premarital sex, confronts one with the paradox that sex is seized by force more frequently in precisely that group of the population in which it is most readily attainable without the use of force. This would seem to suggest that rape is both highly situational and that it is fostered by a cultural milieu.

In the black ghettos and in other slum areas, there flourishes what Wolfgang and Ferracuti have named a subculture of violence.[13] This violence—taught, admired, institutionalized—becomes associated with masculinity in peoples whose males have been systematically robbed of their manhood and who are determined to reassert it in many ways. That a few of them choose violent rape as an expression, not of their sexual frustration, but of their general alienation and anger is not surprising. That the black woman should be the victim is more a matter of "convenience" than choice.

Both rapists and their victims in the Amir studies were rather young, most of the offenders being between fifteen and twenty-five years, most of the victims between ten and nineteen. But while both white and black rapists generally seemed to choose victims of their own age or younger, there were a number of older victims too, and "Negro offenders tend to be at least ten years younger than their white victims." It is possible that the older women were victimized during burglaries and similar property crimes.

Alcohol was found by Amir to be a factor in one-third of the rapes, but in this one-third it was usually present in both the victim and the offender. However, rape cases with alcohol involved must be interpreted carefully, for several different factors can be significant: the semi-intoxicated victim as aggressor in a drinking bout, the role of alcohol in lowering inhibitions, the decision of the offender to take advantage of a situation in which the potential victim is not completely sober, and finally, the use of alcohol as an excuse to mitigate responsibility and guilt.

In about 50 percent of the instances in the Philadelphia study, identified rapists had a previous arrest record, but only a fifth of those with an arrest record had committed crimes against the person, and a still smaller percentage had been arrested for rape or for other sexual offenses. About 20 percent of the *victims* had an arrest record, mainly for sexual misconduct. With few exceptions, the offenders seem to be individuals who commit rape under conditions and in situations conducive to it, and who have insufficient controls against it or experience relatively little deterrence in the form of expected punishment.

Reiss has called attention to the phenomenon of adolescent group rapes, or gang bangs, and suggests that "most lower-class adolescents" have been involved in such events at one time or another.[14] The use of "most" is subject to some doubt, and there is a question whether these are forcible rapes or statutory rapes. The nature of the proceedings is conveyed by Rosenberg and Silverstein through an interview with the male participants in a group rape:

If you got a really good friend, and the girl is willing if she's really bad off or somethin', you know what she will do. She'll pull the train.
Pull the train?
Yes, that's what we call it: pulling the train. You take one chance. Then another guy takes a chance. You know.
Usually, how many guys are there?
Two.
Not like ten guys with one girl?
Oh, depends on what kind of a girl . . . . I been in a situation with about six guys.[15]

These adolescent gang bangs have sometimes been interpreted by Freudians as having unconscious homosexual meaning to the males. A man who inserts his penis into the vagina so soon after his friend, while his friend's odor is still permeating the female body, may be unconsciously obtaining satisfaction from this, while on a conscious level he is fully protected from homosexual panic by the knowledge that he is copulating with a girl.

Almost half "of the identified victim-offenders [in the Philadelphia study] were known to each other to the extent to constitute a 'primary' relationship," writes Amir, and 14 percent of all the rapists had what Amir calls "intimate" contacts with their victims. This does not mean that all the victims had invited the situation; some were neighbors, others were strangers who had permitted themselves to be picked up by a young man who had a car.

Amir employs the term "victim-precipitated" rape, an extension, as he notes, of Wolfgang's victim-precipitated homicide, "to refer to those rape cases in which the victim actually (or so it was interpreted by the offender) agreed to sexual relations, but retracted before the act or did not resist strongly enough when the suggestion was made by the offender." He likewise applies the term when a victim "enters situations charged with sexuality." He came to the conclusion that 19 percent of all forcible rapes studied during this period in Philadelphia could be described as victim-precipitated.

The major empirical study of all sex offenders and their offenses was conducted by the Institute for Sex Research, and contains considerable information on forcible rape and other aggressive sexual acts, performed against adults, adolescents, and children.[16] In this study, Gebhard and his colleagues place great emphasis on the borderline cases between force, suggestion, and persuasion. Gebhard writes of the socially approved pattern for female response, in which the woman is supposed to put up at least token resistance. He writes: "Any reasonably experienced male has learned to disregard such minor protestations, and the naive male who obeys his partner's injunction to cease and desist is often puzzled when she seems inexplicably irritated by his compliance." Furthermore, Gebhard continues, women on occasion "desire to be overpowered and treated a little roughly,"[17] or so, at least, many men believe, and some, following this line of thinking, find themselves accused of rape. This is probably an extreme instance of Amir's victim precipitation, and should simply not be treated as rape at all.

Gebhard encountered many convicted rapists "who believe in their innocence and are honestly mystified about why the woman brought charges against them." These men were interviewed in prison, following conviction, and Gebhard believes they are "victims of self-delusion and projection; they have in their minds minimized the violence and wishfully interpreted the woman's ultimate acquiescence as cooperation and forgiveness."

Like Amir, Gebhard found alcohol frequently associated with rape. Also, about three-quarters of the females studied were found to be strangers to the offender, and most were young. Some of the men complained, "It wasn't rape—she took her clothes off!" In most cases where there was resistance, it was ineffectual. Only 57 percent of the convicted men fully admitted their aggression, either to the authorities or to the Institute's researchers; 14 percent completely denied their guilt. The men were usually not "sex maniacs," although one man "had since puberty been sexually excited by stories of rape" and had a history of window-peeping and previous assaults.

Several types of rapists are recognized by Gebhard. The assaultive use unnecessary violence, and the violence is itself exciting to them. The amoral pay little heed to social controls "and operate on a level of disorganized and egocentric hedonism" (these include some intoxicated men). The explosive are average, law-abiding men who suddenly snap and then become extremely dangerous. The double-standard men want to marry a virgin but feel little guilt when they force themselves upon other girls—"bad females who are not entitled to consideration if they become obstinate."

Finally, some of the convicted rapists are mental defectives. Some are characterized by Gebhard as "unquestionable psychotics," and the remainder as a mixture of many types and varieties. "Many are suffering from personality defects and stresses which ultimately erupt in a sex offense. A few . . . appear to be statistically normal individuals who simply misjudged the situation."

One of the many problems in the prosecution of a case of forcible rape, and in many other types of sexual criminality as well, is the frequent absence of evidence other than the identification and charge of the complaining victim. At best, eyewitness testimony is suspect, for the act takes place under conditions of such intense emotional stress that one can easily err.

Even more complex is the question whether the act was voluntary on the woman's part or whether she was forced to submit by violence or the threat of violence. Courts and juries have been influenced by the race and, in many instances, by the previous reputation of the girl. Also, juries misunderstand that to find a man not guilty is not to imply that the woman is guilty; it simply means that *he* could not be adjudicated as guilty *beyond a reasonable doubt*.

It is a general rule of evidence that uncorroborated testimony of the complainant is insufficient for determination of guilt. It would seem to me that, in a case where the male insists that the act was entirely voluntary, and in the absence of *strong* evidence to the contrary, a man should not be convicted on a charge of forcible rape.

When a rape occurs during the commission of another crime (what Amir terms felony-rape), it may lead to other serious crimes, particularly murder, which may be committed to silence a victim who might otherwise identify the rapist. While unpremeditated murder following rape does not seem to account for a large proportion of homicides, it is of sufficient significance to make this a major consideration in the prevention of rape.

Violent homosexual rape, outside of prison, mental institutions, and other such settings, is relatively unusual. However, in prison it reaches alarming proportions, for it is countenanced by the authorities, who see the satisfaction of the aggressive males as a mechanism for keeping such "troublemakers" happy. Sometimes the victims are heterosexual and, in addition to the pain, violence, and humiliation, they suffer tremendous trauma, disgust, and psychological damage. Little sympathy is felt by the guards, wardens, or public; they assume that the convict must be a criminal and therefore had it coming to him. When the victim is homosexual, rapists regard him as fair territory, just as heterosexual defenders of the double standard see it as their right to possess the "bad" girl. One overtly homosexual ex-convict told me that, when assigned to a well-known prison, he was given as a present to a cell block in return for the prisoners' good behavior! This in a field that has changed its name from penology to corrections.

PLAYING CHECKERS—IT'S YOUR MOVE

Like rape, the sexual molestation of a child is the subject of strong general condemnation and receives little institutional support in most societies.[18] In the studies conducted by Gebhard and his colleagues, offenses against children under the age of twelve are differentiated from those against minors.[19]

Generally, the concealment of age by the younger of the partners, in a willing relationship, has been frowned upon as a defense in sex cases involving minors. However, the American Law Institute has made what appears to be a reasonable distinction.[20] It suggests that the defense "I didn't know she (or he) was that young" should not be acceptable if the child is under the age of ten, but is acceptable for a minor between ten and the legal age of consent, provided it is substantiated by the minor's general appearance.

Most of the offenders studied by Gebhard were not old: the average age was thirty-five, with only one-sixth over fifty. These figures possibly suffer from a certain bias because more young adult offenders (in their twenties or thirties) may be reported to authorities, and older ones ignored or perhaps handled with "psychiatric compassion." The cases studied showed a relatively high degree of recidivism: 40 percent had at least one previous sex offense, and nearly 20 percent more than one, but these previous offenses were not always, or necessarily, child molestation. We are here apparently dealing with psychiatrically disturbed, often compulsive, individuals.

Many of the offenses took place in a home, and not infrequently the man was known to the girl—sometimes as a friend, a casual acquaintance, a neighbor, or a relative (but not one close enough for the case to be studied as incest). Some offenses occurred outdoors, or in school buildings or automobiles, and some in theaters, where a man sits down next to an unaccompanied girl, and if she rebuffs his advances, he makes another move, an activity called "playing checkers."

The girls in the Gebhard studies were of an average age of eight, and the activities usually consisted of fondling, heavy petting, exposure, masturbation, and some oral-genital contacts. In a relatively small number of cases, there was attempted coitus, and in about 2 percent of the instances under study, successful coition.

As Table 1 indicates, the degree of resistance or encouragement on the part of the female is described very differently in the official record of the case (based primarily on the victim's version) and in the account given by the offender to the investigators of the Institute for Sex Research. The interviews were conducted long after adjudication of guilt and incarceration, and assurances of confidentiality were given. For several reasons, these figures can be misleading. We are here dealing only with cases that were not considered to be forcible rape (which, for analytic purposes, was studied as a separate category). Hence the percentage resisting is far lower than it would be if all reported cases of sexual offense against children were included.

How can the discrepancy between the report given by the child and the one given by the offender be explained? Both are suspect. The child is old enough to understand that she will exonerate herself if she claims resistance or lack of encouragement in the courtroom; and since she is a prosecution witness, the prosecution encourages her in that direction in order to obtain a conviction. On the other hand, the defendant is anxious that the court, the researcher, and even he himself believe that he was led on. Indeed, some

Table 1

	RESISTED %	PASSIVE %	ENCOURAGING %	CASES Number
According to record	75.4	8.2	16.4	61
According to offender	14.6	36.9	48.4	157

offenders denied their guilt, not only in court, but to the investigators as well. They did not adduce mitigating circumstances (such as encouragement or intoxication), but maintained "their innocence in the face of ample testimony and evidence to the contrary, and one often felt that they could not admit the truth even to themselves. Their explanations were generally unconvincing and frequently contained a paranoid theme concerning their having been 'framed.' "

Researchers were here dealing only with those who had been found guilty in a court of law and were currently in prison. While the picture of a prison system filled with innocent men is indubitably an exaggeration, there probably were some truly guiltless prisoners among those stoutly denying their culpability.

Who are the offenders? In addition to the stereotype of dirty old men, two other types are recognized: the oversexed individual and the extraordinarily timid. At times the same person can combine both characteristics. The timidity may explain the male who is fearful of approaching adult females, lest he be rebuffed; the oversexuality may explain the compulsive person for whom the sex drive is beyond control, and who will approach anyone at all.

While there were inebriates, psychotics, mental defectives, and senile deteriorates among these people, the most important from the point of view of social policy are the group that Gebhard labels pedophiles, and who constitute between one-quarter and one-third of the offenders. The term itself, Gebhard writes, "is somewhat unfortunate since these men evidently did not consciously prefer children as sexual partners, but simply found them acceptable." Some of these pedophiles are repeaters, many making passes at children for as long as twenty or more years. For those who find children acceptable but not preferable as sex partners, therapy, whether in prison or out, has been said to be particularly successful. Many of these men can be convinced that they are capable of finding gratification elsewhere, and that the sexual approach to the child is self-defeating and easily controlled. They can simply *decide* to refrain, because they are not compulsively driven to it.

But the child molester lives with a stigma that goes far beyond that associated with any other offenses. Although prison authorities may try to conceal records, and the prisoner himself may tell a cover story, word of the nature of his crime soon gets around. Those convicted of other crimes shun him, maltreat him, and, if he is reasonably young, may give him a piece of his own medicine by conducting gang rapes on him.

With homosexual offenders against children, a somewhat different pattern emerges. Some are men who have had a great deal of activity with other males (older boys, generally teen-agers). Some are pedophiles interested in minors in whom secondary sexual characteristics have not yet become obvious.

The Gebhard study shows that the median age of the male victims was slightly higher than that of the females. On the average, the homosexual offender is just past thirty, is almost always unmarried, and presumably can easily locate homosexual partners of his own age. He is frequently interested in young boys, preferably in their teens. Seldom was force or threat used, and it would appear that some of the youths were consenting or willing partners, if not actually the "aggressors," unless one takes the position that, as children, they were legally incapable of giving consent. *Both the official records and the offender's report* agreed that 70 percent of the boys were either passive or gave encouragement; in another 19 percent of the cases, there was agreement that the boy had resisted. Since apprehension and arrest are more frequent when the boy has resisted, it can be assumed that in an overwhelming majority of homosexual relations between a man and a young boy, the latter is either passive or encouraging. While not reported by Gebhard, many of the adult-child, and even more of the adult-minor, homosexual cases involve a fiduciary transaction.

A major problem concerning adult-minor sexuality is the effect that such behavior has on the life patterns of the victim at a later age. Almost as if in contradiction, the seduction of a girl has been blamed for her turning away from men and toward other women, while the seduction of a boy has been blamed for his being inducted into the world of homosexuality. There may be no contradiction, however. The girl who is unwillingly seduced may be left with a feeling of repulsion against men as "beasts." The boy who is seduced—and we are here speaking of a child of twelve or fourteen—is in an unformed state, seeks an unspecified sex outlet, and discovers it in what may have been at first an unexpected and later an easily obtainable form.

One other major study of child molestation was carried out by Charles McCaghy.[21] Whereas Gebhard studied incarcerated offenders, McCaghy studied all those who had been found guilty of a sexual offense with a child in certain counties of the state of Wisconsin, and who were either incarcerated or on probation. To accomplish this, "the records of persons convicted under all statutes, ranging from disorderly conduct to rape, which might logically be applicable when convicting a child molester," were studied. His final sample consisted of 124 incarcerated men and 57 on probation.

Verifying many of Gebhard's findings, McCaghy established that the men were not old, that many of them knew the children, and that in 76 percent of the cases, there was no evidence of any type of coercion. Those involved with the very young often denied the sexuality of the event; those involved with older children more often denied culpability on the grounds that the child "wanted it." Molesters of boys, McCaghy found, were more candid than molesters of girls, and less frequently used drunkenness as an excuse for their behavior. The homosexual molesters, it appears, had already accepted their deviant sex role in society. Since they had made "a drastic departure from the sexual norms of conventional society," the accusation of child molestation did "not constitute a threat to their present self-concepts as sexual deviants."

When subjected to therapy, the members of the McCaghy sample seemed particularly adept at manipulating the situation to gain early release from incarceration. They soon found out that denial of the act, placing the blame on the victim for having enticed them, and other mechanisms were of no avail. They saw that what they had to do was learn the language of therapy—

recognize that they had deep problems, often of an unconscious nature, and convince the world that they now knew how to act out their problems in a socially acceptable manner. Inasmuch as many a molester had an indeterminate sentence, and had an interest in terminating his stay as quickly as possible, his problem became how to express himself "in a manner that will convince staff members that he is making progress toward his release date." This does not in itself prove that therapy is ineffective, but simply that it may turn into a mutual put-on.

General statements about molesters and molestation are still difficult to make. Research seems to point to overreaction on the part of social control forces, sometimes to the detriment of the child;[22] oversimplification of stereotypes (the senile and the highly sexed, particularly); a high degree of personality maladjustments, neuroses, and psychoses among those whose interests are directed to the extremely young; and relatively "normal" heterosexual or homosexual interests on the part of teen-agers who become involved with someone only slightly below the age of frequent social interaction.

Few child molesters seem to be career molesters, in the sense that this is their identification. Therapy frequently consists in teaching them to reorient their drives toward the slightly older in order to avoid conflict with the law. That this is not as difficult to accomplish as a reorientation from homosexual to heterosexual, for example, has been shown by its high degree of success. As McCaghy puts it: "Society's attempts to alter molesters' motives are on the whole successful. Under conditions in which accepting responsibility for the offense is a prerequisite for release, molesters come to embrace new, and presumably socially acceptable, explanations for their conduct."[23] Do they accept these explanations or do they offer them? Perhaps they start by offering them, and in the effort to delude (or convince) therapists and social control agents, they end by accepting them. And, once accepted, the new motives seem to become guides for new modes of behavior. Or so we hope!

SEX WITH MANY, SEX FOR MONEY

If there is considerable consensus and a degree of uniformity in the penal codes with regard to violent rape and child molestation, the same cannot be said for prostitution. The United States is the only country in which the prostitute is punished, although in many others she is arrested for street solicitation. Furthermore, in twenty-one states, the customer is also subject to arrest (although the ordinance is seldom invoked); this, too, is a legal condition almost unknown elsewhere. Finally, one state (Nevada) has local option, with each county deciding for itself whether prostitution shall be legal.[24]

Prostitution is not easy to define. Generally, it is the selling of sexual favors for money, preferably cash or its equivalent. Some have emphasized the indiscriminate nature of the act, and others (e.g., Polsky) maintain that it is the pursuit of such acts as a career or profession that constitutes prostitution.[25]

In America, the nature of prostitution has changed over recent decades, and there is every likelihood that it will continue to change. As late as 1951, Lemert was able to write that prostitution was essentially a female profession, although a few males were involved in it.[26] However, today male prostitution, widespread in almost all large American cities, and in many small ones as well, may be offering considerable competition to female prostitution.

Houses of prostitution, or brothels, declined in the United States between the First and the Second World War, and almost but not quite disappeared after the Second World War. If they did not disappear, they went underground in most cities—no longer advertised, but, like the speakeasies of Prohibition days, known to their own clientele and protected by the police. Brothels have been replaced in a variety of ways. In addition to streetwalkers, there are high-class prostitutes, generally known as call girls, who are discriminating in their customers and charge fifty to one hundred dollars a night, or any part thereof.[27]

Arrest records on prostitution shed light on law enforcement activities in a given area, but offer almost no key to the extent of the crime. This point is brought out in a report by the President's Task Force Commission on the economic impact of crime:

This illegal service [prostitution] was once an important source of revenue for organized crime. Changes in society and law enforcement techniques, however, have rendered it much less profitable, and today organized crime is no longer interested to the extent that it was formerly. Although diminished, commercialized vice has not disappeared from the scene. In 1965 there were an estimated 37,000 arrests nationally, male and female, for prostitution and commercialized vice. These arrests touch mainly the most obvious cases. Expensive call girls are rarely arrested. Like arrests for gambling and other illegal goods and services, it is clear that the arrest figures understate the number of persons involved in prostitution. If it were assumed that the total number of persons associated with prostitution and commercialized vice were about 45,000 and that the average annual income was around $5,000 the total received would be about $225 million. It is not clear how much of this would wind up in the hands of organized crime.[28]

In 1968, 10,403 persons were charged with prostitution in a sampling of the United States covering about one-third of the population. About three-quarters of these pleaded guilty to the offense charged, a very small number to a lesser offense, and somewhat less than one-fourth were acquitted or dismissed.[29] It is difficult to extrapolate these figures to the nation as a whole, because the sampling includes most of the larger cities. Another source of distortion of the statistics is that many of those arrested for prostitution may be charged with disorderly conduct or some other offense. Winick, who has studied this problem, suggests that in a typical year in the 1960's about 95,000 different women were arrested for prostitution or for solicitation for the purpose of committing prostitution.[30]

Several factors can be investigated in the study of the prevalence and distribution of prostitution: the number of prostitutes, the number of their customers, the average frequency of the interaction, and the amount of money paid for the service. Even if a census were possible, it would require considerable skill to differentiate between the prostitute living entirely off her earnings from sex and the one supplementing her earnings from some other occupation. A figure on the number of women involved in prostitution *as a regular career* is as hazardous a guess as one on the number of narcotics addicts. An arrest figure can be misleading, because many are arrested more than once, and many are never arrested at all. Clinard estimates that there are about 300,000 full-time prostitutes in the United States;[31] this is approximately one percent of the female population between the ages of fifteen and sixty, a figure that easily doubles if the upper age limit is reduced to forty.

The frequency of interaction with customers differs; the call girl usually has fewer customers than the streetwalker. Winick estimates that a prostitute at the lower socioeconomic level has an average of three customers a day, works six days a week, and charges ten dollars per session.[32] If we accept his figure of 95,000 prostitutes arrested, we can calculate that the group would have about 89 million encounters a year, or a little more than one per male over the age of fourteen. Obviously, only a minority of all males have an experience with a prostitute in any given year, while many males have such experiences frequently. With a ten-dollar average fee, the annual take would be 890 million dollars.

If, on the other hand, we accept the Clinard figure of a third of a million as full-time prostitutes, we would be dealing with about three times as many encounters, and a total expenditure of some 3 billion dollars. When part-timers and male hustlers are added, the size of the enterprise is seen as considerable.

Male prostitution is common, and in many cities the youthful hustlers have special streets and special bars that they frequent. There are houses with call boys, who are usually sent out to the home of the customers. Some work through a telephone answering service, while others use the facade of the masseur. Many newspapers carry ads inserted by male models, who offer their services for a specified amount.

An estimate of the number of males involved as prostitutes is even more difficult to arrive at than the number of females, not only because of the subterranean nature of the life, but because so many of these males are part-timers. Probably the total number of people involved over a given period in one or more prostitutive transactions is greater for male prostitution than for female heterosexual prostitution. But the number of men making a regular career of prostitution is probably extremely small compared with the number of women. Thus, following Polsky's definition, there would be few male prostitutes, but a great many sporadic promiscuous prostitutive relationships.

Prostitution exists because there is a market for it. The heterosexual market consists of several types of men: some single men, without regular outlet, or unwilling to devote the time and attention necessary to obtain it; some believers in the double standard and in the concept of good and bad girls;

some married men who seek variety of partners, and partners with whom there will be no involvement or entanglement; men seeking the excitement of interracial sex; some men who have a need to pay in order to obtain gratification; and finally, and perhaps most important, a group of men who seek noncoital sex of a peculiar, bizarre nature with females.[33]

Who are these girls, and why have they embarked on a career so strongly condemned and so fraught with dangers? Call girls may be office workers, business executives, teachers, who supplement their income by prostitution. Many full-time prostitutes are probably streetwalkers, who come from and remain in the lowest socioeconomic class. From the mid-fifties onward in the United States, narcotics addiction increased among these women, and sex became a means of earning money to support their own habit and that of their pimps.

That prostitution is strongly condemned in the United States is beyond question, although Esselstyn finds that public outcries have diminished and are mainly directed against public solicitation.[34] Nonetheless, prostitution is definitely discouraged, and the woman herself is seen as someone who ought to be rehabilitated. The reason for the hostility to prostitution, Esselstyn points out, is that society "senses the seeds of social collapse in promiscuous, commercialized, and uncontrolled sexual congress," and as a result develops "a folk wisdom [that] commands that no one should make love for money. . . . All other arguments [against prostitution]—vice, crime, disease, white slavery—are important, but actually they are disguises."[35]

What can be done about prostitution, other than condemn it or regulate it? The police have several alternatives. Prostitution can be ignored, while it remains illegal, and simply given sufficient police surveillance to reduce to a minimum the victimization of either the prostitute or her client. But this is a policy that leaves it to the police to decide what laws to enforce, and how vigorously, and leads to the evils that always accompany unenforced crime (graft, payoffs, protection, and the like). The police can pursue the eradication of prostitution with the utmost vigor, which will almost certainly drive the prostitutes to a neighboring county or even to another part of town. Or the police can harass the prostitute with occasional arrests, and with what amounts to "justice without trial," by holding the accused for several hours, or a night, and then releasing her without charge. This practice of arresting and releasing prostitutes, LaFave contends, is of doubtful legality: "Most of the arrests [in the state of Michigan where the study was made] fail to meet the probability of guilt requirements as those are customarily defined."[36] Furthermore, in some states, but not in Michigan, the courts "have said that a release by police following an arrest otherwise proper makes the arrest and detention illegal." LaFave points out that the harassment policy has resulted in the arrest of black women, merely because they were in the company of white men.

Prostitution brings with it a number of secondary deviances and criminalities. When legally regulated, as in many parts of Europe, it is said to give a sense of false security to customers and community, particularly with regard to the spread of venereal disease.[37] In regulated cities, most prostitutes never register; on the basis of studies made in Paris, Bremen, Hamburg, and elsewhere, it is generally believed that only about 10 percent of all prostitutes are registered with the police and have a license for their activities. The greatest argument against regulation is that it implies moral approval.

Abolition, the alternative to regulation, has been accepted by the United Nations as its official position. What is meant is abolition of regulation, but without illegalization. It suggests a moral campaign against prostitution, but not arrest of either the prostitute or the customer.

For the United States, there is no problem of abolition (except in Nevada), for this country does not have regulation. The problem is rather one of decriminalization. It is pointed out that the United States has a strong puritanical and prohibitionist tradition, and that many types of behavior only discouraged in other societies have been prohibited here. Prostitution, it is said, brings with it police corruption, in the form of payments for protection and bribery to avoid arrest. Moreover, it is a crime of a consensual nature, and nonconsensual crime, now so widespread, must be the focus of most police efforts. Hence the attitude: if two people, of proper age and by mutual consent, want to have sex of an impersonal nature, with an exchange of money, so be it. Such seems to be Schur's view,[38] and it accords with the recommendations of the American Law Institute that sex between consenting adults be ignored by the law.[39] But it need not be ignored by society, which has the obligation to warn the participants of the dangers of their activities, and to offer alternatives so that this behavior will become infrequent.[40]

THE SEX IS RIGHT, BUT THE GENDER'S WRONG

In general, the definition of homosexuality is easier than the definition of a homosexual, but both involve complications. Of homosexuality, one can say that it is erotic behavior consciously engaged in by two persons of the same sex. However, on rare occasions, one of the parties may not know the sex of the other (because of transvestism, for example); or the aggressor-inserter may have a peculiar conception of the act, defining it as homosexuality for the other but not for himself. It would seem best to restrict the term "homosexual" to those who have a chronic and strong *preference* for erotic satisfaction with a person of the same gender (regardless of the physical nature of the act preferred or accepted by that person).

Homosexuality has become a serious and important part of the study of sexual criminality, for many reasons: the number of people involved, the pressure by organized forces to change the law, the numerous concomitant problems (disease, blackmail, extortion, stigmatization, and the victimization of the homosexual in extremely serious crimes, including murder), the high incidence of adult homosexual interest in teen-agers, the view of homosexuality as an almost ideal-typical example of crime without victims, and the failure to distinguish between consenting adults acting in private or acting in public.

On the number of people involved in a sporadic or chronic homosexual pattern, much authority attaches to the famed statistics of Alfred Kinsey, now a generation old.[41] There is good reason to believe that Kinsey's figures on the incidence of homosexuality among white American males are somewhat high. But Kinsey established that this type of behavior is extraordinarily prevalent, that it does not exclude heterosexual activity by most of those participating in it, and in fact may be completely abandoned by some after years of participation, and embraced by others who previously led a heterosexual life.

Homosexuality between consenting adults is a classic example of a crime without a victim.[42] In England, the age of consent has been set higher than for heterosexual relations.[43] In the United States, the American Law Institute has suggested that the age not only of the younger but of the older participant be taken into account and that determination of criminality be based on the age differential when one participant is below and the other above the age of consent.[44]

Following many years of agitation in England as a result of the Wolfenden Report, which suggested that homosexual relations between consenting adult males no longer be subject to criminal sanctions (similar relations between adult females had been legal for many years in England), the British law was changed.[45] In the United States, Illinois repealed its laws against this type of behavior as well as against street solicitation (for "immoral" purposes, but not for money).[46] Similar action was later taken by a few other states.

The homosexual is subject to harassment, on the job, in social relations, and in such ways as discrimination by official governmental bodies. Though a high court has officially stated that "it is not a crime to be homosexual"[47] — the implication being that the "crime" lies in the acts and not in the status or the desire—it is doubtful if a person admitting homosexuality would be accepted into a police department, for example.

Arrests for homosexual acts between adults follow almost exclusively upon open solicitation on the street or in some public place, or apprehension during the commission of an act in a public area, such as a washroom or park. The first type of arrest is usually effected by a police decoy or plainclothesman. In a series of decisions, the courts have ruled that a defendant should not be convicted by the uncorroborated testimony of a police agent; and that an agent who, under false pretenses, goes to the house of a man suspected of homosexual activities is inviting the action and is guilty of entrapment.[48] Furthermore, when the agent "invites" or "encourages" a homosexual to make "a pass," the latter can hardly be accused of sexual assault, for this term suggests an unwilling partner.[49]

The call for repeal of the antihomosexual laws is all too often a smokescreen. Despite some deplorable raids on bars (a well-publicized one took place in New York City in 1969), the overwhelming majority of homosexual arrests and prosecutions are for solicitation *and activities* in public and semipublic places. It has been argued that these events occur only when the area is deserted except for the willing participants and a concealed police voyeur.[50] But it is doubtful if the number of homosexual arrests would diminish in our large cities if the American Law Institute proposals were enacted into law. The problem here is whether public restrooms and sections of parks should be virtually declared off limits to the straight population, or even to homosexuals who find this type of sex in public repugnant, in order to accommodate the needs and desires of a special group.

More serious from the viewpoint of major crime are the problems of homosexual murder and robbery. Here the homosexual is almost always the victim and not the perpetrator, although in some instances both parties may be homosexual. Homosexual murders do not seem to be rare. They are protected by the anonymity of the encounter. Often the motive is robbery, but frequently there is also rage, anger, homosexual panic (by the self-imaged heterosexual), and a sense of self-righteous outrage fed by years of conditioning against the degenerate other. In addition, when a homosexual is the victim of robbery, assault, and even murder, the aggressor often rationalizes that the "queer got what was coming to him."

PERIPHERAL PROBLEMS: DRUGS, DISEASE, PREGNANCY

Sexual offenses cannot be discussed without some consideration of the by-products of these acts: unwanted pregnancies and venereal disease. Today, pregnancies can be prevented with ease, and there is no need to discourage sex solely on the grounds that procreation might be a result of the activity. Prostitution rarely results in pregnancy, nor is there danger of pregnancy in child molestation, although the seduction of a teen-ager may result in impregnation. Of the sex crimes, only rape and incest are likely to produce pregnancy, and it is now common practice to handle such cases by abortion.

The question of venereal disease (V.D.) is not quite so simple. By V.D. is meant a disease that is transmitted primarily by sexual contact. The chief examples are gonorrhea and syphilis. A major cause of the spread of V.D. is unquestionably prostitution. The prostitute, no matter how careful, cannot know whether she is dealing with an infected client, and she may not be aware that she has herself been infected until she has had intercourse with numerous other clients in the interim. The man does not know the source of his ailment, and the woman cannot locate either the person who infected her or those to whom she passed the disease.

The spread of V.D. by heterosexual contact, particularly prostitution, increased with the use of the pill, when girls began to lose their sense of insecurity about unwanted pregnancies. The pill replaced the condom, and while it gave new and possibly greater protection against pregnancies, it increased the dangers of V.D.

Another major source of venereal disease is homosexuality, and here casual nonprostitutive homosexuality is probably more important than "gay hustling." Shame and stigma, as well as fear of social reprisal, restrain the diseased from cooperating in the naming of partners who may have infected him or may have contracted the ailment during its incubation period. Even physicians specializing in a homosexual clientele are reluctant to cooperate with public health authorities. What complicates this situation is that a homosexual may not be aware of the infection for a considerable period, particularly if he has been the "passive" partner (the insertee) in anal intercourse at the time when he was infected.

Regulation, criminalization, or illegalization of various acts have been ineffective in stopping venereal diseases. Conceivably, V.D. can be reduced by a strict moral code—but that does not seem to be in the offing; by public education; and by assurances that strict confidentiality governs all cases. But it is more likely that V.D. will be with us until effective immunization techniques have been developed.

A problem of recurring interest in sex crime is the effect of alcohol, marijuana, LSD, and other drugs on the participant. The matter is complex, first because these substances cannot be grouped into one category and treated as if their effects were all alike, second, because they may have different effects on different persons. Those who commit sex crimes are even more likely to blame intoxicating or psychedelic substances for their act than are those who commit other types of crimes; it is difficult for the researcher to determine how many do so justifiably.

It seems that alcohol frequently, and other drugs from time to time, are "unfairly" blamed, particularly in cases of child molestation and, according to McCaghy, especially when the child molested by a man is a female.[51] But many sex crimes take place during a brunken brawl, particularly when the victim is drunk and hence easy prey, or when both victim and perpetrator are drunk and involved in dyadic relationship that deteriorates into a criminal act. This would seem to be frequently true of forcible rape.[52]

By and large, drugs seem to have two contradictory effects so far as sexual criminality is concerned. They seem to lower inhibitions with regard to acts that would otherwise be tabooed by the individual, and at the same time they serve as antiaphrodisiacs, lowering the libidinal drive.

Hard-core narcotics, particularly heroin, are not a cause of sex crime in the usual cause-and-effect sense; rather, some persons who are already addicts resort to sex crime in order to support their habit. This is specifically true in prostitution, especially heterosexual prostitution. However, many women who have already become prostitutes learn from pimps and other associates to use drugs. This could be a specific example of both differential association and secondary deviation.

SEXUAL CRIMINALITY AND CRIMINOLOGICAL THEORY

Despite the fact that an entire group of offenses can be conceptualized as sexual crime and can be differentiated with some degree of accuracy from other types of criminal acts, it is doubtful if a single criminological theory can properly cover these acts, which traditionally were conceived of as being either of genetic origin or of psychological origin. Sociological theory does not exclude either of these interpretations; the former, particularly, is currently being given serious attention.

The entire gamut of sexual crime might be understood in terms of the moral ambiguities governing sex training, upbringing, and opportunities in America. Nowhere is the puritan tradition so strongly preached and so widely flouted. This contradiction has existed since the early colonization of America by the Europeans and is attributable particularly to the influence of Calvinism in the shaping of American morals. More recently, with the growth of literacy, urbanization, and the pseudosophistication that came with movies and television, a sharpening awareness of the discrepancy between the moral posture and the reality has become translated into a widespread cynicism.

Within this society, the subculture of violence that permeates underclasses acts to neutralize the normative restraints against force, and probably accounts for a considerable amount of rape.[53] Culture conflict theory, as originally elaborated by Sellin,[54] stressed that people in different subcultures act in a manner normative in their group but criminal in the dominant society. This difference in norms would not explain any of the major areas of sexual criminality, although it may account for much of the consensual fornication among youths. However, in a broader sense, culture conflict theory helps one understand a society in which sexual crime thrives in an atmosphere of breakdown of the moral order, a breakdown due at least in large part to the resentments that such a disunited society as ours fosters in an environment of racial and ethnic hostilities.

Whatever value anomie may have as a theoretical explanation for crime and deviance generally, it seems unproductive as a theory of sexual criminality, when interpreted in the narrow framework of Merton, and of Cloward and Ohlin,[55] to refer to the use of illegitimate means to gain legitimate ends. When applied to sexuality, the means-ends dichotomy breaks down. For the ends are not legitimated in the social sense. It might be suggested that homosexuality, adolescent homosexual prostitution, and heterosexual prostitution in its beginnings are means of attaining other, more legitimate, ends: heterosexual outlet or money; and the career development might then be explained in terms of learning theory. But the ends-means paradigm can tell us little about rape, child molestation, or homosexual acts that involve explicitly illegal patterns, such as sex in public places or violence committed in the course of gay encounters.

Differential association may account for the general attitudes one learns toward the moral order, and it is possible that certain types of behavior can be attributed to early association with persons who have a negative attitude toward certain sex norms.[56] The theory may help explain induction into homosexuality and prostitution, but it can hardly explain violent rape, and even less, child molestation. On the other hand, association with those who already have a negative attitude toward certain norms may contribute to a readiness and willingness to perform violent acts against "queers."

Labeling theory, and with it secondary deviance,[57] can account for some types of sex crimes, but hardly for rape (or our attitudes toward it), and perhaps not for child molestation either. It is true that acts become crimes when they are so defined by the moral enforcers, but there are certain types of sex crimes that would outrage any society; they are acts that do not outrage the group because they are crimes, but are crimes because they outrage the group.

SOCIETAL AND LEGAL REACTION

Sexual criminality has been dealt with by highly punitive societies for hundreds, perhaps thousands, of years. Alleged rapists have been lynched, when they were not legally executed; and homosexual offenders, even when their activities were conducted among adults and in private, have been sentenced to very lengthy prison terms. But legal reactions have been merely a reflection of social attitudes, with stigmatization, derision, and casting the offender out of the community, if not out of humanity.

Perhaps like crime itself, sexual crime is too wide a rubric, and all offenses and all offenders falling within it cannot be treated in the same manner. If we "desexualize" these crimes, rape can be seen as a form of aggravated assault upon a person, child molestation as an unauthorized intrusion into the life of a child too young to be able to make choices, voyeurism as invasion of privacy, and exhibitionism (and perhaps prostitution) as an interference with the maintenance of public order. The concept of sex crimes as such would be set aside, but it would be recognized that many crimes (including murder, burglary, and shoplifting, as well as rape) can have sexual explanations and motivations. This approach would bring the subject out of the hysterical realm for discussion and for the formulation of policy.

One of the ways suggested for dealing with certain types of sex crimes is to legalize the acts. Decriminalization, a complex problem, would apply mainly to consenting adults, and more specifically to homosexuals. What is being made legal and what remains illegal must be defined accurately. Decriminalization, however, is hardly a desirable way of reducing the arrest statistics for child-adult sexuality or violent rape. Given the social and economic conditions in this country, the age of consent in many jurisdictions is illogical; however, this is not the same as decriminalization of acts of an overtly sexual nature between adult and child. In fact, nothing more is involved than a redefinition of the term "child."

On the other hand, it might be advisable to legalize heterosexual prostitution, while making public solicitation illegal. As for homosexual relations between consenting adults, it must be specified whether decriminalization would legalize washroom activities.

The arguments invoked for the legalization of certain previously illegal practices are usually of two types: 1. The act is immoral or undesirable, but illegalizing it produces little good and much harm: blackmail, shakedowns, police corruption, gangland activities, continuation of the act under surreptitious and uncontrolled conditions, disease, victimization of one or both of the parties, all without reduction of the quantity of such activities. 2. The act is as normal as any other, and the *only* evil that results from it is the evil emanating from its being illegal. For a variety of social and historical reasons, the drive for decriminalization of prostitution has used the first argument, that for decriminalization of homosexuality, the second.

It is difficult to remove the onus of criminality from both prostitution and homosexuality without moving toward social acceptance of the acts. A further complication is that the major nonlegal mechanisms for social control are at least as undesirable as the legal ones: namely, stigmatization, discrimination, derision, the making of an outcast out of a useful citizen. The humane alternative to criminalization and social stigmatization seems to be the medical approach: view certain activities as unhealthy and undesirable, without stigmatizing them, and handle them like other medical, including psychiatric, nonsexual problems.

Packer suggests that both decriminalization and nonenforcement promote the behaviors in question:

When the threat of punishment is removed or reduced, either through legislative repeal or (as ordinarily occurs) through the inaction of enforcement authorities, conduct that has previously been repressed (in two senses of the word) tends to increase. We are so familiar with the phenomenon that there may be no more convincing demonstration than this of the effectiveness and complexity of deterrence. When, for example, laws repressing certain kinds of sexual conduct are no longer enforced with regularity, the conduct in question is promoted, not merely because people feel that a threat has been removed but also, and probably more significantly, because the subtle process of value reinforcement through the rites of criminal stigmatization comes to a stop.[58]

It is my belief that the conduct in question does not *have* to be promoted because the threat of punishment is removed; it may be discouraged by education and by substituting other, more attractive, institutionally approved modes of behavior.

On the other end of the spectrum, numerous states have had for many years so-called "sex psychopath laws," which permit indeterminate sentences for those convicted of certain sex crimes; the offenders are held until therapists are ready to release them.[59] Whatever merit these laws have, they must be looked on with suspicion, because they single out sex crimes alone of all crimes for indefinite incarceration, and because they are subject to great abuse on the basis of race, social class, and other factors.

To reduce the incidence of violent rape, the most serious of the sex crimes, would take far-reaching social measures affecting the still-spreading subculture of violence that permeates large sections of this country. A program for reduction of violence in America has been proposed by the Presidential

Commission on Violence,[60] and this aspect of the problem is discussed at length in the work of Wolfgang and Ferracuti.[61]

A program of "voluntary" castration of certain sex criminals, especially the violent ones, has been studied in Europe, particularly in Scandinavia.[62] However, the voluntarism is limited in that the criminal's alternative is continued incarceration. In the operation the sex drive is reduced, but not annihilated. According to Stürup, these operations, performed on violent, compulsive, uncontrollable recidivists, have proved successful, not only in reducing the violence, but in the general rehabilitation of the subjects.[63]

Most types of sex crimes that cannot be decriminalized lend themselves to rehabilitative therapy. The sex criminal is usually not an incorrigible menace. He is often a nuisance, and sometimes no more than a nonconformist. Ellis and Brancale found that the majority of convicted sex offenders they studied were fairly harmless, "minor" deviates, rather than dangerous "sex fiends."[64]

Modern societies, in the midst of a more relaxed attitude toward sexuality itself, are getting more tolerant toward the transgressor. However, sex crime is still sometimes exploited both by organized crime and by politicians running on a platform of crusading purity, and much of it is associated with serious nonsexual antisocial activities such as narcotics addiction, transmission of disease, robbery, rolling, blackmail, and murder.

"We can have as much or as little crime as we please," writes Herbert Packer, "depending on what we choose to count as criminal."[65] Yes and no. Some things can never count as anything but criminal, such as rape.

We must be careful that in ceasing to react to most deviant behavior as crime, we do not cease to see it as personally unfulfilling and socially undesirable (as I believe homosexuality and prostitution to be); and that when we do react to other aspects of behavior (e.g., child abuse or forcible rape) with a sense of outrage, we do not again fall into the age-old error of confusing sex crime with sex as crime.

NOTES

1. See, for example, Fred Rodell, "Our Unlovable Sex Laws," in John H. Gagnon and William Simon, (eds.), *The Sexual Scene* (Chicago: Aldine, 1970).

2. Edwin M. Schur, *Crimes Without Victims* (Englewood Cliffs, N.J.: Prentice-Hall, 1965).

3. Alan J. Davis, "Sexual Assaults in the Philadelphia Prison System," in Gagnon and Simon, op. cit.

4. K. Davis, "Sexual Behavior," in Robert K. Merton and Robert A. Nisbet (eds.), *Contemporary Social Problems* 2nd ed.

5. Uniform Crime Reports: Crime in the United States, 1969.

6. Uniform Crime Reports: Crime in the United States, 1968.

7. *Ibid.*

8. Uniform Crime Reports.

9. See Calvin C. Hernton, *Sex and Racism in America* (New York: Grove, 1966); John Dollard, *Caste and Class in a Southern Town* (Garden City, N.Y.: Doubleday-Anchor, 1957); Joel Kovel, *White Racism: A Psychohistory* (New York: Pantheon, 1970).

10. Haywood Burns, "Can a Black Man Get a Fair Trial in This Country?" *New York Times Magazine*, July 12, 1970, pp. 5ff.

11. Frank E. Hartung, "Trends in the Use of Capital Punishment," *Annals of the American Academy of Political and Social Science*, 284 (November 1952), pp. 8–19.

12. Menachem Amir, *Patterns in Forcible Rape* (Chicago: University of Chicago Press, 1971). A paper by Amir bearing a similar title is published in Marshall B. Clinard and Richard Quinney (eds.), *Criminal Behavior Systems: A Typology* (New York: Holt, Rinehart & Winston, 1967), pp. 60–75; references and quotes in the present article are from this paper.

13. Marvin E. Wolfgang and Frank Ferracuti, *The Subculture of Violence: Towards an Integrated Theory in Criminology* (New York: Barnes & Noble, 1967).

14. Albert J. Reiss, Jr., "The Marginal Status of the Adolescent," in John H. Gagnon and William Simon (eds.), *Sexual Deviance* (New York: Harper & Row, 1967).

15. Bernard Rosenberg and Harry Silverstein, *The Varieties of Delinquent Experience* (Waltham, Mass.: Blaisdell, 1969), p. 65.

16. Paul H. Gebhard, John H. Gagnon, Wardell B. Pomeroy, and Cornelia V. Christenson, *Sex Offenders: An Analysis of Types* (New York: Harper & Row, 1965).

17. *Ibid.*, p. 177.

18. Clellan S. Ford and Frank A. Beach, *Patterns of Sexual Behavior* (New York: Hoeber, 1951). A rare instance of defense of adult-child sexuality is found in René Guyon, *The Ethics of Sexual Acts* (New York: Knopf, 1934).

19. Gebhard et al., *op. cit.* The material on child molestation (heterosexual and homosexual) from this work is reprinted in E. Sagarin and D. MacNamara, (eds.), Problems of Sex Behavior (New York: Crowell, 1968).

20. Model Penal Code, American Law Institute.

21. Charles H. McCaghy, "Child Molesters: A Study of Their Careers as Deviants," unpublished Ph.D. dissertation, University of Wisconsin, 1966. A paper bearing the same title, prepared from this thesis by McCaghy, is published in Clinard and Quinney, *op. cit.*, pp. 75–88; references and quotes in the present article are from this paper.

22. See particularly William R. Reevy, "Child Sexuality," in Albert Ellis and Albert Abarbanel (eds.), *The Encyclopedia of Sexual Behavior* (New York: Hawthorn, 1961), and the work of Lauretta Bender and her colleagues, cited by Reevy.

23. McCaghy, in Clinard and Quinney, *op. cit.*, p. 88.

24. Charles Winick and Paul M. Kinsie, *The Lively Commerce: Prostitution in the United States* (Chicago: Quadrangle Books, 1971).

25. Ned Polsky, *Hustlers, Beats, and Others* (Chicago: Aldine, 1967). See also Winick and Kinsie, *op. cit.*; also K. Davis, *op. cit.*; and Harry Benjamin and R. E. L. Masters, *Prostitution and Morality* (New York: Julian Press, 1964).

26. Edwin M. Lemert, *Social Pathology* (New York: McGraw-Hill, 1951). The chapter "Prostitution" from this work is reprinted in Sagarin and MacNamara, *op. cit.*

27. Harold Greenwald, *The Call Girl* (New York: Ballantine, 1958); and *The Affluent Prostitute: A Social and Psychological Study* (New York: Walker, 1970).

28. President's Commission on Law Enforcement and Administration of Justice, *Task Force Report: Crime and Its Impact—An Assessment* (Washington, D.C.: U.S. Government Printing Office, 1967), p. 53.

29. Uniform Crime Reports, 1968.

30. Winick and Kinsie, *op. cit.*

31. Marshall B. Clinard, *Sociology of Deviant Behavior* (3rd ed.; New York: Holt, Rinehart & Winston, 1968), p. 372.

32. Winick and Kinsie, *op. cit.*

33. The best analysis of the market remains that of K. Davis, op. cit. Charles Winick has written on the clients of prostitutes, "Prostitutes' Clients' Perceptions of Prostitutes and of Themselves," International Journal of Social Psychiatry, 8 (1962), pp. 289–297.

34. T. C. Esselstyn, "Prostitution in the United States," Annals of the American Academy of Political and Social Science, 376 (March 1968), pp. 123–135.

35. Ibid., p. 125.

36. Wayne R. LaFave, Arrest: The Decision to Take a Suspect into Custody (Boston: Little, Brown, 1965), p. 463.

37. See Winick and Kinsie, op. cit.

38. Schur, op. cit.

39. Model Penal Code, American Law Institute.

40. See E. Sagarin, "Sex, Law, and the Changing Society," Medical Aspects of Human Sexuality, 4 (October 1970), pp. 103–107.

41. Alfred C. Kinsey, Wardell B. Pomeroy, and Clyde E. Martin, Sexual Behavior in the Human Male (Philadelphia: Saunders, 1948).

42. Schur, op. cit.

43. As recommended by the Wolfenden Committee.

44. Model Penal Code, American Law Institute.

45. The new law was passed on July 4, 1967. The full text of the Wolfenden Committee's Report relating to homosexuality is given in Sagarin and MacNamara, op. cit.

46. Penal Code, State of Illinois.

47. The case is cited in Edward Sagarin and Donal E. J. MacNamara, "The Problem of Entrapment," Crime and Delinquency, 16 (October 1970), pp. 363–378.

48. Ibid.

49. Ibid.

50. This position is taken by Laud Humphreys, Tearoom Trade: Impersonal Sex in Public Places (Chicago: Aldine, 1970).

51. McCaghy, op. cit.

52. Amir, op. cit., and Gebhard et al., op. cit.

53. Wolfgang and Ferracuti, op. cit.

54. Thorsten Sellin, Culture Conflict and Crime (New York: Social Science Research Council, 1938), Bulletin 41.

55. See Marshall B. Clinard (ed.), Anomie and Deviant Behavior: A Discussion and Critique (New York: Free Press, 1964).

56. Edwin H. Sutherland and Donald R. Cressey, Criminology (8th ed.; Philadelphia: Lippincott, 1970).

57. See particularly Lemert, op. cit.

58. Herbert L. Packer, The Limits of the Criminal Sanction (Stanford, Calif.: Stanford University Press, 1968). A portion of Packer's book is reproduced in Donal E. J. MacNamara and Edward Sagarin, Perspectives on Correction (New York: Crowell, 1971); quote, p. 109.

59. See Edwin H. Sutherland, "The Sexual Psychopath Laws," Journal of Criminal Law and Criminology, 40 (January-February 1950), pp. 534–554, and "The Diffusion of Sexual Psychopath Laws," American Journal of Sociology, 56 (September 1950), pp. 142–148.

60. Hugh Davis Graham and Ted Robert Gurr, (eds.), Violence in America: Historical and Comparative Perspectives (New York: Bantam, 1969).

61. Wolfgang and Ferracuti, op. cit.

62. Georg K. Stürup, Treating the Untreatable: Chronic Criminals at Herstedvester (Baltimore: Johns Hopkins University Press, 1968).

63. Stürup, address delivered before the American Society of Criminology, Philadelphia, 1966.

64. Albert Ellis and Ralph Brancale, *The Psychology of Sex Offenders* (Springfield, Ill.: Charles C. Thomas, 1956).

65. Packer, in MacNamara and Sagarin, *op. cit.*, p. 98.

8/ THE CRIMINOLOGY OF DRUGS AND DRUG USE*

ERICH GOODE

INTRODUCTION

What is a drug? Most of us assume that anything called a drug must *do* something to the human body, which automatically puts it into that category. Now, any adequate definition should (1) unambiguously group together all elements sharing a given characteristic, and (2) unambiguously exclude all elements not sharing that characteristic. What does a pharmacology textbook tell us? On the first page of the standard reference work on pharmacological therapeutics, we encounter the following definition: ". . . a drug is broadly defined as any chemical agent that affects living processes. . . ."[1] This is sufficiently inclusive to encompass almost any conceivable substance, from a glass of water to a bullet fired from a gun.

In actuality, the term "drug" is a social fabrication. The fact is that no formal, objective pharmacological characteristic of chemical agents will satisfy both criteria of an adequate definition simultaneously. *There is no effect common to all drugs* that, at the same time, is not shared by substances not considered drugs. Some agents called drugs are psychoactive, while some are not. Some affect the central nervous system, and some do not. Some drugs are physically dependency-producing—are "addictive"—while some are not. Some drugs are extremely toxic, while many, in the doses typically taken, are comparatively innocuous. This does not mean that drug effects are not "real." Drugs, of course, have chemical and pharmacological properties; they do act on human tissue. But the way they act has relatively little to do with how they are viewed and defined. Society's attitudes toward a given substance have very little to do with its laboratory-identified properties—and a great deal to do with sentiment and emotion. Society, or rather certain segments of society, define what a drug is, and the social definition, the linguistic device, largely determines our attitudes. The statement "He uses drugs" calls to mind only certain specific *kinds* of drugs. If what is meant by that statement is "He smokes cigarettes and drinks beer," we are disappointed; cigarettes and beer are not part of our stereotype of what a drug is, even though we will find a description of the effects of nicotine and alcohol in any pharmacology textbook.

A given substance may be a drug within one definition or sphere of interest, but not another. If we were to study ethnopharmacology and ethnobotany, agents such as kava-kava, peyote, yage, betel nuts, cocoa leaves,

---

*I would like to thank Dr. Mark Segal and Professor Alfred Lindesmith for their useful comments on an earlier draft of this chapter.

and Amanita muscaria would be important, but if we were to survey a current work on therapeutic medicine, these substances would not appear anywhere. Penicillin has probably been the most useful drug in medical therapy—but it is not used illicitly on the street. Alcohol is a drug if we restrict ourselves to psychoative effects in defining what constitutes a drug, but not if we adopt the definition of mainstream conventional society: no one who drinks liquor thinks of himself as a drug user, and hardly anyone who does not drink alcohol looks upon drinkers as drug users. A substance is a drug, not according to any abstract formal definition, but only within specific behavioral and social contexts. Which substances we elect to examine in any treatment of drugs is always arbitrary, and depends on our purposes.

Not only the term "drug" itself but nearly all terms relating to drugs and drug use reflect social, ideological, and moral attitudes. Physicians, for example, commonly employ the term "abuse" to refer to drug use outside a medical context. This term is a moral rather than a scientific designation, implying, as it does, that drugs should be used only for therapy and that such purposes as euphoria, pleasure, relaxation, or mind transformation are illegitimate. By this definition of abuse, any use of marijuana constitutes abuse, since this drug is not approved for therapeutic purposes, at least not by the most powerful and numerous members of the medical fraternity.[2] Marijuana is a mild hallucinogen that has some salutary, legitimate medical uses, which were one time recognized as such, but has fallen into disrepute for "moral" and political reasons.[3]

ADDICTION

The heroin addict and the weekend pot smoker are placed in a similar category legally, as well as in the minds of a major segment of the American public. Put in a very different legal and moral category are the alcoholic and the barbiturate-dependent housewife. And yet, medically and pharmacologically, heroin, alcohol, and the barbiturates share a great many characteristics, while marijuana is in a totally separate class of drugs. The framers of the law react not to objective properties of drugs, but to the prevailing social and moral assumptions.

Pharmacologically the broadest category, containing the largest number of drugs of interest to the criminologist, is that of the *depressants,* whose general characteristics are described below. One large subcategory of depressants is the narcotic analgesics, or simply *narcotics.* Not all drugs are narcotics, but since the public mind equates narcotics with "dangerous" or "bad," labeling a wide range of drugs as narcotics serves an ideological function in discrediting their use. For instance, marijuana is in no pharmacological sense narcotic, but law enforcers and politicians wish to retain the absurd label because it is useful as a propaganda device.[4] Heroin is a narcotic, as are all derivatives of opium (opiates): morphine, from which heroin is derived chemically, codeine, paregoric (a weak, alcohol-based tincture of opium), and, of course, opium itself. There are also a host of synthetic and semisynthetic narcotics (opioids): meperidine (or Demerol), methadone (Dolophine), dilaudid, as well as a number of other less well known substances.

A second subcategory of depressants includes the *sedatives* and *hypnotics*. While narcotics are used to kill pain, sedatives are used for their soothing, calming effect, and hypnotics are used to make sleep possible. Hypnosis and sedation are closely related functions—in fact, degrees of the same function—and the same drugs could, and are, used for both. The best known of the sedatives and hypnotics are the barbiturates; phenobarbital (whose trade name is Luminal), amobarbital (or Amytal), pentobarbital (Nembutal), and secobarbital (Seconal) are popular examples. The barbiturates are classified according to the speed and duration of their effectiveness, from ultra-short-acting to long-acting. The tranquilizers, such as Librium, Thorazine, Miltown or Equanil, and Doriden, share some fundamental characteristics with the barbiturates, though they possess some additional traits as well; for instance, some are useful in suppressing certain symptoms of mental illness. Tranquilizers are classified as "major" and "minor" tranquilizers.

Alcohol is also a depressant, but it is not a useful therapeutic tool. It was employed in the last century as an analgesic—as any fan of Westerns and old war movies knows—but the effective dose is so close to the lethal one that alternative methods were accepted as soon as they were developed. Alcohol acts as a fair tranquilizer and sedative.[5]

In varying degrees, all depressants share the following pharmacological characteristics.

1. All are physically addicting, or produce a physical dependency.[6] This means that withdrawal symptoms appear upon discontinuation of heavy, relatively long-term use. The delirium tremens of the alcoholic is an example of these withdrawal symptoms. The "cold turkey" symptoms (so called because of the appearance of gooseflesh upon withdrawal) of the "kicking" heroin addict are well known. Nausea, convulsions, muscular spasms—hence the term "kicking"—diarrhea, extreme irritability and nervousness, insomnia, and bodily aches and pains are typical withdrawal symptoms after physical dependency on any of the depressants. There is some evidence that the severity of these symptoms is greatest with the barbiturates. It must be emphasized that the alcoholic and the barbiturate-dependent are addicts—"junkies"—in every physical sense, and in this respect do not differ from the heroin addict; it is only because of our society's partial tolerance of the first two, and its complete rejection of the third, that addiction is thought to involve only the narcotics. In fact, in sheer numbers, addiction to alcohol and barbiturates is a problem of far greater magnitude than addiction to heroin.

2. All depressants are *tolerance-producing*—as are a number of nondepressants and nonaddicting substances as well. This means, first, that the body will be able to "tolerate," without apparent toxicity, a larger and larger dosage of a given drug over a period of continued use. Thus the amount of morphine, say, that would produce coma and death in someone who has never used the drug—about 150 milligrams—could be taken by an addict almost without

toxic effect. (There are, of course, limits in this process.) Second, it means that the individual habituated to one of the depressants requires an increasingly large dose to obtain the same degree of psychological satisfaction from it.

3. All substances classified pharmacologically as depressants tend to reduce nervousness and tension in the user, and produce a soothing, calming effect in moderate doses. All, that is, have something of a sedative influence on humans. In larger doses, they are soporific; they induce hypnosis, or sleep.

4. The depressants are, in varying degrees, analgesics: they tend to deaden the body's sensitivity to pain (and pleasure as well) at therapeutic levels. The narcotics are by far the most effective in this regard, and are universally employed for this purpose. The hypnotics, such as barbiturates, are not nearly as effective for analgesia, but tend to be significantly more so than a placebo. Sometimes sedatives will be used to potentiate analgesia, and would be employed in conjunction with a narcotic.

5. All depressants depress or inhibit the body's respiratory functions. Thus an overdose of heroin, Seconal, or vodka would typically produce coma and respiratory failure. There are between five and ten thousand overdoses a year in the United States from barbiturates—over half of which are suicides.

6. All depressants produce some degree of mental clouding, or a diminution of cognitive functioning—alcohol and the barbiturates more markedly than the narcotics.

7. All depressants to some degree lower the ability to perform motor skills, such as driving, although, again, alcohol and the barbiturates are far more debilitating in this regard than the narcotics—if, indeed, narcotics debilitate motor skills at all.

Although the "objective" laboratory-tested characteristics of any given drug explain to some extent why and how it is used by humans, as well as what they do and think under that drug's influence, these characteristics are only a small part of the picture. Take the question whether heroin is a "dangerous" drug. The medical literature on heroin use is replete with a wide range of extreme pathological sequelae, including hepatitis, tetanus, pneumonia, nutritional deficiencies, and, of course, overdosing, resulting in coma and often death.[7] The death rate of heroin addicts is several times as high as that of the general population of comparable age. We might very well conclude that heroin is, indeed, an extremely toxic and dangerous drug.

Such a generalization would be simpleminded, however. Whether heroin, or any other drug, is or is not a dangerous drug depends almost entirely on the context in which it is used. Consider overdosing. Since heroin is typically mixed, or "cut," with comparatively inert substances, such as lactose, any given sample may contain no heroin at all, or 1 percent, or as much as 75 percent. Although a high percentage of samples will contain roughly 3 percent, the addict is nearly always injecting a drug of unknown potency into his system. It is largely because of the great variability in the strength of the doses purchased that addicts will overdose. If high-potency samples are sold, a sudden rash of overdoses and even deaths will crop up in one neighborhood. (And addicts will flock to that neighborhood to purchase those strong, deadly doses—since, if they killed anyone, they must be good, or "righteous," dope.) One addict may be used to 3 percent heroin, and one day receive a packet of 20 percent—which may be fatal to his individual system. If the samples of street heroin were magically standardized as to strength, the problem of overdosing would be reduced dramatically.

Hepatitis and tetanus are consequences of using unsterilized needles communally, rather than a specific consequence of taking heroin; the same diseases are frequently observed among "speed freaks," or chronic amphetamine users, who also inject their drug of choice. Were care taken to use only sterilized needles, these diseases would not crop up among addicts. Inept handling of the needle may produce injected bubbles into the veins, which is dangerous, and may be fatal. Or a novice may inject heroin into the arteries instead of the veins, which will result in gangrene. Other diseases, such as pneumonia, are largely a result of the hectic, frantic, scrambling, hand-to-mouth existence of the junkie, who is committed to raising anywhere from $10 to as much as $150 a day to support a habit that would cost a few pennies a day if the drug were manufactured legally.

Many of the broad features of the chronic use of the amphetamines are identical to those of heroin addiction, and yet the pharmacological effects of the two drugs are directly opposite: heroin is a depressant and the amphetamines are stimulants.

The condition of the physician narcotics addict[8] contrasts sharply with that of the street junkie. Various estimates place the incidence of addiction among physicians at about one or two in a hundred, which is far higher than for the population at large. (There are about three or four thousand physician narcotics addicts in the United States.) Physicians typically use meperidine (Demerol), an artificial narcotic, although methadone, dilaudid, or morphine will sometimes be used. Addicted physicians very rarely suffer any of the negative physical consequences that street junkies suffer, because (1) their dosage is standardized as to strength and purity; (2) their needles and other paraphernalia are sterile; (3) they are aware of nutritional requirements (narcotics depress the appetite, and junkies are typically uninterested in food); (4) they do not have to search for drugs and money to maintain their habit, and therefore do not have the various health problems of the street addict; (5) they can be sure of a continued supply, and therefore do not have to undergo withdrawal—a painful and dangerous process—as the street junkie often does.

Physicians have been known to be addicted for forty or fifty years without medical complications. To say, then, that narcotics are dangerous is an oversimplification. What is unquestionably dangerous is the typical street narcotics scene. One of the more interesting medical facts about heroin and the other narcotics is that, aside from the danger of overdosing, they are relatively nontoxic drugs. Unlike alcohol, the amphetamines, and the barbiturates, which are toxic to the body, given relatively heavy long-term use, the narcotics are comparatively safe. The organs are not damaged, destroyed, or even threatened by even a lifetime of addiction. No major malfunctions of the body, no tissue damage, no physical deterioration, can be traced directly to the use of any narcotic, including heroin. "Opiate addiction per se causes no anatomical changes in the body," writes a physician working at Lexington's Addiction Research Center.[9] Another medical expert puts it this way: "No irreversible organic damage to the nervous system or viscera is known to occur as a result of opioids per se."[10] At the same time, it must be realized that the largely "artificial" dangers of heroin addiction connected with the present legal and logistic entanglements are every bit as real and powerful as the "natural" dangers attributable to the drug in its action on human tissue. That is why anyone addicted to heroin today stands an extremely high chance of destroying himself.

Given the obvious social and medical pathologies associated with addiction, a question that immediately comes to mind is: Why should anyone want to become involved with narcotics? Why should a young person—with the facts staring him in the face—wish to experiment with dangerous drugs? In the past, the great majority of works on addiction adopted an externalistic and "objective" posture toward the addict. They nearly always ignored the most important potential source of information—the drug user himself. Increasingly, however, current attempts to understand the addict have involved actually getting out into the street with him, into his world, his natural habitat. Obviously, the method selected to study the addict influences the nature of the observations. Data collected from "caught" criminals, for example, are likely to be heavily slanted. The prison is not the street, and reliance on prison addict populations inevitably leads to distortion of the whole drug scene.[11] Any valid study of drug use must rely on information secured outside an institutional context. Fortunately, these studies have become increasingly common in the past few years.

A twenty-two-year-old college senior provided me with a detailed firsthand account of her involvement with heroin. Her experiences are at once singular and representative of those of many middle-class college heroin users. Although she never became addicted, and discontinued using heroin about a month before she wrote her paper (in May 1970), she was a weekly user for almost two years. Her account confirms that heroin use, especially one's initial experience, is almost exclusively a group experience. "I did it because my boyfriend did it," she explains. "He did it because his two closest friends did it." On her return from a vacation with her family, she tells us, "my boyfriend had a surprise for me. He said that he had shot heroin. Suddenly, all of the conventional stereotypes were forgotten. I was more mad about not being there when the first shots were fired than anything else. Instantly, I said I wanted to try it too." Accounts of being "turned on" to the use of drugs invariably mention friends as introducing the novice to drugs for the first time, and not drug sellers (or "dealers"). Whether the drug is heroin or marijuana, it is friends who turn on friends. It is precisely because the use of drugs is initiated among intimates that it appears almost impossible to stop their spread.

A kind of bizarre status ranking seems to have emerged among many drug-oriented youths. Our informant tells us:

. . . there was in our group an unofficial competition, usually unverbalized, concerning who could do [take] the most drugs. . . . I was taken over to the house of a friend who . . . was given to stating that he intended to be the most outrageous drug addict in town, no matter what the drug was. (He was one of the few who talked openly about the competition.) As an example, the best show I ever saw him put on was the night he swallowed some LSD and shot a couple of bags of dope [heroin], after which he shot several more LSD trips, shot at least four more bags of dope, smoked hash [hashish] all night, and took some amphetamines as a nightcap.

This case is obviously extreme, but there seems to be no question that experience with, and ability to handle, various types of drugs have formed a new ranking system, partially replacing athletics, sex, and the ability to "hold your liquor" among some young men who require affirmations of their masculinity. Thus, daring and bravado play some part in the lure of many drugs.

In a community such as the Haight-Ashbury, being the biggest freak in a community of freaks is not an easy task. Pride in one's ability to shoot massive doses is reflected in the following statement from such a speed [methedrine] freak: ". . .This was a down to the death dope shooting contest. One of the two of us was supposed to die when the thing was all over. He'd shot a half a gram and I'd shoot a gram, and he'd shoot one and a half, and I'd shoot two grams, and he'd shoot two and a half, and I'd have to shoot three. Nobody would back out, we'd die before we'd back out."[12]

It is a cruel irony that many of the values of the drug subculture appear to be almost a mirror image, somewhat distorted to be sure, of some of the most sacred values of conventional mainstream America: competition and success. A country that urges its adolescents to achieve, to do better than their fellows in school and in every other area of endeavor, is going to be a country with a competitive drug subculture.

Drug users will often contrast the excitement of the drug world with the banality of the "straight" world—particularly that of their parents. My informant writes:

I tend to think that the primary target of my striving for deviance is possibly the sterility and blandness of the life I had always been exposed to. . . My parents . . . gave me a life devoid of real, deep feeling. I wanted to feel! I wanted to play in the dirt. I wanted to transgress those lily-white norms, break those rules designed to make me a good little Doris Day. And when the first transgression was followed not by the wrath of God . . . but by a feeling of being alive, and free, and different, that I had never known before, then I guess after that, all rules and norms lost their meaning and power over me. . . . I knew that there was a way for me to declare my independence from the straight, conventional and BORING! life my mother wanted me to lead. . . . When I shot up, I felt so superior, so wicked, so unique. . . . I though I had found the ultimate rebellion, the most deviant act possible. I was drawn to it because it set us apart from, and above, everyone—

even the other drug users, the "soft" drug users. . . . I was . . . irresistably attracted to and proud of the deviance and anti-sociability of the act. . . . The "badness" of shooting heroin was precisely why I did not hesitate to do it.

No activity, including sex, is inherently pleasurable; enjoying something is the consequence of a learning experience. Just as the marijuana user *learns to enjoy* his drug of choice,[13] the heroin user, too, goes through a process of becoming sensitized to the nuances of a heroin high, and to discount or underplay aspects that he finds unpleasant. Not uncommonly, the first experience will convince a neophyte that taking heroin is a distasteful and unappealing experience, and he will not try the drug again.[14] But often the negative aspects will be explained away. My informant describes her first shot, taken with her boyfriend, as follows:

I am truly surprised that we both didn't die that very first night. I was more physically miserable than I had ever been before. The whole night was spent vomiting. The thing that surprises me is that we didn't forget about heroin right then and there. It was horrible! But we later decided that our dear friend had given us too much. So I decided to give it another chance. . . . *My friends were all doing it, and it had become a question of prestige within our small group.* [*Italics mine.*]

Aldous Huxley described his mescaline experiences in shades of "heaven and hell"—the title of one of his books. Heroin users and addicts, too, paint the pleasure and pain as the most acute that life has to offer. But the Manichaean nature of the drug controversy does not allow propagandists to recognize any positive features in illegal drug use; even so primrose an experience as euphoria becomes reinterpreted as something insidious, false, and artificial.

Extreme pleasure, then, is part of a large proportion of heroin experiences. My informant says about her first few experiences, after the initial shot: "I can't describe the rush to you. . . . At the time, *it was better than orgasm.*" In fact, sexual imagery and analogies are prominent in the descriptions by junkies of their drug experiences. The needle being inserted into soft, yielding flesh, the wave of ecstasy flooding the body just after the injection, the feeling of calm satisfaction and well-being after the initial period of euphoria—all these sensations have sexual overtones. In fact, for many junkies, heroin becomes a substitute for sex. (Addiction to heroin produces disinterest in sex, and often temporary impotence.) In evaluating the appeals of heroin, one would be remiss in omitting its hedonistic component.

However, typically, continued use of heroin entails a cellular adaptation such that the euphoriant properties become attenuated. It becomes necessary to increase the dosage to achieve pleasure. This is a major feature of drug tolerance. Eventually, the user who once injected heroin because it was pleasurable no longer derives as much pleasure from it. My informant tells us:

Luckily, it was no longer feeling good enough to make it worth getting busted for. . . . I could tell from the rush I got (weak) and the time I stayed high (short) that heroin had lost its immense power over me. . . . It simply wasn't worth it. . . . The magic ceased to happen long ago. There's only the memory, and the hope to get it back again like it was. . . . Right now I'd rather go out for a good dinner than shoot a bag of heroin.

The so-called "honeymoon" period eventually terminates for all, or nearly all, long-term users and addicts.[15] Thus the motive for continued use, and especially addiction, must be different from the motive for initial experimentation.

The life of the average heroin addict seems wretched in the extreme. Why, it is often asked, should anyone want to lead such a life? The question assumes that the addict previously had the desire, whether conscious or unconscious, actually to *become* addicted. This is not the case:

The individual user never believes he himself will become addicted. Perhaps we see here the same mechanism that allows a soldier on the battlefield to surge forward and continue fighting while he sees soldiers around him dying from wounds. One can be firmly set in the belief that the self is inviolable, unique, and not subject to suffering, accident or death. It is unlikely that traditional ground wars could be fought unless men believed that they personally would not die on the battlefield.

This is, I think, the first ingredient that makes addiction possible for those knowledgeable about the legal, moral, and addicting aspects of narcotic usage. It is important to keep in mind that this quality is a common one. Most possess the firm belief that "Nothing like that could happen to me." . . . the "decision" to become an addict is very questionable. One no more decides to become an addict than one decides to die on the battlefield.[16]

Alan Sutter, a sociologist who studied street drug use firsthand, quotes one of his addict informants on this point:

It seems as if every junkie . . . goes through a stage of feeling that he can take it or leave it alone. I have yet to meet a . . . dope fiend that started out to get hooked. "I'm not going to get snatched up by this thing," and then they proceed to chippy [use drugs sporadically] again. I did. I used two–three days a week on weekends, then would be back away from it and not even think about it until the next Friday. I did this successfully for about three years after that. But you know, I have never been able to chippy since the first time.[17]

Sutter terms this naive belief that others may become addicted, "but not me," a "faith in the chippy habit."

Young drug users who have never experienced addiction, and addicts who will not admit their addiction, have a magical belief that one can "chippy around" (use heroin intermittently) without getting hooked. . . . Some addicts, while on the street, present the image of using heroin as a luxury, not as a necessity. If a person knows from experience that he has always been able to control his drug use and still "take care of business," he will be convinced of his strong "will power" and will believe that only "weak-minded people get hooked." This very belief lays the groundwork for addiction.[18]

Like nearly all drugs used on the street—marijuana is an exception—heroin builds tolerance rapidly. The cellular adaptation that occurs, diminishing euphoria, necessitates larger and larger doses taken increasingly frequently. To derive continued pleasure, the user must begin to take doses at levels and frequencies that are often addicting. Yet even a daily user of heroin does not automatically perceive himself as an addict. Many are cellularly dependent without realizing it (just as many are not physiologically addicted, but think of themselves as addicts). The most crucial process in addiction comes when the drug user realizes that (1) without heroin he suffers withdrawal sickness and (2) heroin relieves his distress.[19] Sutter quotes one addict who pinpointed this realization dramatically:

I'm sick in bed with a cold. My bones ached, my eyes were watering, my nose running, and man, I felt miserable. Then this broad comes back from hustling. "What's the matter with you, man?" I told her; she says, "Oh, you're hooked." I says, what do you mean I'm hooked? I got a cold. So she gets in there and cooks up some stuff and fixed me. Poom, everything was gone. So from then on, I knew I didn't have to feel like that, because a fix would take care of it.[20]

Sutter concludes: "The perception of withdrawal symptoms as being due to the absence of opiates will generate a *burning* desire for the drug."[21]

It is difficult for a nonaddict to understand the almost religious quality of addiction; to an addict who is a member of the drug subcommunity, heroin is an *absolute,* something that transcends utilitarian calculation. A journalist quotes an addict (who was also an undercover agent working for the police) on the value of heroin versus the value of money:

A good stash is a lot better than money. Money is phony stuff. . . . It's not a commodity. But heroin's a real commodity. Get a couple of kilos of clean, pure heroin and you've got a lifetime security. Better than gold. You've got gold, you've got to spend it to get dope—if you can get it. You've got dope, you've got everything you need. Gold, you can always get it if you've got dope.[22]

The addict's view of the heroin seller, or "dealer," differs markedly from the popular stereotype. Public wrath is reserved for the peddler who profits from human misery by selling the junkie heroin. Sentences ranging up to death have been designed for him. The addict, on the other hand, often sees the dealer as a kind of savior—a faith healer, a medicine man, a source of health and comfort. Now, the police, the psychiatrist, and the public will condemn this view, but the fact is, it exists, and must therefore be taken into account.

Besides a physiological and psychological dependence, the heroin addict suffers a kind of social dependence. If "turning on" is a matter of going along with the group, "turning off" is a matter of breaking with the group. My college informant tells us:

Whenever I saw my friends, they were shooting up, too. . . . The problem with kicking heroin . . . is that all of your friends aren't kicking at the same time. . . . A three months' abstention was accomplished only by almost total isolation from friends in the drug world.

It is a simple matter to apply conventional judgments and evaluations to the world of the addict. A society that has decided that a given activity is undesirable will impute to it negative causes and consequences, and will enlist the services of experts and professionals to validate these imputations. Thus psychiatrists will proclaim that the addict is immature, irrational, and that he has a compulsion to avoid responsibility. An earlier school of sociologists built an entire theoretical edifice on the assumption that addiction (this is often stretched to include all illegal drug use) is a "retreatist" adaptation to the problem of social adjustment, and that the addict is attracted to his drug because he is a "double failure,"[23] unable to achieve success by legitimate or criminal means. These views rest on the assumption that to conform to society's expectations is "normal" and that to do otherwise requires an explanation invoking a pathology or a dysfunction of some kind.

Addict behavior is considered irresponsible because addicts generally do not do what society defines as responsible. The addict, however, will have a different definition of what constitutes responsibility. From his point of view, the responsible addict is the one who is able to hustle the money necessary to maintain a $100 a day habit. "Prestige in the hierarchy of a dope fiend's world is allocated by the size of a person's habit and his success as a hustler."[24] Addicts are acutely aware that they are masters in areas where the "square" would be a hopeless failure. But the popular imagination, under the influence of a distinctly dated picture of the Chinese opium smoker, sees the addict as existing in, or "retreating into," a state of dreamy somnolent idleness, a euphoric temporary death. This state of oblivion does, indeed, typify a certain portion of the addict's day, and is known as "going on the nod." (Its occurrence is, however, dependent on the quality of the heroin administered.) But it represents only a small portion of the addict's day—the climax so to speak—and the hectic hustle and bustle of the entire day is oriented toward this brief moment of transcendence. Far from taking the addict out of contact with the world, addiction "plunges the newly recruited addict into abrasive contact with the world."[25] Fiddle calls the kind of life the typical street addict lives "a pressure cooker universe."[26] Paraphrasing the addict's own rejection of the "retreatist" theory of drug addiction, Fiddle writes: "Could a square survive . . . in the kind of jungle we live in? It takes brains, man, to keep up a habit that costs $35 to $40 a day—every day in the year."[27]

SOLUTIONS

If a large cross section of the public—laymen and law enforcement officials alike—were to be asked the reasons for the existence of the drug laws, the one most commonly offered, by far, would be protection of the population against harm, both bodily and psychic; society has to prevent the damage the drug user might inflict on himself as well as on others were he allowed unlimited access to drugs. Presumably, the more dangerous a drug is, or would be if used by significant numbers of individuals, the stronger would be the legal attempts to prevent its use outside a medical context. Drugs whose potential for damage is low would, supposedly, be far less likely to fall within the orbit of criminal law.

There are, of course, many different ways of measuring the damage a drug might do. Joel Fort has elaborated a scheme for measuring the "hardness" of a drug; according to him, the main dimensions of hardness are brain and other organic damage, insanity, addiction, the generation of violence, accidents, particularly vehicular, and, obviously, death.[28] These are "nonpolitical" dimensions, since nearly everyone would agree that they are undesirable; on this point, at least, there should be no controversy.

According to these criteria, probably the most dangerous drugs are alcohol, the barbiturates, the amphetamines, nicotine (in cigarettes), and cocaine. Any individual who is a heavy, chronic user of any of these drugs runs a high risk of eventually damaging his body or his mind. Not only are these drugs potentially damaging, but, except for cocaine, they are very commonly used. Drugs of moderate damage potential, given fairly frequent, long-term, high-dosage use, include all of the narcotics (because of overdosing, addiction, and the agonies of withdrawal) and the hallucinogens (because of some degree of risk of temporary psychosis in some users). Finally, the damage due to caffeine, aspirin, and marijuana is relatively infrequent and superficial. This is not to say that these drugs are completely safe; *no* drug—indeed, no chemical agent of any kind—is *completely* safe, and that includes water. There are hundreds of aspirin poisonings each year, mainly of very young children who swallow massive doses.

Of the five extremely damaging drugs, two (alcohol and nicotine) are readily available to anyone above a certain age; two (amphetamines and barbiturates) are available by prescription (and very commonly so obtained, for largely nonmedical, or pseudomedical, reasons); and only one (cocaine) is completely criminalized. Possession of the moderately dangerous narcotics and hallucinogens is a crime, although illegalization efforts are more heavily concentrated on heroin than on LSD. The possession of any quantity of marijuana, a comparatively nondamaging chemical agent, is a crime; possession of as little as a quarter of an ounce in some jurisdictions, as well as any sale or transfer, including handing along a joint in a circle of friends, constitutes a felony, punishable by a prison sentence ranging anywhere from two years to life.

In at least one state, Rhode Island, the minimum penalty for the sale of marijuana to a minor is thirty years; the maximum is life imprisonment. The severity of this penalty is surpassed only by that for first-degree murder and treason. It is a harsher penalty than for rape, second-degree murder, arson, and armed robbery.[29] (A separate but related question is whether or not these penalties are carried out. But the symbolic and deterrent functions of the severity of the law cannot be discounted.) This penalty is not a leftover from an earlier, less enlightened age, but was a result of a revision of the penal code in 1962; no doubt a later scrutiny will produce a reversal. Now, if we wish to make the claim that selling someone twenty years old a couple of joints of marijuana *is more damaging to him than murdering him,* without premeditation, then we may argue that the penalties are consistent with damage. But not otherwise.

Thus, instead of an intimate and causal connection between damage and the law, what we see is an extremely loose relationship between the two. Legislators and agents of social control believe that they create and enforce drug laws *because* drug use is "dangerous." Actually, the imputation of danger and damage *follows* the belief that the use of certain drugs is wrong, evil, undesirable—and should be outlawed. Most people do not believe that a drug should be criminalized because it is dangerous; they believe it is dangerous because they oppose its use, because they think it is immoral to use it, and, in part, specifically because the use of the drug is illegal. The "rational" argument is superimposed on what is essentially a moral and ideological conviction.

This is not to say that some forms of crime outlawed by society do not harm members of that society. Murder is an example. But the degree of harm is an incidental feature of the law. Many forms of criminal behavior—perhaps most—harm no one, not even the perpetrators of the crime.[30] These are the "crimes without victims." What is more, many forms of criminal behavior extremely destructive to society and its individual members are quite legal. The record of damage of alcohol consumption is probably without equal, but the list of activities prohibited to the drinker is fairly small; he may destroy himself in private, but not in public. Warfare, to take an example outside the realm of drugs, is always catastrophic, but far from rendering it illegal, politicians have nearly always made the *refusal* to fight a criminal act. Shoddy and unsafe products have been manufactured by corporations and distributed to the public for generations, and yet only in the past few years have laws, of the most timid sort, been enacted. Legal efforts to eradicate pollution and environmental degradation are weak or nonexistent; yet pollution is an incomparably greater threat to life than drug addiction. The view that laws are passed and enforced after an objective appraisal of the danger presented to society by a given behavior is not only extremely naive, but flatly fallacious.

Behind the passage of every drug law in existence is a well-organized and effective lobby which has convinced lawmaking bodies and agents of social control that drug use is a threat to public safety and health. In no instance were medical, pharmacological, psychological, or sociological researchers asked to prepare a thorough evaluation of the potential or actual dangers of the drugs in question. In fact, the main "expert" testimony in favor of the passage of the laws was often presented by the moral entrepreneurs themselves; this was true in the Marijuana Tax Act of 1937, for example, which was supported by Harry Anslinger; one account holds that he did this in an attempt to expand the operations of the Federal Bureau of Narcotics.[31] Where lawmaking bodies did receive expert testimony from drug research specialists, this testimony would invariably come from handpicked figures known to be in agreement with the lawmakers. If any expert expressed a contrary view, his competence and legitimacy would be called into question. The process of criminalization invariably entailed a search for evidence that the drug was damaging; if the search was thorough enough, some scraps of proof could be dredged up, even if, typically, the behavior brought into evidence was relatively harmless. Getting a law passed always involves *making a case,* rather than an objective assessment of all available evidence. And making a case is, inevitably, one-sided and biased.

The social image of the drug addict has turned almost full circle since the Civil War.[32] Addiction to morphine following serious surgery, such as amputation, was common during and after the Civil War; it was known as "Army disease" or "soldier's disease." Late in the nineteenth century, many over-the-counter preparations contained addicting substances, such as opium and morphine, and many respectable middle-class housewives were addicted to them. Because of the connection between medical therapy and addiction, the drug addict was seen in the late 1800s as a helpless victim, an unfortunate sick person in need of medical attention. But by the 1920s, the public image of the addict was that of a criminal, a willful degenerate, a hedonistic, thrill-crazed pleasure-seeker deserving imprisonment and severe punishment. Curiously enough, many afflictions, such as leprosy, epilepsy, and insanity were gradually being labeled strictly medical problems, after being long considered stigmata of immorality and depravity, at the very time that addiction was losing the character of a disease in the public mind and acquiring a taint of moral corruption.[33] (This trend has begun to reverse itself again, at least among physicians and some segments of the public.)

It is unfortunately impossible to estimate with any precision how many addicts the freely available over-the-counter narcotic preparations called into being. Figures kept on addiction around the turn of the century are notoriously unreliable, and estimates vary from a low of 100,000 to a high of several million.[34] In 1919 the Treasury Department issued a report that approximately a million persons were addicted to narcotics at that time, largely as a consequence of the laissez-faire policy previously in effect. Let us accept this figure as roughly accurate. The decrease in the proportion of addicts in the American population—at present, estimated at about a quarter of a million individuals out of a population of 200 million, as opposed to a million out of a 1900 population of 100 million—is taken by many observers of the drug scene, especially the supporters of existing laws, and above all the police, as evidence that punitive coercive policies work, that prison sentences for drug infractions are an effective deterrent. Discussing the putative drop in addiction rate from the inception of the narcotics laws to just after the Second World War, a team of physicians employed by the government wrote: "This reduction has been largely due to the vigorous enforcement of the Harrison Act and to Federal facilities for the treatment of addicts."[35]

Actually, a close look at the facts demonstrates precisely the opposite: existing legislation and policies have, from their inception to the present, been a contributing factor in worsening the drug problem; punitive approaches have been an almost unrelieved failure.

Before we can determine the impact of the narcotics laws, we must be clear about the social composition of the population of addicts. In the late 1800s, as opposed to the 1970s, addiction was largely a consequence of medical problems, and was not related to a search for euphoria and peer-generated excitement. As a result, the middle aged, rather than the young, were addicted. In addition, women were more likely to be addicts than men. Whites were more likely to become addicted than blacks before 1900; the reverse is true today. Whereas addicts used to be distributed over the entire social spectrum (with a somewhat higher proportion, perhaps, in the middle class), most addicts are now found in the lowest social stratum—a situation that is changing, however. Where addicts were once drawn from the entire rural-urban continuum, they are now concentrated in the large cities.

What we have here, then, is not diminution of a once large addict population, but a different population altogether. Legislation and enforcement, far from reducing the problem, appear to have created a problem out of whole cloth. To support this view, let us examine the role of the sedatives and hypnotics today. It is interesting that the barbiturates began to be used on a more or less widespread basis about the same time that the narcotic over-the-counter drugs became criminalized. The current use of the sedatives—including all of the barbiturates and the tranquilizers—probably equals, and possibly even outstrips, the use of the narcotic over-the-counter preparations at the turn of the century. Approximately a million pounds of the barbiturates, as well as over a million pounds of one of the tranquilizers (under the trade names Miltown and Equanil), were manufactured and used in the United States in the late 1960s. If we assume that about five barbiturate pills per day (or about 500 milligrams) taken for any extended period will produce an addiction,[36] then it is possible that we have as many as a million or more sedative addicts in the United States—users who would suffer severe withdrawal symptoms if their supply of drugs were discontinued—the large majority of whom are taking their drugs legally, under medical supervision.

It should be clear, then, that as a result of the legislation outlawing over-the-counter narcotics the sedatives have become the *functional equivalent* of the drugs so promiscuously handed out at the turn of the century. Three groups seem to have been created by illegalizing drugs. The first group comprises the majority of middle-class addicts, mostly women—originally the nervous, distressed housewives who turned to the use of barbiturates, under the care of a physician, when opium and morphine became unavailable. The second group, which most likely took in the least addicted of the addicts, discontinued use altogether. Thus the legislation probably helped only those easily susceptible of being helped. The third group constitutes our present street addict population. A certain proportion of the earlier addicts refused to discontinue use of narcotics and, unable or unwilling to avail themselves of legally obtainable drugs, became dependent on an illegal supply. In the early 1900s the addict population that could be characterized as criminal was extremely small; there was no particular link between narcotics and crime. It is obvious, then, that criminalizing narcotics use has had the unanticipated consequence of swelling a tiny and insignificant criminal drug-using population to substantial size. The addicts of the early 1900s who did not discontinue the use of narcotics automatically joined the ranks of the criminal underworld. A few, a minority, were already a part of that world. Most were law-abiding. But whatever their origins, the law defined them as criminals. This set the stage for a criminal narcotics subculture.

In December 1914 Congress passed the Harrison Act, which outlawed over-the-counter narcotic preparations and placed the addict in the hands of the physician. Whatever the intent of the law, most addicts were able to continue receiving drugs, from their physicians, instead of directly from the pharmacist, as was true prior to the law. Thus, by itself, the law would not have changed anything. It was the Supreme Court which, drawing a restrictive interpretation of the law, made maintenance illegal. In a series of rulings from 1919 to 1922, the Court ruled maintenance beyond the pale of legitimate medical practice. It is interesting that the courts, and not the medical profession, decided what constitutes good medical practice.

Because of the police harassment of physicians after the passage of the Harrison Act, and the wave of arrests that followed the Supreme Court's decisions, most physicians became unwilling to shoulder the legal risks attendant on administering narcotic drugs, and treating addicts.[37] The few who did treat them, whether for idealistic or for mercenary reasons, predictably attracted a sizable clientele—and, predictably, were charged with "trafficking" in narcotics.

Perhaps the problem was dimly perceived by some officials, for ambulatory clinics were opened in 1919, clinics that dispensed narcotics to patients, supposedly with a view toward their rehabilitation and cure. The programs were highly variable in method and effectiveness. In the New York clinic, which received the most publicity, drugs were handed out more or less indiscriminately; reporters posing as addicts found that they could receive addicting narcotics almost upon demand. A public outcry was raised; campaigns were launched to close the clinics down. The program began in 1919. At its height, there were forty-four clinics. All but one had closed by 1921, and by 1923 the project was entirely abandoned. Actually, the New York clinic, the object of the most numerous and vigorous criticisms, was the least well run. The two in Louisiana (in New Orleans and Shreveport), on the other hand, appear to have been successful in their stated goals: (1) relieving the addict's suffering; (2) offsetting the illegal drug trade; (3) keeping addiction from spreading; (4) reducing the criminal activity of addicts. These efforts, however, received little public attention.

The apparent failure of the public clinics was exploited to galvanize popular sentiment against the strictly medical approach to addiction.

Subsequently, public feeling supported the view that the addict has to be dealt with punitively, that addiction is a matter for the police, not the physician. In 1919, when the clinics started their operations, there were only 1,000 federal arrests on narcotics charges. By 1925, over 10,000 federal arrests were made.[38] Thus the early 1920s witnessed the sudden dramatic emergence of a criminal class of addicts. The link between addiction and crime—the definition of the addict as a criminal—was forged.

What are some of the consequences of the punitive approach to addiction? It cannot be doubted that criminalizing narcotic drugs had the immediate short-run result of lowering the number of addicts in the population. But what about the long-run trends?

Probably the most important contribution the police have made to the reality of addiction is *the creation of an addict subculture.* It must be emphasized that prior to 1914 no addict subculture of any size existed. Addicts displayed no particular cohesion as a group, possessed no lore concerned with the acquisition and administration of drugs, no ideology elaborating the qualities of various drug "highs," no justification for using drugs, no status ranking unique to addicts, no rejection of the nonaddict world. During the formative 1920s, these elements of the addict's subculture did begin to emerge. *It was the criminalization of addiction that created addicts as a special and distinctive group, and it is the very groupness of addicts that gives them their recruiting power.* The period between 1920, when police policies began to take effect, and 1946, when the number of addicts began to rise dramatically, can be viewed as the incubation phase of the heroin subculture. Prohibition, when organized criminal activity was concentrated on the distribution of another drug, alcohol, the Depression, when there was very little for a supposed addict to steal to support his habit, and the Second World War, when supply channels were cut off, all probably delayed addiction as a way of life for a large number, far more than anything the police were doing. In fact, during and just after the Second World War, it was thought that addiction had ceased to be a problem of any magnitude. It is not unreasonable to view the postwar wave of addicts, and even more the spectacular rise in addiction since 1967, as largely due to the recruitment powers of a gradually developing subculture of intensely committed addicts. And it was through the efforts of the police that this subculture came into being in the first place.

A second consequence traceable to the punitive approach is *the criminal activity of addicts.* The view that addicts are "inherently" criminal is without foundation. Almost every addict—aside from the wealthy and those in medical professions—is also a criminal, engaged in some illegal moneymaking venture.[39] A "slave" (argot for a legitimate conventional nine-to-five job) does not pay enough to support a heroin habit, but many "hustles" do. "Boosting" (stealing from a store) and burglary are probably the most common forms of theft for male addicts, although armed robbery, "snatch and grab" street tactics, and automobile theft are also common. Most junkies have also sold heroin, although access to large quantities of drugs—inexpensive on a per unit basis but extremely costly in total outlay—is dependent on more cash than most addicts can scrape together at one time. A number of other hustles, such as pimping, confidence games, and heavy high-level narcotics dealing and smuggling, are not uncommon, but require more skill and ingenuity than most addicts possess. Most female addicts prostitute themselves, although many will "boost" in addition.

The police, in an effort to justify the existing punitive approach to drug prevention, claim that the typical addict's career in crime began *before* his involvement with heroin, and thus, "it is generally the criminal who turns to addiction rather than the addict who turns to crime."[40] The conclusion that is supposed to be drawn from this observation is that addiction is a criminal, and not a medical, matter: "Any intelligent layman who becomes convinced of this fact . . . will see no solution to a crime problem by providing free drugs to criminal drug addicts. How can they be expected to live useful, productive lives on narcotics when their lives were enmeshed in crime before they became addicted?"[41] The problem with this position is that it is true but irrelevant, a non sequitur. As many researchers have pointed out,[42] most addicts *are* engaged in criminal activities prior to addiction, and typically have a prior arrest record. (This is, however, a comparatively recent development; the addicts of a generation ago were most commonly addicted before they engaged in a life of crime.[43]) But addiction clearly increases stupendously the *frequency,* the *rate,* and the *seriousness* of crimes, as well as the likelihood of arrest. It is questionable whether any addict would see the sense in stealing hundreds of dollars' worth of merchandise daily for a clinic-maintained habit costing a few pennies a day. The clinic addict's rate of crime would, of course, be higher than that of the population at large. But it would be far lower than the addict crime rate under police-controlled policy. It is impossible to argue against the position that a maintenance program would reduce the rate of urban crime dramatically.

If the deterrence logic were valid, someone who has been arrested and punished for a narcotics violation would be very unlikely to continue using drugs after the experience. However, the opposite is true. In one study of 9,000 addicts in Chicago, 86 percent had been previously arrested on narcotics charges.[44] Various studies of the recidivism rate of addicts who have served prison sentences—or have been detained in government-supported narcotics "hospitals"—testify to rates of readdiction ranging from 97 percent to occasional lows of roughly 50 percent. Most studies show a recidivism rate among addicts of about nine in ten.[45] If each instance of possession, sale, and/ or use of narcotics is taken as a separate crime, then the recidivism rate of addicts who are supposedly treated by the prisons is higher than for any conceivable type of crime—except, possibly, homosexual acts. Even if actual addiction is used as an indicator of relapse, released ex-addicts have one of the highest rates of recidivism of any category of criminal. In fact, in many ways, prisons serve to intensify the addict's commitment to narcotics, since the majority will associate only with other addicts and their one topic of conversation is drugs. The marginally involved narcotics user will often find himself immersed in a genuine addict subculture, whose attitudes and values he will gradually acquire. The lesson to be learned from follow-up studies of ex-addicts released from prisons and federal hospitals is, overwhelmingly, that relapse is the rule rather than the exception. Punishment appears to have virtually no effect on deterring the addict. Prison is not the answer.

It is obvious that efforts at criminalizing addiction have failed. *Any agency with as high a rate of failure as law enforcement would be forced to reevaluate its methods.* Since the police are to some degree insulated from criticism, they may safely ignore a factual assault on their methods. When a given form of purposive behavior fails to achieve the stated goals of its participants, the sensible observer begins to look for unstated goals, unanticipated consequences, latent rewards, and intellectual blind spots. I am often asked by my students in criminology, deviance, and delinquency if the police do not receive very large payoffs from organized criminals, if·this is not the reason, perhaps, for the inability of society to rid itself of the drug problem. My feeling is that this explanation is far too facile. While it is true that more than a few narcotics police receive sums of money directly from the criminal underworld, this does not in itself account for the continuation of the obviously unsuccessful drug programs in force today, although it might explain why this or that drug peddler is not arrested. (It is true that corruption is extremely common among narcotics squads. During the summer of 1969, one-sixth of the New York office of the Federal Bureau of Narcotics— or 50 out of 300 agents—were forced to resign in the wake of a scandal exposing widespread drug peddling among law enforcement agents.) My feeling is that the following factors help explain why the agents of social control, as well as a majority of the public, view their efforts as reasonable and efficacious—and claim that any reform of the system represents an erosion of justice.

1. A policy is not only a practical attempt to achieve clearly demonstrable goals—in the case of the drug laws, supposedly deterrence and rehabilitation. *It is also a statement of one's own ideological stance.* Punishing the wrongdoer affirms one's undaunted opposition to drug use. To take a less severe stance would, somehow, imply that one approves of taking drugs, that, at the very least, one tolerates drug use.

2. Ideological considerations so severely limit one's perceptions—on any side of a controversy—that one is unable to see the destructive effects of one's own actions, or the actions of parties that one supports. The fact that many efforts to stamp out crime actually strengthen it will not be recognized by those who initiate those efforts. Policemen will reject the contention that the death penalty does not deter homicide—even with the data supporting that assertion a matter of public record.[46] In the same way, it is extremely unlikely that anyone involved in pursuing or supporting existing drug policies will recognize that these policies have decisively increased the dimensions of the drug problem.

3. Vengeance is a powerful motive in the desire to punish the deviant and the criminal. A strict observer of the law and existing morality will perceive an imbalance in the moral economy when deviant and criminal manage, in

his view, to beat the system. The desire on the part of the law-abiding citizen to punish the transgressor need bear no relation to criteria of effectiveness, because punishment is seen as an end in itself.

4. It is not unreasonable to view deviance and crime, and deviants and criminals, as a vast *resource* for social control agencies. It has been noted repeatedly that the agents and agencies whose supposed goal is to stamp out antisocial behavior, and to "correct" individuals who commit antisocial acts, often do their best to insure that these individuals persist in the behavior which attracted the attention of these agencies in the first place. Whether we are talking about prisons, mental asylums, the courts, welfare agencies, reformatories, schools, or any one of a dozen such agencies, there appears to be an almost self-perpetuating effect to their efforts. This is not as contradictory as it sounds at first blush. The deviant is defined as the special area of competence of the agency, which receives public funds to exercise that competence. Deviance is a domain, a sphere of interest, a "turf," an area of control, power, resources, and expertise. A correctional agency should not be too successful, lest it eliminate the very reason for its existence. Drugs and drug users are a domain that the police are not going to give up easily or willingly. It has profited them too handsomely.

It is a common fallacy to assume that a single drug program will be effective—and that all others will not. Especially those involved in administering some one program will be inclined to tout that program as *the* solution, and to discredit others as ineffective. However, a more reasonable view is that different programs may be effective in quite different ways, for different groups, or according to different criteria. Some programs will cost a great deal more than others. Some programs aim at partial rehabilitation, while others seek nothing short of a total adaptation to the social mainstream. Still others will have as their goal the rehabilitation of respectable society—and only secondarily that of the addict. Some programs would give a high degree of autonomy to the community and grant the police little or no control or supervision. Clearly, the criteria of what constitutes an effective program depend partly on one's values. It is impossible to judge any program in absolute terms.

Nonetheless, there are a number of goals about which there would be general agreement: (1) a diminution of the recruitment of new addicts; (2) a decrease in drug selling by the criminal underworld; (3) a lowering of the crime rate of addicts; (4) relief of the addict's suffering, and a virtual elimination of addiction as a cause of death; (5) the employment of addicts in legitimate jobs.

The failure of imprisonment and detention of addicts in government-sponsored "hospitals" is already manifest; neither technique has helped solve the drug problem—on the contrary. Two alternative methods, both of them largely experimental, have the potential for eventually becoming official policy. These are (1) the therapeutic community, and (2) methadone maintenance.[47] Therapeutic communities, such as Synanon, Phoenix House, Daytop Lodge, have not been fully evaluated. The incomplete data we have indicate that, as a means of rehabilitating the ex-addict, this method is promising, but extremely variable in its outcome. (I will return to the therapeutic community shortly.)

Methadone is a synthetic narcotic. It is addictive; the patients in the maintenance program would undergo withdrawal pangs if administration were discontinued. However, the proponents of the program claim that taking methadone is not simply substitution of one drug for another. They theorize that addiction is the result of a *metabolic,* and not a psychiatric, problem. Opiates, according to the Dole-Nyswander view, cause or touch off in some narcotics users an irreversible physiological change in the body chemistry such that narcotics are needed to feel normal—in much the same way that a diabetic's body needs insulin to feel normal. Methadone acts as a stabilizer, normalizing an existing deficiency. The addict who suffers from this deficiency *cannot* be cured, according to this view, by conventional methods—just as a diabetic cannot be cured, but must continue to take insulin—because his body will continue to crave opiates, regardless of the technique used to treat him. Thus, giving the addict methadone is administering a medication in the strictest sense, and not providing him with a drug in the popular sense of the term. This theory is, of course, highly speculative, and it completely ignores psychological and social influences, reducing the problem to a single factor. But whatever the validity of the physiological theory, methadone maintenance shows the greatest promise of any therapeutic program yet proposed for dealing with heroin addiction.

If administered orally, methadone does not produce any significant degree of euphoria or lethargy, as heroin and morphine do. (However, if injected, methadone does produce these symptoms.) Thus the patient feels basically normal under its influence, and not "doped up." He is able to lead a productive and active life, receiving at first a twice-daily, later a once-weekly dose. Moreover, methadone seems to block the effects of other opiates. The patient's cells no longer crave heroin, since methadone renders heroin relatively ineffective. And there are no known pathological effects. (It is possible to overdose with methadone, but since the dose is stabilized, there is no inducement for taking ever-stronger doses.) Finally, methadone is extremely inexpensive. A dose costs a few pennies—in contrast to the $15 to $100 or more a day that the heroin addict steals from the public and spends to maintain his habit.

Studies of the methadone program, although not definitive, indicate that a significant proportion of patients give up the use of heroin. (Urine analyses are taken periodically to check drug use.) And nearly all of the minority of "cheaters" considerably reduce their use of heroin below their premethadone level. Moreover, the patients in the program typically discontinue a life of crime. The arrest rate drops dramatically. The contrast between the addict population and the methadone patients is striking. The proportion employed increases considerably; very few addicts can hold down a "square" job— something that becomes possible on methadone. And possibly most important, the deadly, degrading life of the addict is exchanged for one that allows some dignity and self-actualization.

Estimates of the total number of addicts in the United States, and of the cost of thefts committed by them, differ widely.[48] Some commonly accepted figures—which, however, could be very wide of the mark—are a quarter of a million addicts in the nation and 100,000 to 150,000 in New York (it is believed that half of all addicts are in New York). It is calculated that in large cities with high addiction rates, such as Chicago, New York, and Washington, roughly half of all serious property crimes—particularly armed robbery, burglary, larceny, and shoplifting—are committed by addicts. Estimates of cost range from a low of a quarter of a billion to a high of several billion dollars. To the monetary cost of addict crime must be added even larger costs, such as multiplied police enforcement, treatment facilities, and the incalculable human cost in misery, degradation, and death. In contrast, the cost of a methadone maintenance program is now less than a thousand dollars a year per addict, and as the clinics become institutional-ized and routinized, the cost will eventually be cut in half. In every conceivable way, and not merely in dollar savings, the introduction of this program must represent an enormous gain to society, and to the addict.

Proponents of the therapeutic community approach feel that methadone deals not with the addict's underlying problems, but merely with his symptoms. The addict is not really cured by methadone; he is still addicted to, and dependent on, a chemical. He is just as insecure, just as sick, lonely, and frightened, just as immature and alienated, as he was prior to metha-done. The therapeutic community seeks a completely drug-free existence for the addict, as well as the psychiatric cure of the underlying emotional disorder that impelled him to use drugs in the first place. Narcotic addiction is seen as

. . . largely . . . a symptom of a character disorder—which results from or is exacerbated by faulty socialization of the person. The individual suffering from this form of disorder typically reacts to . . . stress by withdrawing into a protective shell, namely, drugs. This kind of behavior is seen as immature, and as reflecting problems of felt inadequacy or incompetence in dealing with stress. In response to these feelings of "shithood," the addict overcompensates by developing an inflated self-image and a false sense of superiority. Consequently, he does not relate openly and honestly with others, attempts to manipulate them through a show of dependency, and lacks any real concern for them.[49]

For advocates of the therapeutic community, the methadone program is by definition a failure, since their goal is a completely drug-free existence. But with this loftier goal comes a much greater investment in time, energy, commitment, emotion, and, of course, money—along with a much lower rate of rehabilitation. While all patients in the methadone program are ambula-tory—they live at home and can pursue employment and a normal family life—members of the therapeutic community live in a drug treatment center for at least several months, and often as long as several years. The cost has been estimated as high as $25,000 per patient per year.

Ideally, everyone in the treatment center is an ex-addict, including the directors. The reasoning is that the addict undergoing treatment will achieve rapport only with therapists who have "gut level" experience with addiction, and that he will not succeed in "conning" an ex-junkie. More conventional methods are doomed to failure, the thesis goes, largely because of the inability of the nonaddict to understand the mentality of the junkie. Such is the ideology of all Synanon-type programs.

That the therapeutic community concept does not work for all addicts, that its effectiveness is limited, is underlined by a study of one such program (Daytop),[50] which reports that roughly three-quarters of all addicts accepted into the program left against the advice of the staff; most probably returned to the life they led before entering. Motivation evidently plays a considerable role in the success of such a program; it plays a far lesser role with methadone. The addicts who submit to the program to begin with—and, even more emphatically, those who remain in it for any meaningful length of time—are the least involved with drugs, are younger than the average addict, have been addicted for a shorter period, have smaller habits, have been arrested fewer times, and are the most hopeful of treatment. They are, moreover, likely to have a middle-class background. Thus the therapeutic community concept works only for a segment of the addict population. It cannot provide a total solution, but may very well be the answer for certain kinds of addicts.[51]

No single drug rehabilitation program should be regarded as a panacea—and that includes methadone maintenance. Making the addict drug-free is a desirable, if perhaps too ambitious a goal. Research should continue to seek more effective ways of dealing with the drug problem. The public should not be deluded into thinking that the financial support of a few methadone clinics has, or will, solve the heroin problem. Unless a program is backed up with job placement and psychiatric care, its value will be limited at best. At the same time, it should be clear that reliance—especially, exclusive reliance—on punitive techniques can only aggravate the drug problem. Unless some combination of methadone maintenance (for the older, long-term, more heavily involved addict) and the therapeutic community (for the younger, less involved addict) is adequately, meaningfully, and swiftly funded, the volume of human suffering will increase, more and more deaths will occur, the rate of crimes and violence in the cities will grow apace, and addiction will continue to rise.

It would be naive to believe that drug addiction can be eliminated completely. Attacking a given problem always involves balancing one value against another; no problem exists in isolation. Effective solutions to the drug problem depend on the resolution of a number of related questions: At what cost? By neglecting what other problems and values? And employing what definition of a "solution"? If law enforcement agents were given virtually unlimited powers to deal with the narcotics traffic, and laws such as the "no knock" bill were passed to make their work easier, and drastic measures, such as the death penalty for all addicts, were put into effect, then the illegal use of heroin could probably be brought to a virtual halt—but only at the cost of a desecration of justice and civil liberties on a scale previously unheard of in this country. Thus the question is not simply how to deal with the drug problem, but under what conditions. As with a drastic operation, the most "effective" method may well destroy the patient.

Society has already decided that certain categories of addicts cannot (and should not) live without their drug of choice. We allow the alcoholic access to his addicting drug, and the nervous and distressed access to hypnotics and sedatives. We have decided that the alcoholic is not, by definition, a criminal, and that addiction to the barbiturates is only a *medical* matter, not a matter for the police. Heroin addiction, in strictly numerical terms, is a relatively minor (although growing) problem. Public hysteria over a quarter of a million addicts contrasts oddly with relative indifference to some ten million alcoholics, who are far more destructive to themselves and to others. The decision to permit some addicts to continue using their drug, but to deny the same privilege to others—indeed, severely penalizing one addiction but not another—is based on factors having to do, not with public safety, but with the relative respectability of the addictions. American society has decided that if the addict is young, and especially if he is black and from a working-class background, and if he expresses himself in hedonistic terms, he must be harassed and imprisoned. But if he is middle-aged, middle-class, manages a medical or therapeutic vocabulary—or supports a powerful "legitimate" industry—he may take his drug of choice without fear of prosecution.

NOTES

1. Edward Fingl and Dixon M. Woodbury, "General Principles," in Louis S. Goodman and Alfred Gilman (eds.), *The Pharmacological Basis of Therapeutics* (4th ed.; New York: Macmillan, 1970), p. 1.

2. For a contrary view, see Tod H. Mikuriya, "Marijuana in Medicine, Past, Present and Future," *California Medicine*, 110 (January 1969), pp. 34–40.

3. See Erich Goode, *The Marijuana Smokers* (New York: Basic Books, 1970), pp. 300–312.

4. See Claude Pepper, *Marihuana: First Report by the Select Committee on Crime* (Washington, D.C.: U.S. Government Printing Office, 1970), pp. 13–14.

5. William Dock, "The Clinical Value of Alcohol," in S. P. Lucia (ed.), *Alcohol and Civilization* (New York: McGraw-Hill, 1963).

6. The World Health Organization has adopted a terminology in which "dependency" replaces "addiction." See Nathan B. Eddy, H. Halbach, Harris Isbell, and Maurice H. Seevers, "Drug Dependence: Its Significance and Characteristics," *Bulletin of the World Health Organization*, 32 (1965), pp. 721–733.

7. See Milton Helpern and Yong-Myun Rho, "Deaths from Narcotism in New York City," *International Journal of the Addictions*, 2 (Spring 1967), pp. 53–84, and Donald B. Louria, "Medical Complications Associated with Heroin Use," *International Journal of the Addictions*, 2 (Fall 1967), pp. 241–251.

8. Charles Winick, "Physician Narcotic Addicts," *Social Problems*, 9 (Fall 1961), pp. 174–186. A

somewhat different perspective is adopted in Herbert C. Modlin and Alberto Montes, "Narcotic Addiction in Physicians," *American Journal of Psychiatry*, 121 (October 1964), pp. 358–365.

9. Harris Isbell, "Medical Aspects of Opiate Addiction," in John O'Donnell and John C. Ball (eds.), *Narcotic Addiction* (New York: Harper & Row, 1966), p. 62.

10. Abraham Wikler, "Drug Addiction: Organic and Physiological Aspects," in *International Encyclopedia of the Social Sciences* (New York: Macmillan, 1968), p. 292. See also the last chapter in John C. Ball and Carl D. Chambers, *The Epidemiology of Opiate Addiction in the United States* (Springfield, Ill.: Charles C. Thomas, 1970).

11. Robert K. Merton and M. F. Ashley Montagu, "Crime and the Anthropologist," *American Anthropologist*, 42 (August 1940), pp. 384–408. See also Ned Polsky, "Research Method, Morality and Criminology," in *Hustlers, Beats and Others* (Chicago: Aldine, 1967; Garden City, N.Y.: Doubleday-Anchor, 1969).

12. Roger Smith, "The World of the Haight Ashbury Speed Freak," *Journal of Psychedelic Drugs*, 2 (Winter 1968–1969), pp. 185–186.

13. Howard S. Becker, "Becoming a Marijuana User," *American Journal of Sociology*, 59 (November 1953), pp. 235–242.

14. Claude Brown, *Manchild in the Promised Land* (New York: Macmillan, 1965), pp. 105–108.

15. Seymour Fiddle, *Portraits from a Shooting Gallery* (New York: Harper & Row, 1967), pp. 117–118.

16. Troy Duster, *The Legislation of Morality: Drugs and Moral Judgment* (New York: Free Press, 1970), pp. 70–71.

17. Alan G. Sutter, "The World of the Righteous Dope Fiend," *Issues in Criminology*, 2 (Fall 1966), p. 194.

18. Alan G. Sutter, "Worlds of Drug Use on the Street Scene," in Donald R. Cressey and David A. Ward (eds.), *Delinquency, Crime and Social Process* (New York: Harper & Row, 1969), p. 820.

19. Alfred R. Lindesmith, *Addiction and Opiates* (Chicago: Aldine, 1968), p. 8.

20. Sutter, "World of the Righteous Dope Fiend," op. cit., p. 195.

21. Ibid.

22. Brian Keating, "Four Junkies," *Village Voice*, April 1, 1970, p. 30.

23. Robert K. Merton, "Social Structure and Anomie," *Social Theory and Social Structure* (3rd ed.; New York: Free Press, 1968). The "double failure" hypothesis is more fully elaborated in Richard Cloward, "Illegitimate Means, Anomie and Deviant Behavior," *American Sociological Review*, 24 (April 1959), pp. 164–176, and in Cloward and Lloyd Ohlin, *Delinquency and Opportunity* (New York: Free Press, 1960).

24. Sutter, "World of the Righteous Dope Fiend," op. cit., p. 200.

25. Alfred R. Lindesmith and John H. Gagnon, "Anomie and Drug Addiction," in Marshall B. Clinard (ed.), *Anomie and Deviant Behavior* (New York: Free Press, 1964), p. 179.

26. Fiddle, op. cit., pp. 55–63.

27. Ibid., p. 82.

28. Joel Fort, *The Pleasure Seekers* (Indianapolis: Bobbs-Merrill, 1969), pp. 98–99, and "A World View of Marijuana: Has the World Gone to Pot?" *Journal of Psychedelic Drugs*, 2 (Fall 1968), pp. 1–14.

29. Roswell D. Johnson, "Medico-Social Aspects of Marijuana," *Rhode Island Medical Journal*, 51 (March 1968), pp. 171–178, 187.

30. See Howard S. Becker, *Outsiders* (New York: Free Press, 1963), pp. 121–163, and Richard Quinney, *The Social Reality of Crime* (Boston: Little, Brown, 1970), chaps. 2 and 3.

31. See Donald T. Dickson, "Bureaucracy and Morality: An Organizational Perspective on a Moral Crusade," *Social Problems*, 16 (Fall 1968), pp. 143–156, and John Kaplan, *Marijuana: The New Prohibition* (New York: World Publishing Co., 1970), pp. 89, 90, 96, 98, 233–234.

32. Charles E. Terry and Mildred Pellens, *The Opium Problem* (New York: Bureau of Social Hygiene,

1928; Montclair, N.J.: Patterson Smith, 1970). Other works include Alfred R. Lindesmith, *The Addict and the Law* (Bloomington: Indiana University Press, 1965) and *Addiction and Opiates* (Chicago: Aldine, 1968); Duster, op. cit.; Roger Smith, "Status Politics and the Image of the Addict," *Issues in Criminology*, 2 (Fall 1966), pp. 157–175.

33. Duster, op. cit., p. 10.

34. Terry and Pellens, op. cit., p. 40; Lawrence Kolb and A. G. DuMez, "The Prevalence and Trend of Drug Addiction in the United States and Factors Influencing It," *Public Health Reports*, 39 (May 23, 1924), pp. 1179–1204. Lindesmith, *The Addict and the Law*, op. cit., pp. 104–122.

35. Victor H. Vogel, Harris Isbell, and Kenneth W. Chapman, "Present Status of Narcotic Addiction," *Journal of the American Medical Association*, 138 (December 4, 1948), pp. 1019–1026.

36. See Fort, *The Pleasure Seekers*, op. cit., p. 128. For tranquilizers, see Leo Hollister, Francis P. Motzenbecker, and Roger O. Degan, "Withdrawal Reactions from Chlordiazepoxide ('Librium')," *Psychopharmacologia*, 2 (1961), pp. 63–68.

37. New York Academy of Medicine, Committee on Public Health, "Report on Drug Addiction—II," *Bulletin of the New York Academy of Medicine*, 39 (July 1963), p. 432. See also Lawrence Kolb, *Drug Addiction: A Medical Problem* (Springfield, Ill.: Charles C. Thomas, 1962).

38. Lindesmith, *The Addict and the Law*, op. cit., p. 143.

39. See Florence Kavaler et al., "A Commentary and Annotated Bibliography on the Relationship Between Narcotics Addiction and Criminality," *Municipal Reference Library Notes*, 42 (April 1968), pp. 45–63 and Jeremy Larner and Ralph Tefferteller (eds.), *The Addict on the Street* (New York: Grove, 1965), as well as in Fiddle, op. cit.

40. Henry L. Giordano, "Keynote Address," in the International Narcotic Enforcement Officers Association, *Sixth Annual Conference Report*, September 26 to October 1, 1965 (Albany: INEOA, 1966), p.2.

41. *Ibid.*

42. See John A. O'Donnell, "Narcotic Addiction and Crime," *Social Problems*, 13 (Spring 1966), pp. 374–385.

43. Arnold Abrams, John H. Gagnon, and Joseph J. Levine, "Psychological Aspects of Addiction," *American Journal of Public Health*, 58 (November 1968), p. 2147.

44. *Ibid.*, p. 2142.

45. See John A. O'Donnell, "A Follow-up of Narcotic Addicts," *American Journal of Orthopsychiatry*, 34 (October 1964), pp. 948–954; O'Donnell, "The Relapse Rate in Narcotic Addiction: A Critique of Follow-up Studies," in Daniel M. Wilner and Gene G. Kassebaum (eds.), *Narcotics* (New York: McGraw-Hill, 1965), pp. 226–246; Henrietta J. Duvall, Ben Z. Locke, and Leon Brill, "Followup Study of Narcotic Drug Addicts Five Years After Hospitalization," *Public Health Reports*, 78 (March 1963), pp. 185–193; G. Halsey Hunt and Maurice E. Odoroff, "Followup Study of Narcotic Drug Addicts," *Public Health Reports*, 77 (January 1962), pp. 41–54.

46. See Thorsten Sellen (ed.), *Capital Punishment* (New York: Harper & Row, 1967).

47. Herman Joseph, "Heroin Addiction and Methadone Maintenance," *Probation and Parole*, 1 (Spring 1969), pp. 18–40; Joseph and John Langrod, "Analysis of the Methadone Maintenance Report Issued by the New York State Council on Drug Addicts" (New York: New York State Committee Against Mental Illness, August 28, 1969; unpublished ms.); Jerome H. Jaffe et al., "Experience with the Use of Methadone in a Multi-Modality Program for the Treatment of Narcotics Users," *International Journal of the Addictions*, 4 (September 1970), pp. 481–490 and 5 (September 1970), entire issue.

48. John C. Ball, David M. Englander, and Carl D. Chambers, "The Incidence and Prevalence of Opiate Addiction in the United States," in Ball and Chambers, op. cit., pp. 68–78; Max Singer, "The Vitality of Mythical Numbers," *Public Interest*, 23 (Spring 1971), pp. 3–9; Carl D. Chambers, *An Assessment of Drug Use in the General Population* (New York: Narcotic Addiction Control Commission, 1971).

49. Edward R. Hammock, Charles Devlin, and Walter V. Collier, *An Evaluation Report on the Therapeutic Program of Daytop Village* (New York: Daytop Village, February 1970), p. 3.

50. *Ibid.*

51. See Alexander Bassin, "Daytop Village," *Psychology Today,* 2 (December 1968), reprinted in *Addictions,* 17 (Summer 1970), pp. 30–44; Lewis Yablonsky, *Synanon: The Tunnel Back* (Baltimore: Penguin, 1965); Alexander Bassin and Joseph Shelly, "Daytop Lodge—A New Treatment Approach for Drug Addicts," *Corrective Psychiatry,* 11 (July 1965), pp. 186–195; Bassin and Shelly, "Daytop Lodge: Halfway House for Drug Addicts," *Federal Probation,* 28 (December 1964), pp. 46–54; Dan Waldorf, "Social Control in Therapeutic Communities for the Treatment of Drug Addicts," *International Journal of the Addictions,* 6 (March 1971), pp. 29–43; Leon Brill, "Some Comments on the Paper, 'Social Control in Therapeutic Communities,' " *International Journal of the Addictions,* 6 (March 1971), pp. 45–50.

9/ THE CRIME CORPORATION

GUS TYLER

ROOTS OF ORGANIZED CRIME

The appeal of organized crime is ecumenical, reaching out to all kinds of people. It is basically a business, a way of making a living, that flourishes naturally—almost inevitably—in any subculture trying to move up. This subculture may be economic, ethnic, or geographic: it is generally all three, composing a kind of nation within a nation (in twentieth-century metro-America, a city within a city) with a distinct piece of native turf, its own language, and its own class attitudes. Within this subsociety, there arises the antisocial gang, generally made up of young men and boys. This is the seed of organized crime.

To the young, gang life comes naturally. At some point, the adolescent wants to sever the umbilical cord and knot new ties to his peers. For the moment, this is his new family. If he does this in college, he joins a fraternity, or S.D.S., or a rock group, or a hippie commune. If he stays home, he joins a gang—formal or informal—on the block. Instinctively, he organizes his own street-corner society.[1]

The tendency of such a gang to turn violent is, again, quite natural. In a group, there is an increase in suggestibility, a gain in collective power, and a loss in individual responsibility. Oedipus is reenacted en masse. In settled times and restraining circumstances, the generational conflict is palliated; in troublous hours, the gap becomes a bloody gash.[2]

When the young gang grows up in a depressed, oppressed, or repressed subculture, its tendency toward antisocial action is spurred to open violence. Many of these disadvantaged young are raised in an ambience of anger and brutality. To the frustration of family repression is added the frustration of economic deprivation. The end result is the war of the little society (the gang) against the big society (the government).[3]

When such a gang represents some special ethnic group, with its own language or special pigmentation, its organized war against society becomes even more compulsive. Coming out of a common culture—nationality, religion, race—it coheres compulsively, united by its own brand of xenophobia. The generational and class ties are reinforced by ethnic bonds.

Needless to say, not all the young who grow up in such a subculture turn to organized crime as a career. Many, indeed most, go "social." They get a job, marry, settle down. Others go revolutionary: join protest movements of a mild or wild character. Some go union, conforming while at work and protesting while on strike. But some never outgrow the juvenile gang that has turned against society—and they make it a way of life.

Organized crime is the criminal gang grown up. In the course of its maturation, the gang acquires respect, power, and status. The community from which it emerged finds that, in their way, the bad boys have done good things for the neighborhood:

. . . *the great gangs—with their constant threat to a free society—have, in their time, perversely exercised a democratizing influence: redistributing wealth and political power. They won toleration because they did—and do—something more than commit crimes: they provide jobs, organize political clubs, develop pull, elect candidates, sponsor community projects, donate to the charities. Within their confusedly aspiring subcultures, they win toleration and even admiration quickly, and, ultimately, thanks to those universal solvents— money and votes—win acceptance in the greater civilization.*[4]

In a provocative essay on ethnic mobility, James M. O'Kane of Drew University assigns to "crime" a major role in the upward movement of the Irish, Jews, and Italians:

Each of the minority groups utilized three core modes of movement from the lower classes to the dominant society, each of which is interrelated and interdependent. These can be identified as labor, crime and politics. Each of these offered a route of upward mobility to the newcomers and their children.[5]

The story of how the boys on the block evolved into a giant syndicate of crime is the fascinating history of a business that has flourished and grown in America for many generations. It is the tale of the bouncer becoming banker; of the executioner turned executive; of the killer crowned king.

The rise of organized crime in America is the rise of a new class, once servant, now master; once poor, now rich; once rough, now refined; once despised, now respected. In the long chronicle of America's upward mobility, there is no chapter more startling or revealing than that of the underworld become overlord.

Although organized crime in the post-World War II period has been largely identified with Sicilian names (for reasons enumerated later), in the 1970s new ethnic rivals appeared, propelled by the same impulses as earlier ethnics of the underworld. The new entries are black, Puerto Rican, Cuban, and Mexican-American. Like the Germans, Irish, Jews, and Italians before them, the newly arrived and aspiring people reach upward through "labor, crime and politics."

During the 1950s and 1960s, Negroes and Puerto Ricans were used for menial chores by the syndicates. In 1967, it was reported that "in a major lottery business that operated in black neighborhoods in Chicago, the workers were black; the bankers for the lottery were Japanese-Americans; but the game, including the banking operation, was licensed, for a fee, by a family member (of the Cosa Nostra)."[6]

Former Congressman Adam Clayton Powell publicly bemoaned this racial discrimination in the underworld and in 1960 declared that he was "going to fight for the Negro having the same chance as an Italian" to play the banker's role.[7] In May 1969, an economics professor told a Black Economic Conference of 350 militants in Detroit that "racketeering, prostitution, and the numbers, if they are to continue, must be put into the hands of the black community."[8]

Noting the rise of new ethnic elements in the world of organized crime, Ralph Salerno, who served for many years with the Central Intelligence Bureau of the New York City Police Department, commented that in the central cities the Italian-Jewish Syndicate "is fighting a carefully planned rearguard action as newer racial groups—Negroes, Puerto Ricans, Japanese, Mexicans, Chinese—move up in the power structure." In the world of organized crime, as elsewhere, history repeats itself—playing out old scripts with new actors.

SIZE OF THE ENTERPRISE

In 1933 a witness before a Senate committee, Dr. Clayton Ettinger, submitted figures estimating the annual cost of crime at $13 billion a year (this sum including free-lance as well as organized crime).[9] The committee chairman, Senator Royal S. Copeland, noted that this meant that one dollar out of every four spent in the United States was picked up by criminal enterprise.

By 1950 a Senate Crime Investigating Committee headed by Senator Estes Kefauver concluded that organized crime ran a business with an annual income of $22 billion.[10] Eight years later, Virgil Peterson, the veteran director of Chicago's Crime Commission, reported that, despite the highly publicized and diligent efforts of the Committee, crime—especially organized crime—continued to grow. "Since 1950, major crime has been increasing at a rate four times as fast as population and the particularly frightening aspect of this picture is the one of organized crime, a vicious underworld that is waxing fat on both legitimate and illegitimate sources."[11]

The dimensions of criminal enterprise were dramatized by Dr. Daniel P. Moynihan when he reported in 1961 that the underworld payoff to police was greater than the total payroll of all police departments.[12]

In 1968 the Research Institute of America reported an annual income for organized crime of approximately $40 billion. "Knowledgeable observers," it added, "consider it inevitable that organized crime is reaping a *higher net income* than any single *legitimate industry*."[13] The figure of $40 billion in 1968 is about 5 percent of the G.N.P.

In 1969 the properties of organized crime were estimated to be worth $150 billion. Wayne Hopkins of the National Chamber of Commerce Crime Prevention and Control Division noted that "in another fifteen years, on the basis of 5 percent appreciation, organized crime will have about $600 billion worth of equity."[14]

This business leviathan had inauspicious beginnings, on the order of a Piker Ryan peddling a "punching" for two bucks. Out of two bucks and out of a variety of enterprises that rested on nickels and dimes, the syndicates—like Woolworth's—built an empire.

PARALLELS WITH CAPITALISM

The evolution of organized crime in America recapitulates the origin and development of Western and, more particularly, American capitalism. In the beginning, capitalism, like its bastard brother, organized crime, was ruthlessly violent. Karl Marx's *Das Kapital* and John Hobson's *The Evolution of Modern Capitalism* detail the gory process by which the bourgeoisie started its accumulation of capital. "Behind every great fortune," wrote Balzac, "there is a crime."

The ruthless routine behind the first great American fortunes has been described by Gustavus Myers *(Story of Great American Fortunes)*, Matthew Josephson *(Robber Barons)*, and Stewart Holbook *(Age of Moguls)*. The epithet "robber barons" was well earned:

Original accumulations of capital were amassed in tripartite deals among pirates, governors, and brokers. Fur fortunes were piled up alongside the drunk and dead bodies of our noble savages, the Indians. Small settlers were driven from their lands or turned into tenants by big ranchers employing rustlers, guns, outlaws—and the law. In the great railroad and shipping wars, enterprising capitalists used extortion, blackmail, violence, bribery, and private armies with muskets and cannons to wreck a competitor and to become the sole boss of the trade. [15]

The parallel between the financial and the criminal syndicate is striking: beginnings in bloodshed and rise to respectability. Indeed, it is one of the great ironies of organized crime that its ultimate success depends on the *containment* of violence, running a *peaceful* and prudent business, establishing *law and order* on its turf. Organized crime, unlike much free-lance crime, seeks to put the dirty deed behind it so that it may enter the charmed circles of financial, commercial, religious, and social acceptance. Organized crime prefers to turn the chaos of the underworld into a civilization after its own design. But, in the beginning, it is violent—for many reasons.

The gangster early discovers that existing law is not tailored to his requirements. The first commodity he has to peddle—raw violence—is not legal. The enterprises that hire him—houses of prostitution, gambling parlors, opium dens—are generally illegal. Hence he must operate as an outlaw, writing his own law with his fists.

To these violent pursuits, he brings a set of moral imperatives justifying his brutal acts—very much in the manner of a patriot serving his country or a revolutionary serving his cause. The violent gang, especially in its adult stage, arises from a subculture whose frustration has now turned to *revenge*—the most ancient apologia for man's inhumanity to man.

The gangster notion of violence is not the same as that of the more gently reared. The hood generally comes from a brutal background: much physical suffering, high infant mortality, not to speak of family fisticuffs, street brawls, and barroom donnybrooks. What others consider inhuman horror, the hood considers horseplay.

Because the breakthrough of some new subculture into organized crime is never a planned event, but occurs as a rashlike outbreak of little gangs, no coordinating committee is available, at the outset, to map jurisdictions or to serve as an intramural arbiter. The result is a sort of feudal war—in which gang wars against gang for a preferred spot in the still-undetermined pecking order of the underworld. This rivalry of persons, families, ethnic groups, adds to the violence.

The elements of violence manifest in the rise of each new ethnic group in the underworld are characteristic of other social movements—whether the rise of capitalist enterprises or socialist states. But just as these movements ultimately become institutions (corporations or one-party governments), organized crime, too, tends to become institutionalized.

In the beginning, the gangster is local, small, and attached to some service trade like a saloon, whorehouse, opium den, or gambling joint. He comes in as a hired hand—a big brutal paw. Once he becomes aware of his clout and of his potential role, he asks for a junior partnership. Now he is in business and—if he is a tribal chieftain—he can place his gang braves in other locations. Soon he can move up to senior partner or sole owner. Then he can force entry into other enterprises to become the boss not solely of a "house" but of all the "houses" in the neighborhood. He is a corporate giant in the making.

The sector of the economy into which he moves most readily is the service trades. These require minimum fixed capital investment. To become a pimp requires one girl and one mattress. The best of these service trades to enter are the illegitimate ones. In this shadow economy, the gangster (and his gang) can quickly establish a local monopoly or, if he is challenged, an oligopoly.

Just as the big shot in a local business tries to establish some political influence (usually for a good economic reason), the gangster, too, reaches out for political power. In this effort, he starts with natural advantages. The "boys" in the gang are a natural political club: same neighborhood, similar ideology, strong camaraderie, dedication to the common interest. They vote early and often; intimidate foes; impress friends; count right; heel the ward.

The merger of local operations into national ones and the establishment of a supersyndicate took place in the years between the First and the Second World War. A series of disconnected events concurred to bring the underworld abreast of its more legitimate corporate brethren.

TRUSTIFICATION OF THE GANGS

The Prohibition Amendment of 1919, forbidding the manufacture and sale of alcoholic beverages in the United States, created a vast national market for a new illegal service trade. Americans, by the millions, demanded bootleggers; and the underworld responded to the demand.

While the national economy oscillated in the 1920s, the trade of bootlegging boomed. Because thought of the forbidden fermented fruit heightened the national thirst, the market for alcohol skyrocketed. As Groucho Marx put it: "I was T.T. until Prohibition." Because the commodity was illegal, the price was high—high enough to make any risk cheap. The underworld throve.[16]

By its nature, bootlegging required national (even international) organization. The liquor came from Canada or Europe, necessitating an extranational arrangement. It rode at anchor outside the territorial limits in bottoms belonging to the underworld. It had to be picked up by small craft to be smuggled ashore. The contraband had to get by coast guard, customs, and cops. The cargo had to be loaded on trucks, carried across bridges and highways, protected against hijackers, delivered to warehouses, redistributed to retailers. And somewhere, somehow, there had to be collectors, bookkeepers, accountants, enforcers, personnel men, and masterminds to make the rum-running pay.[17]

And pay it did. Thus one bootlegger, William Vincent (Big Bill) Dwyer, rose from dock walloper to millionaire in two years, able to boast that he cheated the federal government of $100,000 in taxes in 1922, of $800,000 in 1923, and of $1,200,000 in 1924. Big Bill understood that big business must do things in a big way. On one occasion he bribed the crew (or captain) of a coast-guard cutter to pick up his contraband shipment of cargo for him and to land it safely at a dock near Canal Street.[18]

A business as big, complex, risky, and capital-hungry as the bootlegging of alcohol in the 1920s demanded cartelization. Among other things, hijacking had to be eliminated on both land and sea. The coast guard, customs, and the police had to be bought *collectively* to avoid double payment and double cross. The market had to be allocated to avoid cutthroat competition and flooding. The gangs had to gang together for their mutual good: the hoods needed a brotherhood—their counterpart of the Steel Institute or the American Medical Association.

On the East Coast, port of entry for much of the wares, an underworld cartel was organized, known as the Big Seven. The composition of its board of directors reveals much about the ethnic composition of the alcohol import and distribution business in the 1920s.[19] By ethnic count, the Jews were dominant; then came the Italians, then the Irish. In reality, it was the Irish—the "early settlers" of the underworld on the East Coast—who were on top, handling the "clean" political and financial end of the game; the Jews were the "managers," occupying the operational second-management level; the Italians handled the dirty end of the business.

Although the Italian gangs had been noticeable for many years, their numbers increased during the 1920s when Mussolini's orders to exterminate the Sicilian Mafia spurred a mass migration of Mafiosi and other Sicilian leaders to the United States.[20] These newcomers brought more than numbers; they brought skill and leadership with a way and a wisdom refined by centuries of experience.[21] If Mussolini found the Mafia indigestible in his totalitarian state, he was not the first. Sicily by virtue of its geographic location was a steppingstone for every ambitious prince or expanding empire from Africa to Europe, from the Levant to Spain, and vice versa. As foreign despot followed foreign despot, the "people" (or their natural tribal leaders) created a government of their own, a subnation with a code of conduct, a corps of enforcers, a system of defense and justice through vendetta, an inner cohesion secured by the *omerta* (silence to the death). In time, the sophisticated ruler made his peace with this real government; others fought it; still others surrendered to it.[22]

In part because of the Sicilian influx, the 1920s were a time of transition for the Italian sector of the underworld. There was a generational struggle between the old-timers and the new breed. No doubt, it was motivated by the age-old rivalry between sons and fathers, spurred by the grab for pelf and power. But there was also a real conceptual conflict over corporate policy. The new breed saw the need for the cartel: a merger with the Jews, Germans, Bohemians, Slavs, and Syrians; a unification of the Italian gangs; a shift of tactics from fists to finance, from carrying guns to carrying elections; a change of dress from the ostentatious to the unnoticeable.

In April 1929 a number of gangsters of Sicilian origin convened at the President Hotel in Atlantic City, New Jersey. According to the Federal Bureau of Narcotics, they made four major resolutions: (1) map a national trust with a well-defined hierarchy and jurisdiction; (2) establish a system of internal government and justice with its own brand of due process; (3) establish a ministry of external affairs to relate to other "powers"—legal and illegal; (4) set up a scholarship fund to sponsor young sophisticates for the future.[23]

The major obstacle to the implementation of these eminently sensible corporate decisions was, of course, the old guard—the "greasers." They had to be eliminated. And on September 11 and 12, 1931, they were, Some thirty to forty gang leaders were purged in those two days to make way for the new day.[24]

THE CONGLOMERATE CORPORATION

During the twenties, organized crime spread from the service and trade sector of the economy to industrial racketeering. In the period after the Second World War, it reached out to finance with a series of operations ranging from loan sharking to banking. By the 1970s, organized crime—like other giants in the economy—had become a hydra-headed conglomerate.

The various enterprises of organized crime can be grouped under the headings of theft, traffic in illegal goods and services, racketeering, control of unions and businesses, political graft, corporate finance and ownership. Through each of these enterprises, organized crime levies its toll on the community. To carry them forward, it has evolved methods and established power relations that, collectively, undermine the foundations of American democracy.

Thievery

Thievery, as practiced by organized crime, rarely consists of the simple kinds of acts that clutter police blotters, such as pickpocketing, holdups, mugging, housebreaking, rifling parking meters, or burglarizing small shops. That kind of retail activity is generally left to loners, to the free-lancers of the criminal world. Organized crime is more inclined toward the wholesale operation, with a sizable market and a steady income. Such a business requires organization, involving flowcharts, accounting procedures, and ordered distribution of the gross take, as well as the special skills of craftsmen, bookkeepers, managers, and planners. The thievery of organized crime is not the irrational or sporadic act of some bad egg, but part of the underworld's planned economy.

One kind of thievery that lends itself to organized operation is pilferage. This operation is so massive that there are cases where carloads of material, and sometimes even the car itself, disappear from docks and railroad depots. In one celebrated case, the missing car carried government weapons that the underworld needed either for resale or for its own arsenal. Docks, trucks, lading platforms, shipping rooms are natural targets for wholesale pilferage. The "organization" is useful not only to facilitate the pilferage but also to expedite the sale of the stolen goods.

Tied in with pilferage is the "fence," fundamentally a merchandising operation. Quantities of items must be secretly checked in, evaluated, judged for resale value, paid for in cash, warehoused, transported, resold, converted into new cash to make way for a new quantity of items. All this must be done "under the table," and yet in such a way that neither the thief nor the ultimate retailers nor any of the hirelings or agents paid off along the way lose faith in the fence.

A specialized thievery that leans very heavily on the fence is the trade in stolen cars. These autos are generally too hot to be resold in the local market; hence they are often either transported to a distant market or disguised with a motor or body job. In addition, they must be furnished with proper identifications: engine number, registration, and so on. By meshing selective stealing with selective fencing, the underworld auto trade often runs a smooth operation. One such operation was "so refined that a customer who placed an order for a specific car at 9 a.m. could get delivery, *with all the necessary papers,* by 11 a.m."[25] In 1968 the business of stealing and selling automobiles ran to about $800 million.[26]

A by-product of pilferage, thievery, and fencing is the almost inevitable attempt to buy off the police. To conduct a massive traffic in stolen goods requires an unseeing or a cooperative constabulary. In 1969 an official estimate of the sum for corruption of agencies and operations that "have a direct bearing on the enforcement and enactment of criminal laws and procedures" was set at $2 billion.[27] In a few cases, the entente between the outlaw and the law becomes so intimate that local police join actively in hijacking and pilferage operations with the criminals.

It is a mark of organized crime that it is constantly alert to new opportunities, changing with changing times. Thus while early gangs made a regular sport of bank holdups, the criminal establishment of today appears to be leaving this highly risky business to loners or unattached bands. Organized crime itself is moving toward snatching portfolios stuffed with negotiable securities and from check forgery to stealing, forging, using, and selling credit cards. The modern thievery of organized crime is not the poor robbing the rich to give to the poor, but the rich robbing the people, including the poor, to give to the rich of the underworld.

Illegal Goods and Services

Less risky than thievery is the traffic in illegal commodities and services. The risk is lower because the community demands these goods and services, and the supplier, though technically an outlaw, is not exposed to the same kind of social ostracism as the thief. No one boasts of his friend the burglar, but many have boasted of their friend the bookie or the bootlegger.

The earliest gangs found a congenial roost in the houses of pleasure with their gambling and prostitution. While prostitution is looked upon as a moral, as well as a legal, transgression in our society, gambling is not— although widely outlawed. Hence public participation in gambling is as widespread as its illegality. The risk is very low; the penalties are minuscule; enforcement is more than lax; the cash turnover is enormous, and the net income rewarding.

The major activity of organized crime in gambling no longer takes place in the gaming parlor. The operation has successfully reached out for a mass market, through bookies and "numbers." Catering to desperation and dreams, the underworld sends its runners out with paper bags to pick up bets in nickels and dimes. It has long discovered the riches that can be made in running a five-and-ten-cent store.

While organized crime invites everyone to gamble, the managers of the operation do not see it as a gamble at all. For them it is a business. While bets are being taken on horses, they devise ways and means to get early results, to fix outcomes, to stack odds so that the gamble is a one-sided gamble—for the customer only. In the numbers and policy rackets, the idea is to set the odds in favor of the house and (where possible) to rig the winning number to minimize payment by the house. In short, this kind of gambling is just another form of taxation levied by organized crime on the society, very often a viciously regressive tax levied on the poorest.

The gambling industry must protect itself against the unregulated small-time competitor. Little capital is needed to enter this business: all you need is a paper bag. If the first paper bag yields a profit, a new gambling entrepreneur is born. If, however, the self-starter is unable to pay off the bet as promised, he is not only bankrupt but a black eye to the whole industry. The "organization" seeks to discourage fly-by-nights either by getting them off the street altogether or by suggesting that they join the big outfits and, by responsible diligence, work their way up in the syndicate structure.

To get rid of small-time competitors, the syndicate can either report the small-fry gambler to the police (an action as effective as it is ironic) or suppress him with violence. The latter method is preferable, since a law enforcement agent is purchasable by both sides. In the late 1950s, as the underworld belatedly discovered the potential power of the financier, organized crime developed a way of absorbing the independent bookie without any resort to force—legal or illegal.

Just how big the income from gambling is, nobody knows—because the underworld conceals as much as it can—but all authorities agree that it is large: from $7 to $50 billion per annum.

In a category with gambling, in terms of return per hour invested, is the trade in drugs: opium, marijuana, heroin, and, more recently, the psychedelic drugs (LSD). While the army of pushers is composed of little people, loners and lost ones, the great suppliers are men of capital, able to grow, refine, smuggle, and distribute among the retailers. The wholesale end demands the large-scale operations, skill, finances, and contacts of organized crime. According to William H. Tendy, chief of the narcotics unit of the U.S. Attorney's office for the Southern District of New York, "80% to 85% of the import and distribution of hard narcotics in the U.S. is controlled" by organized crime; "fifteen men, all members of the Mafia, control nearly all the dope traffic in the U.S."[28]

In recent years, loan sharking (5 percent per week) has become so lucrative to organized crime that some believe it has replaced gambling as the top earner. Loan sharking is a clean and easy way to make money quickly—until it comes to collecting from delinquents. Here the mob plays rough: it cannot collect by legal action; so it finds another way of getting its pound of flesh. When a small businessman in the food business found that he could not pay back with the required interest, he was told what might happen to him by the collecting hood:

He showed me a story about a man whose body was found in Jamaica Bay with weights on it, and he said it could happen to me. He said, "If this house gets on fire one night how are you going to get the kids out? Your whole family will go up. I know the school your kids go to; they can get hit by a car. Accidents do happen!"[29]

When a businessman is in such desperate straits, what can he do? He can turn over his business to the mob, or manage the business for them, or turn pusher himself—"putting mob money out as a loan shark himself. He knows his industry. He knows the people who are marginal and need money badly. So he turns into a loan shark, at mob direction, and he traps others into it."[30]

Loan sharking is a way of hooking otherwise honest people to do the work of organized crime. A longshoreman on the hook can be pushed to point out "valuable cargo for hijackers or to help smuggle illicit goods into the country. A businessman in debt to a loan shark may help the underworld dispose of stolen goods ranging from liquor to stocks and bonds."[31] A city official who has turned to the underworld for fast financing may become an agent for the mob in a massive racket of city contracts and kickbacks.

Guns for hire are another item in the business of organized crime—although far less today than formerly. Muscle and murder are enlisted for industrial disputes, for personal revenge, and for political purposes. At one time, the hired hood was as common an item on Election Day as the paper ballot. The use of the musclemen in industrial and political disputes, while an evil in itself, is merely the first step in the assault of organized crime on our political and economic institutions. The strong-arm man enters as a janissary to become, in too many cases, the emperor.

Racketeering

The term "racketeering" is here used in a restricted sense to refer to *industrial* racketeering: the use of underworld methods to bleed or control a business or some area of business enterprise.

Historically, this operation is identified with petty preying on small businesses. The method is simple. If a shopkeeper does not want to find his windows or his head broken, he must take out "insurance" with the Underworld Underwriters. For a set sum per week or month, he avoids "accidents."

Parallel with the effort to terrorize a trade through the retail end has been the drive to control it through shipping. Because a retailer (or manufacturer) cannot operate without supplies, control of transportation is equivalent to a thumb on the jugular. At one time, shipping meant the railroad. Today, shipping means the truck. Even when bulk cargo is sent by rail, water, or air, the cargo must be carried by truck to loading points from the place of origin.

Control of trucking, or any significant sector of it, is especially effective when the material in hand is perishable. This can mean fruits and vegetables; or it can mean hardware like building materials, which unless delivered, can hold up other work or delay building beyond the construction season. Other items that need rapid handling are garbage, linen supplies, food for restaurants and hotels, newspapers. Because all these trades are so sensitive to interruptions in the system of truck transport, the underworld has found penetration in these areas easy and lucrative.

Indeed, very early in the development of organized crime in America, it became apparent that such control, combined with terrorization of the small retailer or producer or supplier, could give the underworld the deciding voice not only in a given firm but in a trade as a whole, through the trade association. Hence, what started as undirected preying on individual businessmen turned into well-organized capture, control, and management of trade associations.

As the underworld has grown in wealth, expanded in influence, and matured in method, it has perfected ever more sophisticated ways to reach out for control of given firms, trades, or industries. It can come to a businessman with a full portfolio of services covering capital, labor, raw materials, outlets, transportation, an edge against competition, legal defense, and immunity from law enforcement. Indeed, it comes equipped to serve a company as if it stood *in loco republicae.*

The underworld can provide capital. Hot cash is sometimes available; factoring agents can be brought in; a bank loan may be underwritten by a third party who is a front of the underworld. One of the most refined operations is to provide enough swift and ready capital to give a firm interim financing, to establish a record of stability and growth, to encourage the firm to go public, to stimulate a demand for the stock by pushing a few of the underworld buttons, and then to cash in on the stock rise and report it as capital gain.

The underworld is highly skilled at handling labor situations. In industries that farm out work, the underworld can make a labor supply available and generally does it at bargain rates. The operators of the underworld know where cheap labor plants have been set up (in some cases criminal money is in control of such plants), and they know how to evade unions and union standards. When a firm is having difficulty with a legitimate union, the underworld can be called in to maintain labor "peace," either by a bribe or by a beating or killing. On a more sophisticated level, the underworld acts as mediator: getting a little more out of the employer than the union might have by itself and checking the union better than the employer might have himself, while collecting the difference, sometimes from both sides. Where an employer sees trouble ahead with a legitimate union, the underworld can provide an illegitimate union, a "racket" union with "sweetheart" agreement and a bar, both legal and criminal, against outside interference.

The underworld can make needed raw materials more accessible. While it may on rare occasions be able to indicate the best and cheapest source, it generally speeds raw materials in a negative way, that is, by not impeding steady shipment. Hijacking, blowouts, delays, stoppages, lost trucks and lost cartons, damaged materials, and shrinkage in transport can be worrisome to manufacturers. A contract with the underworld has been written by thousands of American companies, including some of the biggest, to insure safe and speedy transport.

Similarly, the underworld can supply outlets for manufactured goods. In part, this influence stems from its power on the highways. But, in addition, the underworld penetration of retailing—small shops and their associations—makes a recognized factotum in the underworld a good man to place on a company's payroll as a salesman. A man with such a background can be most persuasive. He knows how to make himself heard—and felt.

The trucking service itself is a most useful item in the portfolio of organized crime. Largely through political know-how and well-cultivated contacts, the gangs can provide special services. They can park where others can't; they can speed over highways where others can't; they can drive competing trucks off the road; they can provide special guarantees against hijacking. In short, they can provide better transportation—at a reasonable price.

Organized crime is a useful ally in a commercial war. It can help a firm dispose of a competitor in innumerable ways, legal and illegal. The rival's production can be halted, his shipment delayed, his plant sabotaged, his customers scared, his person threatened.

Finally, organized crime is able to defend lawbreakers against the law. The political contacts of the underworld can be, and are, used at many levels: with building and sanitation inspectors, with labor and health agents, with the police and the courts, and with district attorneys and mayors.

In sum, the underworld is a business partner well worth having—if one is ready to pay the price. This price has gone up over the years. At one time, the gangster was a day hand, to be paid for a rough job and then forgotten, a harlot for hire. Today, the gangster seeks respectability, a marriage with the master.

Corporate Finance and Ownership

Racketeering is not the only method available to the underworld for the penetration and ultimate control of a company or a trade. A much more sophisticated approach is the legal one of direct investment. There are several good reasons why organized crime seeks to convert its bad money, derived from illegal activities, into good money, invested in legal undertakings.

First, the volume of money derived from illegal activities is too great to be reinvested solely in outlaw undertakings. The spillover needs larger channels. Thus an original accumulation of capital derived from bootlegging goes into legitimate liquor manufacture; funds drawn from preying on bars goes into buying or erecting hotels.

Second, the transfer of funds to legal enterprises is the path to respectability. The retired gangster can live the honorable life on his fully legitimized investments.

Third, the legitimate enterprise is a channel for moving illegal money into the legal arteries of the economy. Too much bad money can choke its owner. He is afraid to spend it, lest he be asked how he got it. The legitimate business is the front, the alleged source of the income.

Fourth, this front allows the rich criminal to make his settlement with the tax collector. The men of organized crime pay taxes; at least, they pay on that portion of their income that they deem it proper to report.

While a few of these legitimate concerns are in the name of their underworld owners, most are in the name of a dummy or dummies and run by a trustee. In the business community, such companies have a distinct advantage over their competitors. They have the underworld—its contacts, methods, and influence—at their disposal. They can combine the legal with the illegal. Their business ties are reinforced by social, political, and criminal ties.

The types of business penetrated or owned by organized crime are various. Hardly a sector of the economy is immune. Those who once ran a nightclub now own a hotel; the loan shark goes into factoring and then banking; the hoodlum who served apparel employers now owns a string of apparel companies; the gangster who beat up retailers is now a merchant prince; the organizer of mass pilferage at the dock now owns the shipping company.

An Internal Revenue Service survey of 98 persons prominent in the underworld revealed that they were involved in 159 businesses including 32 casinos and nightclubs, 17 land investment and real estate groups, 11 hotels and motels, 10 vending machine companies, 8 restaurants, 8 trucking companies, 7 wholesale food distributors, 7 businesses in sports and entertainment, and 6 finance institutions. These holdings were but the tip of the iceberg, since they do not include ownership through dummies.

According to the Department of Justice, organized crime now "has links with tens of thousands of businesses and businessmen in such widely ranging fields as electronics, trucking, banking, construction, real estate, and food and health services."[32]

The underworld, in its more recent reliance on finance to accomplish its goals, has directed increasing attention to the infiltration and control of banks and brokerage and investment houses. New York Attorney General Louis J. Lefkowitz has outlined the methods of influence and penetration. The member of the underworld may operate the firm himself, under his own or an assumed name, or he may put a figurehead in ostensible charge and supervise the operation by giving himself or a lieutenant a job in the organization. There are other possibilities:

An artful device for underworld infiltration of the securities industry involves direction of stock-price manipulation activities. In such cases, the underworld seeks control of a spurious company and several avenues for "unloading" its fraudulent securities. The principal earmarks of the success of such a venture are the establishment of fictional market prices and use of high-pressure literature or phone calls to "unload" the stock. . . .

An insidious method by which the underworld cancer has spread into some corners of Wall Street is loansharking. By carrying insolvent brokers, or "warehousing" their debt obligations, at enormous interest rates—sometimes as high as 60 per cent initially—the gangster has in the past become virtual ruler of several over-the-counter securities firms.[33]

Turning to the international aspects of criminal syndicate finance, Lefkowitz added: "The tentacles of the underworld in the securities business reach not only over the United States and Canada and Latin America, but also to places such as Switzerland, Italy, Lebanon, Liechtenstein, France, England and West Germany."

THE SECRET GOVERNMENT

To operate its various income-producing enterprises, organized crime must develop political muscle and know-how. As it becomes involved in the political game, it learns that politics per se can be a most profitable business.

With control of clubs and precincts, it can "sell" nominations for public office. It can put in the "fix" for a fee. It can win contracts for its own operations. It can place its henchmen in sinecures, where they can indulge in official extortion. In short, the underworld, once it enters politics, can play the game of political graft at its worst.

For this usurpation of the public service, the citizenry must pay the price—in needless taxes, in shoddy administration, in perverted justice, in corrupt government.

But organized crime presents a more profound threat to a free society. Freedom in the American culture flows from the interplay of free individuals and institutions. The world of business knows the interplay of company with company, retailer with wholesaler, manufacturer with supplier, entrepreneur with financier. The world of labor knows a similar interplay of individual leaders and unions. In government, a vast number of power centers are subject to a measure of control through a system of checks and balances. Among these great institutions—business, labor, government—there is constant push and pull, each checking, spurring, challenging and moderating the others. It is precisely this free interplay of autonomous institutions that can be seriously imperiled if organized crime is permitted to go unchecked. The organized underworld becomes a secret and private government covertly in control of large segments of business, labor, and government, molding all these to the requirements of what may eventually become a gangster state.

The Business World

As a nation, we are committed to promoting free enterprise in an atmosphere of competition. We have laws and enforcement agencies for dealing with monopolies and oligopolies. But where organized crime establishes concentrated control, there is no monopoly owner to proceed against, since the underworld is neither a person nor a corporation. The underworld is legally nonexistent. It cannot be asked or ordered to divest itself of its holdings. Indeed, it is almost impossible to prove that it has wide holdings. And whatever properties it may own or control are held in the name of different individuals some of whom, if not most of whom, show no criminal record at all.

In the world of business, then, the underworld eludes the grasp of our existing body of legislation, holding and running a vast sector of the American economy: a true conspiracy in restraint of trade and commerce.

The Labor World

A union is a collective bargaining agency for its members. Its dues are to be used to promote their interests and concerns; its welfare funds are designed to provide essential services; its constitution and bylaws are intended to promote inner democracy.

In the hands of organized crime, a union becomes an instrument for extortion. Its dues become a means for enriching the criminal boss; its welfare funds become an instrument for financing private undertakings; its constitution and bylaws become a paper screen behind which gangsters run the union by terror.

Administration of the Law

The system of due process is a basic element in the preservation of American freedom. Due process is the guarantee to the lone citizen that he will not be crushed in the fist of an overpowering state. It is our way of balancing the scales of justice, of seeing to it that the individual is not denied his inalienable rights by the society—even if he should be a heinous criminal.

When a henchman of organized crime comes before the judicial bench, however, a new element is introduced that upsets the delicate balance between "the people" and the accused, embodied in our system of due process. The accused in this case is not just an individual. He is an agent of the "organization," of a private government. Because he is backed by the resources of a powerful institution, it may be almost impossible to convict him. For instance, valid proof generally depends on witnesses, without whom a case cannot be made. Yet precisely these indispensable witnesses can be and have been either silenced or destroyed by the underworld where its interests were at stake.

In society's combat against inimical organizations, it is not unusual for law enforcement agencies to infiltrate the antisocial institution. This infiltration provides leads and, at a later stage, witnesses who cannot be terrorized. It is the peculiar strength of organized crime that because of its organic structure—recruitment from family and old friends—it is extremely difficult, almost impossible, to penetrate the core of the underworld in the same way that it has been possible to infiltrate the Communist party or the Ku Klux Klan.

In frustrating justice, the underworld can bring various other devices into play. It can provide any number of false witnesses who will furnish synthetic alibis. It has a massive apparatus with which to bribe and threaten members of the jury. It can protect the truly guilty—the mastermind—by throwing a stand-in to the wolves of justice; the stand-in takes the rap (usually in exchange for an appropriate reward), while the big fish escapes.

In sum, the underworld—as an organized group—can and repeatedly does violate the constitutional rights of American citizens, even while it can and repeatedly does escape efforts on the part of government to protect the individual citizen against criminal violation. In the hands of organized crime, due process tends to become a license to violate individual rights—to take from citizens life, liberty, and property *without* due process of law.

Government

Organized crime can bring three indispensable items to a political campaign: money, manpower, and muscle.

In a 1952 study, Alexander Heard calculated that the underworld is responsible for about 15 percent of all political money in the United States. Of necessity this is only an estimate, since the underworld is one of the few great institutions that are able to conduct almost all their business on a cash basis. The ready money is a double boon to a candidate: he can exceed his legal allowance with impunity and use the money in illegal ways with ease.

The underworld can provide manpower. Its employees in both its legal and illegal enterprises can be made available—to vote, to electioneer, to turn out the vote, to man headquarters, to speed mailings, to do the many indispensable chores of the volunteer on a full-time paid basis.

The underworld can provide muscle—if and when needed. Moreover, in the numerous subcultures of America, the gangster is often the community leader.

With all its resources, the underworld can effectively support its kind of people for public office: for district attorney, for judge, for mayor. The outlaw tries to become the law—and often succeeds!

LIMITATIONS ON ORGANIZED CRIME

The totalitarian potential of that octopus—organized crime—is implicit in its ceaseless drive for control both in the economic and in the political sector. For when organized crime runs both corporations and unions, when such underworld-controlled organizations have electoral and lobbying power and in turn benefit from their political influence, when underworld-infiltrated local governments are in league with the criminal—then the play of countervailing forces essential to the preservation of a democratic society comes to an end.

There are a variety of counterforces, however, whose effect is to limit the aggrandizement of the underworld. The political strength of organized crime tends to be predominantly local, since routine policing in the United States is a local matter. The primary and instinctive drive of the underworld in politics is to win over the parochial powers of law enforcement. Higher levels of government find it possible as well as necessary to intervene. In addition, the underworld is torn by its own internal dissensions: eternal jurisdictional disputes; generational struggle between the Young Turks, who are hungry and violent, and the old men, who are sated and statesmanlike; the conflict, ever renewed, between the latest subculture, trying to break through, and the old underworld, dominated by an erstwhile subculture that has become acculturated. At the level of law enforcement, there is a growing sophistication about the nature of the underworld and about ways to combat it through police methods and through social action.

These and other factors have served to limit the power and influence of organized crime over the whole society. But the danger of the gangster state is real.

NOTES

1. William Foote Whyte, *Street Corner Society* (Chicago: University of Chicago Press, 1943).
2. Herbert Block and Arthur Niederhoffer, *The Gang* (New York: Philosophical Library, 1958).
3. Gus Tyler, *Organized Crime in America* (Ann Arbor: University of Michigan Press, 1962.)
4. ———, "An Interdisciplinary Attack on Organized Crime," *Annals of the American Academy of Political and Social Science*, 347 (May 1963), pp. 109–110.
5. James M. O'Kane, "Ethnic Mobility and the Lower-Income Negro," *Social Problems* (Winter 1969), pp. 302–311.
6. *The Challenge of Crime in a Free Society* (1967). Report of the Presidential Commission on Law Enforcement and the Administration of Justice.
7. Quoted in Ralph Salerno and Ralph Tompkins, *The Crime Confederation* (Garden City, N.Y.: Doubleday, 1969), p. 379.
8. *Ibid.*, p. 376.
9. U.S. Congress, Senate Subcommittee of the Committee on Commerce, *Hearings: Investigation of Racketeering*, 73rd Congress, 1933, vol. 1, part 1, p. 252.
10. U.S. Congress, Senate, Special Committee to Investigate Organized Crime in Interstate Commerce, *Third Interim Report*, May 1, 1951.
11. Virgil Peterson, "Fighting Nationally Organized Crime," *Vital Speeches*, October 15, 1958, p. 150.
12. Daniel P. Moynihan, "The Private Government of Crime," *The Reporter*, July 6, 1961.
13. Research Institute of America, *Protecting Your Business Against Organized Crime*, April 15, 1968, pp. 4–5.
14. Business News Service, Chamber of Commerce of the United States, Washington, D.C., June 20, 1969.
15. Tyler, *Organized Crime*, op. cit., p. 44–45.
16. Kenneth Alsop, *The Bootleggers and Their Era* (New York: Doubleday, 1962).
17. See Hank Messik, *The Silent Syndicate* (New York: Macmillan, 1966), pp. vii–xii.
18. See Fred J. Cook, *The Secret Rulers* (New York: 1966), Duell, Sloan and Pearce, pp.72–80.
19. *Ibid.*, p. 75.
20. See Danilo Dolci, *The Man Who Plays Alone* (New York: Pantheon, 1968).
21. See Norman Lewis, *The Honored Society* (New York: Putnam, 1964).
22. See Tyler, *Organized Crime*, op. cit., pp. 321–362.
23. See Cook, op. cit., pp. 77–80.
24. *Ibid.*, p. 81
25. *Wall Street Journal*, January 10, 1969, p. 1, col. 8.
26. *Ibid.*
27. Victor Riesel column (New York: Hall Syndicate, December 12, 1969).
28. *Daily News*, June 27, 1970, p. 7.
29. *New York Post*, June 8, 1968, p. 30.
30. *Ibid.*
31. *Ibid.*
32. *Wall Street Journal*, August 12, 1969, p. 1.
33. Louis J. Lefkowitz, "New York: Infiltration of the Securities Industry," *Annals of the American Academy of Political and Social Science*, 347 (May 1963), p. 53.

10/AMERICAN YOUTH GANGS: PAST AND PRESENT

WALTER B. MILLER

. . . at any and all hours of the day there are multitudes of boys wandering about and congregated on the corner of the streets, idle in their habits, dissolute in their conduct, profane and obscene in conversation and gross and vulgar in their manners. If a female passes one of these groups she is shocked by what she sees and hears . . .

Report in Brooklyn newspaper, 1865

I'm afraid to let my daughter go out on our street. Gangs terrorize the block and drag race down the street. I'm sick with fear. Is there anything you can do?

Letter to Philadelphia newspaper, 1970

The youth gang is viewed in a variety of often contradictory ways. It is seen as a major instrument for the perpetration of crime—and as an ingenious device for containing criminal behavior within tolerable limits; as a body forged in conflict and relentlessly dedicated to the pursuit of violence—and as a relatively peaceful group whose very structure serves to limit the exercise of violent activity; as a fleeting congeries of casual acquaintances—and as the very epitome of close, loyal, and solidary mutual ties; as a rare and fragile blossom, appearing rarely and sparsely—and as a hardy perennial, ubiquitous and enduring. Such diversity of opinion with respect to a social form which is not, after all, a mysterious product of some remote and exotic tribal society calls for some sort of explanation.

One major area of disagreement about gangs is the degree to which they should be defined in terms of behavior violating legal and moral standards. Although specifically illegal activities generally comprise a comparatively small proportion of a gang's total repertoire, such activities are often represented as a dominant preoccupation or even as the major basis of the gang's éxistence. Thus, when youth groups in a particular community appear clearly to present a problem, they are perceived as gangs; when they do not, that community has "groups," not "gangs." The present paper treats illegal and problematic behavior as significant aspects of gang life, but does not conceive youth gangs primarily as instruments for committing crime, or grant the status of "gang" only to those groups whose behavior is clearly problematic.[1]

Another source of disagreement about American youth gangs is that they vary tremendously in such basic features as size, age composition, sex composition, life span, and internal differentiation.[2] For one person, the only

210

"real" gang is one highly organized, close-knit, and autocratic in leadership; for another, only those groups involved in serious criminality—particularly fighting—merit the designation of "gang."

A particularly pervasive source of distortion is that the youth gang is anything but a "neutral" phenomenon, that, on the contrary, it arouses strong emotions and engages deeply rooted values. The youth gang and the family both play important parts in the socialization of youth, with the gang taking a particularly active part during adolescence, when it provides a context for the learning of independence and adult sex roles. Most parents, however, perceive the gang not as a benign and helpful partner but as a malign and dangerous competitor, with a frightening potential for sabotaging attitudes and behavioral practices inculcated with considerable care and at considerable cost.[3]

Insofar as gangs are perceived as agencies of crime and other forms of disapproved behavior, their existence and activities are interpreted in the light of ideological values similar to those applied to criminal behavior in general—values generally mirroring partisan political positions. The "conservatives" commonly regard gang behavior as a reprehensible consequence of excessive liberality or permissiveness, reflecting insufficient control and discipline by the youths themselves, by their parents, and by official authorities. The "liberals" tend to regard gangs and their behavior as symptoms of critical deficiencies in the larger social order. Reasoning from a causal theory which attributes deviant behavior to social ills such as poverty, racial discrimination, injustice, corruption, and the like, they perceive the gang as the signal of a clear mandate to pursue urgently needed programs of social reform. Inevitably, the present treatment of gangs reflects the author's personal, professional, and political values, but one of its primary objectives is to offer a balanced view, one in which gangs are presented neither as evil and self-willed instigators of reprehensible behavior nor as innocent and pitiful victims of malign social forces beyond their control.[4]

Any attempt to present a factually accurate picture of gangs in the United States is currently much hampered by the lack of any established agency, public or private, responsible for the collection, analysis, and dissemination of information on youth gangs. Thus reliable data on the most fundamental aspects of the national gang situation—the numbers, sizes, and locations of gangs—are simply not available, let alone more refined information on the types and current activity patterns of gangs in American communities.

This circumstance has several important consequences. For one thing, it is impossible for any writer on gangs as a national phenomenon to draw generalized descriptive and/or statistical conclusions with any degree of certainty. Any attempt to do so, including the present one, must be evaluated with this in mind.[5] Furthermore, the paucity of "hard" national data, along with the lack of agreement on definitions, provides an unusually propitious climate for the kinds of value-influenced perceptions just discussed. Statements on the numbers, sizes, and activities of gangs are often influenced to a far greater degree by the interests, motives, and values of the observer than by considerations of factual accuracy. For example, a politician running for office may attempt to indict an incumbent administration by claiming that dangerous gangs are running rampant, or a police department with a gang-control program may attempt to demonstrate its effectiveness by claiming that gangs have been completely eradicated. Similarly, liberals or conservatives may claim that gangs are numerous or rare, menacing or benign, proliferating or vanishing, in an attempt to bolster ideologically influenced assertions about current social conditions.

Owing in part to the lack of adequate information, any account of gangs as a national phenomenon tends to be disproportionately influenced by the local community or communities with which the writer is most familiar. One might say that there is a Chicago-colored picture of the American youth gang, a New York-colored picture, and so on. (The author happens to be most familiar with Boston and Philadelphia.) An observer familiar with gang conditions in a particular city must guard against the tendency to extend to other communities generalizations developed primarily from his own. The particular circumstances of Chicago (high ethnic diversity, large black slum neighborhoods, development of "lateral" gang alliances) have had an especially strong influence on national conceptions of gangs for well over thirty years, since a larger number of influential scholarly accounts have been devoted to Chicago gangs than to those of any other city.[6] During the 1950's the situation in New York City ("fighting gangs," black–Puerto Rican conflict, high media attention) exerted a dominant influence on national conceptions.[7]

The other face of the tendency to characterize the national situation as the local situation writ large is a tendency to conceive local conditions as essentially unique. And the gang situation does indeed differ in significant respects from one urban area to another, but it is also alike in many important ways. A balanced treatment requires the identification of both generic, cross-community characteristics and local, individual characteristics.

A prime source of misconceptions about gangs is the mass media. Almost everyone except those whose professional activities bring them in direct and continuing contact with gangs depends for information on media coverage. What the media choose to report about gangs, the kinds of gangs they select for attention, and even whether they choose to report on gangs at all, are determined by considerations only indirectly related to the actual situation. Most of what the average observer "knows" about gangs stems from a series of editorial decisions oriented primarily to the question "What is newsworthy?" rather than "What is accurate?"[8]

Since the youth gang would appear to manifest an unusual degree of stability during many historical periods and in the face of many social changes, initial sections of this paper will focus on the American youth gang as a continuing associational phenomenon. But since youth gangs, along with other associational forms, are sensitive to changes over time in a variety of social conditions—population movements, racial and ethnic migrations, war and peace, depression and prosperity, fashions of the adolescent subculture, ideological and political trends—later sections will discuss the gang in the light of recent social developments—with "recent" referring to a period extending roughly from the middle 1960's to the early 1970's.[9]

THE CRUCIAL QUESTION OF DEFINITION: WHAT IS A "GANG"?

A major reason for renewed attention to the question of definition is that the general conception of "the gang" underwent a significant transformation during the 1950s—a change not fully appreciated by most laymen and many scholars. This change came with the emergence in and around New York City of a highly specialized form of youth gang, partly real, partly manufactured— the "fighting gang." Subject to unparalleled publicity, it produced a new image of "the gang" which made a deep imprint on public consciousness. Prior to this, the term "gang" in the United States evoked at least two images. The first, that of the "corner boy," is embodied in popular songs of the turn of the century celebrating "that old gang of mine" "down on the corner"—a bunch of good pals who shared affecting moments but could be rough and ready when the occasion demanded. The other is the desperado image—typified in American folklore by the James gang and the Younger brothers—an image of quasi-heroic men, capable withal of great cruelty and violence. The classic sociological treatment of gangs, developed primarily by Frederick Thrasher in the 1920's, in large measure reflects the corner-boy image rather than that of the desperado.

The unprecedented publicity accorded the New York fighting gangs of the 1950's brought about a major shift with respect to earlier sociological trends. The gangs of the era that produced *West Side Story* were widely represented as hard, cruel, sadistic, and heartless. For many writers and some scholars the brilliance and appeal of the fighting-gang image virtually extinguished the corner-boy conception, and established the desperado image.

It is obvious that intangible characteristics such as *"esprit de corps,"* "a sense of we-ness," "morale," "group awareness," "tough self-image," and the like, while not irrelevant, are of limited utility in a definition of gangs, since their attribution depends so heavily on subjective judgments. Nor must the definition incorporate hypotheses or speculations as to origins or developmental history ("originally formed spontaneously," "integrated through conflict"), but must depend, rather, on contemporaneously observable characteristics.[10]

The development of a satisfactory definition would require extensive information, of a high order of detail and specificity, concerning gangs and related groupings, not only in the major urban centers of the United States, but also in the many locales in other countries where gangs are and have been prevalent. Ideally, both national and cross-cultural data should have some degree of historical depth. Such information would make possible not only an adequate and generally acceptable definition, but also the development of a taxonomy—a classification of types and subtypes of gangs and related groupings.

As already stated, information of this order is not now available. In its absence, it is essential to delineate as precisely as possible the sense in which the term "gang" is used in the present paper. This definition is based primarily on the substantive findings of the author's own studies, but it also incorporates findings of other empirical studies.[11] Two orders of characteristics will be distinguished—"defining criteria," which serve to define the unit and remain stable over time, and "variable characteristics," aspects or attributes of gangs that may vary over time or in different localities without destroying the identity of the unit as here defined.

The Urban Youth Gang: Defining Criteria

Five major criteria serve to define the urban adolescent street gang, as the term is used here.[12] These are presented in Table 1, along with subcriteria intended for amplification or clarification. These criteria apply both to the more inclusive or independent units ("aggregates") and to recognized subunits ("subdivisions," "segments").[13]

"Recurrent congregation," the paramount defining criterion of the urban adolescent street gang, can be described as "the practice of leaving one's home at recurrent intervals and assembling with others of one's age at designated locales."[14] The locales for hanging out vary from gang to gang and for the same gang at different times ("the" corner, a local store, a hamburger or pizza shop, a playground, a poolroom, a parking lot) and may be indoors or outdoors depending on the season or other circumstances, but they are almost invariably "extraresidential." The propensity to assemble away from the residential unit reflects conditions of at least two subcultures—adolescent and lower-class. A central requirement of adolescent peer congregation is that it be sufficiently removed from the household to allow, among other things, freedom from adult supervision and attention, and the conduct of mating activities. The other factor is that at lower status levels, particularly the lowest, much activity takes place out of the home, in barrooms, on door stoops, at street corners.

The gang is not an "open" group, but maintains well-developed criteria for inclusion and exclusion.[15] These criteria are not formalized, and can seldom be readily articulated, but exert a compelling influence nonetheless. Nor is the gang a transient assemblage. It maintains continuity of affiliation over time. As in most groups, the degree of continuity may vary both over the short and the long run. Membership varies with the season, and there is always some turnover in the course of a year. A group formed in early adolescence will seldom include all the same individuals when it starts to dissolve in late adolescence. Nevertheless, under conditions of average residential stability, a sizable core of persons may almost always be depended on to be "out on the corner" during most of their adolescent years.[16]

Table 1 The Urban Adolescent Street Gang: Defining Criteria

1.   Recurrent congregation

    a.   Extraresidential

    b.   Self-defined inclusion–exclusion criteria

    c.   Continuity of affiliation

2.   Territorial basis

    a.   Customary frequentation locales

    b.   Customary ranging areas

    c.   Self-defined use-and-occupancy rights

    d.   Residential–proximity recruitment basis

3.   Age basis

    a.   Age-limited affiliation

    b.   Subgroup delineation by age

4.   Versatile activity repertoire

Central role of:

    a.   Extended periods of "casual" interaction ("hanging out")

    b.   Mating involvement

    c.   Illegal activities

    d.   Recreational-athletic activities

5.   Intra–unit differentiation

By authority, roles, prestige, cliques

The territoriality of the youth gang has several aspects. The bulk of membership is drawn from nearby residential areas; in urban communities most "regulars" live within walking distance of the major assemblage locale or locales. The automobile has to some degree weakened the powerful influence of territoriality and localism on traditional modes of gang life, but has by no means eliminated it. Members of suburban gangs, for example, who tend to be completely motorized, operate within specific "ranging areas," whose major activity locales (the movie, the hamburger stand, the lovers' lane, the bowling alley) are highly routinized.[17]

Perhaps the best-known manifestation of territoriality in gang life is what Table 1 designates as "self-defined use-and-occupancy rights." Many species of animals, including man, carve out geographically delimited areas or zones within which they exercise certain special rights of occupancy and use.[18] The "turf" concept has caught the fancy of popular writers, who often misleadingly represent the "gang turf" as a rigidly defined no-trespass zone into which outsiders may intrude only at the risk of serious danger. As in the case of other subcriteria discussed here, the sense of territory varies among different gangs. The territoriality of most gangs is selective. For example, the "trespass at your own risk" ethic applies primarily to male peers, and seldom affects adults. However, all gangs *do* make some sort of claim of special rights of occupancy and use for what they define as "their" territory, and this phenomenon serves as a major defining criterion of the street gang.

The adolescent gang is, preeminently, an assemblage of age-mates. Age serves in diverse and complex ways to define the limits of gang aggregates and to order internal relationships. One of the principal ways in which age affects gang composition is that it establishes the approximate upper and lower limits of the adolescent "hanging-out" phase. In most instances, the lower limit runs from about ten to thirteen, and the upper limit from about eighteen to twenty-two for males and sixteen to eighteen for females.

Age also exerts a decisive influence in the delineation of gang subgroups. Subaggregation by age is a complex process involving interaction between several sets of variables, including the number of individuals in the aggregate; local statutes respecting age of school attendance, work force participation, and armed services membership; age levels within adolescence; and characteristic gang activity patterns. Total size of the aggregate is very important. By and large, the greater the number of congregating individuals, the more sensitively age serves to delineate subgroups. When the local community can support only one or a few gang units in a given locality, the age-span within the unit is wider than when larger numbers are present. Similarly, the age-spread within units tends to be wider at the oldest (and sometimes the youngest) age levels, and narrower for middle-adolescent units.

The adolescent street gang is conceived here as a stable and conventionalized associational form—one of a number composing the totality of social arrangements in urbanized societies. The gang, like the family or child-rearing unit, is "multifunctional"; that is, instead of focusing on single or restricted concerns, it engages the lives of its members in multiple and diverse spheres of endeavor. Table 1 selects from this range four kinds of activity sufficiently intrinsic to gang life to qualify as "defining" criteria. These are hanging out (or hanging), mating, recreational-athletic activity, and illegal activities. Each of these forms, in turn, takes in a diversified set of subforms.

Hanging out, the central form of gang activity, is often perceived as aimless and amorphous—as "loafing" or "doing nothing" or "killing time." This perception is reinforced by the tendency of gang members themselves to characterize this activity in similar terms. Hanging out is in fact a highly complex and diversified form of activity, which includes arguing, discussing, teasing, ranking, repartee, horseplay, flirting, and gambling. Recreational activity, with its important components of athletic spectatorship and participation, is a dominant activity for gang members as it is for most American adolescents. Among the more common forms of collective recreation for both sexes are expeditions to beaches or amusement parks, dancing, and listening to popular music. Music and dancing are a persistent aspect of gang life, but the actual forms current at any time vary greatly, being highly susceptible to fashion. Mating activity—all those forms of behavior related to the process of establishing mating partnerships—is a dominant concern of the larger adolescent subculture, too.

Of all the customary activities of the street gang, illegal activity is perhaps the most misunderstood. The term "delinquent gang" is highly misleading; as generally used, it implies the existence of two distinct kinds of gangs—one whose members engage primarily or exclusively in criminal behavior and another whose members are law-abiding. In point of fact, there is no street gang whose members do not engage in some form of illegal activity, nor does specifically illegal activity comprise more than a minor portion of any gang's total range of customary activities.[19] The repertoire of illegal activities engaged in by the average gang includes various forms of theft, assault, drinking, drug use, property destruction. There is, however, wide variation in the forms and frequencies of illegal activity—among different gangs, at different age levels, in different communities, at different periods. Like tastes in popular music, preferred forms of crime are strongly influenced by fashion. For some gangs during certain periods drugs may be more fashionable than drinking, with different kinds of drugs, as well as different kinds of alcohol, moving in and out of favor. The frequency of organized intergang conflict is particularly subject to time-and-place variation; for example, the "rumble" was "in" in some cities during the 1950's, and in others in the 1970's.

Like other kinds of human groups, the street gang is characterized by internal differentiation. The differentiation may be in terms of authority, prestige, roles, or cliques. There is considerable misconception about the first of these—authority, or "leadership." Many see the "true" gang as an exemplar of autocratic despotism, with a single dictatorial leader imposing his will on compliant followers; others see it as a highly organized system of hierarchical authority, with presidents and war councillors, and the efficient execution by subordinates of decisions originating at the command level. Like other stereotypes, gangs approximating the "dictator" and "chain-of-command" conceptions do appear occasionally, but such manifestations represent extremes in a range of variation, and are far from typical. Authority or leadership in the average gang is complex, fluid and responsive, more diffuse than concentrated, and depends in large part on the particular activity being conducted.[20]

Related to but not identical with differentiation by authority is differentiation by prestige. Members of gangs are mutually evaluated with respect to ability and esteemed personal qualities.[21] Some writers have pictured the gang as a rigid and stable pecking order. While the allocation of prestige is quite sensitive, it is considerably less rigid than implied by the pecking-order image and, like leadership, may vary over time and according to situation. The gang is also differentiated by role; that is, well-defined types occur with remarkable consistency from gang to gang: the lover, the clown, the scapegoat, the battler, the operator. Finally, all gangs include cliques or subgroups of varying sizes and mutual relationships—ranging from pairs and triads to relatively stable six- to eight-person groups. Both leadership and prestige are related to one's position in a particular clique.

Variation in Gang Characteristics

Which characteristics of the youth gang remain constant, and which vary? The defining criteria are constants in a broad sense, but as we saw in the preceding section, they encompass numerous variations both over time and from place to place. Here we shall elaborate on some of these, before turning to variations in characteristics other than the defining criteria.

In a gang's total activity repertoire, hanging out is always an important component, but the frequency and duration of hanging periods show considerable variation, particularly by season. The amount of time and attention devoted to mating activity varies both by age and sex, with females devoting proportionately more attention to such activity than males and with intensified concern generally starting at an earlier age.[22]

While theft in its various forms shows a high degree of persistence as a major component of a gang's repertoire of illegal activity, certain forms of assault—particularly intergang assault—show much variation both in frequency and scope.[23] It is important to bear in mind that involvement in collective assault—like other forms of gang activity—may be more or less prevalent without reflecting the prevalence of gangs. As to the equipment of assault, weapons may or may not be used, and the kinds of weapons utilized at different times and among different gangs (zip guns, shotguns, knives, chains, clubs) may vary greatly.

Involvement by gang members in political and politically oriented activities appears to show cyclical variation in response to changes in the political climate. During most periods political activity does not play an important part in the customary activities of gangs. However, during the heyday of the big-city political machines, gang members often became involved in local political activity, acting as runners and performing a variety of tasks (posting bills, transporting voters) during election time. Not infrequently gangs were partially subsidized by local ward bosses.[24] Similarly, at the height of the black rights movement of the 1960's, some black gangs, particularly older males, became involved in a variety of activities relating to one or another of the constituent enterprises of the movement.[25]

Gangs are essentially "informal" association units; that is, their many kinds of role differentiation, leadership arrangements, subunit formation, and modes of operation are not governed by or delineated in a codified charter. Under some circumstances, however, smaller or larger parts of a gang may adopt one or more of the features of a formal organization—with codified rules and bylaws, elected officials, committees, and so on.[26] Yet, in spite of such elements, the basic congregating unit may still be readily identified as a "gang" on the basis of the defining criteria presented in the preceding section.

Variation also affects nondefining characteristics, among them *names, language, attire, size, number,* and *ethnic composition.* Gang names,[27] often colorful and striking, appear to provide a simple and obvious indication of the presence of gangs. The actual relationship of formal names to gangs is, however, quite complex. Many gangs that meet all the definitional criteria have no formal name. Some are designated by locality (the kids that hang out at Ace Variety; the gang at 12th and Poplar), others by key members (Digger and them kids). Some gangs assume a name for some purposes and not for others, or assume different names under different circumstances. Athletic teams whose membership overlaps that of a gang may assume the gang name, if there is one, or a different one. Some gangs eschew formal names for a variety of reasons (kid stuff, passé, increased vulnerability to arrest). Both the use of names and the types of names used are subject to changing fashions. When a gang decides to drop its name, outsiders may infer the dissolution of the gang, when in reality nothing has gone but the name. Gang names are in no way intrinsic to the existence of gangs.

There is little in the way of a special or distinctive gang language independent of the larger subcultural systems of which gang members are a part. Most usages current among gang members but not encountered in the schools derive from one of several subcultures, primarily those of adolescence and the social class of gang members. Grammatical usage in particular is affected by social status (lower lower class, "I seen them guys"; higher lower class, "I saw them guys"; middle class "I saw those guys"). An additional set of terms in common usage by gang members derives from the drug subculture (a bust, the fuzz) and the subculture of the prison and/or adult crime (stoolie, packing, a hustle). A further set of terms does derive primarily from gang life itself (turf, rumble, rep), but is relatively small. Like other gang characteristics, language patterns show a fascinating mixture of stability and change; some of the terms cited by Thrasher in 1927 are still current (punk, jackrolling); others are quite passé. Variations in terminology from area to area and period to period (jam, rumble, bopping, punch-up, japping, jitterbugging) have little relation, of course, to the formal features of gangs.

Persons seeking to locate or identify gangs or gang members through any distinctive "uniform" or mode of dress are generally disappointed. From time to time some article of clothing or mode of adornment becomes particularly fashionable among members of urban street gangs (pachuco marks, West Coast 1950's; leather jackets, 1950's), but such fashions are never universal, and are generally short-lived. The attire and adornment of gang members generally reflect fashions current in adolescent and lower-class subcultures and, like other "extrinsic" gang characteristics discussed here, may vary widely without affecting the formal character of the gang.

The size of gangs[28] is, of course, subject to wide variation. With respect to the lower limits of gang size, present usage would apply the term "gang" to any regularly congregating group where the potential recruitment pool numbers six or more persons; five would represent a borderline case. General statements about the upper limits of gang size are difficult to make. Gang members, for a variety of reasons, frequently make highly exaggerated claims for the size of their own and other gangs, and some observers take these at face value. The size of congregating units is elastic, depending largely on participation in particular activities. It is most unusual for the number of gang members associated with a particular "corner" or other hangout locale to exceed 100 or 120 persons, and a group of this size seldom if ever assembles at the same place at the same time. Gangs in some cities sometimes claim extensive "lateral" or cross-territorial alliances or aggregations, but these claims are usually questionable, and, even if valid, apply only to very limited kinds of association or collective endeavor.

The size of gangs in different neighborhoods, different cities, and different countries at different times is affected by many factors, including seasonal variations, birth rates, age distribution of the population, local population density, and rates of population movement. Since the propensity to form gangs is higher at lower social-status levels, one would expect to find the largest gangs in areas with relatively large lower-class populations.

Factors affecting the numbers of gangs are similar to those affecting gang size—size of local populations, age distributions, residential density, rates of population movement. Here, too, the prevalence of lower-status populations is of critical importance; roughly, the more prevalent the lower-class populations, the more gangs. The effect of public service operations on the number of gangs is poorly understood. More intensive police action in areas with larger gangs may result in a larger number of smaller congregating aggregates, thus reducing size but increasing numbers. Action by social welfare agencies appears to have limited effect on the numbers of gangs.[29]

The ethnic and/or racial composition of gangs also varies according to the kinds of demographic variables that affect size and numbers. Observers of any given period tend to relate the characteristics of gangs to those of the particular ethnic groups prominent in the urban lower class during that period. Gangs were thus seen as distinctively "Irish" or distinctively "Italian" in the late nineteenth and early twentieth century; subsequently they have been associated with urban lower-class blacks and Spanish Americans. Although the ethnic composition of particular gangs may affect some of their nondefining characteristics (Jewish gangs in the 1910's used many Yiddish phrases; Puerto Rican gangs in the 1950's spoke Spanish), it has limited influence on the form or basic pursuits of gangs. The degree to which the several ethnic populations retain lower-class status (Italians and blacks more; Jews and Japanese less) affects the number of gangs in various ethnic communities, but the general influence of ethnic status is minor compared with that of class status.

The prevalence of gangs is often misjudged because of a widespread tendency to force groups into one of two discrete and mutually exclusive categories—"gangs" and "nongangs"—depending on the presence or absence of one or more elements seen as essential to the "true" gang. Thus changes in the forms or frequencies of particular characteristics such as leadership, involvement in fighting, or modes of organization are perceived not in terms of normal variation in time and/or space, but in terms of the disappearance or emergence of the gangs themselves; typological variation is confused with existence and nonexistence. The evidence indicates, however, that core characteristics of youth gangs manifest *continuous* variation in time and from place to place without affecting their identity as gangs.

PERCEPTION AND GANG PREVALENCE

Perceptions of gang prevalence, like many other kinds of perception, are closely related to the "class" interests and subcultural concerns of persons in different age, sex, social-status, occupational, and other categories, and to the kinds of information ordinarily accessible to them. The following pages will discuss some of the influences affecting the perceptions of four categories of persons—middle-class adults, "service" personnel such as police and social workers, ex-gang members, and gang members themselves.

To the average middle-class adult the street gang is something dangerous and distasteful whose existence he would ordinarily prefer to ignore. On the other hand, the shocking and spectacular aspect of gang activities constitutes a salable product for which middle-class adults provide an important part of the market. The media, catering to a middle-class adult audience, do not report the day-to-day activities of gangs, nor pay much attention to their routine criminal involvements. Indeed, the very existence of gangs is ignored except when they manifest extreme and atypical forms of behavior such as violent conflict. This artifact of media reporting—silence during periods of ordinary gang activity and focus during times of atypical activity—fosters an impression of abrupt appearance and disappearance of gangs and, in general, a distorted and inaccurate picture of their prevalence and way of life.

Adults whose occupational responsibilities bring them in direct contact with gangs are generally in a good position to provide data with respect to gang prevalence. This is especially true of service workers such as juvenile police officers or social workers whose special area of responsibility is youth and/or gangs. However, unless a specialized research branch is available to them, their estimates as to the prevalence of gangs must be accepted with considerable caution. For such workers tend to recognize as gangs only those aggregates which are perceived as appropriate objects of the kinds of services they render; others are accorded little attention and generally do not figure in counts of gangs. In addition, a particular policeman or area social worker, while knowledgeable about the gang situation in his own district, might be poorly informed as to other districts. Unless careful counts are furnished by special administrative or research personnel, workers in local urban areas are generally unsatisfactory sources of information as to the number of gangs in the total metropolitan area, and quite unreliable as to numbers in other cities.[30]

Young adults or older adolescents who formerly belonged to gangs are often sought out as sources of information concerning gangs and gang prevalence. It would seem reasonable that their status as ex-gang members should qualify them for the role of expert—a role readily offered by adults such as reporters, social workers, and sociologists, and generally accepted with little reluctance. The kinds of information generally furnished by ex-gang members, while of considerable value, are at the same time significantly influenced by the subjectiveness of their point of view. For example, a nineteen- or twenty-year-old might say, "The gangs are all breaking up"; a twenty-three- or twenty-four-year-old, "The gangs have all broken up." What this means is that *his* gang and those of his peers have passed through the traditional developmental sequence of the adolescent street gang. He will often give reasons: all the fellows are getting jobs instead, or becoming involved in narcotics or prostitution, or getting married, or going into the service, or have just generally "wised up." These activities are perceived as newly discovered alternatives to gang life rather than as a natural consequence of moving toward adulthood.

Questioned about the "younger kids" who are still hanging out, the same person might say: "Oh, them. They ain't wised up yet. Still acting like idiots like we used to." With few exceptions, older ex-gang members insist that "gangs today" differ markedly from the gangs of their adolescence—in increased use of weapons, greater foolhardiness, less fear of authorities, and so on. Whatever the reality of actual generational changes, the perspectives of the ex-gang member are colored by a powerful perceptual process whereby changes in behavior which arise naturally from age-passage are seen as general trends which affect everybody. The character and flavor of many of his gang experiences are often recalled by him in vivid detail, but these experiences are recast into a largely ritualized framework which better serves the purposes of adulthood than those of factual accuracy. An ex-gang member generally loses real familiarity with details of the gang situation among the "younger kids" a surprisingly short time after his own gang experience has ended, even in the neighborhood he once knew most intimately.

But what of the "younger kids" themselves as a source of information? Surely it must be the gang member himself who is in the best position to provide reliable and accurate information as to the prevalence and activities of gangs. Unfortunately, this is not the case. While any informed treatment of gangs must of course ascertain and take into account the verbal testimony of gang members, it is folly to accept that testimony at face value. The capacity of the gang member to furnish accurate estimates, descriptions, or explanations is significantly affected by strong perceptual influences related to his age, his social status, his locality.

The average gang member sees himself as inhabiting a circumscribed zone of relative safety surrounded by a mysterious and menacing terrain alive with malign and threatening forces. Perception tinged by fear predisposes him to exaggerate the numbers, size, and prowess of gangs in other areas. He is an eminently parochial being, who ordinarily possesses surprisingly limited knowledge of the gang situation even in neighborhoods close to his own, let alone throughout the city.

In addition, gang members have a propensity, especially pronounced at lower-status levels, to foresee unbounded calamity in the near future. Year after year they proclaim themselves privy to absolutely reliable inside information as to unprecedented carnage or terrors about to explode. And very often there *is* trouble, some of it serious, but as a rule only a small proportion of the catastrophes predicted ever materialize.

Subculturally influenced perceptions also affect the kinds of explanations for their own behavior gang members customarily offer. Through the years gang members have been confronted with a set of standardized questions for which they have developed equally standardized answers.

Q: Why do you join gangs?
A: We *have* to! With that other gang threatening us it's a simple matter of self-defense.
Q: Why do you get in trouble?
A: Boredom! There's nothin' to *do* around here. It's so dead we get into trouble just for a little excitement.
Q: Why do you fight?
A: We gotta show *them* they can't step all over us.

It is surprising how often these traditional and ritualized "horse's mouth" explanations are sought, granted credence, and reported in all seriousness.

Another factor affecting the accuracy of information obtained from the gang member derives from his estimate of what kinds of information are appropriate for different categories of questioner. A gang member soon senses the interests of a reporter looking for a sensational feature, and will the more readily provide lurid details of enormous gangs, shocking violence, and outrageous happenings as he is eager to represent his gang as important and powerful: "We got 250 kids right here we can get together in twenty minutes, and we got branches all over the city. I'd say we got 1,000 kids altogether, maybe 2,000." The same boy might tell a policeman or attendance officer: "There's no gangs around here. We got about nine or ten kids that hang around together, but there ain't no *gangs*." Information subject both to situation-biased perception and to audience-adapted formulation must be interpreted with particular caution.

Information obtainable from each of the sources cited above—media reporters, service workers, ex-gang members, and gang members—can and do contribute valuable facets of the total picture, and it is obvious that information derived from several or all of these and similar sources will be better founded than that derived from a single source. But it is also clear that all these sources are systematically affected by particular kinds of perceptual bias, which must be corrected for. Detailed, balanced, accurate information on gangs can be obtained only through intensive systematic research conducted by highly competent personnel.

YOUTH GANGS IN THE URBAN CRISIS ERA

The 1960s marked a kind of domestic watershed in the United States. For Americans of African background this period brought an acceleration of efforts to achieve civil equality; a new militancy in the pursuit of black interests and objectives; a wave of the most extensive and destructive civil disorders in the history of the country; drastic changes in the makeup of the population of major cities and in the relation of the suburbs to the metropolis. The magnitude of these developments and the problems they posed—particularly as they affected the cities—prompted some to designate this period as the era of "urban crisis."

Among American youth, particularly college youth, opposition to the war in Southeast Asia fueled an unparalleled involvement with pacifism and associated ideological movements. There was intensified concern with social justice as it affects blacks and other groups; a heightened emphasis on "inner experience" and the value of warm interpersonal interaction, and a concomitant devaluation of "middle-class values"—achievement, material success, the prevailing technological orientation. Other important developments in the youth subculture were a marked increase in the use and acceptability of drugs of various kinds, predominantly marijuana, and increased stress on sexual freedom, with more widespread acceptance of sex relations before marriage. To some, these and related developments were of sufficient significance to merit the designation "counterculture," and some even talked of a radically new order of "consciousness" among youth of the urban crisis era.[31]

How did these developments affect the youth gangs of the United States? Some observers thought that the character of gangs had been radically transformed, others that they had become a predominantly black phenomenon; a few even believed that gangs had disappeared entirely. The following sections will explore the impact of the urban crisis on gangs.

Present-day Gangs: Prevalence and Publicity

Accurate information as to the current prevalence of gangs in the many communities of the United States is not, as noted earlier, presently available. It will be instructive, however, to examine briefly the pattern of media coverage of gangs in recent years—both because of the clues furnished by such coverage as to actual gang prevalence, and for a better understanding of the bases of media coverage.

The media during the 1950s—newspapers, magazines, television—devoted a good deal of attention to youth gangs—with New York and its "fighting gangs" a major focus. Although most research evidence indicated that gangs of this type were relatively rare both in New York and elsewhere, an impression was created that they were prevalent throughout the nation. In the early 1960s New York media attention to gangs began to wane, and by the mid-1960s had ceased almost entirely—a trend paralleled in the national media. This period of low media attention fostered a belief in some quarters that gangs had died out entirely, or at least experienced a major change in behavior.

In the early 1970s the New York media rediscovered the youth gang. Initially attention was confined to particular areas and types of gangs (August 1970: "Wave of Youth Gang Wars in Chinatown"; November 1971: "The Rat Packs of New York"), but by 1972 the rediscovery had burst into full flower. A March 1972 story in the *New York Times,* reporting a killing in a fight between the "Savage Nomads" and the "Galaxies," stated that there were 100 violent gangs in the South Bronx, and a few weeks later *New York* magazine, in a story bannered "Are You Ready for the New Violence?" officially announced the "Return of the New York Street Gangs."

It is clear that the gangs lost and then regained the attention of the New York media, but had they actually disappeared? Just over one year prior to the *Times* report of 100 gangs in the Bronx and many more in other boroughs, police and Youth Agency officials stated conclusively that the last gang had disappeared from the streets of the city, and that there was *no* gang problem in New York.[32] Assuming that it is unlikely that the number of gangs in the South Bronx grew from zero to 100 in a year's time, how can the sudden "reemergence" of the gangs be explained?

The condition allowing city officials to claim that there were no gangs, and allowing the media to reflect this claim, was the adoption by officials of a special and restricted definition of gangs. In the early 1960s the pattern of names, jackets, and large-scale fighting which had received so much publicity during the 1950s was essentially abandoned in those areas where it had been adopted. But despite changes in these fashion-susceptible practices, gangs, as defined here, remained prevalent.[33] By choosing to regard as gangs only those groups which exhibited characteristics of the outmoded pattern of the 1950s, officials with an interest in controlling gangs were able to proclaim their elimination during the very period when messages were being dispatched to New York patrolmen informing them that "disorderly groups of youths are in the streets fighting with knives."

Apart from New York, the city with the most intensive media coverage has been Philadelphia, where headlines proclaimed, in 1965: "245 Teenage Gangs Roaming City; 49 Capable of Killing"; 1969: "Teen Gang Carnage Reaches Peak; 47 Dead, 519 Injured in 17 Months"; 1972: "Is There No Way to Halt the Mad Violence of Gangs?" In Chicago major press attention in the 1960s focused on a few well-publicized "politicized" gangs. In Los Angeles the media maintained fairly consistent if not extensive coverage of gangs (1969: "Mexican-Americans, Negroes Clash Again"), but in the early 1970s a series of highly publicized gang-connected killings sparked an upsurge in media attention resembling New York's.[34] Stories about gangs have also appeared in the press of Baltimore, Indianapolis, Milwaukee, San Francisco (Chinese gangs), and Newark, but no clear pattern is evident with respect to other major cities. Groups of three to six or more youthful thieves or muggers have received attention in a number of cities—notably Washington, D.C., but the media generally do not apply the term "gang" to such groups.[35] Why the media cover gangs in some cities but not in others, the basis for coverage when it occurs, the relation between the actual gang situation and what the press reports—all these are questions to which we have only partial answers.

During the 1950s the domestic scene in the United States was relatively peaceful, and against this backdrop gang fighting provided the media with one of the more newsworthy forms of domestic violence. In the 1960s, however, gangs and their activities were, in effect, driven off the front pages by the advent of far more serious and spectacular forms of domestic violence—massive urban riots, dramatic student demonstrations, armed conflict between police and black militants, and, later in this period, a wave of ideologically motivated bombings and other forms of terrorism.

By the 1970s, despite unequivocal predictions that each of these forms of violence represented the start of a continuing or increasing national trend, they had subsided sufficiently to draw little media attention, and the media returned once again to publicizing the activities of the ever-present youth gangs. While the absence of media coverage in a particular locality does not necessarily mean that gangs are absent, coverage almost certainly indicates well-developed gangs. On the basis of evidence both from the media and other sources, it would appear that of the nation's ten largest cities, gangs are numerous and active in the four largest—New York, Chicago, Los Angeles, and Philadelphia. Of the remaining six, evidence of gangs is convincing for Baltimore and Washington, and absent or ambiguous for Detroit, Houston, Dallas, and Indianapolis.

More direct evidence from two urban areas, Philadelphia and Boston, provides an opportunity to compare information available through public sources with research findings based on direct field reports. In Philadelphia gangs are well publicized by the media; in Boston, virtually ignored. What do the field data show?

In August 1970 a major Philadelphia daily averaged one youth gang story every two days, and several front-page headlines concerned gangs. With good reason. The Philadelphia area in the latter 1960s and early 1970s was swarming with youth gangs of every description—large and small, violent and peaceful, male and female, black and white. In 1969 a crime commission concluded that there were in municipal Philadelphia about seventy-five gangs, mostly black, comprising about 3,500 members, sufficiently "active" (primarily in fighting) to be of continued concern to the police.[36] Social agencies put the estimated number of gangs at about 200.

Between October 1962 and December 1968, gang members were reportedly involved in 257 shootings, 250 stabbings, and 205 "rumbles." Between January 1968 and June 1969, 54 homicides and over 250 injuries were attributed to armed conflict between gangs. Assailants ranged in age from thirteen to twenty, with 70 percent between sixteen and eighteen. Only a minority of these gangs bore names, the majority being designated according to their major congregation corner (12th and Poplar; 21W's, for 21st and Westmoreland). In the year following the crime commission report, the number of "active" gangs estimated by the police increased from seventy-five to ninety, and the number of gang members from 3,500 to 5,000.[37] Moreover, the rate of gang-connected homicides established in 1968 and 1969—three per month—continued at a similar or higher level during the next three years.

It is important to note that the Philadelphia gangs responsible for so striking a record of violent assault do not conform to the *West Side Story* image of the "fighting gang" of the 1950s. Most gangs do not have names. There are no gang jackets. There is little evidence that gangs are specifically "organized for conflict," or even "organized," in the sense of having formalized chain-of-command titles ("warlord" etc.), specialization of function, and the like. Instead, the Philadelphia gangs in most significant respects approximate the classic corner groups of the 1910–1960 period, whose major defining criteria are summarized in Table 1. Intergang fighting appears as only one of a range of gang activities—an activity pursued by different gangs with greater or lesser frequency, and with more or less serious consequences.[38]

A particularly interesting aspect of the Philadelphia gang situation concerns its relation to the racial issues of the urban crisis era. The great majority of the more violent gangs in Philadelphia are black, during a period when issues involving race relations have been more of a national focus, and more highly charged, than at any time since the Civil War. Given this ideological climate, one would expect that the major conflicts would pit blacks against whites—particularly in a city where migration patterns and the spatial distribution of the races appear to create so fertile a climate for interracial conflict. Instead, the great bulk of gang clashes involve blacks versus blacks, and the great bulk of injuries and homicides involve black perpetrators and black victims.

The reasons advanced for involvement in gang fighting have few ideological overtones; they are, rather, the traditional ones—territorial defense, maintenance of personal and collective honor, and achieving prestige by besting one's peers. Similarly, the actual conduct of gang fighting generally follows the classic pattern of provocation, attack, and counterattack, also described as traditional.[39] Few engagements between gang members involve massed encounters with large numbers of participants, possibly including allies. They generally take the more traditional form of gangster-style attacks by passing assailants (sometimes in cars) on single or paired members of rival gangs. One aspect of the Philadelphia situation does differ clearly from many past situations: firearms are widely used; the shotgun is a favored weapon. It is this fact, in all likelihood, rather than any special viciousness or bloodlust on the part of Philadelphia youth, that accounts for the high incidence of gang-related homicides in Philadelphia.

It must be emphasized that the gangs involved in violent conflict, however well publicized locally, comprise only a minority of Philadelphia's youth gangs. Field research shows that scores of street corners, parks, and schoolyards throughout the city provide hangouts for a wide variety of less violent gangs, whose activities, nonetheless, are regarded with dismay by local householders and businessmen. Pursuing the practices of the classic youth gangs discussed earlier, and of concern to local police less for homicide and armed conflict than for vandalism, drinking, and general disturbance, these gangs are not confined to the central city, but abound in inner suburbs, some of which have long been considered among the "better" residential sections of the city. Moreover, youth gangs are prevalent in scores of outer suburbs as well. Since these are predominantly white, the gangs are predominantly white, although black gangs are not uncommon in some of the larger ring cities such as Reading, Norristown, and Pottstown.

The most extensive current survey of gangs in a major urban region covers the area of metropolitan Boston.[40] This area contains ninety-four cities, towns, and urban districts, each with its own name and police headquarters. Fifteen of these are named districts of municipal Boston (pop. 20,000–100,000); thirty-seven are incorporated cities and towns (pop. 20,000–100,000), located for the most part within an "inner" metropolitan zone beyond municipal limits; forty-two are towns (pop. 2,500–20,000), located in an "outer" metropolitan zone.[41] Between 1965 and 1971 information as to the presence of gangs was collected on a continuing basis for all ninety-four communities. Data were obtained through a variety of sources, with primary reliance on direct field observation and routine police reports.

What is the youth gang situation in the many communities of the metropolitan area? In municipal Boston itself, gangs are present in all fifteen districts. They are, in general, more numerous, active, and better-developed in lower-status areas. The district with the most persistent tradition of active gangs is not black; it is, rather, the predominantly Irish district of South Boston, past homesite of the Kennedys, McCormicks, and other eminent political families. In fact, in contrast to Philadelphia, where gangs are clearly most numerous in black neighborhoods, gangs in Roxbury, Boston's best-known black district, are considerably less active than gangs in lower-status white districts such as East Boston, Charlestown, and South Boston.

The pattern of gang-connected youth offenses—those forms of gang activity which routinely call forth police action—shows a high degree of stability over a five-year study period. The most common offense is "creating a disturbance"—roughhousing, obscene conversation, impeding public passage, and the like. Next most common are relatively mild forms of assault and property damage—stoning passing vehicles, small-scale set-tos, breaking school windows. Third and fourth are drinking and theft of various kinds, such as stripping autos and ransacking public buildings. Gang fighting follows the "traditional" pattern; that is, it occurs with some frequency and regularity when viewed as a city-wide phenomenon (although rather rarely from the point of view of the life history of particular gangs), but seldom results in serious injuries or commands much general notice. One major reason is that the use of firearms is rare; stones, sticks, clubs, and fists still comprise the main weapons. It is likewise of interest that during a period of increasing drug use by adolescents, use of or involvement with drugs only rarely provides a basis for police action with respect to gangs.

It is striking that gangs are present in every one of the thirty-seven cities outside municipal Boston. As in the urban center itself, gangs are more prevalent, active, and better developed in cities with larger lower-status populations and, within these cities, in lower-status neighborhoods. The pattern of offenses dealt with by the police also resembles that of the main urban center, drug use seldom providing a basis for police action.

The forty-two communities with populations of 2,500 to 20,000 vary widely, ranging from small residential villages with predominantly higher-status populations to industrial towns with sizable working-class populations. The gang situation presents a correspondingly mixed picture. Recurrently congregating groups occur in about half the communities. None of the gangs are black, since the population in this suburban zone is about 95 percent white, and children of local black residents are unlikely to form part of local adolescent groups. The pattern of youth group offenses dealt with by police resembles that already described, with the less serious forms of group disturbance constituting a relatively higher proportion of police-handled offenses; action involving drugs, while still infrequent, is somewhat more common than in the more urbanized areas.

In many of these communities, as well as in the urban-ring cities and towns, the shopping plaza has replaced the street corner for youth gangs, thus inheriting many of the problems traditionally associated with the "kids on the corner" in the cities. And this phenomenon is hardly confined to the Boston area; in fact, the suburban supermarket or shopping-mall youth gang has become highly prevalent throughout the nation.[42]

A comparison of the gang situation in Philadelphia and Boston suggests several important conclusions with respect to gangs and information about gangs in the United States today. The two metropolitan areas resemble each other in that youth gangs in large numbers and of a wide variety are present in both, with locality-based groups most common; patterns of gang activity in the scores of communities surrounding the major urban center resemble those of the center itself; gangs are more in evidence in lower-status communities; congregation patterns in the suburbs of the two areas are very similar; the racial and ethnic composition of the gangs reflects that of their local communities. On the other hand, gangs are predominantly black in municipal Philadelphia, predominantly white in municipal Boston; and whereas a minority in a relatively small proportion of Philadelphia gangs have engaged in violent intergang combat resulting in a large number of gang-related homicides, the fighting activities of the Boston gangs have seldom been lethal and have produced no widely publicized homicides in recent years. The primary differentiating factor, then, lies not in the presence, numbers, or distribution of gangs in the two urban areas, but, rather, in the frequency and severity of gang-connected violence.

It is this factor, primarily, which accounts for the striking difference between the two cities in the availability of information about gangs. Even a casual reader of the Philadelphia dailies is well aware that gangs are numerous and active in the city; even the most careful reader of the Boston dailies has no idea whatever, unless he has access to other sources, that literally hundreds of youth gangs are present both in the municipal city and in over fifty of the nearby suburban communities. The conclusion must be drawn that while continuing media coverage of gangs is virtually always an accurate indication that gangs *are* present (and generally in larger numbers than indicated by the media), the absence of media coverage is by no means an accurate indication that gangs are *not* present, for gangs can flourish in an urban area in the complete absence of media attention. That the media ordinarily give no hint of the existence of gangs in Boston suggests that a similar situation might well obtain in cities like Detroit, Cleveland, and Houston, where gangs are similarly ignored by the media.

Change and Continuity: Is There a "New Gang"?

There is a tendency, when attempting to explain social phenomena, to assign disproportionate weight to contemporary developments. Thus youth gangs in the late 1800s were seen as a direct product of massive waves of foreign immigration; in the 1930s, as one of the results of a grave national economic depression; in the 1940s and 1950s, as a consequence of basic changes in the family unit.

In the urban crisis era, there are those who feel that contemporary events have affected gangs so fundamentally that continuity with the past has been drastically weakened or even lost.[43] Three developments in particular have been adduced to account for the emergence of the "new" gang: increased militancy and readiness to employ force by urban blacks; increased political and/or ideological activism by residents of low-status communities; and increased use of drugs among adolescents, accompanied in some instances by a "countercultural" ideological perspective.

Since these developments directly involve groups—the young, urbanites, and low-status populations—whose circumstances affect the existence and nature of gangs, they could scarcely fail to have an impact on present-day gangs. But the issue here is not whether they have had any impact, but rather whether that impact has been sufficient to justify one's speaking of a "new" gang, whose form, orientation, and customary pursuits represent a sharp break with the past. The following sections will consider these developments in their effect on gangs.

TRANSFORMATION THROUGH PROTEST: YOUTH GANGS AND CIVIL DISOR-DERS. Chief among the forms of domestic violence which marked the urban crisis era was a kind of collective social event designated, in formal terms, as a "civil disturbance" or "civil disorder" and, less formally, as "rioting." The basic pattern was set in 1963 and 1964; the rioting reached a peak in 1967–1968, and diminished thereafter. The disorders ranged from massive outbreaks involving scores of deaths, countless injuries, and extensive property damage, to small-scale commotions scarcely distinguishable from routine slum-life disturbances. They were the subject of voluminous reports by many writers, several governmental commissions, and dozens of social analysts.[44]

What part did youth gangs play in the disorders? Participation by youth gangs in urban rioting is nothing new; the activities of gangs during the "race riot" period of 1915–1919, in particular, have been well documented.[45] The basic and most obvious fact about gangs and riots in the urban crisis era is that both the locale of the major riots (urban slum areas) and the social characteristics of the most active rioters (male youths and young adults) are coterminous with those of the classic urban youth gang. The riots occurred in their own home territory; the gangs were there, the riots were there, and hundreds of groups of black males were clearly in evidence, active and ubiquitous.

The character of gang participation in the rioting—what gang members did as well as what they did not do—deserves attention because of the light it throws on the nature both of the gangs and of the rioting. In virtually no instance did the gangs "start" the rioting—either in the sense that they agitated actively for the advent of riot conditions, or that incidents involving gangs served as major trigger events.[46] Once the riots were under way, however, gang members were among the most ardent and energetic participants.

The zeal of gang participation in the riots should come as no surprise. To the average member of the average black gang the riot represented an extraordinary convergence of desirable conditions—people milling in the streets, buildings in flames, police and fire vehicles rushing to and fro, the crash of breaking glass, the hubbub of police radios, the unstilled clangor of unattended burglar alarms. Observers of gang behavior during the rioting were struck by what appeared as a current of enormous excitement—an almost ecstatic perception that all things were possible, and all delights within grasp. It was the sense conveyed in certain ritualized events—the bacchanalia, the mardi gras, the corroborree—when ordinary rules of conduct are suspended and one is granted special license to pursue with fervor what is denied in ordinary times. Even where the triggering incident was most unequivocally perceived as a racial affront, the dominant emotions of most gang members appeared to be closer to elation than anger.[47]

Analyses based primarily on a careful examination of the forms and frequencies of gang-member activity during the riots reveals a degree of regularity, rationality, and patterning which does not accord with a conception of youthful riot behavior as an irrational and uncontrolled outburst of long-suppressed emotions. The targets of theft, assault, and property destruction reflect a process guided by orderly principles of selection. In particular, riot-period gang behavior does not support the thesis that racial hatred was the dominant motive for the rioting. Racial hostility was clearly a significant factor, but it was only one of a complex of motives, many of them common to American youth of all racial and ethnic backgrounds. Moreover, to those familiar with the behavior of urban low-status youth in ordinary times, the riot-period behavior of gang members seemed less a unique condition than a logically continuous extension of customary motives and concerns. Of course, riot conditions provided an extraordinary climate of opportunity for the actualization of those concerns, but the fact that gang members chose to pursue more avidly during the riots the same kinds of ends they ordinarily pursue attests to the enormous influence of motives derived from their subcultural status as males, as adolescents, as city dwellers, and as residents of low-status communities. Rather than releasing some radically new or untapped source of motive energy, the riot experience served to illuminate with great clarity the potency of those forces which engender gang behavior during ordinary times.

TRANSFORMATION THROUGH COMMITMENT: GANGS AND POLITICAL ACTIVISM. The notion of "transforming" gangs by diverting their energies from traditional forms of gang activity—particularly illegal forms—and channeling them into "constructive" activities is probably as old, in the United States, as gangs themselves. Thus, in the 1960's, when a series of social movements aimed at elevating the lot of the poor through ideologically oriented, citizen-executed political activism became widely current, it was perhaps inevitable that the idea be applied to gangs. Two major models of activism existed—a more radical "militant" model, which saw gangs as a spearhead in the attempt to undermine established sources of power (often white power), and a less radical "social betterment" model, which conceived gangs as the basis of a kind of indigenous community-service enterprise. The simplicity of this notion, and the obvious desirability of social/political activism by low-income citizens, impelled many to predict—and some to assert the existence of—a new type of "politicized" gang, replacing the "conflict" gang of the past.[48]

Prominent among the groups publicized were, on the "militant" model, the Black Panthers (black) and the Young Lords (Hispanic); on the "social betterment" model, the Blackstone Rangers and Devils Disciples of Chicago and the Real Great Society of New York.[49] But the predicted transformation of American youth gangs never occurred. Even during the peak period of politicization, the actual proportion of youth gangs involved was small, with the great majority of gang youth remaining essentially unaffected by political/social activism. Even among those most affected, there is little evidence that activism *replaced* illegal and/or violent pursuits; rather, traditional activities such as theft, assault, extortion, and various "hustles" were carried on in conjunction with, and frequently as an intrinsic part of, political and social reform undertakings.[50]

Moreover, even in the areas most affected, politicization appears as a relatively short-lived development. By the early 1970s, for example, in those areas of Philadelphia and New York where hopes had been highest that political activism would replace gang fighting, levels of lethal intergang conflict were high or even increasing. Furthermore, even at its height, political activism and its associated ideologies had very little impact on the average "prime-age" gang member. While the prime age for male gang involvement in most localities runs from about thirteen to eighteen,[51] all but a few of the publicized politicized gangs were composed largely of young men in their twenties or even thirties. Often the politicized gang was *not* the product of a direct progression by an established prime-age gang from traditional to political activities; instead, older males, generally with prime-age experience in other gangs, frequently assumed leadership in new groups after a period of separation from gang life as such.

By far the greatest amount of publicity concerning political activism by gangs centered on Chicago. During the 1965–1970 period the Chicago police estimated that there were approximately 900 "youth groups" in the city, of which about 200 were sufficiently troublesome to be designated "gangs," and about twenty difficult enough to be termed "hard core."[52] A generous estimate of the number of identifiable units and/or subdivisions affiliated in some manner with the major politicized gangs in Chicago (Rangers, Disciples, Vice Lords, a few others) would indicate something on the order of eighty units—less than 10 percent of the total number of youth gang units in the city. Thus, if during the heyday of the politicized gang in the city with the highest number of such gangs, about 90 percent were *not* significantly involved in political activism, the politicization of the gang could hardly be said to represent a major national development.

One product of the civil rights movement was the addition of a new kind of *justificatory vocabulary* to the traditional modes for explaining gang activity.[53] This new vocabulary incorporated basic ideological tenets of the black rights movement and applied to customary forms of gang behavior concepts such as exploitation by the power structure, restitution for past injustices, and brutalization by the system.[54] But verbal behavior must be distinguished from actual practice. By and large, black gang members continued to do the kinds of things they had always done.

TRANSFORMATION THROUGH ENHANCED EXPERIENCE: GANGS AND DRUG USE. Given the widespread perception that "drug abuse" had become endemic among youth, it was perhaps inevitable that the phenomenon should be linked with youth gangs. In fact, the prospect of increased drug use by gang members was suggested as early as the 1950s, but, like the predicted emergence of the "politicized" gang, that of "drug-using" or "drug-addicted" gangs failed to materialize, although a relatively small proportion of all gangs do use drugs.[55]

During the urban crisis era, drug use figured prominently in an elaborate explanation of both the death *and* rebirth of the "fighting gang." According to this explanation, the fighting gangs of the 1950s were knocked out by the advent of hard drugs—particularly heroin, taken primarily out of frustration engendered by the exclusionism of a discriminatory society. Then in the 1960s, through the civil rights movement, gang members came to realize that one *could* take action against the system instead of retreating into drugs, that the drug traffic was another means used by the power structure to exploit the poor, and that it served the interests of the establishment to cripple potential activists by pressing them into addiction. By the late 1960s, increasingly disheartened by the apparently deliberate ineffectiveness of officialdom, gang members decided to take upon themselves the policing functions necessary to purge their communities of drugs. However, rather than devote their aggressive energies to driving out the pushers and exposing corrupt police- men, they began to direct them instead—for reasons not fully understood— toward their fellow gang members. Thus occurred a rebirth of a pattern of intergang violence much like the one abandoned ten years before—with frustration-engendered violence intensified, if anything, by the failure of the recently attempted activism to effect any really significant changes in the social order. The need for devising this rather imaginative scenario—fighting gang to narcoticized gang to politicized gang to fighting gang in ten years— arose, as shown earlier, from a prevalent impression that gangs had somehow flourished, been knocked out, and then revived—an impression not supported by available evidence.

Far from stimulating the emergence of new or markedly different kinds of gangs, or undermining the bases of gang formation itself, the increased availability of certain drugs appears to have fitted readily into an established niche. The "versatile repertoire" of gang activities noted earlier traditionally involves the use of what might be called "experience-enhancing" substances— substances serving to heighten the excitement of participation in recreational and other activities. The average gang member wants something easy to get, which will provide a quick but not too potent "high" at minimum cost. Traditionally this demand has been met primarily by alcohol, especially beer. However, use of drug and/or narcotic substances (particularly pill-popping, glue sniffing, "bennies," cough medicine containing codeine) has been familiar to gang members in many locales for a long time.[56] Many gangs have employed a pragmatic mix of alcohol and drugs. A major consequence of the increasing acceptability of drug use among adolescents (principally marijua- na) and the concomitant increased availability of certain drugs (again, primarily marijuana) has been to increase the proportion of drugs to alcohol in the drug-alcohol mix of many gangs.

What is the relationship of gang-member drug use to other forms of crime? Two apparently inconsistent positions are current. The first sees drug use as inhibiting crime, the second as enhancing it. The inhibition thesis is that drug use serves as a surrogate for more serious forms of crime, in that drug users are generally content with legally benign activities such as rapping, whereas alcohol serves to spur more aggressive activities such as fighting. The enhancement position is that the use of relatively inexpensive "soft" drugs inevitably leads to costly "hard" drugs and the necessity to engage in serious crimes in order to support a drug habit. Whatever the validity of the inhibition and the enhancement positions, they appear to have little application to gang-member crime. Certainly the contemporary gangs of Philadelphia, the Bronx, and Los Angeles are not abstaining from violence as a consequence of drug use (inhibition position), and there is little evidence linking rising rates of robbery and burglary with increases in the use of drugs by gang members (enhancement position). But evidence in this area is fragmentary.

Conclusion: Cyclical Elaboration and Perceptions of Newness

The major developments of the urban crisis era would appear to have had an unusual potential for altering established societal forms. Yet this paper has concluded that none had very much impact on American youth gangs. Both at the beginning of the period and at the end, youth gangs, some quite violent, flourished throughout the nation, particularly in the slum areas of the largest urban centers. The basic forms and characteristic pursuits of these gangs—while certainly reflecting the changing fashions of the larger adolescent subculture—showed a high degree of continuity. If one grants validity to this conclusion, two additional questions at once present themselves. First, why do gangs persist, and why do their characteristic pursuits retain considerable stability under changing circumstances? And, second, how can one account for recurring representations that gangs have changed radically or even disappeared altogether?

Answers to the first question can be presented here only in the most summary form. The youth gang persists because it is a product of conditions basic to our social order. Among these conditions are division of labor between the family and the peer group in the socialization of adolescents; emphasis on masculinity and collective action in the male subculture; stress on excitement, congregation, and mating in the adolescent subculture; the importance of toughness and smartness in the subcultures of lower-status populations; and the density conditions and territoriality patterns affecting the subcultures of urban and urbanized locales. It is these social conditions and their related subcultures which generate the American youth gang, and insofar as they persist, the gang, too, persists.

How, then, account for recurring perceptions that gangs come and go, and that current manifestations represent new forms? The average youth gang, as has been shown, is a generalized rather than a specialized form, with a versatile rather than a constricted repertoire of activities. Gangs, like other generalized and versatile societal forms, are sensitive to a wide variety of environmental developments, which are reflected in periodic modifications in their characteristics.[57] These modifications, however, are for the most part stylistic elaborations of existing forms, rather than genuinely original additions to or changes in traditional features.

The fate of these elaborations varies. In some instances they remain localized; in others they spread to gangs in other areas through media publicization and other means. In the 1950s some gangs in other cities in varying degrees emulated the New York fighting-gang model; in the 1970s some New York gangs began to pursue the intensified patterns of homicide by firearms evolved in Philadelphia some five years before. The bulk of the elaborations are relatively short-lived, for as a rule, gangs do not long sustain elaborations which interfere substantially with their customary patterns of activity.

Once certain types of elaboration achieve a sufficient degree of development, they begin to engage the attention of societal agencies, to whose characteristic reactions gangs respond in turn in a complex process of mutual feedback. Among these agencies are agencies of control (police, probation agents), social service (social workers, youth workers), and government (elected officials, bureau personnel). Agencies whose responses bear most directly on the perception-of-newness phenomena are the communications/information specialists, to whom "newness" is money in the bank. These specialists typically represent contemporary elaborations either as the emergence of previously nonexistent forms or as the advent of *the* new type of gang of our times. Meanwhile youth gangs are continually scanning, selecting from, modifying, and absorbing available subcultural materials, and as the new gang of today's writer becomes the old gang of tomorrow's historian, continue to thrive as a vital and adaptive form.

NOTES

1. See Malcolm Klein, *Street Gangs and Street Workers* (Englewood Cliffs, N.J.: Prentice-Hall, 1971), pp. 13–14; M. Klein, "Violence in American Juvenile Gangs," in D. Mulvihill and M. Tumin, *Crimes of Violence* (National Commission on Causes and Prevention of Violence, 1969), 13, p. 1428.

2. See Frederick Thrasher, *The Gang* (Chicago: University of Chicago Press, 1927), p. 45.

3. W. B. Miller, *City Gangs* (New York: Wiley, in preparation).

4. ———, "Criminal Justice and Ideology," Robert A. Pinkerton Memorial Lecture, May 1972.

5. James F. Short, Jr. (ed.), *Gang Delinquency and Delinquent Subcultures* (New York: Harper & Row, 1968), p. 10.

6. About 100 published titles on gangs in the Chicago area are listed in Dorothy C. Tompkins, *Juvenile Gangs and Street Groups—A Bibliography* (Berkeley: University of California, Institute of Governmental Studies, 1966), pp. 36–47. See also Thrasher, *op. cit.*; Clifford R. Shaw, *Delinquency Areas* (Chicago: University of Chicago Press, 1929); Solomon Kobrin, "The Chicago Area Project—A 25-Year Assessment," *Annals of the American Academy of Political and Social Science*, 322 (March 1959), pp. 19–29; James F. Short, Jr., "The Nature of Street Corner Groups: Theory and Research Design," *Chicago Youth Studies Program*, Spring 1960; Gerald Suttles, *The Social Order of the Slum: Ethnicity and Territory in the Inner City* (Chicago: University of Chicago Press, 1968).

7. Published materials based on New York gangs are listed in Tompkins, *op. cit.*, pp. 55–67.

8. See Klein, 1971, *op. cit.*, pp. 15–18.

9. Besides drawing on a wide range of published materials, this paper bases its conclusions on (1) a ten-year study of youth gangs in an inner-city district of Boston; (2) a five-year study of urban and suburban delinquency in 94 communities of the Boston metropolitan area, sponsored by the M.I.T.-Harvard Joint Center for Urban Studies; (3) visits of varying lengths to about 220 urban-area communities in 21 states, the most extensive to the Philadelphia and Albany-Troy-Schenectady areas.

10. The first major sociological effort to define "gang" is that by Thrasher (*op. cit.*, chap. 3), from whom most of the quoted phrases are taken.

11. See Tompkins, *op. cit.*; William Kirkwood, Jr., "Delinquent Gangs: A Selected Bibliography," in *International Bibliography of Crime and Delinquency* (Washington, D.C.: U.S. Department of Health, Education and Welfare, vol. 3, August 1966).

12. See Peter Scott, "Gangs and Delinquent Groups in London," *British Journal of Delinquency*, 7 (July 1956); Lewis Yablonsky, "The Delinquent Gang as a Near-Group," *Social Problems*, 7 (Fall 1959); Howard L. and Barbara G. Meyerhoffs, "Field Observations of Middle Class Gangs," *Social Forces*, 42 (March 1964); Gerald D. Robin, "A Study of Delinquency of Gangs and Conflict Group Members," Department of Sociology, University of Pennsylvania, mim., n.d.; Bernard Cohen, "The Delinquency of Gangs and Spontaneous Groups," in T. Sellin and M. Wolfgang (eds.), *Delinquency: Selected Studies* (New York: Wiley, 1969); Klein, 1969, *op. cit.*, especially pp. 1427–1428.

13. The terms "aggregate" for the larger group and "segment" for subgroups were introduced in 1957 (W. B. Miller, "The Impact of a Community Group Work Program on Delinquent Corner Groups," *Social Service Review*, 31 [December 1957], p. 398). The present paper for the most part uses the term "subdivision," but other writers favor the terms "division," "clique" (also used to designate the more inclusive group), "faction," "age-level," "age-grade," "branch," "affiliate," or "auxiliary."

14. Miller, *City Gangs*, *op. cit.*, "The Corner Gangs of Midcity."

15. W. B. Miller, "Lower Class Culture as a Generating Milieu of Gang Delinquency," *Journal of Social Issues*, 14 (1958), pp. 5–19.

16. According to the author's field research, membership continuity for shorter periods is on the order of 80–85 per cent, and for longer periods on the order of 70–80 per cent.

17. See Theodore Goldberg, "The Automobile: A Social Institution for Adolescents," *Environment and Behavior*, December 1969.

18. See Robert Ardrey, *The Territorial Imperative* (New York: Atheneum, 1966) and David Davis, "The Phylogeny of Gangs," in E. L. Bliss (ed.), *Roots of Behavior* (New York: Harper & Row, 1962).

19. Statistics bearing on the proportion of illegal to legal forms in the behavioral repertoire of gangs may be found in Miller, *City Gangs*, *op. cit.*, "Theft Behavior," "Assaultive Behavior," "The Patterning of Illegal Behavior." See also statistics relative to "assault-oriented behavior" in W. B. Miller, "Violent Crimes in City Gangs," *Annals of the American Academy of Political and Social Science*, 364 (March 1966), pp. 100–101.

20. Klein, 1971, *op. cit.*, pp. 91–99; Miller, 1957, *op. cit.*, p. 402; Miller, 1969, *op. cit.*

21. Miller, 1958, *op. cit.*; (W. B. Miller, H. Geertz, and H. S. G. Cutter, "Aggression in a Boys' Street Corner Group," *Psychiatry*, 24 (1961); Bertram Spiller, "Bases of Prestige Among High and Low Delinquent Street-Corner Groups," unpublished Ph.D. dissertation, Sociology Department, Boston University, 1961; Spiller, "Delinquency and Middle-Class Goals," *Journal of Criminal Law*, 56 (December 1965), pp. 463–478.

22. Miller, *City Gangs*, *op. cit.*, "Female Sexual and Mating Behavior," "Male Sexual and Mating Behavior."

23. See references cited in note 19. Also Miller, in Klein, 1967, *op. cit.*

24. See Thrasher, *op. cit.*, pp. 452–486.

25. See Richard W. Poston, *The Gang and the Establishment* (New York: Harper & Row, 1971).

26. See W. B. Miller, "The Place of the Organized Club in Corner-Group Work Method," Boston Youth Project, 1956; Miller, 1957, op. cit., pp. 403–405; Nadine Brozan, "For Hundreds of Girls in the City, Street Gangs Offer a Way of Life," New York Times, May 9, 1972, p. 48.

27. Thrasher, op. cit., p. 257; Ruth Shonle Cavan, Juvenile Delinquency: Development, Treatment, Control (Philadelphia: Lippincott, 1969), p. 269; Klein, 1971, op. cit., pp. 105–106.

28. See Klein, in Mulvihill and Tumin, op. cit., p. 1432; also Klein, 1971, op. cit., chap. 3.

29. See Klein, in Mulvihill and Tumin, op. cit., p. 1453.

30. Police department files on gang control have been used by several researchers; see Robin, op. cit., and Cohen, in Sellin and Wolfgang, op. cit. See also Solomon Kobrin, "Sociological Aspects of the Development of a Street-Corner Group," American Journal of Orthopsychiatry (October 1961), and T. M. Gannon, "Dimensions of Current Gang Delinquency," Journal of Research in Crime and Delinquency, 4 (January 1967).

31. See Theodore Roszak, The Making of a Counter Culture: Reflections on the Technocratic Society and Its Youthful Opposition (Garden City, N.Y.: Doubleday, 1969), and Charles A. Reich, The Greening of America (New York: Random House, 1970). See also Philip Nobile (ed.), The Con III Controversy: The Critics Look at the Greening of America (New York: Pocket Books, 1971).

32. Interviews with officials of the New York City Police Department, Planning Division, and of the Youth Services Agency of the Human Resources Administration, November 1970.

33. Direct field observation by the author, conducted in conjunction with police radio reports.

34. D. Janson, "Violence by Youth Gangs Found Rising in Three Cities," New York Times, April 15, 1972.

35. See Shane Stevens, "The 'Rat Packs' of New York," New York Times Magazine, November 28, 1971; and G. Rae, "Rat Packs," Man, (Spring 1972).

36. Gang Violence in Philadelphia (Harrisburg, Pa.: Pennsylvania Crime Commission, Department of Justice, July 31, 1969).

37. Testimony by Police Commissioner Frank L. Rizzo to U.S. House of Representatives Select Committee on Crime, reported in the Philadelphia Bulletin, July 16, 1970, p. 1.

38. Gang Violence in Philadelphia, op. cit., p. 5.

39. Miller, 1957, op. cit., pp. 398–399; Miller, 1958, op. cit., pp. 17–18; Miller, 1966, op. cit., p. 110. See also Klein, in Mulvihill and Tumin, op. cit., p. 1449.

40. So far as is known, the present report on gangs in the Boston metropolitan area is the first published report based on a survey of all named communities in a Standard Metropolitan Statistical Area as defined by the U.S. Bureau of the Census.

41. See U.S. Bureau of the Census, Census of Population, and Housing: PHC (1)–18, Census Tracts, 1960 (Washington, D.C.: U.S. Government Printing Office). Categorization of towns and cities was based on population counts of the Federal Census of 1960 and the Massachusetts State Census of 1965.

42. See Seth L. King, "Supermarkets Hub of Suburbs," New York Times, February 7, 1971.

43. See, for example, Lewis Yablonsky, The Violent Gang (New York: Macmillan, 1963), especially chap. 1; Gannon, op. cit.; Poston, op. cit.; R. Bragonier, "A New-Style City Gang," Life, August 25, 1972; G. Weingarten, "East Bronx Story: Return of the Street Gangs," New York, March 27, 1972. See also the balanced treatment by Klein, 1971, op. cit., p. 20.

44. Selected studies and reports include S. Lachman and B. Singer, The Detroit Riot of July 1966: A Psychological, Social, and Economic Profile of 500 Arrestees (Detroit: Behavior Research Institute, 1968); Report of the National Advisory Commission on Civil Disorders (New York: Bantam, 1968); Marvin E. Wolfgang, "Violence, U.S.A.! Riots and Crime," Crime and Delinquency, 14 (October 1968); H. Hubbard, "Five Long Hot Summers and How They Grew," Public Interest, 1969; Civil Disorder Digest (Cambridge, Mass.: Civil Disorder Research Institute, vol. 1, no. 1, September 1969); Gary T. Marx, "Riots," Encyclopedia Britannica, 1970; J. Baskin, et al., The Long, Hot Summer: An Analysis of Summer Disorders, 1967–1971 (Waltham, Mass.: Lemberg Center for the Study of Violence, Report no. 2, 1972).

45. See, for example, Thrasher, op. cit., pp. 201–203; Elliot M. Rudwick, Race Riot at East St. Louis, July 2, 1917 (New York: Meridian, 1966); A. Meier and E. M. Rudwick, "Black Violence in the Twentieth Century," in H. Graham and T. Gurr, The History of Violence in America: A Report to the National Commission on the Causes and Prevention of Violence (New York: Bantam, 1969).

46. This conclusion is based on an examination of accounts of "trigger events" in Report of the National Advisory Commission on Civil Disorders, op. cit., chap. 1, and in the Lemberg Center's "Race-Related Civil Disorders, May-August 1968" and "April Aftermath of the King Assassination," op. cit., 1968.

47. See, for example, observations of media reporters during the Watts riot of 1965 and the Newark riot of 1967.

48. See Gilbert Geis, "Juvenile Gangs," President's Committee on Juvenile Delinquency and Youth Crime, June 1965.

49. See, for example, L. Mouat, "Teen Gangs Vie for Reputations," Christian Science Monitor, November 12, 1966; J. Blank, "Make Way for the Real Great Society," National Civic Review, December 1968; J. McPherson, "Chicago's Blackstone Rangers," Atlantic Monthly, May 1969; A. Lupo, "Efforts by Street Gangs to Help Cities Ready but for $750,000," Boston Globe, June 17, 1969; J. Laing, "A Chicago Gang Strives for Political Potency but Clings to Violence," Wall Street Journal, September 15, 1969; F. Browning, "From Rumble to Revolution: The Young Lords," Ramparts, September 1970.

50. See, in particular, Laing, op. cit., and Poston, op. cit.

51. See Klein, 1971, op. cit., p. 76; W. B. Miller, "The Corner Gang Boys Get Married," Transaction, 1 November 1963; Miller, 1966, op. cit.; and Miller, City Gangs, op. cit., "Characteristics of City Gangs."

52. Figures furnished by officials of the Gang Intelligence Unit, Youth Division, Chicago Police Department, 1966 and 1971.

53. On ideologically formulated vocabularies of justification, see G. Sykes and D. Matza, "Techniques of Neutralization: A Theory of Delinquency," American Sociological Review, 22 (December 1957), and D. Matza, Delinquency and Drift (New York: Wiley, 1964), especially chap. 10.

54. See, for example, Browning, op. cit.

55. See Randall Russell, " 'The Mob': A 'Participant' Observation Study of a Drug-Oriented, Non-Addicted Peer Group," Special Projects Section, National Institute of Mental Health, Adelphi, Md., n.d. See also I. Chien, "Narcotics Use Among Juveniles," Social Work, 7 (April 1956); J. Klein and D. Phillips, "From Hard to Soft Drugs: Temporal and Substantive Changes in Drug-Usage Among Gangs in a Working Class Community," Journal of Health and Social Behavior, 9 (June 1968).

56. See Thrasher, op. cit., p. 340; Klein and Phillips, op. cit.

57. See W. B. Miller, "Generalized Theoretical Orientations to the Study of Gang Delinquency," International Newsletter in Mental Health, 1 (October 1959), p. 4.

II / **VIOLENT BEHAVIOUR**

MARVIN E. WOLFGANG

As a sociologist-criminologist and Research Director of the National Commission on the Causes and Prevention of Violence during most of this past year, I have been writing, reading and thinking about violence in a variety of forms, so that what I can say now is but a resumé of many previous thoughts of my own and of others.[1] I take no credit for original thinking, only the responsibility for the peculiar twists of the language to express some ideas.

I have been torn in my preparation for this paper between wanting to cover material from the laboratory on aggression, the psychological studies of reactions to films, electronic impulses imposed on critical centres of the brain, the influence of the XYY gene syndrome, to interesting analyses of assassinations, firearms, crimes and student violence. There are types and degrees of violence which England does not share with the United States, and you should be grateful but watchful. So extensive in scope and intensive in detail is our present national inquiry into violence that I can but hope that some of the dozen or so volumes that we expect to publish this summer will have some interest to scholars and the public in general, here as well as in the United States. My own remarks are highly selective and generally devoid of the statistics needed to buttress argument. I shall concentrate on only a few general areas of concern.

When the dictatorial Duke of Athens was compelled by an angry mob to flee Florence in 1343, some of his political assistants were grabbed on the street, tortured, and murdered. The apex of the mob fury was reached in the scene described as follows by Machiavelli:

Those who could not wound them while alive, wounded them after they were dead; and not satisfied with tearing them to pieces, they hewed their bodies with swords, tore them with their hands, and even with their teeth. And that every sense might be satiated with vengeance, having first heard their moans, seen their wounds, and touched their lacerated bodies, they wished even the stomach to be satisfied, that having glutted the external sense, the one within might also have its share.[2]

This mob action helped to sustain Machiavelli's insistence that 'the rage of men is certainly always found greater, and their revenge more furious upon the recovery of liberty, than when it has only been defended.'[3]

My reason for referring to this scene is patent: to draw upon an example of riot and violence from a beautiful city at the most glorious time in its history, to show the brutal side of man's behaviour in the midst of another period's affluence, political enlightenment, and highly humanistic culture.

Man is not innately criminal, violent, or aggressive. He responds to people, events, or other kinds of stimuli that precipitate violative, violent, or aggressive behaviour. But he learns what is fearful or frustrating so that the things to which he reacts are interpreted by him as such, and the resolution of events which he defines as problems is also learned. Cats, dogs, and monkeys do not shoot their adversaries because they cannot or have not learned to use guns. Only man has the capacity to make and to use such artificial weapons designed to destroy himself and others.

This general introduction leads to my first major topic, which is the socialization into violence, with an emphasis on the fact that our culture provides a variety of learning processes that develop an acceptance of the use of violence, often labelled legitimate. Much of my concern is with America because I know it best and because I am involved in a national scrutiny of my own society. If I sound a bit critical of the United States at times it is because we are critically analysing our posture relative to violence.

I shall also speak much about youth because youth is a time of movement and physical activity, and acts of physical aggression, whether performed by monkeys or homo sapiens, whether or not injurious to others, are most likely to be performed by the young.

SOCIALIZATION INTO VIOLENCE

Legitimized Violence

Violence can be viewed as physical injury to persons and damage or destruction of property, and abstractly is neither legitimate nor illegitimate. Judgement of legitimacy is based on the agent, the target, the ends sought and the context in which violence occurs. Whether physical force is good or bad is always decided within a culture value setting. The positive or negative, eufunctional or dysfunctional, aspects of violence depend on the observer's perspective.

There is, however, no society that does not contain in its normative system elements of acceptable limits to violence. Thus, the use of physical force by parents to restrain and punish children is permitted, tolerated, encouraged, and is thereby part of the normative process by which every society regulates its child-rearing. There are, of course, varying degrees of parental force expected and used in different cultures and times, and there are upper limits vaguely defined as excessive and brutal. The battered child syndrome is an increasingly recorded phenomenon in several Western societies.

The point is, however, that our norms approve or permit parents to apply force largely for their own ends against the child. The application of force is a form of violence and may be used consciously to discipline the child to the limits of permitted behaviour, to reduce the domestic noise level, to express parental disapproval, and even unconsciously as a displacement for aggression actually meant for other targets. This model of parent-child interaction is a universal feature of all human societies. The model is one that the child himself comes to ingest: i.e., that superior force is power permitting manipulation of others and can be a functional tool for securing a superordinate position over others, for obtaining desires and ends.

The violence in which the child himself engages is but an expressed extension of the basic model. The use of physical restraint and force is not a feature only in lower-class families, although studies have shown that its persistent use, and use in greater frequency over a longer span of childhood, is more common in that social class. The substitutions, by middle-class parents, of withdrawal of rights and affection, of deprivation of liberty and of other techniques, are designed to replace the need for force. They are also ways of masking the supreme means of control, namely, physical force.

Violence and the threat of violence form the ultimate weapons of any society for maintaining itself against external and internal attacks. All societies finally resort to violence to solve problems that arise from such attacks. War is aggressive force between nations and is legitimized within each. Relativity of moral judgements about violence is quite clear in the case of war. When the American colonies collected themselves together in the eighteenth century to sever metropolitan ties, we called the action revolution and good despite the violence it engendered. When some states in the nineteenth century sought to bifurcate the nation, we called the action civil war and bad and lamented the bloodshed. The Nazis gave justice to our bombs and enlisted the world's generation of youth to react violently to violence. Violence becomes viewed as a rapid collective problem-solver, from the three-and-twenty stabs in Caesar, according to Suetonius, to riots in city streets or college grounds.

There are international conflicts in which our countries have been involved and for which the label of legitimacy has been seriously questioned by substantial numbers within our own territory. Vietnam is such an episode. And when this happens, a society becomes more conscious of the process of socializing its own youth to accept violence as a mode of response. When war is glorified in a nation's history and included as part of the child's educational materials, a moral judgement about the legitimacy of violence is surely and firmly made.

Socialization means changing the individual into a personality; it is the process of cultural transmission, of relaying through the social funnel of family and friends a set of beliefs, attitudes, values, speech and habits. When the front-line instruments of war become part of the physical features of a child's life space, when cannons, rifles, grenades and soldiers are moved from real battlefields to the mind of the child and the plastic world of his playroom, and are among the objects touched and manipulated by the child in the process of becoming, then some set of values associated with the legitimacy and recognition of the superiority of violent activity is also transmitted.

It is our youth who man the weapons of war. But they must be trained to have reduced fear and increased anger, to rationalize their being mobilized into a phalanx of force. Youth must be socialized into acceptance of the collective will that drives and flies them into battle against their individual desires. From Roman troops who marched through Britain to United States soldiers who struggle in Vietnam, the still-forming limbs of youth have been used to push political philosophies through history.

It is always an older generation that thrusts its younger ones into battle. Decisions made with maps and oval tables in the conference halls of power are made by men whose own youth has passed. Not privy to the policies that formed their own fate, the young are used to play the games of violence imposed on them by their elders. I am not here questioning, but only describing, the process which creates its own cultural justification. But I am implying that the process and the justifications that envelope it are part of the socialization of generations into violence. We might question whether the generation that designs, or the generation that fights, war is the truly violent one.

There are many other areas of social life which witness the protection of order by representatives of control. In their roles and persons, they corporealize the actual or potential use of legitimized violence. The police and national guard are the most obvious of these agents, but there are also the less visible and more silent cadres of guards in prisons, mental institutions, banks, parks and museums. Even less seen but subjectively self-legitimized, are unofficial groups like the lynching mobs of yesteryear, the Minutemen and vigilantes of the rural South and urban North, and certain black militants who have armed their members for assault. The presence of all these groups, ranging from the culturally prescribed to the barely tolerated, has diffusive effects that are part of the socializing experience of youth into the acceptance of violence as a means of control. The more these agents of real or potential aggression are used, the more impact such use has in socializing others to the functional utility of violence. If the official legitimacy of violence is stressed many of the young generation exposed to such values will have heightened acceptance of its use. On the other hand, many who are identified with the targets of officially legitimized violence will respond in like manner, thereby confirming their need to use violence to combat violence. And this message is passed on to yet another group of the younger generation who learn to attack the guardian executors of the larger society with their own contrived version of legitimate violence.

Masculinity

Social scientists, psychologists and psychiatrists have often stressed the importance of the theme of masculinity in American culture and the effect this image of the strong masculine role has had on child-rearing and the general socialization process. The middle-class child today has some difficulty if he seeks to match himself to the old masculine model and he may sometimes become neurotic and insecure. Among the lower classes, says Walter Miller, the continuity of the physically assertive male is still one of the 'focal concerns'. The desire to prove one's masculinity, added to the desire to become a successful male adult member of the lower-class culture, requires adolescent 'rehearsal' of the toughness, heavy drinking and quick aggressive response to certain stimuli that are characteristic of the lower-class adult male. Such rehearsal involves activities not necessarily delinquent but often participation in conduct that is defined as delinquent by the middle class. *Machismo* is still a viable term in various cultures, and especially among the young in the lower class, that equates maleness with overt physical aggression. The genesis reaches far into the biological evolution of the species, into the history of civilization; it was found on the peripheries of expanding colonial powers, on the frontiers of America, and it has been at the core of the less verbally articulate classes. Efforts to explain its persistence include rejection by the male child of female dominance at home and school, and rejection of the association of morality with femininity; the result is the antithesis, that of being physically aggressive, which in turn often leads to delinquency and crime.

Males commonly carry the role of committing the required deeds of assault, of investigating homicides and suicides, being mortician assistants, handling the injuries of highways; in short, men are required to assume responsibility for the physical public injuries and tragedies of humanity. Women are protected and faces are turned from such displays. It is also the male who is expected to use violence in prescribed ways and at prescribed times, during which he must be sufficiently desensitized to the pain he inflicts, whether in the street or playground, on a battlefield or in a bomber. It should not be unexpected, therefore, that most delinquent acts of physical injury are also committed by males.

The Mass Media

Other features of our culture in general, such as the mass media, may promote acceptability of male violence or make violence so banal that large segments of the population are no longer sensitive to expressions of violence. At least these features fail to encourage nonviolence. Whether viewing television or otherwise vicariously experiencing violence functions as a catharsis is not a scientifically resolved issue. The weight of most research seems counter-indicated. The sheer frequency of screened violence, its intensity as well as context, and the myriad forms it takes, cannot be claimed to instil firm notions of nonviolence in the children who are witnesses. Unless the logic of the assertion that violence in mass media encourages violent behaviour is destroyed by scientifically acceptable evidence, we play dangerous games with the socialization process and its adult products.

Automobile Advertising

Even automobile advertising in America evokes many of the attributes of aggression, particularly male aggression, and seeks to affect purchasing habits by drawing upon the existing pool of socializing forces. Despite pamphlets distributed to young drivers by car manufacturers to encourage courteous driving habits, these same manufacturers advertise aggression behind the wheel by linking their cars and the drivers to masculine might. In a short time I can only give the tenor of their appeal.[4]

Glamour and thrill in the cars are meant to be associated with speed and power through such verbs as *roars, growls;* adjectives like *dynamic, powerful, exciting, wild, ferocious, swinging;* nouns like *missile, rocket, tiger, stinger.* Phrases of advertising include: *just pull the trigger, start billing yourself as the human cannon ball; want action?; fire the second stage; aim it at the road.* Longer excerpts make clear the intended associations: (a) *For stab-and-steer men, there is a new 3-speed automatic you can lock in any gear . . . make small noises in your throat. Atta boy tiger;* (b) *Bring on the Mustangs, Wildcats, Impalas . . . . We'll even squash a few Spyders while we're at it. Dodge has made it a little harder to survive in the asphalt jungle. They just uncaged the Coronet;* (c) *This year let yourself go for power;* (d) *All new! All muscle! . . . with Advanced Thrust engineering . . . and an almost neurotic urge to get going. Drive it like you hate it—it's cheaper than psychiatry;* (c) *Nobody said a nice car can't play mean now and then.*

There are appeals to virility and masculinity: *Get with man-sized Dart; Sleek, lean, muscled new style . . . improved cat-quick handling; Burly and businesslike; Go ahead, be rebellious. Demand more 'big'. More 'hot'; Come rid yourself of prematurely gray driving; The 300 has muscle; Bold Plymouth Fury; A man's kind of action! Bold! . . . It's the man's car for men who like their action big . . . gives a man that 'in charge' feeling.*

It is difficult to factor out the contribution this kind of advertising makes to the traffic accidents of the young, both as victims and agents. That the association is present is clear. Traffic accidents are the leading cause of death among children and youth. Of all youth 13 to 25 years of age who died in a recent ten-year span, 42 per cent died as the result of traffic accidents. The young are our worst drivers, as reflected in part through insurance rates. Persons under 25 are 19 per cent of all licensed drivers but cause over 30 per cent of the accidents. Two-fifths of all teenage drivers are involved in traffic accidents each year.[5]

Such advertising, through car magazines read by thousands of youth, reaches into the later adolescent socializing process and can be faulted for adding to the violence in our culture if not on the road.

Guns

Much the same can be said about guns in American society—a problem so well controlled in England. The appeal to masculinity is again present, and the general awareness of young males about guns forms yet another part of the socialization into violence. The best current estimate is that there are at least 100 million guns in the United States. If evenly distributed there would be one for every male in the country. But they are not evenly distributed. The South East and South Central regions have highest gun possession, as do males under 25. These are also the regions and the age group of highest rates of homicide.

Nearly 3,000 persons in the United States are fatal victims of firearms accidents each year, and at least another 20,000 are injured by firearms accidents. About 65 per cent of our criminal homicides involve firearms.

The ease with which guns can be purchased is well documented. During the past decade about 30 million new guns have been added by domestic production and importation. Weak or unenforced control statutes on possession or use make guns available to almost anyone who wants one. And to this availability is added the stimulus of advertising not unlike that which I have read about automobiles.

Mail-order advertisement in America, the highest gun-to-population ratio in the world, the virtual glorification of guns in our history, and the daily displays on television of guns in the hands of heroes, can surely play no role in minimizing violence in the socialization process.

I have spoken of guns, automobile advertising and legitimized violence because they are features given scanty attention among the socializing forces that mould the personalities, shape the values and form the mentality of many youth in our society. As we unpack the mixed bag of culture inputs presented to youth, we become increasingly aware that a high proportion are violence-laden, and that they are often offered for absorption with the palliative of legitimacy and social acceptability. They can now be seen more clearly as further extensions of the basic model of physical force found in parent-child interaction. Violence, thus viewed, is a continuous variable, measured in degrees of severity and intensity, legitimacy and illegitimacy.

Illegitimate violence is not qualitatively different from but is continuous with and dynamically similar to legitimate violence. It is to the clearly illegitimate forms of violence—the delinquencies and crimes—and the more blatant criminogenic forces of our society that I should now like briefly to turn, to understand another dimension of the relation between culture and violence.

URBAN VIOLENCE

The Subculture of Violence

The forces that generate conditions conducive to crime and riots are strongest in our urban communities. Urban areas with mass populations, greater wealth, more commercial establishments, and more products of our technology also provide more frequent opportunities for theft and greater chance of violence. Victims are impersonalized, property is insured, consumer goods in more abundance are vividly displayed and are more portable.

Urban life is commonly characterized by population density, spatial mobility, ethnic and class heterogeneity, reduced family functions, and greater anonymity. When, on a scale, these traits are found in high degree, and when they are combined with poverty, physical deterioration, low education, residence in industrial and commercial centres, unemployment or unskilled labour, economic dependency, marital instability or breaks, poor or absent male models for young boys, overcrowding, lack of legitimate opportunities to make a better life, the absence of positive anticriminal behaviour patterns, higher frequency of organic diseases, and a cultural minority status of inferiority, it is generally assumed that social-psychological mechanisms leading to deviation, crime and violence are more likely to emerge.

It is abundantly clear even to the most casual observer that Negroes in American society are the current carriers of a ghetto tradition in our cities. More than any other socially defined group, they are the recipients of urban deterioration and the social-psychological forces leading to legal deviation. And for this reason, concern with crime in the American city is commonly a concern with Negro crime.

Although there are good reasons for raising serious questions about criminal statistics that report the race of the offender, and the fact that official crime rates about Negroes are in general three or four times higher than white rates, and although Negroes probably suffer more injustices than whites in the law enforcement process from arrest to imprisonment, it is no surprise that the most valid efforts to measure crime still find Negro crime rates high. When the untoward aspects of urban life are found among Italians, Germans, Poles, or almost any other group, their crime rates are similarly high. Relative deprivation and social disqualification are thus dramatically chained to despair and delinquency.

All of this is not meant to obscure the fact that poverty also exists in small towns and rural areas. But when multiplied by congested thousands and transmitted over generations, poverty, as Oscar Lewis has claimed, becomes a culture. The expectations of social intercourse change, and irritable, frustrated parents often become neglectful and aggressive. The children inherit a 'subculture of violence'[6] where physically aggressive responses are either expected or required by all members sharing not only the tenement's plumbing but also its system of values. Ready access and resort to weapons in this milieu may be essential to protection against others who respond in similarly violent ways. Carrying a knife or some other protective device becomes a common symbol of willingness to participate in violence, to expect violence, and to be ready for its retaliation.

A subculture of violence is not the product of cities alone. The Thugs of India, the *vendetta barbaricina* in Sardinia and the *mafioso* in Sicily have existed for a long time. But the contemporary American city has the major accoutrements not only for the genesis but also for the highly accelerated development of this subculture, and it is from this subculture that most violent crimes come.

The use of violence in such a subculture is not viewed as illicit conduct, and the users do not have to deal with feelings of guilt about their aggression.

Violence can become a part of the life-style, the theme for solving difficult problems and is used primarily between persons and groups who themselves rely upon the same supportive values and norms. A carrier and user of violence will not be burdened by conscious guilt, then, mainly because the recipient of his violence shares in the same subculture and has similar class, occupation, residence, age, and other attributes which characterize the subuniverse of persons sharing in the subculture of violence.

Delinquency in a Birth Cohort

Now there is a relatively small cadre of young citizens who are born into and grow up in a subculture pocket of residential propinquity, poverty and psychological depression, ungoverned households and wedless mothers, where the subculture of violence is nurtured and transmitted across generations as well as city streets. Yet, this relatively small group, fostered by inadequate urban renewal, occupational, educational and housing programmes, and unchecked by community service agencies or correctional strategies, can and does inflict most of the serious, violent social harm on a community.

Relative to this assertion are some new kinds of evidence about juvenile crime and particularly violence that are being analysed by the Center for Studies in Criminology and Criminal Law at the University of Pennsylvania under support from the National Institute of Mental Health. The data constitute a unique collection of information in the United States about a birth cohort of boys born in 1945. Approximately 10,000 males born in that year and who resided in Philadelphia at least from ages 10 to 18, have been analysed in a variety of ways. Using school records, offence reports from the police, and some military information, the Center has, among other things, followed the delinquency careers of those boys in the cohort who *ever* had any contact with the police. The cohort is probably typical of other urban cohorts in the United States.

Some of the findings from this Philadelphia study are particularly pertinent for more understanding about youth and crimes of violence. Of the total birth cohort of 9,946 boys born in 1945, about 85 per cent were born in Philadelphia and about 95 per cent went through the Philadelphia school system from first grade. From the entire cohort, 3,475, or 35 per cent, were delinquent, meaning that they had at least one contact with the police before reaching age 18. Of the 7,043 white subjects, 2,017, or 29.64 per cent, were delinquent. Of the 2,902 nonwhites, 1,458, or 50.24 per cent, were delinquent. It is a dramatic and disturbing fact that slightly more than half of all Negro boys born in the same year were delinquent—more than were nondelinquent.

Of special significance is the fact that only 627 boys were classified as chronic offenders, or heavy repeaters, meaning that they committed five or more offences during their juvenile court ages. These chronic offenders represent only 6.3 per cent of the entire birth cohort. Yet, these 627 boys were responsible for 5,305 delinquencies, which is 52 per cent of all the delinquencies committed by the entire birth cohort.

Chronic offenders are heavily represented among those who commit violent offences. Of the 815 personal attacks (homicide, rape, aggravated and simple assaults), 450, or 53 per cent, were committed by chronic offenders; of the 2,257 property offences, 1,397, or 62 per cent, were from chronic offenders; and of 193 robberies, 135, or 71 per cent, were from chronic offenders. Of all violent offences committed by nonwhites, 70 per cent were committed by chronic boys; of all violent acts committed by whites, 45 per cent were performed by chronic boys.

Clearly, these chronic offenders represent what is often referred to as the 'hard core' delinquents. That such a high proportion of offences—particularly serious acts of violence—is funnelled through a relatively small number of offenders, is a fact that loudly claims attention for a social action policy of intervention. Under the assumption that these offences are the most serious and the ones to reduce in any deterrence or prevention programme, and that most of the other forms of delinquency are relatively trivial, the pivotal point of social cost reduction appears to be when juveniles have committed their first offences. To produce delinquency desisting at this stage in the biography of the child might thus be considered the most efficient procedure. More nonwhites go on after the first offence, and perhaps the major concern should be with this racial group. Nearly 30 per cent of the nonwhite boys, compared to only 10 per cent of the white boys, fall into the chronic offender category of having committed five or more offences.

Urban Riots

There is a still more serious form of violence today—that of group violence. The United States has recently experienced race riots that offer fundamental threats to the entire social system. To deny the political utility of such violence would be neither easy nor valid. Not until violence erupted did the United States Congress move to enact the first major rights legislation since the Civil War.

Nearly every major city in the land has experienced riots and civil disorder during the past few years. There were 239 violent outbursts by Negroes that involved at least 200,000 people and resulted in more than 8,000 casualties, including 191 deaths, most of them Negroes. More than 30,000 white Americans have taken part in violent clashes with civil rights demonstrators, causing more than 150 injuries. Some 200 major acts of white terrorism against blacks and civil rights workers have resulted in some 20 deaths and more than 100 serious casualties.[7]

When men perceive oppression as their lot and know of others not oppressed, when ordered avenues of change are blocked by kings or legislators or some vague variety of any social system, the oppressed will either resign themselves to fate or rise up to taste the fruit of freedom, and having tasted will want the feast.

Like whites, Negroes are men who have learned of their oppression. By forced migration they became slaves. The politics of war redefined their citizenry but scarcely changed their status. Slaves became servants in the economics of change. The quiet process of elevation has been too slow for all but a trickle of black humanity to enjoy white privilege, and today colour is a description not of the skin but of one's status. That status is a depressed, deprived, and now frustrating one.

But group violence is not a new phenomenon in American society. Our history suggests violence as severe as or worse than now. We might discount the Revolution and the War between the States, the latter of which took approximately half a million lives. But we cannot neglect the Shays and Whiskey Rebellions over debts and taxes; the slaughter and subjugation of American Indians; the Know-Nothings who fought rising Irish political power, who had a 48-hour orgy of mob violence in St Louis in 1854 in which a dozen persons were killed and 50 homes of Irish Catholics wrecked and looted, who killed 20 persons in a two-day riot in Louisville the next year and burned two churches and two parochial schools in Philadelphia; and the Irish antidraft riot in New York in 1863 that killed nearly 2,000 and injured 8,000 in four days.

There were the bloody railroad strikes in 1877 that killed 150; the Rocky Mountain mining wars that took the lives of 198, including a governor, at the turn of the century; the brutal Molly Maguires, a secret band of Irish miners in Pennsylvania; the Wobblies, or Industrial Workers of the World;. the industrial and railroad police who brutally beat labourers from Pennsylvania to California; the garment workers' strike in Chicago in 1910 that resulted in seven deaths, an unknown number of seriously injured, and 874 arrests; the 20 lives lost in the Illinois Central Railroad strikes in 1911; the 1919 steel strike in which 20 persons perished; the national cotton textile labour dispute of 1934 that spread from Georgia and South Carolina to Alabama, even to Rhode Island and Connecticut, with 21 deaths and 10,000 soldiers on strike duty.[8]

By 1871 the invisible empire of the Ku Klux Klan had a membership of over half a million, and a Congressional investigation that year uncovered hangings, shootings, whippings, and mutilations in the thousands. In Louisiana alone, two thousand persons had been killed, wounded, or injured in a short few weeks before the election of 1868. The commanding general of federal forces in Texas reported: 'Murders of Negroes are so common as to render it impossible to keep accurate accounts of them.'[9]

That violence is not unique to the United States is an assertion that needs no more than a few illustrations. The aftermath of the French Revolution had a kind of terror and bloodshed never witnessed in this country; the 1843 student riots in France spread throughout Europe; assassinations occurred from Austrian Archduke Francis Ferdinand in 1914 to Prime Minister Verwoerd in South Africa. The Nazis need not even be mentioned. Still fresh in history are the tortures in French Algeria; the Stalinist terrors of a generation; the mob violence and riots off and on for another generation involving Pakistanis and Indians; the current Nigerian civil war; the student and union violence in France; the *violencia* of Colombia for nearly 20 years that resulted in the assassination of Dr. Jorge Gaitan in 1948 and an estimated 200,000 deaths up to 1967; the confused 'cultural revolution' in mainland China; and the horrendous, little-publicized massacre of 400,000 persons in recent years in Indonesia.

Violence in America's past, in the past and present of other nations, does not diminish it in our current scene. But its present dimensions and our instant explanations should be viewed within these perspectives.

While not having a firm political ideology any more than students who riot on campus, the 'young militant' Negroes responsible for the fire-bombing and the sniping—the bitter and alienated activists—surely perceive the bureaucrats and the broader social order as distant impersonal targets for distaste and disruption. Having seen that it is possible to get attention and dethrone the complacency of the white establishment, and having gained hope that their lot can be improved, they regard their present deprivation as unendurable. In referring to the French Revolution, de Tocqueville said: 'A people which has supported without complaint, as if they were not felt, the most oppressive laws, violently throws them off as soon as their weight is lightened. The social order destroyed by a revolution is always better than that which immediately preceded it . . . . The end which was suffered patiently as inevitable seems unendurable as soon as the idea of escaping from it is conceived.'[10]

To riot is a crime in any state penal code definition. To incite to riot, to loot, burglarize, set on fire, destroy property, rob, assault, shoot, carry deadly weapons—each of these is a crime. Surely the unrecorded number of crimes and of unapprehended offenders in riots is enormous.

But in another sense, not compatible with a legalistic proximate cause notion, the white society, as the Kerner Commission noted, is responsible for inciting to riot. While displaying before the Negro poor the democratic idealism of opportunity, it has inflicted on them the prejudice, the economic blockage of opportunities, the subjugation, and the alienation from power and participation in democracy that have produced among Negroes the power to respond, exploding now in attacks to express their feelings. The urban riots thus far are a mixed bag of some confusing revolutionary ideology among a few, anomic acts expressive of social malaise among many, and almost adventuresome play among still others. Should there be another round of riot, it will be either moderate skirmishes in more muted tones, reflecting a turn towards dissipation of the ghetto thrust, or more violent guerilla warfare that can result only in more stringent repressive force by the state. If riots . . . are few or more moderate, we might conclude that the massively diffused efforts for better police-community relations, coalitions of white businessmen with the Negro community, and all our other strategies of solution that reject tokenism and gradualism are beginning to pay off.

I am inclined to link the causes of urban riots and those of urban crime. Where riots have begun, crime rates have been highest, especially crimes of violence. The social forces that have generated crime overlay the forces that erupt into riot. The players in both dramas are the same or similar. The parallelism is too strong to ignore or deny. Correct the conditions causing the one phenomenon and we change the other concomitantly.

STUDENT VIOLENCE

Student violence is yet another and slightly different form of group violence experienced in most societies today. England may have a much lower homicide rate than the United States, but she is sharing the pains of student protest in not dissimilar ways.

I can only touch lightly on this topic but I would like to underscore the element of cultural contagion and the fact that many protests are peaceful demonstrations. But some escalate into violence, often as a result of excessive reaction by the police.

During 1967–68 in the United States, about 700,000 antiwar and antidraft protesters staged more than 170 demonstrations in cities and universities across the country. Of these, only 36 involved violence, including 15 in which counter-demonstrators initiated violence. Only eight resulted in reported injuries, a total of 800. [During 1968] student demonstrations on war and campus issues involving more than 100,000 participants, occurred on more than 100 campuses. About 220 demonstrations took place. A few resulted in seizure of university facilities, police intervention, riot, property damage, injury, and even death; and several institutions were brought to a halt.[11]

Here are a few descriptions commonly reported in news accounts:

Over 4,500 police with shields rushed into [the] University early this morning and, using tear gas, tried to force out 300 students barricaded in . . . the main building.

Hundred of students today ransacked the office of [the] University Rector and tried to throw him out a window . . . After a wild meeting of 2,000 students in the central university building, about 500 rushed toward the rector's office, painting slogans on the walls as they went.

. . . a month's old student strike was complicated by a partial walkout by teachers. Mounted police charged groups of students along off-campus streets; rocks flew and the toll of arrests and injuries climbed steadily.

The Dean . . . was imprisoned for eight days in an occupied university building and subjected to 'mass collective bargaining' until he was finally allowed to leave, exhausted, on a stretcher.

A hard core of about 150 radical students caused havoc at the . . . University . . . today. They smashed doors and windows, broke into cupboards, flung files around, piled up furniture as barricades, and manned hoses ready to fight the police.

These are a few typical reports of student violence during the early part of this year. There is at least a score of specific criminal offences lodged in these activities. The locale in each report has been deleted in order to demonstrate clearly how widespread and similar is the violence. The difficulty one has in distinguishing the universities attests to the extent and similarity of the conditions.[12] In some cases it is instrumental violence to obtain clarified parochial goals; in other cases it is a generalized effort at sheer confrontation for the sake of disruption. Often, in either case, 'The commitment to violence is clear-cut. Said an anarchist leader of the . . . students who first began the dispute . . . : "Simply, the situation is a battle against the entrenched and direct power of the State. This power equals violence. To fight back we must employ direct violence. There is no other choice."'[13] This is a quotation from a student at Tokyo University, but the comment is heard in similar tones from San Francisco State to the Sorbonne.

It is important to keep in mind that most student protest has not been violent, that it has captured the sentiments of many who are no longer young, and that the social effects of youthful protest are systemic. Most students are not radically, wholly or injuriously involved in the activism on campuses. Reports rather consistently indicate that only about one or two per cent of all students in America and in England are actively involved in protests. This figure may be most misleading, however, for some students weave in and out of periods of activity, but the ardour and forcefulness which the active members bring to their tasks have indeed attracted international, political and economic attention. Events seem to move more swiftly than the pen. The analysis made last month, however sophisticated at the time, may seem outmoded this month. The liberal who gained his stance ten years ago for integration of the races is today fighting a new-style segregation suggested by the militant blacks who want not only separate Afro-American departments, faculty and budget for black students at San Francisco State College, but who want separate black dormitories there, at Yale, and elsewhere. Black power is a term that takes on more meanings as time goes on, adding money and guns to the former meaning of dignity and identity. The desire to participate in decision-making episodes affecting one's own life shifts partly to a wish for confrontation. Dialogue changes into duologue, a term Abraham Kaplan uses to refer to two parties who talk *at*, rather than *to*, one another without listening. Responses to student demands range from repression to reasoned arguments that student leaders often do not heed.

Whether student protest becomes violent depends on the intensity of the protesters' feelings, the response of the forces who try to control the protest, the leaders' rhetoric and many other things. But escalation into violence is not the usual pattern of demonstrative protest.

Nor should student activists necessarily be viewed as rebelling against the values of their parents. On the contrary, our current studies in the United States (and apparently in England as well) indicate that the students appear to be trying to implement those very values through their action. Student activists are recruited from the better students, they were raised in families that have valued aesthetic and intellectual interests over money and material success, and have transmitted to the children notions of humanitarianism and free expression that sometimes question authority, convention and tradition.

It is not 'permissiveness' so much as parental interests in political and socially conscious activity that are commonly related to this group of active youth.

The growth and complexity of university structure have combined with increasing involvement in issues of national policy and inadequate channels for expression of disagreement and participation of student and faculty in the decisions that affect their lives on campus. At the same time, radical student activists concerned with these issues have been attracted to such movements as the Students for a Democratic Society (SDS), which claims 7,000 dues-paying national members and about 35,000 members in its several hundred local chapters.

Scores of other single-issue groups on campuses across the United States and in England range from civil rights support groups to leagues for sexual freedom. They are generally not involved in violence around these issues but their numbers reflect increased student participation in public affairs and the volatile potential of campus politics. They are showing, instead, their desire for more personal autonomy and greater latitude for self-expression.

Until recently, Negro university students were smaller in number, politically impotent if not indifferent, and considerably individualistic. Black power groups on campus have offered direction and organizational vehicles for young educated Negro students to find collective expression of grievance, and identification with the black community as well as with fellow black students. Black Student Unions and Afro-American Associations have recently emerged on many campuses with increasing numbers of black students. The black student leaders are as militant and violent or more so than the white radicals, especially in terms of tactics used. The principal difference appears to be that black student groups wish to negotiate specific reforms and concessions while the white student radicals often seek only to confront authority with their protests, and serve no guiding ideology or specific target. Militancy and violent tactics of black students seem to augment the militant stance of white students. Moreover, internecine battles for power are beginning to occur among the black organizations and may occur eventually between white and black radicals. The white radical commitment to justice and equality is often answered with derision and scepticism by blacks.

Much of the white student movement and whatever violence it engenders is without many ideological supports. There are, nonetheless, values expressed but not always followed: compassion instead of coercion, people above property, total involvement (to the point of holding administrators hostage or running risks of urban guerilla fighting), distrust of constituted authority (white or black), sexual freedom, privacy of one's own organism (to ingest what one wants, including drugs), rejection of bureaucratic hierarchicalism, and hypocrisy. From an earlier external interest in poor blacks in Mississippi, students from relatively affluent middle-class families shifted to more militancy as they became interested in the Vietnamese. Then, almost suddenly, they were fighting less for others and more for themselves. Abstract principles of justice and equality through student power, and the problems of the war in Vietnam, were made concrete by specific objections to university military contracts, and were personalized by threat of the draft. And in the process of these shifts increasing use of violence was the accompaniment. Ironically, a kind of romantic element has mixed with the personal as attention is also focused on the sterility of the power structure and an emphasis on human values. Dissent finds targets in mass production, creature comforts, and industrial technocracy. But these features of the New Left have little thrust toward politicization that could resemble an earlier era's underpinning of labour unrest with Marxism.

Some observers have noted that violence most often erupts, or occurs in most intense fashion, when the university authorities and police overreact. Perhaps this is a lesson learned from the Columbia and recent Harvard riots. Daniel Bell, my colleague in Sociology at Columbia, views the behaviour of the police as the major cause that 'radicalized' the Columbia student body.

Confrontation is a militant and violent means of arousing moderates to join in the movement and the action. It is used to alert the public to the issues. And it may dislodge the qualities of patience and quietude from young middle-class radicals whose traditional ethics of nonviolence have been politically inhibiting. Confrontation can cause many of the otherwise docile students who have been living only the quiet revolution of thought to commit themselves seriously to the revolution of action, however violent it may become. These are a few of the tenets of the tactics used by the SDS and other radical students. They are the kind of tactics that elicit, if not encourage, violence.

Because many students are still committed to pacifist or liberal democratic ideals and are as much concerned with university courses as with causes, they are becoming disturbed by the new waves of violence, uncomfortable with the rude, uncouth attacks and the increasingly anti-intellectual stance of the radical student movement. As this movement becomes more militant with its strategy of confrontation, it may grow more isolated and lose, and fail to attract the large cadre of moderate students whose sense of social justice is being offended by a violence more 'nasty and brutal' in its Hegelian prepoliticality than the power structure they at first rejected.

The response to student protest places the major burden on the universities themselves. University administrators are the front-line forces who must cope with the challenges of most of the protest of middle-class youth when it becomes violent.

The university today appears to have accepted the assertion that it is a microcosm of society. The university is also a step beyond this mini-mirror of its context. It is a community of young citizens and of scholars who not only harbour and enrich the knowledge so tediously acquired in the past, but who should engage constantly in questioning and reassessing that knowledge, which includes ideas about the functions and values of the present society. The capacity to inquire and to analyse the results of inquiry is the most fundamental feature of a university. To which I might add Sir Eric Ashby's cogent comment that the university should provide an 'environment for the continuous polishing of one mind by another.'[14] To maintain and strengthen this capacity is the purpose of every university administration.

But the concept of stern authority by the university over the *civil* life of its students is now nearly anachronistic. The traditional intradisciplinary measures used by the university to regulate, in assumed parental role, the personal lives of its younger citizens can little longer be of adequate utility for most universities in the United States. Few, if any, universities enjoy the collegiate loyalty of Cambridge and Oxford. The judicial structure of the contemporary university does not reproduce the rules of evidence, qualified judges, accredited legal counsel, and the other features of legal authority to handle major civil and criminal violations. Many of the violent violations on campus today are far beyond the internal differences of a family affair.

The distinction between academic and civil roles must therefore somehow be made both for the university administration and the students. If students are violent and disruptive they must be judged by the proper role they are taking and by the proper agency of response. If they question what is *academic* in character, the university cannot resort to a claim for allegiance to campus spirit and loyalty to an old-fashioned authority. Their questioning should be honoured with respect and engaged by the administration in full debate if courses, curriculum and other academic affairs are at issue. Where the right of the university to assert authority over certain matters is questioned, it must be earned by argument, if necessary.

CONCLUSION

When violence occurs in crime or protest, youth is often its vehicle. But most crimes and most protests are not violent, even when youth are involved.

There are many different kinds of violence; some of it is legitimized by the norms of the society and ranges from the force used in parent-child interaction to the conduct of national war. The older generations of most societies are not entirely free from the use of violence, either in the earlier version of their own youth or in the context of their later years. The conduct of a war is but one of the more obvious examples. Moreover, an older generation may be but slightly removed from the posture of most proximate cause for various kinds of violence that a society comes to tolerate. Not yet arrived at positions of power where responsibilities are shared, youth cannot be blamed for a society that yields violence because it fails to make automobiles and highways safer, fails to reduce high rates of infant mortality, to move more vigorously to reform cities of blight and organized crime, or to control the manufacture and sale of guns.

Violence is largely a learned response. If in everyday life man witnesses the display of violence in an abundance of styles, it takes on a banality and he may come to accept its use in encounters with his own environment.

It might be said that for all their protest against their established elders, youth in a sense rely on the patience, understanding, tolerance and responsibility of the older generation to check their escalating demands at the crunch point of the utterly impossible. One of the privileges of youth is having the ability to afford to complain and question.[15] The older generation becomes immersed in running the system and must rely upon the younger to provide the pressure needed to question and reform it. Even when they show displeasure at the tactics of student protest and riot, the older generation may have sneaking suspicions that youth could be right about many things. Like the ordinary German who a generation ago slowly became aware that something terrible was going on at the edge of town, so those in middle age are having their conscience aroused by youth and feel that more than a few things around them may not be well. There is merit in some of the disturbance from the student youth who are often idealistic, if not well-clothed with an ideology. 'You'd never believe,' said one professor in the midst of student protests at the London School of Economics, 'that a group could be so dedicated and saintly and such a terrible nuisance.'[16]

If the response to youthful violence is exclusively repression, the response may well assume the violence it seeks to halt. Perhaps, instead, a growing flexibility to change and an understanding of youth's requests will be the older generation's final weapon. The thrust of youth's protests may be dissipated in the soft belly of the establishment. And violence will be dethroned. Whatever the outcome of current crises, the annual layer of each newly arriving cohort folds into the fabric of society and continues to enrich the cloth.

Violence is a means of seeking power and may be defined as an act of despair committed when the door is closed to alternative resolutions. It comes from the failure to have a more abundant repertoire of means to gain a goal.

The lessons to be learned from current collective violence seem clear: as Columbia University officials remarked recently, acts wherein muscles usurp the role of minds are alien to a university. I suggest the same dictum for the larger society. Where reason is ruined and collective violence is viable, the social system has failed to provide the kind of participatory democracy we basically extol.

In the abstract there can be no side of violence [which can be equated] with virtue. The course of the dominant society built on law and intrinsically the inheritor of the value of nonviolence must be to maintain itself. The black militant who would burn cities or the student who would destroy an administration building harbours no better way of life than the Ku Klux Klan-er who would burn crosses or bomb Sunday schools. But the responsibility of that dominant society is to offer alternatives for expression, provide reasonable access to the thrones of power, permit grievances to be known, and execute the provisions of our Constitution with dispatch.

Change occurs in all societies, albeit the change in some may be slow or unplanned. It is when persons opposed to change become intransigent and those who wish to promote change are willing to resort to violence that order becomes disorder. When protest moves to riot and riot to rebellion, dissent is transformed into disruption. The right to exercise dissent peaceably is our basic political guarantee. But when physical harm occurs, another guarantee is called into focus and is used to force assaulters to retreat. This kind of balance is a fundamental which the police and the courts were designed to protect and maintain.

Perhaps Abraham Lincoln asked the basic question about violence most succinctly: 'Must a government of necessity be too strong for the liberties of its own people, or too weak to maintain its own existence?' I trust that both our countries are sufficiently sensitive to the liberties of all to listen, and strong enough to maintain them with justice under the rule of law.

ADDENDUM: RESEARCH

In part, research is a function of policy. The suggested programs, briefly sketched below, for the prevention of violence and delinquency, especially among the poor, all carry a research corollary, a provision for testing the value of the program.

A decision to undertake research is made within a context of prior decisions: (a) that research is a valuable basis for taking subsequent action or making policy decisions; (b) that some set of assumptions is worth implementing and testing. We offer the following suggestions without the elaborate supportive reasoning that should accompany them were they proposals before sponsoring agencies. The earlier sections of this paper should, however, give some indication concerning the theoretical underpinnings.

(1). Public subsidies could be provided to help individual poor families move into dwelling units for sale or rent on the private market. Instead of relocating the families in large public housing developments or high-rise tenements for the poor, the welfare agencies could quietly purchase single dwelling units for them throughout the community. Support should be sufficient to maintain a life-style not unlike that of the original inhabitants of the neighborhood, among whom the new arrivals would in time be accepted and absorbed. The host communities should be rewarded with improvements designed to promote neighborhood pride (e.g., a general beautification program).

The lessons of public housing have taught us that people moved from conditions of poverty need help in adjusting to their new physical and social environments. New notions must be acquired concerning the way space between properties is maintained, the grooming of lawns and sidewalks, the noise level of the neighborhood, the local habits of handling trash, even the street gestures of greeting neighbors. Education for elevation from poverty is a delicate matter, of course, but a required service.

Our research corollary is to follow the families who have been moved. There are literally scores of concerns here that could be formulated as testable hypotheses—for example, the psychological impact of separating families from their friends in poverty, or the receptivity of the new neighborhood. But with a focus here on delinquency and youth crime, we would be particularly interested in tracking the younger members of the newly moved families. A hundred experimental families, scattered throughout a large urban community, would be expected to develop new associations, attitudes, and values in the midst of new norms. Time would be required to determine whether comparative groups, left in their milieu of poverty and delinquent subcultures, have significantly higher rates of delinquency and crime.

(2). Instead of a single social worker, an entire family, including teen-agers, could become the social unit of help to other families. Such a family might have a "caseload" of a dozen other families, dispersed in the community according to the scheme outlined in the preceding section, and could, of course, live in or near the neighborhoods of the "case" families. The association of policy and research in this suggestion is obvious.

(3). Black pride is a current viable concept, but it need not be bred through black separation. Where racial pluralism is a reality, pride in self, family, or race comes from contact with other selves, families, or races. The dispersal program is not meant to bury the black in a surrounding sea of white. Unless there is widespread racial intermarriage, blacks will probably continue to form both formal and informal black associations. But it is in contact with white groups that blacks will best be able to manifest their elevation in status, not because they are white groups but because the whites and blacks together can share occupational, parental, artistic, neighborhood, educational, and other roles. Testing these notions in the context of the dispersal and family worker program is a researchable project.

(4). Demasculinizing violent physical aggression may be a worthwhile enterprise. In fact, there is evidence that some demasculinizing of overt noxious aggression is already current in the younger generation. What we are suggesting is not, of course, making females more violent, but divorcing maleness from pugilism and the symbols of violent and aggressive power in our culture. How successful a planned program can be in redirecting a whole culture's perspective on masculinity is problematic, but the association between maleness and aggressivity could be muted by conscious effort.

(5). Most commonly, group therapy is conducted among groups homogeneous in their deviance, be it neuroticism, delinquency, or drug addiction. Here we are suggesting that any group of a dozen or so members brought together for therapeutic purposes would benefit from a *mixture* of deviants and nondeviants—in our case, delinquents and nondelinquents. We are suggesting that value change, resocialization, model imitation, will be encouraged and accelerated by the mixture. The proper ratio probably depends on the character of the deviancy, but a three-to-one ratio of deviants to nondeviants might provide an initial experiment. The enormous burden of producing value shifts is now placed on the therapist and the slow emergence (if it ever occurs) of collective wisdom of the deviants themselves. The mere numerical increase of carriers of nondelinquent norms and values, who are peers of the delinquents in age, sex, and social class, could contribute much to the process of promoting conformity to lawful behavior. Research would follow traditional lines using representative or matched samples of experimental and control groups for comparison of outcome and description of the therapeutic process.

(6). Plans exist throughout the country for using former offenders as agents for helping to reform current offenders. Former inmates are known to be working with prisoners and parolees. This kind of activity should be expanded and tested for efficacy in many different settings.

(7). As an extension of the preceding, we would suggest that an ethos of service to others be cultivated among delinquents. A mixed group of delinquents and nondelinquents in the community might be brought together for planning ways to use their young talents and energies in constructive service to the handicapped, the mentally deficient, the aged, the unemployed. The public health service and many other welfare agencies in most communities have an abundance of tasks that must be done and could be performed by subprofessionals.

The touch of grace in being even minimally responsible for a smile on the face of an aged woman is a reward to which almost everyone is sensible. Delinquents so often come from a family, a neighborhood, a class, subject to welfare service. What we are here suggesting is that the ethos of service be transferred to them. The research to accompany a program of this kind would surely require psychological study of any personality change as well as alteration of delinquent conduct.

These policy-research suggestions have focused on violence and delinquency, mostly among youth from the lower social and economic class. They have not been addressed to the more affluent middle-class young who are involved in student protest that occasionally erupts into violence. The university, as a microcosm, is itself a kind of social laboratory for experimentation in structural and functional change, and many experiments in handling youth violence on campus have been undertaken.

NOTES

1. I am drawing upon materials from the National Commission on the Causes and Prevention of Violence, especially from the Task Forces on Individual Acts, co-directed by Melvin Tumin and Donald Mulvihill, and Group Violence, directed by Jerome Skolnick.
   I used some ideas that appeared in my previous writings, such as 'Violence, U.S.A.', *Crime and Delinquency* (October 1968), pp. 289–305, and *Youth and Violence*, a report I submitted to the Office of Juvenile Delinquency and Youth Development, Department of Health, Education and Welfare.
2. Niccolo Machiavelli, *History of Florence and of the Affairs of Italy* (London: M. Walter Dunne, 1901), Book II, p. 100.
3. *Ibid.*
4. A report entitled 'Automobile Safety; Speed and Racing Advertising', submitted to the U.S. Federal Trade Commission, 15 November 1966, by C. B. Yarley and C. A. Sweeney. A careful comparison between the automobile industry's safe-driving publications and magazine advertisements has been made by Jeffrey O'Connell, 'Lambs to Slaughter', *Columbia Journalism Review* (Fall 1967), pp. 21–28.
5. O'Connell, *op. cit.*, p. 21.

6. For a fuller description of this thesis, see Marvin E. Wolfgang and Franco Ferracuti, *The Subculture of Violence* (London: Tavistock, 1967).

7. These compilations have been made by the staff of the National Commission on the Causes and Prevention of Violence and appear in the Progress Report.

8. Most of this history of labour violence has been abstracted from Philip Taft, 'Violence in American Labor Disputes', *Annals of the American Academy of Political and Social Science* (March 1966), pp. 127–140.

9. Arnold Forster, 'Violence in the Fanatical Left and Right', *Annals of the American Academy of Political and Social Science* (March 1966), p. 143.

10. Alexis de Tocqueville, *L'Ancien Régime*, trans. M. W. Patterson (Oxford, England: Basil Blackwell, 1949), p. 186. Cited and brought to my attention by Judd Marmor, 'Some Psychological Aspects of Contemporary Urban Violence', n.d. (mimeo).

11. See note 7.

12. The following list identifies the source of information and the universities where the student violence occurred: *The Times* (London), 18 January 1969–Tokyo University; *International Herald Tribune*, 18 January 1969–Barcelona University; *Time*, 17 January 1969–San Francisco State College, California; *The Times*, 8 January 1969–Tokyo University; *The Times*, 24 January 1969–Free University of Berlin.

13. *The Times*, 19 January 1969.

14. Quoted by *Time* magazine, international edition, 18 April 1969, p. 40.

15. These are perceptive comments from Richard Lorber and Ernest Fladell, 'The Generation Gap', *Life*, 17 May 1969.

16. *The Sunday Times* (London), 26 January 1968.

12 / CRIME, PUNISHMENT, AND PSYCHIATRY

THOMAS S. SZASZ

RELATIONSHIP BETWEEN PSYCHIATRY AND LAW

There has long been a close association between psychiatry and law, and especially between institutional psychiatry and criminal law. Traditionally, psychiatrists have been enlisted to assist lawyers, judges, and juries in determining whether a person was or was not insane or mentally ill, and "dangerous to himself or others," and hence whether it was or was not justifiable to commit him to a mental hospital. They have also aided in ascertaining whether an accused pleading not guilty by reason of insanity was or was not insane when he committed the criminal act. More recently, psychiatric assessments of the defendant have been utilized in every phase of the criminal law, from pretrial psychiatric examination to the administration of psychiatric treatment programs in prison. Nevertheless, psychiatry has been conventionally defined, and is defined with special emphasis now, as a medical specialty concerned with the diagnosis and treatment of mental diseases. These two facts point to certain basic problems—to certain unresolved moral, philosophical, and semantic controversies—regarding the very nature of law, of psychiatry, and indeed of man himself. It may be best to begin by trying to clarify these problems.

If psychiatry is just another medical specialty, then why should there be any closer connection between law and psychiatry than there is between law and urology, or law and dermatology, and so on? Psychiatry differs from nonpsychiatric medicine in that it deals with (abnormal) behaviors of (deviant) persons[1] rather than with diseased bodies. In addition, certain modern definitions of psychiatry assign to it the study and treatment not only of mental diseases but also of behavioral disorders.

Since the concern of criminal law is behavior that is abnormal or deviant according to specific criteria, we can see the close connection indeed between psychiatry and the criminal law. Both law and psychiatry are applied sciences or policy disciplines, their common basis being ethics.

Criminal law is concerned with behavior that violates criminal laws, and with the social disposition of persons who are accused or convicted of such violations. Psychiatry (especially institutional psychiatry) is concerned with behavior that violates the norms of mental health, and with the social disposition of persons diagnosed as suffering from such mental disorders. Both disciplines are thus involved with (1) the study of certain kinds of "bad" human behavior; and (2) the social control of certain kinds of "bad" persons. The criteria for intervening in the lives of persons who are said to be criminally guilty or psychiatrically sick overlap, and the methods of intervention are often similar. Psychiatry and criminal law do not deal with different subjects; they apply different strategies to the same subject—human behavior and misbehavior. Let us now spell out the perspective of psychiatry.

The criminal law makes numerous common-sense and legal distinctions among various types or degrees of responsibility. For example, when a gangster ambushes and kills a rival, he will be considered responsible for criminal intent and first degree murder. Whereas, if an intoxicated driver crashes into another car and kills someone he does not even know, he will be considered responsible, at most, for criminal negligence and manslaughter. In the first instance, the defendant's responsibility is for the murder; in the second, for the negligence. Although both victims are equally dead, the criminal law distinguishes—without recourse to psychiatric examinations, explanations, or experts—between two radically different acts.

There are, however, many circumstances in which psychiatric considerations are deemed relevant to assessing the defendant's criminal responsibility. Since in practice these assessments center on and culminate in judgments about whether or not the patient is mentally ill, insane, or psychotic, it is necessary to briefly review what these concepts mean.

What is mental illness? First, its crucial manifestations are behavioral (for example, asserting unusual fears or claims), not bodily (for example, displaying fever or jaundice).

Second, it may be attributed to bodily disease or injury. For example, a person with neurosyphilis may be said to be insane or to have an organic psychosis; or a drunk person may be said to suffer from a delirium or a toxic psychosis. In such cases, mental illness is attributed to anatomical or chemical alterations in the brain. Some people—psychiatrists and criminologists among them—believe that all so-called mental illnesses are of this type, and that it is only a matter of time before their organic causes are demonstrated.

Third, mental illness may be attributed to psychological or social disorder or stress. For example, a young adult who neglects his personal hygiene and refuses to study or earn a living may be diagnosed as schizophrenic. In such cases mental illness is attributed to, and is also the name of, a so-called disorder or malfunctioning of the personality. Individuals exhibiting such malfunctioning are considered sick even though it is admitted that they do not suffer from any demonstrable disease or injury of the body.

Fourth, mental illness may be used as a convenient strategic label to disqualify a person from a role, or to qualify him for another. For example, attorneys or judges involved in the trial of a politically controversial defendant may claim that, because of mental illness, he is unfit to stand trial; and they may thus avoid an embarrassing public spectacle. Or a pregnant woman wishing to have an abortion in a state permitting it on the ground of mental illness but not on demand may claim that she will kill herself rather than bear her child; she and her physicians may thus be able to obtain a legal abortion. In making these claims, all the participants may know, and even admit, that they do not consider the ostensible patient sick in any way, but are merely complying with the requirements of a complex medical-psychiatric-legal game imposed on them by a bureaucratic state.

The examples just discussed illustrate the differences between the theoretical and the practical definitions of the concept of mental illness. Theoretically, it may be defined as unsoundness of mind. Practically, the concept must be broken down into two distinct components: a biological (anatomical, physiological) or behavioral (moral, psychological, social) condition; and a social role. Let us consider each of these components separately.

When we say that a person is ill (bodily or mentally), we mean two quite different things: first, that he displays an abnormal biological or behavioral condition; and second, that he occupies or is cast into a deviant social role.

For example, a person suffering from pneumonia displays signs and symptoms of an abnormal biological condition (cough, fever, increased white-cell count, clouding of the lung fields on X-ray examination). Similarly, a person diagnosed as suffering from schizophrenia may display evidence of an abnormal behavioral condition (unusual speech pattern, neglect of personal hygiene, assertion of a false personal identity). These manifestations, usually elicited and identified by a physician, signify and form the basis for the judgment that the person is in, or has, an abnormal condition called "illness." But regardless of whether a person is or is not ill in this sense, there remains the question of whether he assumes or rejects the sick role—that is, the role of a person who defines himself as ill and as in need of medical assistance.

Typically, the role of medical patient is assumed voluntarily, whereas that of mental patient (especially in situations impinging on the criminal law) is assumed involuntarily. Whereas biological conditions exist regardless of whether they are observed and recognized by human beings, social roles—like that of the medical or mental patient—exist only insofar as they are observed and recognized by human beings.

IMPLICATIONS OF THE SICK ROLE FOR THE PSYCHIATRIST

A person may be ill, but may prefer not to assume the sick role. We often do this when we have a cold but go to the office or theater. Conversely, a person may not be ill, but may prefer to assume the sick role. We often do this when we offer illness as an excuse for avoiding an obligation, such as going to a party or a meeting. Soldiers, housewives, and other oppressed people have traditionally assumed the sick role to avoid the dangers of combat or the drudgeries of child care.

Inasmuch as psychiatrists deal mainly with persons who do not suffer from demonstrable biological abnormalities, they deal with persons who either assume the role of mental patient or are cast into that role by others. An individual may be said to assume the role of mental patient voluntarily if, feeling beset by personal problems, he visits a psychotherapist or seeks treatment in a mental hospital. On the other hand, if a person feels satisfied with his own behavior, but is committed to a mental hospital, then the role of mental patient is ascribed to him.

From the point of view of law, society, and civil liberties, then, the voluntary mental patient resembles the ordinary medical patient, or, for that matter, any client who purchases the services of an expert. I have suggested that this type of psychiatric relationship be designated as "Contractual Psychiatry." On the other hand, from this point of view, the involuntary mental patient resembles the accused or convicted criminal, since he neither initiates nor otherwise controls his relationship with the expert. I have suggested that this type of psychiatric relationship be designated as "Institutional Psychiatry."[2]

Institutional psychiatry and the criminal law are both concerned with defining which roles are legitimate and which are not, and with enforcing conformity to prescribed roles. The criminal law forbids illegal behavior; institutional psychiatry forbids abnormal behavior. When, for example, an uneducated, overburdened housewife escapes from her life of insignificance into the dramatic pretense that she is the Virgin Mary, the psychiatrist calls the woman sick and, with the aid of mental hygiene laws and mental hospitals, interferes with her efforts to play the role she has selected for herself. This prohibition, buttressed by the sanction of incarceration in the mental hospital, is similar to the prohibition of the role of bank robber, buttressed by the sanction of incarceration in prison. This function of institutional psychiatry rests squarely on the fundamental differences between the mental hospital and the medical hospital.

As mental illness is unlike medical illness, so the mental hospital is unlike the medical hospital. In contemporary American society (and Western societies, generally), the relationship of the medical patient to the medical hospital is essentially that of a buyer to a vendor. The medical patient is a voluntary consumer of the hospital's services. He must give "informed consent" to his physician for any diagnostic or therapeutic procedure. Without it, the physician is committing an unauthorized invasion of the patient's body and is subject to both civil and criminal sanctions. In opposition to this is the involuntary mental patient, who may be compelled, through the power vested in the physician and the mental hospital by the state, to submit to psychiatric incarceration and to interventions defined as therapeutic for him.

In this connection it is important to note that excepting death, involuntary psychiatric hospitalization imposes the most severe penalty our legal system can inflict on a human being: namely, loss of liberty. The existence of psychiatric institutions that function as prisons, and of judicial sentences that are, in effect, indeterminate sentences to such prisons, is the backdrop against which all discussion of criminal responsibility and its relation to psychiatry must take place. This is especially true in jurisdictions where there is no death penalty. Does it matter whether or not the accused was, at the time of the offense, sane and criminally responsible, or insane and criminally not responsible? For a comprehensive answer to this question, I shall offer, first, an epistemological analysis of the concept of criminal responsibility; then, a description of the major rules used for ascertaining it; and, finally, an analysis of it as a strategic label to justify the imposition of certain kinds of sanctions on persons accused or convicted of crimes.

THE PROBLEM OF CRIMINAL RESPONSIBILITY

In criminology, law, and psychiatry there is a vast literature devoted to the problem of criminal responsibility.[3] Through the constant use of this term, many students of crime, as well as lay persons, have come to believe that there is such a thing as criminal responsibility. All that is needed is a psychiatrist to ascertain whether or not an offender "has" it. The idea of criminal responsibility is neither synonymous with, nor derived from, the concepts of physical or mental illness. Pneumonia, hypertension, and schizophrenia designate physical and mental diseases; yet these terms provide no definitive clue to criminal responsibility.

Despite these difficulties, it is possible to provide an approximate definition of criminal responsibility. It usually refers to a particular kind of relationship between an offender and the society in which he lives. In other words, criminal responsibility is very nearly synonymous with punishability. The concept refers not only to the offender but also to society's right to punish him. The meaning of the concept must therefore be sought not in a trait or quality of the offender but in his *human situation*.

Before turning to an illustration of the way the term "responsibility" is used in the criminal law, it should be noted that this concept has three separate, though overlapping, meanings. We speak of *descriptive* responsibility when we assign a causal relationship to two events, as, for example, in the statement: "The avalanche at X was responsible for the death of three skiers." We speak of *prescriptive* responsibility when we imply that some action should be taken or avoided, as, for example, in the statement: "Cigarette smoking is responsible for lung cancer." And we speak of *ascriptive* responsibility when we assign blame to a person for an act he is alleged to have committed, as, for example, in the statement: "I am holding John responsible for the murder of James." It is unfortunate that there are not three different words for the three meanings of "responsibility." As matters now stand in law and psychiatry, the three meanings are used interchangeably, without specifying the necessary distinctions between them. A brief illustration may clarify this discussion.

Let us take the statement "John killed James." From the point of view of descriptive responsibility, the report is either true or false. To evaluate the statement, the listener must find out if it is correct or incorrect. Thus there are three possible reactions to the assertion that "John killed James": agreement, disagreement, or indecision.

Criminology and law, however, do not deal with physical facts as such. That is the province of the physical sciences. The province of criminology and law is social relations and ethics, or, more broadly, human rule-following behavior. Thus the questions become: *"How* and *why* did John kill James?" and "Is John guilty or innocent?" To answer these questions, it is necessary to seek facts and motives. Did John kill James in cold blood to rob him? Or did James throw himself in front of John's truck? Or, when James jumped in the river to commit suicide, did John "kill" him by failing to rescue him? And so forth. The point is that special legal, psychological, and social inquiry is often required to discover how and why John killed James. If, for example, John was a soldier and James his enemy, this would not be a legal matter. However, in civil life, "cold-blooded murder" makes prosecution imperative. Under still other circumstances—for example, when the distinction between suicide and homicide is unclear—it may be a matter of choice for the legal authorities whether or not to take action.

From the prototype in religion, both jurisprudence and psychiatry acquired the idea of *responsibility as guilt*. It is, however, senseless to speak of guilt when responsibility is used in the descriptive mode.

Descriptive responsibility for an act may be attributed to a person correctly or falsely. If attributed correctly, the individual is descriptively responsible; if falsely, he is descriptively innocent. In the actual criminal process, ascriptions of both guilt and innocence may be verified or disproved publicly, as by a jury. The following example, which analyzes descriptive and ascriptive responsiblity in terms of four different situations, should help to clarify this.

The charge is that John Doe killed James Smith, in Columbus, Ohio, on January 30, 1957. Is Doe responsible for Smith's death? There are four possibilities in such a case. First, John Doe's responsibility for the act is proved to be both true descriptively and ascriptively. This is the case of the guilty criminal who is arrested and convicted. Second, Doe may have committed the act, but may not be judged criminally responsible for it by those empowered to pass on the matter. This is the case in accidental homicide. John Doe has descriptive responsibility but not ascriptive responsibility in this case. Third, the description of John Doe's responsibility might have been false—for example, he may not have been in Columbus, Ohio, on that date. Nevertheless, responsibility for the act could be ascribed to him. This is the successful frame-up, or the conviction of an innocent man as a scapegoat. Fourth, and last, Doe's responsibility for killing Smith may prove to be false both descriptively and ascriptively. This is the case of the innocent man finding justice in the courtroom. A summary of these four contingencies is presented in Table 1.

Typically, the defense of insanity is raised only in those criminal cases in which the offender's descriptive responsibility for the antisocial act is accepted as true. Of course, this is true only if the defendant himself pleads insanity, which, in essence, means: "Yes, I committed the crime, but I am not responsible because I did not know what I was doing." If the question of insanity is raised by someone else—for example, by the judge or the district attorney, and especially if this is done to avoid trial and, instead, to confine

Table 1 Classification of Acts According to Types of Responsibility

	I	II	III	IV
Descriptive Responsibility	True	True	False	False
Ascriptive Responsibility	True	False	True	False

I: The apprehended and successfully prosecuted criminal.
II: The accident.
III: The successful frame-up, or conviction of the innocent person.
IV: The unsuccessful frame-up, or acquittal of the innocent person.

the accused in a hospital for the criminally insane—then there is doubt of the accused person's descriptive responsibility. Perhaps the defendant has been falsely accused. But if he is not tried, he cannot establish his innocence—that is, his descriptive (factual) nonresponsibility for the crime.[4]

Admission of descriptive responsibility is logically inherent in a plea of insanity. Hence, the argument falls in Group II (Table 1). Such cases are characterized by true descriptive responsibility and false ascriptive responsibility. A verdict in an American court of "not guilty by reason of insanity" states precisely this.

More generally, the verdict could be stated in this form: "Although the death of James Smith was caused by John Doe, he is not guilty (ascriptively) because of X." X may stand for many things, but it usually means one of these three: accident, self-defense, or insanity. Irresponsibility for a harmful act by reason of insanity is thus logically similar to irresponsibility for such an act due to accident or self-defense. The notion of insanity is in the same category as other conditions that excuse the commission of otherwise criminal acts.

THE INSANITY PLEA AND ITS CONSEQUENCES

Most words, and certainly all words used during criminal trials in courts of law, have strategic import. Their meaning must be inferred mainly from the consequences of their use. The consequences of pleading guilty and not guilty are clear and generally well appreciated. But the consequences of pleading not guilty by reason of insanity are neither clear nor generally understood. Briefly, they are as follows. If the defense of insanity is not sustained and the defendant is found guilty, he is sentenced to punishment as prescribed by the law and meted out by the judge, much as if he had entered any other plea. If the defense of insanity is sustained, the defendant's fate varies from jurisdiction to jurisdiction. There are two basic possibilities. One is that acquittal by reason of insanity is regarded as being the same as any other acquittal; the defendant walks out of the courtroom a free man. This is what happened to the fictional hero of Robert Traver's *Anatomy of a Murder*.[5] It is what would have happened to Jack Ruby had Melvin Belli's defense strategy succeeded.[6] However, this outcome is unusual and is becoming rarer every day.

The other course of action, which has been gaining ground rapidly in recent years, is to treat the individual acquitted by reason of insanity as a dangerously insane person from whom society needs the utmost protection. After his acquittal, such a defendant is forthwith transported to an insane asylum where he remains until "cured" or until "no longer dangerous to himself and others."[7] This concept and procedure are exemplified in the District of Columbia, where, "if any person tried . . . for an offense is acquitted solely on the ground that he was insane at the time of its commission, the court shall order such person to be confined in a hospital for the mentally ill."[8] The American Law Institute Rule embodies the same principle of automatic commitment. In a decision relying on this rule, Judge Kaufman wrote:

Throughout our opinion we have not viewed the choice as one between imprisonment and immediate release. Rather, we believe the true choice to be between different forms of institutionalization—between the prison and the mental hospital. Underlying today's decision is our belief that treatment of the truly incompetent in mental institutions would better serve the interests of society as well as the defendant's.[9]

Consider what this means. The judge recognizes the defendant as mentally competent to stand trial; he allows him to enter a plea and defend himself as best he can; and, if found guilty, he considers the defendant sane enough to be sentenced to the penitentiary. But should the defendant be found not guilty by reason of insanity, that verdict immediately transforms him into a "truly incompetent" person whom the judge feels justified in committing to a mental hospital.

In short, tests of criminal responsibility cannot be evaluated without knowing whether acquittal means freedom or commitment. The personal consequences for the defendant of successfully pleading insanity are extremely important. Indeed, preoccupation with the wording of the various rules in both popular and professional discussions of the subject only serves to distract attention from the basic issue of social control through institutional psychiatry. Actually, where a successful insanity defense means commitment, the well-informed defendant rarely feels that the insanity plea serves his best interests. He tends to avoid this plea, preferring punishment in jail to treatment in the mental hospital.

What would happen, in jurisdictions where commitment follows automatically upon acquittal by reason of insanity, if the defendant clearly understood this choice? I venture to predict that such pleas would become very infrequent, and perhaps would disappear altogether. Although this is hardly the intention of the "liberalized" rules of criminal insanity, I would consider it a happy outcome. I do not believe that insanity should be an excusing condition for crime. The sooner the insanity plea is abolished, or the sooner it disappears because of its dire consequences for the defendant, the better off we shall all be.

But even if the defendant does not elect to plead insanity, so long as laws empower physicians to incarcerate people in mental hospitals, the law enforcement agencies of the state will be tempted to make use of these laws. How this has happened can be seen in the District of Columbia following the adoption of the Durham rule (an individual is not responsible for criminal behavior if such behavior was a product of mental disease or defect). Since the plea of not guilty by reason of insanity insured an indefinite stay at St. Elizabeth's Hospital, judges chose in some cases not to allow defendants to plead guilty and receive a minor prison sentence, but insisted instead that they plead not guilty by reason of insanity and, following "acquittal," be committed to the mental hospital.[10] In a decision that sidestepped the constitutional issues involved, the Supreme Court ruled in 1962 that this tactic was improper, and that instead of foisting an involuntary plea of insanity on such defendants, the court ought to initiate proceedings for their commitment.[11] This not only leaves commitment intact as a quasi-penal sanction, but recognizes it as the constitutionally proper alternative to a prison sentence.

Whether or not it is constitutional for the state to use mental hospitals to deprive citizens of their liberty is for the authorized interpreters of the Constitution to judge. Until now, the courts have found such detention constitutional. But we might recall that earlier courts found slavery constitutional.[12] Whatever the courts decide, responsible citizens must judge this moral and political matter for themselves.

The argument is often posed that the involuntary confinement of a person in a mental hospital is itself therapeutic, or that it is a condition necessary for the proper administration of some type of psychiatric treatment (for example, electroshock). In this view, held by many psychiatrists, commitment may be compared to the restraint of the patient on the operating table, necessary for the proper performance of surgical treatment. The obvious difference, of course, is that the surgical patient consents to the restraint, whereas the mental patient does not. How, then, shall we decide? Is personal restraint through commitment therapy or punishment?

In the final analysis, this, too, is a matter of definition. If therapy is defined by those who administer it, and if psychiatrists insist, as they do, that commitment is therapy, then it is therapy; and if punishment is defined by those who are the objects of coercion, and if committed mental patients insist, as they do, that psychiatric incarceration is punishment, then it is punishment.

The landmark forensic-psychiatric case in Anglo-American law is undoubtedly that of M'Naghten. In England in 1843, Daniel M'Naghten shot and killed Drummond, private secretary to Sir Robert Peel, M'Naghten's true object. The defense was insanity. Medical evidence was introduced showing that M'Naghten was "laboring under an insane delusion" of being hounded by enemies, among them Peel. The jury found him "not guilty, on the ground of insanity."[13]

Following this verdict, the question of unsoundness of mind as an excuse for crime was debated in the House of Lords. The judges of England were asked to present their views on the criteria for such an acquittal. The most important part of the judges' answers was the following:

[T]o establish a defence on the ground of insanity, it must be clearly proved that, at the time of the committing of the act, the party accused was labouring under such a defect of reason, from disease of the mind, as not to know the nature and quality of the act he was doing; or if he did know it, that he did not know he was doing what was wrong.[14]

The judges' idea was reasonable. The purpose of the criminal law is, or should be, to punish deliberately or negligently committed wrongdoing. A harmful act cannot be judged by considering only *what* happened. It is also necessary to evaluate *how* it happened. Two hypothetical cases will illustrate this. In the first, a man has an epileptic seizure while driving; as a result, he loses control of his car, and runs down and kills a woman. In the second, a man loses a large sum of money in a card game he believes was crooked; he waits for the winner to cross the street, then runs over him with his car and kills him. In the first case, the man "did not know the nature or quality of the act he was doing"; in the second, he did. The M'Naghten rule was intended to distinguish accidents such as the one caused by an epileptic attack from deliberate acts of mischief. It would be difficult to quarrel with this intention. However, the implementation of this rule—and especially the means of assessing whether or not an offender knew what he was doing, and that it was wrong—has resulted in vast difficulties. Most of them have been due to the concept that so-called mental illnesses are similar to neurological defects. Hence, the belief that mental illness causes a lack of appreciation of what one does.

In the further consideration of this subject, three issues must be kept in mind:

1. M'Naghten's case codified as law the notion that certain acts may result from mental illness and that such illness is similar to bodily disease. It made no distinction among organic defects (for example, congenital idiocy), acute intoxication (for example, drunkenness), or ideologically motivated actions (for example, political crime). This global and undifferentiated conception of mental illness has been accepted even by critics of the M'Naghten rule.

2. The postacquittal fate of the defendant was not explicitly defined. Actually, M'Naghten's fate became a model. Following his "acquittal," M'Naghten was involuntarily hospitalized: from 1843 until 1864, he was held in the Bethlehem Hospital; when the Broadmoor Institution for the Criminally Insane was opened in 1864, he was transferred there. He died in 1865, having been incarcerated for the last twenty-two years of his life. Since then, it has been accepted practice to impose involuntary mental hospitalization, often for life, on persons acquitted on the ground of insanity. In 1857,

fourteen years after M'Naghten was tried, an act was passed in England that decreed that persons acquitted on account of insanity "be detained at her Majesty's pleasure." History does repeat itself: in the District of Columbia, Durham's acquittal in 1954 was soon followed by statutes making the commitment of such persons "automatic."

3. The socioeconomic, political, and ethical implications of deviant behavior were obscured in favor of its so-called medical causes. This, too, has remained a significant issue to our day, even in the modifications of the M'Naghten rule.

Much has been made of psychiatric dissatisfaction with so-called tests of insanity, such as are implicit in the M'Naghten rule. In this connection, Isaac Ray's argument is usually quoted to show that so-called enlightened psychiatric knowledge militates against the use of such tests.[15] Ray's forensic-psychiatric views found expression in the New Hampshire rule. In two celebrated decisions handed down by the Supreme Court of New Hampshire in 1869 and 1871, the relation between mental disease and criminal responsibility was defined as a problem for the jury. In the Jones case the court expressed itself as follows:

Enough has already been said as to the use of symptoms, phases, or manifestations of mental disease as legal tests of capacity to entertain a criminal intent. They are all clearly matters of evidence to be weighed by the jury upon the question whether the act was the offspring of insanity. If it was, a criminal intent did not produce it. If it was not, a criminal intent did produce it and it was crime.[16]

Under this rule, it suffices for a psychiatrist to testify that the defendant has certain standard symptoms, and may therefore be classified as having a particular mental illness. Furthermore, the psychiatrist must testify that the crime was caused by the defendant's condition. This sounds better than the M'Naghten rule, but the improvement is deceptive. Actually, the change may be an ethical retrogression. This rule retains many of the difficulties of its predecessors. It, too, treats some kinds of deviant behavior as illness, and is silent on the disposition of the person acquitted under this rule.

Perhaps the most deceptive yet most significant feature of the New Hampshire rule is the positive valuation it places on the *absence* of a predetermined test of insanity. I think that those who claim that physical and mental illnesses are basically similar should be required to abide by the rules of the game they themselves chose. The presence of a bodily disease like pneumonia or syphilis can be established by publicly demonstrable tests. Following from this, if we are going to talk of mental diseases, then there should be publicly demonstrable tests to establish the presence of such diseases. For without the tests, expert opinion ceases to be scientific (in the instrumental sense of this word), and instead becomes oracular. Indeed, beginning with the New Hampshire rule and culminating in the Durham decision, the oracular pronouncements of eminent psychiatrists have replaced publicly verifiable facts and scientifically acceptable theories. The change from M'Naghten to Durham is thus a move away from a rule of law toward a rule of men.

Before turning to the Durham rule, it is necessary to mention the so-called irresistible impulse test. This test rests on the dual premise that freedom of the will is essential to criminal responsibility, and that there are human conditions or situations in which men lack such will and are instead irresistibly driven to act in certain ways. Such actions are thus placed in the same category as accidents. Neither is purposefully planned and executed. These statements do not, of course, describe observable human behavior. The idea of an irresistible impulse is an example of a common practice in forensic psychiatry, in which theories of behavior and prescriptions of conduct are presented as if they were empirical observations. Criticism of this practice is not our concern here. It should suffice to note that the idea of an act resulting from an irresistible impulse presupposes the idea that action is impulse-motivated, and that some impulses can be resisted whereas others cannot. Sanity is then conceived as the ability to resist antisocial impulses.

The doctrine of irresistible impulse is of American origin and dates from 1834. It was adopted in several states and received its strongest support in a decision handed down in Alabama in 1886. There is a vast literature about these decisions.[17] Most of it deals with the advantages of this test over the M'Naghten formula. To many, the M'Naghten rule implied a cognitive or intellectual definition of insanity. The irresistible impulse test is probably best viewed as an early expression of opposition to the M'Naghten formula, based on the alleged overemphasis of that decision on the cognitive aspects of the personality. Accordingly, there has been a constant agitation, mostly by psychiatrists, for the recognition of the so-called emotional aspects of mental illness.

The Durham rule is a logical sequel to the irresistible impulse test. It reveals a persistent preoccupation with the question of "sickness" in some part of the personality, and with a refutation of the significance of the role of cognition in behavior. It was handed down by the United States Court of Appeals for the District of Columbia in 1954.[18] Its most significant assertion is that "an accused is not criminally responsible if his unlawful act was the product of mental disease or mental defect."[19] This is a semantic modernization of the New Hampshire rule. The decision has been widely hailed by both jurists and psychiatrists as a great scientific advance in criminal jurisprudence. A few legal scholars, and an even smaller number of psychiatrists, have vigorously criticized it and its implications.

Clearly, the Durham decision represents the culmination of what could aptly be called the psychiatrization of the criminal law. It is an attempt to transform into legal reality the notion that there are two modes of existence—one sane, the other insane. Since this rule has had a powerful impact on contemporary American jurisprudence, the psychiatric, legal, and ethical aspects of it will be examined in detail.

According to Judge David Bazelon, who formulated it, the Durham decision was based on the ethical principle that "our collective conscience does not allow punishment where it cannot impose blame."[20] This would seem to be both self-evident and commendable. Actually, it is neither. The statement lays claim to a moral principle as a regulatory force in social behavior. It is not a description of a "natural law," but, rather, a prescription of principles that ought to govern social living.

What is prescribed? That there should be no punishment without blameworthiness. The logical corollary of this is that there should be no reward without praiseworthiness. The fact is, however, that our society is not constructed along these lines. Moreover, acceptance of these principles would change our society into an organization quite unknown to us, and hardly imaginable, in which both punishment for bad performance and reward for good performance would be dispensed with.

There is another source of difficulty. In the Anglo-American, and also Roman, philosophy of law, ignorance of the law is no excuse. How can a person ignorant of the law be held responsible for breaking it? How can he be blamed for committing an act that he did not know was prohibited? The answer is that the well-being of a free society is based on the assumption that every adult knows what he may and may not do. Legal responsibility is an expectation: first, that people will learn the laws of the land; second, that they will try to adhere to them. Thus, if they break the law, we consider them blameworthy.

If we apply this reasoning to offenders who are alleged to be mentally ill, similar conclusions will be reached. If mental illness resembles bodily illness, it will not be an excuse from adherence to the law. If, on the other hand, mental illness is similar to ignorance, as indeed it is, then again it is not a condition that excuses violation of the law. Just as the recognition of ignorance and its correction are the responsibility of the adult citizen, so also are the recognition of mental illness and its correction. Thus, from a purely logical point of view, there are no good grounds for the rule that there should be two types of laws, one for the mentally healthy and another for the mentally sick.

The Durham decision and the attempts to implement it have resulted in many difficulties. Perhaps the most fundamental problem is the idea that to be punished as a lawbreaker, a person must be blameworthy. If we accept this, we must determine whether, and in what measure, an offender may be blamed. To complicate matters further, the Durham decision has created a firm but vague connection between blameworthiness and mental health by the insinuation that only mentally healthy persons can be blamed for what they do. This presumption has created a moral and scientific vacuum, into which the forensic psychiatrist has eagerly projected himself.

According to the Durham decision, if the defense of insanity is raised in a criminal trial, it is a "matter of fact" for the jury to decide whether the offender suffered from a mental illness when he committed the act for which he is charged. However, this will not work. The word "disease" always denotes a theory, not a fact. Thus, if the more complex term "mental disease" is to mean anything at all, it too must refer to a theory, not to a fact. For example, that a patient is jaundiced may be a fact: his skin is yellow instead of pinkish white. But being jaundiced is not the same as having a disease. Whether this hypothetical patient has gallstones, infectious hepatitis, or cancer, his disease is the theory we construct to explain why his skin is yellow. Hence, it would be a perversion of our language to refer to a disease as though it were a fact.

Mental illness, as we have seen, is a more confusing concept than bodily illness. Yet the jury is supposed to determine—as a "matter of fact"—whether the accused does or does not have a mental illness. It is possible for a group of people, such as a jury, to *decide to call* someone mentally ill. But this is then *their theory* of why he acted as he did. It is no more or less than it would be to assert that the accused is possessed by the devil. Indeed, to mistake one's theories for facts is often regarded as a symptom of schizophrenia. Yet this is what the language of the Durham decision does. It reifies some of the shakiest and most controversial aspects of contemporary psychiatry—that is, the definition of mental disease and the classification of such alleged diseases—and by legal fiat seeks to transform inadequate theory into judicial fact.

Further, the Durham formula takes the notion of mental illness and requires the psychiatrist and the jury to determine whether the criminal act was a result of it. This, too, is supposed to be a fact. Unfortunately, not only cannot this be a fact, it cannot even be a rational theory.

To clarify this, let us consider a hypothetical example. A man suddenly pulls a gun in broad daylight and shoots several people sightseeing in front of the White House. When arrested and questioned, he explains that he was protecting the president from communist assassins who were about to throw an atomic bomb on the White House lawn. Many contemporary psychiatrists would readily testify, first, that the murderer suffers from schizophrenia, and, second, that schizophrenia was the cause of his act. But was it?

I submit that what we *call* schizophrenia is a theory to explain how such a thing could happen. After all, people rarely shoot strangers. The occurrence of any crime creates a powerful impetus to construct a theory to explain it. People want to know not only what happened but also why. Each person tends to form his own theory in accordance with his educational resources and personal prejudices. The psychiatrist, by virtue of his education, may formulate a more sophisticated, or at least more complicated, theory than the layman. But it is improper on anyone's part to ask if a murderer's schizophrenia *caused* the criminal act. An explanation or theory can never be a cause.

What, then, did cause the killer to commit the crime? Psychiatrists could no doubt contribute to the answer. The cause of a murder by a schizophrenic might be arranged in a temporal order, beginning with how the offender was treated as a child, and ending with so-called precipitating events a few moments before the crime. For example, the waitress who served breakfast to the criminal may have been gruff, providing a final blow to his precariously weak self-concept and precipitating the paranoid-megalomaniac crime. This, however, is not the sort of cause that would help a jury to assign blame to either the waitress or the criminal.

We thus discover what we should have known all along—that genuine scientific causal theories make it unnecessary and, in fact, impossible to assign moral blame to a person. If we take physics and its various branches seriously, we would conclude—as have most people in our society—that we cannot blame the gods if our crops fail or our cattle die. Similarly, if psychology and sociology were taken seriously—but this few people seem prepared to do—then we should have to conclude two very different things: first, that insofar as it is always possible to regard antecedent events as explanations of human behavior, men should never be blamed or praised for what they do; second, that insofar as men are human beings, not machines, they always have some choice in how they act—hence, they are *always* responsible for their conduct. There is method in madness, no less than in sanity.

It would be a mistake to think that such considerations are judicially nihilistic. On the contrary. They highlight the differences between two different social enterprises. In the one, the goal is to understand people and perhaps help them to live as they see fit. In the other, the goal is to control people and thus help society. It is futile to believe that problems of social control (for which processes of blaming, whether couched in the language of sin or sickness, are indispensable) can be dispelled by better understanding of human behavior and motivation. To be sure, many modern psychiatrists and behavioral engineers have insisted on just the opposite thesis, namely, that scientific understanding of human behavior is an effective and proper means for eradicating both crime and mental illness. The problem is that those who support this view, and those who oppose it, have utterly different concepts of the moral nature of man.

THE EMERGENCE OF THE THERAPEUTIC STATE

Those who see the main domestic business of the state as the maintenance of internal peace through a system of just laws justly administered, and those who see its job as the provision of behavioral reform scientifically administered by a scientific elite have, in fact, two radically different visions of society and of man. Since each group strives after a different goal, it is not surprising that each condemns the other's methods. Constitutional government, the rule of law, and due process are indeed inefficient means for bringing about personality change in criminals, especially if their crime is violating laws regulating contraception, abortion, drug abuse, or homosexuality. Similarly, unlimited psychiatric discretion over the identification and diagnosis of alleged offenders, coercive "therapeutic" interventions, and life-long incarceration in insane asylums are neither effective nor ethical means for protecting individual liberties or insuring restraints on the powers of the government. The legal and the medical approaches to social control represent two radically different ideologies, each with its own justificatory rhetoric and restraining actions. It behooves us to clearly understand the differences between them.

In the legal concept of the state, justice is both an end and a means: when such a state is just, it may be said to have fulfilled its domestic function. It has then no further claims on its citizens (save for defense against external aggression). What people do—whether they are virtuous or sinful, healthy or sick, rich or poor, educated or stupid—is not the business of the state. This, then, is a concept of the state as an institution of limited scope and powers.

In the scientific-technological concept of the state, therapy is only a means, not an end. The goal of the Therapeutic State is universal health, or at least unfailing relief from suffering. This untroubled state of man and society is a quintessential feature of the medical-therapeutic perspective on politics. Conflict among individuals, and especially between the individual and the state, is invariably seen as a symptom of illness or psychopathology; and the primary function of the state is accordingly the removal of such conflict through appropriate "therapy"—imposed by force, if necessary. It is not difficult to recognize in this imagery of the Therapeutic State the old inquisitorial, or the more recent totalitarian, concept of the state, now clothed in the garb of psychiatric treatment.[21]

The impetus that drives men to therapeutize human relations and social conflicts appears to be the same as that which drives them to control the physical world. The history of this process—that is, of the birth of modern science in the seventeenth century and its rise to ideological hegemony in the twentieth—has been adequately set forth by others.[22] I shall confine myself here to illustrating the incipient and developed forms of this ideology through quotations from the works of two of its most illustrious American protagonists: Benjamin Rush and Karl Menninger.

Benjamin Rush (1746–1813), a signer of the Declaration of Independence, was Physician General of the Continental Army and served as Professor of Physics and Dean of the medical school at the University of Pennsylvania. He is the undisputed father of American psychiatry. Quoted below, without comment, are passages from Rush's writings that show how he transformed moral questions into medical problems, political judgments into therapeutic decisions.

Perhaps hereafter it may be as much the business of a physician as it is now of a divine to reclaim mankind from vice.[23]

Mankind considered as creatures made for immortality are worthy of all our cares. Let us view them as patients in a hospital. The more they resist our efforts to serve them, the more they have need of our services.[24]

The excess of the passion for liberty, inflamed by the successful issue of the war [of Independence], produced, in many people, opinions and conduct, which could not be removed by reason nor restrained by government. . . . The intensive influence which these opinions had upon the understandings, passions, and morals of many of the citizens of the United States, constituted a form of insanity.[25]

In the year 1815, a drunkard, I hope, will be as infamous in society as a liar or thief, and the use of spirits as uncommon in families as a drink made of a solution of arsenic or a decoction of hemlock.[26]

. . . Miss H. L. . . . was confined in our hospital in the year 1800. For several weeks she discovered every mark of a sound mind, except one. She hated her father. On a certain day, she acknowledged, with pleasure, a return of her filial attachment and affection for him; soon after she was discharged cured.[27]

Chagrin, shame, fear, terror, anger, unfit for legal acts, are transient madness. . . . Suicide is madness. . . . Physicians best judges of sanity.[28]

There was a time when these things [i.e., criticism of Rush's opinions and actions] irritated and distressed me, but I now hear and see them with the same indifference and pity that I hear the ravings and witness the antic gestures of my deranged patients in our hospital. We often hear of "prisoners at large." The majority of mankind are madmen at large. . . . Were we to live our lives over again and engage in the same benevolent enterprise [i.e., political reform], our means should be not reasoning but bleeding, purging, low diet, and the tranquilizing chair.[29]

Rush's foregoing views provide an example of the early-nineteenth-century medical-therapeutic perspective on political and social conduct. His statements cited above amply support my contention that although ostensibly he was a founder of American constitutional government, actually he was an architect of the Therapeutic State.[30] The leaders of the American Enlightenment never tired of emphasizing the necessity for restraining the powers of the rulers—that is, for checks and balances in the structure of government. Rush, on the other hand, consistently advocated rule by benevolent despotism—that is, political absolutism justified as medical necessity.

In short, as the Constitution articulates the principles of the legal state, in which both ruler and ruled are governed by the rule of law, so Rush's writings articulate the principles of the Therapeutic State, in which the citizen-patient's conduct is governed by the clinical judgment of the medical despot. The former constitutes a basis for expanding the personal liberty of the citizen; the latter, for expanding the political power of the government.

To bring into focus the ideology and rhetoric on which our present-day Therapeutic Society rests, I shall next present, in capsule form, the pertinent opinions of one of its foremost contemporary spokesmen, Karl Menninger (1893–   ). Menninger, a founder of the famed Menninger Clinic and Foundation, a former president of the American Psychoanalytic Association, the recipient of numerous psychiatric honors, and the author of several influential books in the mental health field, is one of the most prominent psychiatrists in America. His views illustrate the contemporary psychiatric mode of viewing all manner of human problems as mental illnesses—indeed, all of life as a disease requiring psychiatric care.

[T]he declaration continues about travesties upon justice that result from the introduction of psychiatric methods into courts. But what science or scientist is interested in justice? Is pneumonia just? Or cancer? . . . The scientist is seeking the amelioration of an unhappy

situation. This can be secured only if the scientific laws controlling the situation can be discovered and complied with, and not by talking of "justice."[31]

Prostitution and homosexuality rank high in the kingdom of evils. . . . From the standpoint of the psychiatrist, both homosexuality and prostitution—and add to this the use of prostitutes—constitute evidence of immature sexuality and either arrested psychological development or regression. Whatever it may be called by the public, there is no question in the minds of psychiatrists regarding the abnormality of such behavior.[32]

The very word justice *irritates scientists. No surgeon expects to be asked if an operation for cancer is just or not. . . . Behavioral scientists regard it as equally absurd to invoke the question of justice in deciding what to do with a woman who cannot resist her propensity to shoplift, or with a man who cannot repress an impulse to assault somebody. This sort of behavior has to be controlled; it has to be discouraged; it has to be stopped. This (to the scientist) is a matter of public safety and amicable coexistence, not of justice.*[33]

[In a society properly informed by "behavioral science,"] indeterminate sentences will be taken for granted, and preoccupation with punishment as the penalty of the law would have yielded to a concern for the best measure to insure public safety, with rehabilitation of the offender if possible, and as economically as possible.[34]

All of the participants in this effort to bring about a favorable change in the patient . . . are imbued with what we may call a therapeutic attitude. *This is one in direct antithesis to attitudes of avoidance, ridicule, scorn, or punitiveness. Hostile feelings toward the subject, however justified by his unpleasant and even destructive behavior, are not in the curriculum of therapy or in the therapist. . . . Doctors and nurses have no time or thought for inflicting unnecessary pain even upon patients who may be difficult, disagreeable, provocative or even dangerous. It is their duty to care for them, to try to make them well, and to prevent them from doing themselves or others harm. This requires love, not hate.*[35]

Do I believe there is effective treatment for offenders? . . . Most certainly and definitely I do. *Not all cases, to be sure.*[36]

As the foregoing quotations show, Menninger focuses systematically on the offender, or alleged offender, who, in Menninger's view, is either "punished" with hostile intention, or "treated" with therapeutic intention. Accordingly, he urges that we abandon the legal and penological system with its limited and prescribed penalties, and substitute for it a medical and therapeutic system with unlimited and discretionary sanctions defined as "treatments."

In short, the "enlightened" and "scientific" behavioral technologist has for centuries sought, and continues to seek, the destruction of law and justice, and their replacement by science and therapy.

MENTAL HEALTH AND THE NEW AUTHORITARIANISM

Whether we want a society in which man has a chance, however small, to develop his powers and to become an individual, or whether we want one in which such individualism is considered evil and man is viewed as a mere mechanism by his scientific masters, are, in the last analysis, basic ethical questions to which we need not address ourselves here. Of course, those who feel deeply about either of these alternatives believe that they are champion- ing man's dearest and most authentic aspirations. According to the libertari- ans, man's greatest need is for protection from the dangers of unlimited government; according to the therapeutists, his greatest need is for protection from the dangers of unlimited illness. Moreover, as so often happens when people become separated by an ideological gulf, the advocates of these two points of view are no longer on speaking terms. In particular, the behavioral engineers and psychiatric therapists, who define their position as the "progressive" and "scientific" one, have ceased even to acknowledge the existence of a large body of fact and thought critical of what I call the "theory and practice of psychiatric violence." This was true of Rush nearly 200 years ago, for in his writings he never engaged those who opposed tyranny, whether priestly or medical; and it is true now of Menninger, who never confronts those who fear and distrust the violence of psychiatrists no less than of politicians.

Among the contemporary scholars who have opposed the behavioristic- scientific forces tending toward "the abolition of man," C. S. Lewis stands high indeed. Until his death in 1963, Lewis was Professor of Medieval and Renaissance English at Cambridge University. He is probably best known for his book *The Screwtape Letters*,[37] which first established him as an influential spokesman for Christianity in the English-speaking world; he is a brilliant critic of modern science and technology as dehumanizing social institutions. Given below are passages illustrative of Lewis' views pertinent to the relations between psychiatry and law.

I am not supposing them [the Conditioners] to be bad men. They are, rather, not men (in the old sense) at all. They are, if you like, men who have sacrificed their own share in traditional humanity in order to devote themselves to the task of deciding what "Humanity" shall henceforth mean. . . . Nor are their subjects necessarily unhappy men. They are not men at all; they are artefacts. Man's final conquest has proved to be the abolition of Man.[38]

. . . Thus when we cease to consider what the criminal deserves and consider only what will cure him or deter others, we have tacitly removed him from the sphere of justice altogether; instead of a person, a subject of rights, we now have a mere object, a patient, a "case."[39]

The Humanitarian theory, then, removes sentences from the hands of jurists whom the public conscience is entitled to criticize and places them in the hands of technical experts whose special sciences do not even employ such categories as rights and justice. . . . The first result of the Humanitarian theory is, therefore, to substitute for a definite sentence (reflecting to some extent the community's moral judgment on the degree of ill-desert involved) an indefinite sentence terminable only by the word of those experts . . . who inflict it. Which of us, if he stood in the dock, would not prefer to be tried by the old system?[40]

Of all tyrannies a tyranny sincerely exercised for the good of its victims may be the most oppressive. . . . To be "cured" against one's will and cured of states which we may not regard as disease is to be put on a level with those who have not yet reached the age of reason or those who never will; to be classed with infants, imbeciles, and domestic animals. But to be punished, however severely, because we have deserved it, because we "ought to have known better," is to be treated as a human person made in God's image. [41]

For if crime and disease are to be regarded as the same thing, it follows that any state of mind which our masters choose to call "disease" can be treated as a crime; and compulsorily cured . . . but under the Humanitarian theory it will not be called by the shocking name of Persecution. [42]

But the Humanitarians remain undaunted. And they remain obsessed with the task of demoralizing and technizing ethical problems in order to justify their psychiatric "management." Edward J. Sachar, Associate Professor of Psychiatry at the Albert Einstein College of Medicine in New York City, writes:

Since the psychiatrist, from a scientific point of view, must regard all behavior— criminal and law-abiding, healthy and sick—as determined, he finds the issue of moral condemnation of the individual to be inappropriate. . . . Just as the functions of the sick body and the healthy body proceed in accordance with the laws of physiology, so sick and healthy minds function in accordance with the laws of psychology. . . . [T]he finding that someone is criminally responsible means to the psychiatrist that the criminal must *change his behavior before he can resume his position in society. This injunction is dictated* not by morality *but, so to speak, by reality [italics added].* [43]

Similarly, experiments carried out at Clinton Prison, in Dannemora, New York, by Ernest G. Poser, an associate professor in the departments of Psychology and Psychiatry at McGill University in Montreal, supported by a grant from Governor Rockefeller's Committee on Criminal Offenders, are described as promising to "help us reach a point some day where the decision whether a person will be put behind bars will be based on the chances of his committing another crime, and *not* his guilt or innocence" [italics added]. [44]

In *The Crime of Punishment*, Menninger insists over and over again that "the secret of success in all [penological] programs, however, is the replacement of the punitive attitude with the therapeutic attitude. A therapeutic attitude is essential regardless of the particular form of treatment or help." [45] From this perspective, a lobotomy performed with a therapeutic attitude is more humane than a money fine imposed with a punitive attitude.

In short, crime is no longer a problem of law and morals, but is instead a problem of medicine and therapeutics. This transformation of the ethical into the technical—of crime into illness, law into medicine, penology into psychiatry, and punishment into therapy—is, moreover, enthusiastically embraced by many physicians, lawyers, social scientists, and lay persons. For example, in a review of *The Crime of Punishment* in the *New York Times*, Roger Jellinek declares: "As Dr. Menninger proves so searingly, criminals are surely ill, not evil." [46]

"Criminals are surely ill" say the behavioral scientists and their followers. "Punishers are criminals," adds Menninger. We are thus asked to believe that the illegal acts of criminals are the symptoms of mental illness, and that the legal acts of law enforcers are crimes. If so, the punishers are themselves criminals, and hence they too are "ill, not evil." Here we catch the ideologist of insanity at his favorite activity—the manufacture of madness.[47]

Anyone convicted of lawbreaking is, by definition, a criminal: not only the hired killer, but also the physician who performs an illegal abortion; not only the armed robber, but also the businessman who cheats on his income tax; not only the arsonist and the thief, but also the gambler and the manufacturer, seller, and often the consumer of prohibited drugs. They are criminals all! Not evil, certainly not good; just mentally sick—every one of them without exception. But remember: it must always be *them*—never *us!*

Because psychiatrists avoid taking a forthright and responsible stand on the problems they deal with, the major intellectual and moral predicaments of psychiatry remain unacknowledged and unexamined. These may be stated succinctly as a series of questions posing fundamental choices about the nature, scope, methods, and values of psychiatry.

1. Is the scope of psychiatry the study and treatment of medical conditions, or the study and influencing of social performances? In other words, are the objects of psychiatric inquiry diseases or roles, happenings or actions?
2. Is the aim of psychiatry the study of human behavior, or the control of human (mis)behavior? In other words, is the goal of psychiatry the advancement of knowledge, or the regulation of (mis)conduct?
3. Is the method of psychiatry the exchange of communications, or the administration of diagnostic tests and curative treatments? In other words, what does psychiatric practice actually consist of—listening and talking, or prescribing drugs, operating on the brain, and imprisoning persons labeled as "mentally ill"?
4. Finally, is the guiding value of psychiatry individualism or collectivism? In other words, does psychiatry aspire to be the servant of the individual or of the state?

Contemporary psychiatry hedges on all these questions. Almost any journal article or book by an accepted psychiatric authority will illustrate this. Two brief examples should suffice here.

In the article cited earlier, Sachar explicitly rejects the view that the psychiatrist is a party to a conflict. He writes:

For whose sake does the psychiatrist attempt to change the criminal? For the criminal's sake or for society's? For the sake of both, he would argue, just as the physician, confronted with a case of smallpox, thinks immediately of saving the patient as well as protecting the community.[48]

In an essay devoted to the defense of the idea that mental illness is a disease, Roy R. Grinker, Sr., Director of the Institute for Psychosomatic and Psychiatric Research and Training of Michael Reese Hospital and Medical Center in Chicago, writes:

The truly medical model is one in which psychotherapy is only a part. The total field in terms of therapy includes . . . the choice of therapeutic environment, such as home, clinic, or hospital; the choice of therapy, such as drugs, shock and psychotherapy.[49]

Grinker speaks of "choice" and yet remains discreetly and strategically silent about all the questions I have listed above. He does not say *who* chooses the "therapeutic environment" or the "therapy"—the patient, the patient's relatives, the psychiatrist, the judge, the legislator? Nor does he say *what happens* when the patient chooses not to be a patient at all, or when the psychiatrist recommends mental hospitalization and the patient refuses to comply.

These omissions are not fortuitous. On the contrary, they constitute the very essence of present-day "scientific" psychiatry. The mandate of the contemporary psychiatrist—that is, of the professionally loyal, "dynamic" or "progressive" psychiatrist—is precisely to obscure, and indeed to deny, the ethical dilemmas of life, and to transform these into medicalized and technicalized problems susceptible to professional solutions.

I have tried to show that psychiatry is a moral and social enterprise. The psychiatrist deals with problems of human conduct. He is, therefore, drawn into situations of conflict—often between the individual and the group. If we wish to understand psychiatry, we cannot avert our eyes from this dilemma: we must know whose side the psychiatrist takes—that of the individual or that of the group.

But most psychiatrists, and indeed most observers of the contemporary scene, describe the problem in different terms. By not emphasizing conflicts between people, they avoid enlisting themselves explicitly as the agents of either the individual or the group. Instead of promoting the interests of one or another party or moral value generally, they promote mental health.

Considerations such as these have led me to conclude that the concept of mental illness is a betrayal of common sense and of an ethical view of man. To be sure, whenever we speak of a concept of man, our initial problem is one of definition and philosophy: What do we mean by man? Following in the tradition of individualism and rationalism, I hold that a human being is a person to the extent that he makes free, uncoerced choices. Anything that increases his freedom, increases his humanity; anything that decreases his freedom, decreases his humanity.

Progressive freedom, independence, and responsibility lead to being human; progressive enslavement, dependence, and irresponsibility, to being a thing. Today it is inescapably clear that regardless of its origins and aims, the concept of mental illness serves to enslave man. It does so by permitting—indeed commanding—one man to impose his will on another.

We have seen that the purveyors of mental health care, especially when such care is provided by the government, are actually the purveyors of the moral and socioeconomic interests of the state. This is hardly surprising. What other interests could they represent? Surely not those of the so-called patient, whose interests are often antagonistic to those of the state. In this way, institutional psychiatry becomes largely a means for controlling the individual. In a mass society, this is best accomplished by recognizing his existence only as a member of a group, never as an individual.

The danger is clear, and has been remarked on by others. In America, when the ideology of totalitarianism is promoted as fascism or communism, it is coldly rejected. However, when the same ideology is promoted under the guise of mental health care, it is warmly embraced. It thus seems possible that where fascism and communism have failed to collectivize American society, the mental health ethic may yet succeed.

NOTES

1. For a full development of my views on this subject, see T. S. Szasz, *The Myth of Mental Illness* (New York: Harper & Row, 1961); *Ideology and Insanity* (Garden City, N.Y.: Doubleday-Anchor, 1970); and *The Manufacture of Madness* (New York: Harper & Row, 1970).

2. See Szasz, *The Manufacture of Madness*, op. cit., p. xvii.

3. In this connection, see the following texts and their extensive references to the pertinent literature: T. S. Szasz, *Law, Liberty, and Psychiatry* (New York: Macmillan, 1963); S. Rubin, *Psychiatry and Criminal Law* (Dobbs Ferry, N.Y.: Oceana, 1965); A. S. Blumberg, *Criminal Justice* (Chicago: Quadrangle, 1967); A. Goldstein, *The Insanity Defense* (New Haven, Conn.: Yale University Press, 1967); and R. Arens, *Make Mad the Guilty* (Springfield, Ill.: Charles C. Thomas, 1969).

4. The consequences of this strategy are explored in T. S. Szasz, *Psychiatric Justice* (New York: Macmillan, 1965); see also Arens, op. cit.

5. R. Traver, *Anatomy of a Murder* (New York: St. Martins Press, 1958).

6. J. Kaplan and J. R. Waltz, *The Trial of Jack Ruby* (New York: Macmillan, 1965).

7. See, for example, D.C. Code Ann., par. 24–301, 1961; Ohio Rev. Code Ann., par. 2945.39, 1954.

8. D.C. Code Ann., par. 24–301 (d), 1961.

9. *United States v. Freeman*, 357 F. 2d 606 (2d Cir.), 1966, p. 626.

10. See *Cameron v. Fisher*, 320 F. 2d 731 (D.C. Cir.), 1963; *Overholser v. Lynch*, 288 F. 2d 388 (D.C. Cir.), 1961. For a comprehensive review and critical discussion of the insanity defense in the District of Columbia following the Durham decision, see Arens, op. cit.

11. *Lynch v. Overholser*, 369 U. S. 705, 1962.

12. For critical discussions of civil commitment, see Szasz, *Law, Liberty, and Psychiatry*, op. cit., especially pp. 39–71; *Ideology and Insanity*, op. cit., pp. 113–139.

13. *Daniel M'Naghten's Case*, 10 Cl. & Fin. 200, 8 Eng. Rep. 718, 1843.

14. Quoted in Goldstein, op. cit., p. 45.

15. For a representative statement, see W. Overholser, "Major Principles of Forensic Psychiatry," in S. Arieti et al. (eds.), *American Handbook of Psychiatry* (New York: Basic Books, 1959), vol. II, pp. 1887–1901.

16. *State v. Jones*, 50 N.H. 369, 1871.

17. In this connection, see H. Weihofen, *Insanity as a Defense in Criminal Law* (New York: Commonwealth Fund, 1963), especially p. 46; and Goldstein, op. cit., especially pp. 68–74.

18. *Durham v. United States*, 214 F.2d 862 (D.C. Cir.), 1954.

19. *Ibid.*, pp. 874–875.

20. *Ibid.*, p. 874.

21. See Szasz, *Ideology and Insanity*, op cit.; and *Manufacture of Madness*, op. cit.

22. See, for example, F. A. Hayek, *The Counter-Revolution of Science* [1955] (New York: Free Press, 1964); and F. W. Matson, *The Broken Image* (New York: Braziller, 1964).

23. B. Rush, "Letter to Granville Sharp, July 9, 1774," quoted in H. Feinstein, "Benjamin Rush: A Child of Light on the Children of Darkness," mimeo., 1969.

24. B. Rush, "Letter to Granville Sharp, Nov. 28, 1783," quoted in Feinstein, op. cit.

25. Quoted in D. J. Boorstin, *The Lost World of Thomas Jefferson* (Boston: Beacon, 1948), p. 182.

26. Quoted in C. Binger, *Revolutionary Doctor—Benjamin Rush, 1746–1813* (New York: Norton, 1966), p. 201.

27. B. Rush, *Medical Inquiries and Observations upon the Diseases of the Mind*, facsimile of the 1812 Philadelphia edition (New York: Hafner, 1962), pp. 255–256.

28. B. Rush, "Lecture on the Medical Jurisprudence of the Mind" [1810], in G. W. Corner (ed.), *The Autobiography of Benjamin Rush* (Princeton, N.J.: Princeton University Press, 1948), pp. 348, 350.

29. Quoted in Feinstein, op. cit.

30. See T. S. Szasz, "Justice in the Therapeutic State," *Indiana Legal Forum*, 3 (Fall, 1969), pp. 19–33.

31. K. Menninger, *The Human Mind* (New York: Literary Guild of America, 1930), p. 428.

32. K. Menninger, "Introduction," in *The Wolfenden Report* (New York: Stein & Day, 1964), pp. 5–6.

33. K. Menninger, *Man Against Himself* (New York: Harcourt, Brace, 1938), p. 69.

34. K. Menninger, *The Crime of Punishment*, (New York: Viking, 1968), p. 108.

35. *Ibid.*, p. 257.

36. *Ibid.*, pp. 260–261.

37. C. S. Lewis, *The Screwtape Letters and Screwtape Proposes a Toast* (orig 1943) (New York: Macmillan, 1967).

38. C. S. Lewis, *The Abolition of Man* (New York: Macmillan, 1947), pp. 76–77.

39. C. S. Lewis, "The Humanitarian Theory of Punishment," *Res Judicatae*, 6 (1953), 224–225.

40. *Ibid.*, 226.

41. *Ibid.*, 228

42. *Ibid.*, 229.

43. E. J. Sachar, "Behavioral Science and the Criminal Law," *Scientific American*, 209 (November 1963), 41.

44. D. Burnham, "Convicts Treated by Drug Therapy," *New York Times*, December 8, 1968, p. 17.

45. Menninger, *The Crime of Punishment*, op. cit., p. 17.

46. R. M. Jellinek, "Revenger's Tragedy," *New York Times*, December 17, 1968, p. 31.

47. See Szasz, *Manufacture of Madness*, op. cit.

48. Sachar, op. cit., pp. 41–42.

49. R. R. Grinker, Sr., "Emerging Concepts of Mental Illness and Treatment: The Medical Point of View," *American Journal of Psychiatry*, 125 (January 1969), 866.

13/AMERICAN SOCIETY AND CRIMINAL JUSTICE REFORM

LAMAR T. EMPEY

The introductory student in criminology is asked to absorb an astounding array of fact, theory, and opinion. Therefore, it might be useful to review what has been said and to attempt to place it into a larger societal context, in order to provide a better comprehension of the issues involved. Especially pertinent is a comment by Henry Steele Commager on the philosophical underpinnings of American thought and character. Reflecting on the conditions in the nineteenth century that contributed to the kind of culture we have in America today, he noted that, above all, Americans have been pragmatists.

Practical, democratic, individualistic, opportunistic, spontaneous, hopeful pragmatism was wonderfully adapted to the temperament of the average American. It cleared away the jungle of theology and metaphysics and deterministic science and allowed the warm sun of common sense to quicken the American spirit. . . . Pragmatism's willingness to break with the past, reject traditional habits, try new methods, put beliefs to a vote, make a future to order, excited not only sympathy but a feeling of familiarity. No wonder that, despite the broadsides of more formidable philosophers, pragmatism caught on until it came to be almost the official philosophy of America.

Modern America's response to crime reflects this pragmatism. On the one hand, its system of justice is based upon principles of the highest order, reflecting the optimism of an earlier era and a desire to protect individual rights as well as community order. On the other hand, because the implementation of these principles leaves much to be desired, and because of an extended period of political and civil unrest, the system is being subjected to attacks of the severest kind, from both the political left and the right. A basic question, therefore, is whether more pragmatism, guided only by the vaguest of notions as to what the basic problems are, is adequate to meet the need for reform. Can America afford extreme and precipitous pragmatism and still retain the democratic principles and concepts of justice that have been fundamental to its system in the past? Would it not be useful to utilize rational and empirical, as well as pragmatic, criteria in attempting to deal with current problems?

In an endeavor to explore these difficult questions, let us review some of the things that have been studied to this point: first, society's problems in defining what crime is; and, second, the limitations of the present system of justice. Once having done this, we can place these problems in the larger context of the complex and pluralistic society in which we live. We may then be in a better position to assess the kinds of criteria we wish to use in studying crime and in seeking ways to deal with it.

WHAT IS CRIME?

Let us here try to see crime through the varying perspectives of the American public. These subjectively determined definitions are often vague and amorphous, yet it is extremely important to take them into account because they are usually the bases upon which political and even legal actions are taken.

The American public is terrorized annually by the latest Uniform Crime Reports released by the F.B.I. These reports employ an index of seven crimes said to represent the most common local crime problems—murder, forcible rape, robbery, aggravated assault, burglary, larceny, and auto theft.

What does the report covering the decade of the 1960's reveal? The total number of these seven offenses increased 120 percent; crimes of violence (murder, forcible rape, robbery, and aggravated assault) increased 104 percent; and crimes against property (burglary, larceny, and auto theft) increased 123 percent. According to the President's Crime Commission (1967a:44), the young more than anyone else committed these crimes.

These cold and abstract statistics are only one aspect of a prevailing climate of fear that makes many citizens unwilling to walk the streets of their own cities at night. Through television, Americans are almost daily witnesses to reports of muggings, rapes, and robberies. In today's social climate, Americans would probably rank juvenile delinquency and crimes involving youths as some of the greatest problems in their communities. It is an unfortunate tendency of older and "middle" America to stereotype most young people and to define all kinds of civil and political unrest, as well as illegal acts, as crime.

THE YOUTHFUL PERSPECTIVE

There is, however, another view of social conditions today. Youth (along with others) point to two kinds of traditional behavior that they believe are not only inconsistent with American ideals but that in many cases add new dimensions to that which has ordinarily been defined as criminal.

The first kind of behavior has to do with political and economic behavior of the broadest kind, and with the fundamental system of priorities upon which American life is based.

In reaction to this behavior, youth, along with some of their older sympathizers, have often engaged in open, and often unlawful, protest. However, establishment groups like the police, firemen, teachers, and social workers, or right-wing organizations like the John Birch Society or the Minutemen, have also engaged in protest through such means as slowdowns, work stoppages, or even violence.

A second kind of "crime" that has particularly incensed the young is what Edwin H. Sutherland (1940) first called "white-collar" crime. It has become normative among many to believe that successful participation in the capitalistic system is impossible without compromising one's ethics, if not one's country's laws. Many of the young and idealistic, like their elders, tend to stereotype, and they often fail to discriminate very well between that which is actually criminal in a strict legal sense and that which they do not like very well. Thus, contemporary America presents a picture of opposition, dissension, and undiscriminating charge and countercharge.

What is the relationship of this social climate to attempts to impose some order, some sense and rationality, on the study of crime? Is everyone a criminal, young or old? Should the judgments of one interest group about another be the basis upon which legislation is to be written and the justice system is to operate? Obviously not. Better standards are required. Otherwise, there is little chance that we can retain a republican form of government in which the rule of law predominates.

Crime, as now defined, is a complex issue. Much contemporary thinking reveals what different investigators have called "pluralistic ignorance" (Cloward, 1956:19) or "shared misunderstanding" (Matza, 1964:35–36). Individuals or groups, young or old, black or white, come to believe that they are the only ones who hold sentiments favoring socially acceptable values. As a result, they tend to attribute greater immorality and criminality to others than is actually the case. In judging others, they fail to understand the complex sets of values and motivations that accompany the behavior of others.

Many of the problems now observable on the American scene are the inevitable result of the conflicting values, life styles, power relationships, and generational differences of an increasingly complex society. And, as yet, Americans have not been willing to face up to these complexities. They have failed to distinguish between fact and opinion, law and morals, and what can and cannot be expected from a formal system of criminal justice.

In seeking solutions for a bewildering and growing set of problems, society has already overburdened the criminal justice system, expecting it to provide answers for problems generated by other institutions in society. However, in order to make improvements, several basic points must be better understood: (1) the way society is organized, and the role of legal rules in that organization; (2) the way crime is defined and legal statutes written; (3) the criminal justice system itself and those who are being processed by it; and (4) the knowledge, the resources, and the effort that will be required if the system is to be an improved and humane one. Let us now consider these issues.

NATURE OF SOCIETAL ORGANIZATION

In order to understand the way society is organized, and the role of legal rules in it, we must ask several questions: How do human groups adapt to their external environment? How do they provide for psychic and social, as well as physical, needs? How can they live together without chaos and confusion? How can they control those deviants who would prey upon them?

One striking thing about social organization is man's skill in developing and transmitting from one generation to the next a host of complex ways for meeting his needs.

As Albert K. Cohen (1966:3) observes:

Whatever people want—food, clothing, shelter, sex, fame, contract bridge—they must get it by working with and through other people. They must take up positions in organized and complex social enterprises: families, clubs, schools, armies, political associations, ball teams. Each of these may be thought of as a way of fitting together the diverse actions of many people so that the work of the world gets done.

Social organization is best understood in terms of several attributes: the prevailing *culture* of a society—its objects, knowledge, technology, values, ideas, and normative ways of doing things that are transmitted from one generation to the next; the variety of *subsystems* into which society is organized—communities, schools, neighborhoods, or work groups; the way aggregates of customs, values, and norms are joined into *broad institutional patterns* that govern life; a system of *stratification* that tends to segregate people in such a way that their socioeconomic and ethnic backgrounds affect their life chances differentially; and informal as well as formal *rules for conduct*. When all these factors are considered, it becomes obvious that legal rules and legal institutions constitute but a portion of those by which social organization is determined. In addition, the degree of societal disruption is dependent upon this whole constellation of factors, not just legal rules.

In attempting to provide a framework within which to analyze all these forces, social scientists have used two contrasting models, a "consensus" model and a "conflict" model. Of the two, the former, which emphasizes the idea that all the elements of social organization—values, norms, roles, and institutions—are a highly integrated and closely-knit whole, has enjoyed the greater popularity, probably because the larger part of man's history has been lived in relatively simple, rural civilizations. Drawing upon Rolf Dahrendorf's analysis (1959:161–162), Richard Quinney (1970:8) has summarized the main assumptions of the consensus model as follows: "(1) society is a relatively persistent, stable structure, (2) it is well integrated, (3) every element has a function—it helps maintain the system, and (4) a functioning social structure is based on a consensus on values." In other words, the consensus model suggests that most people share the same general objectives, agree on basic definitions of right and wrong, and engage in a mutually supportive set of activities. Thus, by definition, a person who is criminal is one who rejects the basic consensus and threatens the stability of the whole.

By contrast, the conflict model of society assumes that: "(1) at every point society is subject to change, (2) it displays at every point dissension and conflict, (3) every element contributes to change, and (4) it is based on the coercion of some of its members by others" (Quinney, 1970:8). Following this model, society is seen as characterized by diversity and change; it is held together, not by consensus, but by force and constraint; and although certain values predominate, they do so because they are enforced by dominant groups and interests (Dahrendorf, 1958:127). There has been an increasing emphasis upon the utility of this model. Present levels of conflict and turmoil in society are significant indications of the fact that vast differences do exist over basic values and norms and over the way societal institutions have been operating.

Definitions of crime, and the way people respond to crime, are to a large extent the result of power struggles among groups with contrasting values and interests. And these definitions and responses change from time to time and place to place. They are not static and universal phenomena with which everyone agrees. Expanding further on this notion, Quinney (1970) documents the idea that legal definitions of crime are derived from the conflicts of varous interest groups in society and the relative positions of power they occupy.

While it is relatively simple to obtain agreement on the idea that a person who knocks down an old woman and steals her handbag is guilty of both assault and theft, it is much more difficult to decide whether a policeman who shoots a burglary suspect is guilty of illegal assault. Consequently, the definitions of and officials' responses to these acts depend very much upon what groups occupy positions of power in society and who the accused are. Persons in power tend to protect their own behavior from sanction while condemning, through statute, certain behavior of those who occupy positions of lower status. Despite this, there is always struggle for accession to power. Legalization of certain activities—for example, the use of marijuana—will reflect the values and expectations of new and emerging interest groups. The new laws will be a result of changing values, norms, and institutional practices.

IMPACT OF DEVIANT TRADITIONS

Some writers have also noted that conflicts in society are not due merely to the emergence of new values and customs but may be inherent in tradition as well. David Matza (1964:33) has argued that modern American culture is not simply rural and puritanical; instead, it is complex and pluralistic. In addition to norms favoring adherence to standard definitions of right and wrong, there are "subterranean" traditions of deviance as well (cf. Matza and Sykes, 1961). These subterranean traditions do not represent ignorance or even negation of the law. They are not separate sets of beliefs that distinguish criminals from noncriminals, or youths from adults. Deviant as well as conformist traditions are held simultaneously by almost everyone. And this may help to explain why increasing numbers of empirical studies suggest that most people, not just official criminals, have engaged in a considerable amount of illegal behavior (for a summary of the literature, cf. Cohen, 1966:26–28; Empey, 1967a:30–32).

Daniel Bell's (1959:115–136) classic analysis of crime as an American way of life may shed some light on this situation. Bell notes that Americans are characterized, on one hand, by an "extremism" in voicing support for traditional standards of moral conduct, yet, on the other, by an "extraordinary" talent for compromising these standards in their everyday behavior. Since crime, or at least unethical conduct, has been a major means by which individuals have sought to achieve success in labor unions, business, or politics, it is clear that crime and conformist behavior have a closer relationship than the older consensus model would lead one to believe. The contradiction between American morality and American behavior form the basis for an intimate relationship between crime and noncriminal activities that creates serious doubts about the beliefs of those who would suggest that crime is easily defined and that criminals are clearly different from noncriminals. American culture supplies all of us with a repertoire of possible behaviors—some conformist and some deviant—which we use from time to time depending upon felt need and circumstance. Normative conflicts do not occur only between different interest groups; they are inherent in our basic cultural traditions and are reflected in our individual behaviors.

Social Organization and Its Implications

This discussion of social organization carries with it several implications. First, the degree of crime in society is a function, not just of the way legal institutions operate, but of the entire social structure. Second, the social process in any complex society is characterized by conflict as well as cooperation. Third, much of the current strife, civil unrest, and lawbreaking in American society is a reflection, not merely of human perversity and lack of respect for law and order, but of a clash of differing political interests over what the law should be and how it should operate.

In seeking some insight into the problems that must be confronted, it might be wise to concentrate directly on the way the criminal justice system now operates. The introduction of reform will depend not only upon the resolution of the broader social and political problems that confront America, but upon the capacity of the justice system itself to incorporate desired changes.

ADMINISTRATION OF CRIMINAL JUSTICE

The criminal justice "system" is highly complex and much-splintered; in fact, it is not really a single and integrated system. For example, in only one metropolitan county—Los Angeles—there are no fewer than forty-six local police units, which are responsible to forty-six different local governments. To this number might be added the State Highway Patrol, various federal agencies, and an untold number of private police who are employed by railroads, private businesses, college campuses, and so on. Added to this are prosecutors, public defenders, local, state, and federal courts, and correctional agencies. Thus, the problems of understanding and improving the functioning of all these disparate units is staggering (cf. Bloch and Geis, 1970:391–393).

In addition, there is a striking contrast between the lofty aspirations held for the "system" and the way it actually operates. For many of those who come in contact with it, the experience is distressing, if not horrifying.

A clogged and inefficient system makes it possible for the most serious offenders to delay or escape prosecution, while the poor and ignorant are prosecuted or treated unjustly. Thus, the system as it presently operates is not only failing to protect society from serious criminals, it is not operating in a just and efficient manner either.

This fact is illustrated by a recent study (McEachern et al., 1970), which was concerned with projections to the year 2000 of what might be expected in Los Angeles County if current trends continue. In 1960, for example, the number of crimes in the F.B.I. index (which includes murder, forcible rape, robbery, aggravated assault, burglary, larceny, and auto theft) reported in Los Angeles County was 140,156. The first question asked in the study was: What would happen if the same rate of increase in these crimes between 1960 and 1968 continued until the year 2000, and if the criminal justice system continued to function as it had in 1968?

Based upon projected population increases in the county, the study estimated that if this trend continued, there would be almost 600,000 of these seven kinds of offenses by 1980, 900,000 by 1990, and over 1.25 million by 2000. Moreover, if other felonies were added to these seven, the total number would reach 1,800,000 by 1980 and would be in excess of 4 million by the year 2000. In addition, studies indicate that misdemeanors committed by alcoholics and other so-called petty offenders are far more numerous than felonies! And despite the tremendous concern at present over the serious offender, the police, courts, and correctional agencies are overwhelmed with a persistent but less dangerous clientele. When that group is added to the felony group, the total constitutes a frightening number of people who must be served.

Where will the manpower resources—the judges, district and defense attorneys, law enforcement and correctional personnel—be found? What will be the fiscal impact of these projected increases? . . . How will the criminal justice system, broadly conceived, process these numbers of offenders? More important, can the concept of justice survive? (McEachern et al., 1970:17)

Because current trends and projections were so preposterous, and because they bode such chaos for the justice system unless changed, they were labeled by McEachern et al. (1970:24) in their study as characteristics of a potentially "absurd" system. In using this term, they were not attempting to denigrate the system but were indicating that if solutions were to be found, vast and innovative changes would be required. What might some of these changes be?

REVISED DEFINITIONS OF CRIME

In response to the tendency of society as a whole to expect the criminal justice system to solve a host of moral as well as legal problems, criminologists have long suggested that the definition of crime be more narrowly circumscribed. As Norval Morris and Gordon Hawkins (1970:2) put it:

We must strip off the moralistic excrescences on our criminal justice system so that it may concentrate on the essential. The prime function of the criminal law is to protect our persons and our property; these purposes are now engulfed in a mass of other distracting, inefficiently performed legislative duties. When the criminal law invades the spheres of private morality and social welfare, it exceeds its proper limits at the cost of neglecting its primary tasks. . . . For the criminal law at least, man has an inalienable right to go to hell in his own fashion, provided he does not directly injure the person or property of another on the way.

Morris and Hawkins (1970:3) argue that public drunkenness should not be a criminal offense; that, while the sale of drugs should be criminally proscribed, the purchase or possession of drugs should not be; that all kinds of nonfraudulent gambling should be made legal; that vague and ambiguous disorderly conduct and vagrancy laws should be replaced by laws that are more precise in their specification of unacceptable conduct; that abortion by a qualified practitioner should be made legal; and that no sexual activities between consenting adults in private should be subject to the criminal law. These writers would also revise the laws governing juvenile conduct so that the juvenile court would retain jurisdiction only over behavior by children that would be criminal were they adults. In other words, legal intervention and penal sanctions would not be applied to juveniles for such things as truancy, "incorrigibility," drinking, or violation of curfew.

Morris and Hawkins (1970:4–25) feel that were these changes instituted, three major benefits would result. The pressures on police, courts, and corrections would be reduced by as much as 3 million cases annually, leaving these agents of social control with much greater means for combatting serious and predatory crime. There would be much less interference in the private moral conduct of the citizen, leaving the resolution of such problems as drunkenness, drug abuse, illicit sex, and gambling to other institutions. And, since the sources of much income for organized crime come from such things as narcotics, gambling, and illicit sex, with these sources dried up, the financial power of organized crimes would be seriously hurt.

Finally, Morris and Hawkins (1970:27) advocate that "every legislature must establish a Standing Law Revision Committee charged with the task of constant consideration of the fitness and adequacy of the criminal law sanctions to social needs." In other words, legal reform would be an on-going process.

While these proposed changes seem admirable, it cannot be stated unequivocally that all the results would be salutary. Experience has taught that the consequences of instituting significant social change may be as disruptive as the problems it was designed to correct. For example, although the removal of public drunkenness as a criminal offense may reduce the burdens of the criminal justice system, it would not really solve the problems of the alcoholic. The burden would simply be shifted from the criminal justice system elsewhere. The alcoholic may be spared the stigma of a criminal label, but both he and society will be faced with the more basic problems that his alcoholism entails.

In addition to the recommendation that the criminal law not be used to control private morals in the areas of alcohol, sex, and even drugs, many legal scholars have also warned against the incautious use of moral judgments in other ways, most notably in the arenas of economic and political life. Norms may be of several types—informal and customary as well as formal and legal. Thus, it is not uncommon to find someone who, although he operates within the letter of the criminal law, may also exhibit adherence to an unpopular political ideology. Using moral, not legal, tradition, it is easy to brand such a person as "criminal." Should this be the case? The late Paul Tappan (1968:369), in discussing white-collar crime, argued that it should not be.

Who should be the white collar criminal? Is it the merchant who, out of greed, business acumen, or competitive motivations, breaches a trust with his consumer by "puffing his wares" beyond their merits, by pricing them beyond their value, or by ordinary advertising? Is it he who . . . is found guilty of an unfair labor practice by a labor relations board of an unfair labor practice? May it be the white collar worker who breaches trust with his employers by inefficient performance at work, by sympathetic strike or secondary boycott? Or is it the merchandiser who violates ethics by undercutting the prices of his fellow merchants?

In general, as Tappan indicated, these acts may not violate the criminal law, and may well be within the framework of ordinary business and labor practice. Yet they are acts of which many people disapprove. It was Tappan's opinion, however, that unless such acts are defined as criminal by the law, and that unless, after due process, an accused person is proven guilty of them, he should not be branded as criminal.

Other acts, such as misrepresentation of corporate financial statements, manipulation of the stock market, embezzlement, bribery, or tax fraud, are more clearly criminal. However, because of the power and prestige of many of those who are accused of such acts, it is difficult to convict them. With acts such as these, a debate centers on how people who are accused of committing them shall be treated. Some criminologists have implied that any persons or organizations that break laws regarding these crimes should be defined as criminal (cf. Clinard, 1952:127; Hartung, 1953). But who shall make this judgment—the public, a crusading newspaperman, a social scientist, or a court of law?

Robert G. Caldwell (1958), along with Tappan, insists that no person is a criminal, white collar or otherwise, until he has been arrested, arraigned, indicted, prosecuted, and found guilty in a court of law. The remedies for the mistakes and inequities of the past are to improve the criminal law, to enforce it vigorously, and to provide an impartial prosecution of the accused.

Such a principle would apply not only to businessmen but to political dissenters as well. During the turbulent years of the 1960's and early 1970's, for example, there have been pressures both from the political left and right to ignore traditional protections and practices. Government officials at all levels have been party to unconstitutional and repressive steps to control dissent over such issues as the Vietnam War, racism in American society, and the priorities prevailing in this country. In response to an enraged and conservative element of society, legislators, police, and other representatives of those in power have often been inclined to make criminal acts out of behavior that was essentially political in character. In some cases, if laws did not already exist to control this dissent, they were enacted. Some of this legislation was later struck down by the courts as unconstitutional because it was designed largely to suppress free expression and open assembly, not to protect our persons and our property.

On the other hand, there were cases in which dissenters did use criminal means. Some were willing to destroy property, or even to injure or kill, in order to make their views felt. By so doing, they may have weakened the cause for which they fought. In addition, they showed that, like those against whom they protested, they were willing to use repressive methods in pursuit of political goals. Moreover, an unanticipated consequence of the excesses, either of a repressive government or its political opponents, is likely to be a rise in predatory crimes committed by people who seize upon current inequities and a climate of unrest as a justification for their own crimes.

It is for these reasons that efforts must be made constantly to separate moral and political issues from criminal issues. The inclination of those in power to equate politicality with criminality tends not only to threaten democratic principles, but to generate violence as well. Also, the tendency for dissenters to justify criminal means because of the goals they seek is also destructive of democratic principles. Hence, there is a constant need to insure that the criminal justice system does indeed perform its major function of protecting our persons and our property, and that at the same time it does not become a catchall device for dealing with society's moral and political problems.

THE NEED FOR FACT

There is a pervasive need for a sense of proportion regarding the crimes about which Americans are most concerned—those that affect their personal safety. Americans are inundated at present with reports of violence; they feel that they dare not step out of their homes at night. But what are some of the facts?

First, America is a violent country; its rate of homicide by gunfire is 2.7 per 100,000. This compares with "the Netherlands, 0.03; Japan, 0.04, West

Germany, 0.12; Canada, 0.52; and the United Kingdom, 0.05" (Morris and Hawkins, 1970:57). Surely, this kind of information indicates the need for improved gun control legislation. Yet, behind these statistics, a second body of information stands out—namely, that the public's perception of where the danger of bodily harm lies may be grossly at odds with the facts. Consider the following:

1. About 70 percent of all willful murders, 66 percent of all aggravated assaults, and a high percentage of forcible rapes are committed by family members, lovers, friends, or acquaintances of the victim. Insofar as these crimes are concerned, therefore, one is probably safer on the street than at home, safer with strangers than with loved ones (President's Crime Commission, 1967a:18).

2. The rates of murder, rape, and assault today are probably lower than they were in the 1870's and 1890's (President's Crime Commission, 1967a:22–23). Although these rates have increased during recent years, they were considerably higher at other times in our history.

3. The number of deaths per 100,000 in motor vehicle accidents is five times greater than the number of deaths by murder. Murder also ranks far behind other common accidents and suicides as a cause of death. Moreover, people who drive while intoxicated are probably involved in more than one-half of all motor vehicle deaths (President's Crime Commission, 1967a:19). Thus, willful murder ranks very low as a cause of death.

4. Finally, if one considers the following information, taken from the President's Crime Commission report (1967a:20), he finds that crimes of violence, especially serious assault and murder, do not even rank among the ten most common crimes.

OFFENSE	PERCENT OF TOTAL ARRESTS
Drunkenness	31.0%
Disorderly conduct	11.5
Larceny (over and under $50)	7.7
Driving under the influence of alcohol	4.9
Simple assault	4.2
Burglary	4.0
Liquor laws	3.6
Vagrancy	2.4
Gambling	2.3
Motor vehicle theft	2.1
Total (ten most frequent offenses)	73.7

If reasonable priorities are to be set, both the public and its elected representatives will have to become far better informed regarding the total configuration of crime. That is why the suggestion made by Morris and Hawkins (1970:27) that every legislature establish a Standing Law Revision Committee to consider constantly the fitness and adequacy of present laws and procedures is a good one. But beyond that, the current climate of fear that grips the nation may never be dispelled until greater attention is devoted to the task of crime prevention.

CRIME PREVENTION

Despite the continuing clamor over the evils of crime, efforts at crime prevention have been minimal. There has been a vast discrepancy between the raucous demands that somebody do something about crime and the resources that have actually been devoted to the problem. As a matter of fact, society has been far more concerned with control of crime—with reacting to it after it occurs—than with preventing crime. But that is only one of several difficulties. To organize a prevention program of any magnitude, three major sets of questions would have to be examined.

1. *Conceptual*: What is meant by crime prevention? Of the many kinds of crime discussed above, which shall be deemed most important for a program of prevention? How shall an attack be mounted?
2. *Organizational*: How does one organize a prevention strategy? If prevention rather than mere control is the objective, should not educational, economic, political, and scientific institutions be involved as well as the legal ones?
3. *Evaluative*: How does one evaluate prevention efforts so that in addition to some assessment of success, there is an accrual of knowledge by which continued improvements can be made?

Let us consider the implications of these matters for the possible planning of a crime prevention program.

Basic to any effective action is some definition of "crime prevention," which, in simple terms, might be any attempt to find the causes for crime and to reduce their harmful effects on potential criminals, especially young people, who now comprise the largest share of the official criminal population. But this definition, by itself, is grossly inadequate because it overlooks so many subtle, yet pervasive, problems.

Some suggestions made by Lloyd E. Ohlin (1970) illustrate this point. Ohlin suggests that the potential offender is subject to four major structures in any society, all of which, or any one of which, may be related to prevention:

1. The legitimate, normative system, including not only informal guides for behavior, but the legal rules and policies that define what deviance and conformity are.
2. The primary socializing institutions, such as the family, school, world of work, or church, all of which are expected to train the young and to prepare them for an effective role in society.
3. The institutions of social control, such as the police, the judiciary, and

corrections, whose responsibility is to deal with those who violate legal rules.

4. The illegitimate structures in society that support delinquency—gambling, vice, drug, criminal, or delinquent subcultures.

Since all these structures can affect deviant behavior in some way, then, in addition to the individual himself, all might legitimately be involved in any prevention effort. Do we wish to engage all or only some of them in that effort? The size and nature of the task would be determined by the answer.

Let us consider the four structures just described in terms of their relation to crime prevention. In relation to the legal system itself, there are some striking implications. Given the catchall nature of the legal statutes that define both crime and delinquency, and the fact that they prescribe a legal course of action for such things as truancy, neglect, gambling, and several kinds of victimless crimes, as well as predatory acts, there are virtually no criminals. If one adds to this list the immoral acts referred to earlier that do not involve a victim, it is clear that a tremendous amount of law-violating behavior could be "prevented" simply by changing legal statutes or policies.

In regard to youth it has been recommended that young people not be prosecuted and given penal sanctions for behavior that would not be prosecuted if exhibited by adults. Furthermore, a recent President's Crime Commission report (1967b:25) seriously questioned the utility of legal statutes that place judges and other legal authorities in the position of having to decide what is moral and immoral conduct for young people, or of having to levy sanctions against youthful fads that wax and wane. Of course, the consequences of such changes are not known. Therefore, there is great merit in Judge Ted Rubin's (1970) suggestion that any alterations, either in the rules themselves or in the administration of them, be tried on an experimental basis. Such an experiment would include the substitution of other institutional resources for those of the social control agencies that would occur if these statutes were changed. The implication, of course, is that the impact on other institutions of changes in legal rules would be great.

This leads to the second of the four structures—the primary socializing institutions in society. In an experimental effort at crime prevention these institutions would be asked to pick up the slack in dealing with nonpredatory types of offenses and even some more serious kinds of acts where young people were involved. Thus, an effort at prevention might be organized around some or all of these institutions, either as separate entities or in conjunction with changes in legal statutes. They would be asked to deal with most of the victimless crimes—drunkenness, drug abuse, sexual acts—for which many adults as well as juveniles are now processed by the legal system.

Since, in the last analysis, it is the primary institutions upon whom society must depend for the basic socialization and involvement of young people, such a strategy would seem to make a great deal of sense. The police, courts, and corrections are a last resort, designed more to control and resocialize a limited few than to socialize and integrate the many. Furthermore, traditional ways of dealing with offenders, especially in jails and prisons, may not only be ineffective in changing them, they may actually increase the identification of juveniles with other criminals and criminal norms.

However, there is a basic irony in this suggested strategy. Ordinarily, the primary institutions in society do not see it as their responsibility to prevent delinquency, and it usually falls to the agencies of the criminal justice system to assume the task. Why is this so?

In the evolution of our institutions in the last few decades, responsibility has been increasingly assigned to the agencies of control, although, in fact, their ability to prevent delinquency has been proven to be questionable. The result of this, we would suggest, has been to contribute to, not to reduce, the crime problem. The agencies of legal control have developed a vested interest in dealing with difficult cases. Their powers, budgets, and bureaucratic structures depend in part on their maintaining that interest. Thus, in a subtle but pervasive way, the likelihood that an individual, especially a young person, will be diverted from an acceptable role in the primary institutions and placed in a stigmatized role within legal structures has been increased rather than decreased. This likelihood underscores the importance of examining the relevance for prevention, first, of altering the legal rules that cause this situation to exist and, second, of redefining the roles of both the primary institutions and the social control agencies. Changes in all three of these major societal structures might be tried, at the very least, on an experimental basis to see if crime prevention might be improved.

The chief impediments to any such effort are inherent in the traditions and politics of change. People are unwilling to switch from a tradition of punishment to a strategy of prevention. However, there are some counter-trends that show promise. For example, an awareness of the pervasiveness of drug use in this country, not just by young people, but by all segments of society, is growing. Increase in research is helping to demonstrate the ways in which the use of drugs may be harmful as well as helpful. Education programs are presenting facts, not shibboleths, to young people. Treatment programs use methadone and other drug substitutes that are less harmful than such drugs as heroin. But this is only a beginning.

Before crime prevention can be successful on any large scale, the general public and its elected representatives will have to come to grips with the need to eradicate the poverty that makes life hopeless for a significant minority. They will have to confront a system of priorities that places much greater stress upon buying creature comforts than upon buying clean air or education. Many of those who prey upon society feel that their acts of senseless vandalism, theft, and violence are justified because they have no power over, or stake in, what is happening to them. On one hand, they are inundated with daily reminders of the "good life"; on the other, many live a miserable existence in which the daily realities are totally inconsistent with what they have been taught to expect. As James F. Short, Jr., and Frank L. Strodtbeck (1965:212–214) have noted, the community "institutions" in which many ghetto youth participate are not the schools, churches, recreational activities, and artistic centers in which middle- and upper-class youth participate, but the pool halls, brothels, and street hangouts of run-down city centers. They have grown used to the pushers, junkies, pimps, and thieves among them; vice and violence become a way of life. The result of the deprivation of ghetto dwellers is an enhancement of a sense of futility, anger, and frustration on their part.

These remarks should not be construed as suggesting that the control agencies should go out of the prevention business. The issue is not whether they have a role to play, in prevention as well as rehabilitation, but the nature of the role. They must occupy a central position in correcting as well as apprehending the offender. However, they could do much more to establish an effective link with the primary institutions so that the placing of penal sanctions results in as little disruption as possible in the offender's chances for education, work, and a constructive existence. Far more could be done to experiment with community alternatives that, while maintaining some controls, would permit the offender to maintain contact with legitimate structures and friends. It seems likely that this would result in better prevention of criminal acts than if the individual is removed entirely from his daily pursuits and placed only with other offenders.

Finally, it will be recalled that a fourth community structure to which greater attention might be paid is that which includes the illegitimate elements of society—the sources of drugs, the criminal subcultures, and the other forms of organized or white-collar crime. If legal rules were changed, and if the primary institutions were given a greater role in crime prevention, more attention might then be paid by the criminal justice system to the control of these structures. Prevention would be devoted to a better understanding of the nature of organized criminal structures and to ways of dealing with them. Despite a growing body of evidence that many illegitimate structures are related in a symbiotic way to prevailing business and political activities, few inroads have been made upon them. For example, there seems little doubt but that large quantities of dangerous drugs produced by legitimate concerns are being fed into illegitimate channels to be sold to young people. The federal government is now beginning to regulate the amounts of dangerous drugs produced domestically, but that is only the beginning. In part, organized and white-collar criminals have been able to operate successfully because of the political and economic power they exercise. Hence, one cannot afford to be overly optimistic. Not only is it difficult to locate and convict the people who provide illegal goods and services, but society itself seems more concerned with controlling the more obvious symptoms of the crime problem—the addicts, the armed robbers, and the muggers who prey directly upon them—than with controlling organized criminal structures.

IMPROVEMENT OF CRIMINAL JUSTICE

Given the climate of fear and paranoia in which Americans now live because of the crime problem, one would think that the stage for reform would be set. However, that is not entirely true. Because society has overburdened the criminal justice system, and because it has placed an excessive and totally unwarranted faith in the power of criminal sanctions to deal with all its problems, the system does not operate efficiently, even when there is harm to persons and property.

In a study of the operation of the criminal justice system in Chicago, Morris and Hawkins (1970:91) found that of approximately 500 possible arrest situations, only 100 arrests were made. Of these 100 arrests, only 40 were considered by court and prosecuting personnel for possible trial. After their deliberations, only 20 were actually tried, and of these 20, only a few were convicted and referred to correctional agencies. To what extent did the whole process represent a careful administration of justice? Of the original 500 arrest situations, nonjudicial personnel—especially the police and to a lesser degree court intake persons—exercised prosecutorial and judicial decisions for 480 of the arrestees. Judges themselves made the decisions for only 20 of them. Why were more of the offenders not referred to court? Were the decisions by the police and court intake personnel wise ones? We do not know. But the study does explode "the mythology that the police make an arrest when they see what they think is a properly arrestable criminal and that they then pass him on to others to handle" (Morris and Hawkins, 1970:91).

Given findings such as these, we can see why better information is required on the policies, practices, and decision-making apparatus of the entire system. "It is impossible to think rationally about the crime problem without constantly bearing in mind the interdependence of the subsystems that make up the criminal justice system" (Morris and Hawkins, 1970:91). Not only is better information required, but an awareness of the varieties of pressures under which the various people in the system operate. Let us consider some of them briefly.

The Police

In a moralistic manner, the public demands that the police atone for all the sins of society, whether there are victims or not. If these extreme demands were honored in the abstract, all of the 500 possible arrestees discussed above might have been arrested. And yet, the police know that an arrest might not be warranted in each case—that young people are sometimes better served by a warning than by a jail sentence; that arrests are fruitless unless grounds for conviction are sound; that correctional facilities are already overcrowded; and that the courts are clogged and overworked. Thus, the police are often placed in an untenable position in which they are asked to please everyone.

As Ben Whittaker (Morris and Hawkins, 1970:89), an English lawyer who studied the English police system, noted:

The public use the police as a scapegoat for its neurotic attitude toward crime. Janus-like we have always turned two faces toward a policeman. We expect him to be human and yet inhuman. We employ him to administer the law, and yet ask him to waive it. We resent him when he enforces the law in our own case, yet demand his dismissal when he does not elsewhere. We offer him bribes, yet denounce his corruption. We expect him to be a member of society, yet not to share its values. We admire violence, even against society itself, but condemn force by the police on our behalf. We tell the police that they are entitled to information from the public, yet we ostracize informers. We ask for crime to be eradicated, but only by use of "sporting" methods.

Therefore, we see that effective reform will require not only improvements in police training, salary, and decision-making capabilities, but a reform of the societal values, legal rules, and informal norms that make their position so difficult. Other institutions in society share blame for many of the problems that the policeman is now expected to resolve; but he cannot do it without their help.

The Courts

The courts, like the police, cannot improve their functions without some changes in the legal rules that define crime, without an increase in the resources at their disposal, and without the willingness of the public and legislators to support court reform. In an article in *Life* (1970:26), Chief Justice of the Supreme Court Warren Burger listed many of the reforms that are needed: enlargement of the court system; changes in our thinking in regard to the way minor crimes are handled; establishment of better standards for plea-bargaining; modifications in the formalism of the adversary system; establishment of a more reasonable balance between the means for protecting individual rights and those means that are used by serious offenders to escape prosecution; and, finally, recognition that courts cannot solve all of society's criminal problems. If the functions of the court system were more narrowly circumscribed, it could provide a more swift and fair adjudication of guilt or innocence, it could better protect society, and it would have a greater deterrent effect.

Corrections[*]

If criminal sanctions are to work, there must be certain prerequisites: (1) there must be some universality in defining the acts that are disavowed, which would be achieved through a more narrowly circumscribed set of statutes concerned with harm to persons or property; (2) the response of the

[*]This statement on corrections is taken in large part from two of the author's prior publications (Empey, 1967b and 1969). Reference can be made to those publications for a detailed analysis.

criminal justice system to such acts must be swift and efficient; and (3) the convicted person must learn from his experience, and be provided with alternatives to crime.

Assuming for the moment that the first two steps could be accomplished through reforms in legal statutes and police and court practices, let us now turn to the third area—the correctional segment of the justice system. It can be seen in historical perspective as a succession of four approaches: revenge, restraint, reformation, and, now, reintegration (Glaser, 1972:102–103).

Revenge—death, disfigurement, and banishment—was the primary response to lawbreaking prior to the eighteenth century. It was gradually replaced at that time by an emphasis upon *restraint*—the use of imprisonment as the major method for correcting offenders. However, it became apparent that imprisonment would not work successfully, and in the late nineteenth and early twentieth centuries, *reformation* became an important objective. Attention was focused upon mental and emotional makeup as the primary sources of difficulty of the offender and efforts were made to alter them. In the current phase in correctional history, *reintegration* is emphasized.

Reintegration is characterized by three major concepts. The first is a focus upon the compelling pressures that are exerted upon the offender by members of his community, by the social groups to which he belongs, by his particular class or ethnic group, and by the overall culture. Since it is this complex set of forces that prescribes his goals, that shapes his perception of the world, and that strongly determines how he will react to it, then it is these forces, as well as the offender's personal characteristics, that should become the objective of correctional attention. If the offender is to be helped, then both he and his interaction with all these forces will have to be reshaped.

The second element of the reintegration philosophy is an emphasis on the idea that crime, and reactions to it, are social products, socially defined. Society, not the individual offender, defines rules, labels those who break rules, and prescribes ways for reacting to the labeled person. This labeling process is often a means of isolating offenders from, rather than integrating them into, such major societal institutions as schools, businesses, unions, churches, and political organizations. Since these institutions provide the major access to a successful, noncriminal career, the offender may remain perpetually an outsider unless the labeling process is changed. Successful reintegration of the offender will depend, therefore, not only upon his own behavior, but upon the community's labeling and reacting processes as well. If they permit the offender to discard his label of "criminal" and to adopt another, the reintegration process will be aided. If not, efforts at correction may fail.

The third idea inherent in the reintegration philosophy is that it is not the severity but the certainty of punishment that will help to deter crime. A number of recent studies have indicated that the fear of punishment, as well as the anticipation of reward, gained by observing others being punished or rewarded has a strong influence on human behavior (Bandura and Walters, 1963; Bandura, 1969:118–216). Even when punishment is considered in the abstract, a belief that its probability is high may directly deter deviant behavior (Jensen, 1969). Hence, these and other studies suggest that punishment need not be severe, but that it is likely to deter if it is overt, personalized, and reasonably probable. Punishment is most likely to be this way if it is made a part of the person's community and neighborhood. Community programs can both provide assistance and exercise some constraints, and, in the long run, this may actually be more helpful than severe sanctions like prisons.

This is not meant to suggest that prisons are no longer needed. Some offenders are a clear danger to the community, which clearly deserves protection. But that number may be much smaller than many anticipate. In fact, we have gone a long way in implementing the reintegration philosophy. In 1965, for example, only one-third of all offenders, the bulk of them felons, were in institutions, while the remaining two-thirds were under supervision in the community (President's Crime Commission, 1967b:1). These figures testify to the existence of a minor revolution in the way offenders are treated.

All these methods are not working satisfactorily, however. One reason is that correctional efforts are piecemeal, underfinanced, and often disorganized. Beyond that, the correctional segment of the criminal justice system is characterized by a mass of myth, misinformation, and ignorance. We do not possess good information on either the causes for crime or the most effective and specific methods for dealing with it. There is a great need for research and a broader base of knowledge in order to make progress in the area of corrections.

NEED FOR RESEARCH

Robert Merton (1957:81) once noted that any attempt to eliminate or alter an existing social structure, such as the criminal justice system, without providing adequate alternative structures for fulfilling the functions previously fulfilled by that structure, is doomed to failure. Hence, if there is one major weakness in all of the reforms that have been suggested, it is the failure to consider Merton's warning. Attempts at reform may be engaging in nothing less than *sociological magic* unless these attempts provide viable alternatives to older patterns.

Unfortunately, there is a prevalent syndrome that characterizes contemporary thinking—the idea that once a problem is recognized, viable solutions are implied. That is nonsense. Although crime is a well-recognized problem, the need for research has not been acknowledged. People somehow assume that the most commonsense kinds of efforts will solve the crime problem. Despite all its wealth and resources, the United States has devoted very little attention to a disciplined assessment of crime and ways to go about correcting it. According to the President's Crime Commission (1967c:1), "More than 200,000 scientists have applied themselves to solving military problems and hundreds of thousands more to innovations in other areas of modern life, but only a handful are working to control the crimes that injure or frighten millions of Americans each year."

This is a paradoxical, even shocking state of affairs; as Stanton S. Wheeler and Leonard S. Cottrell point out (1966:44):

No responsible business concern would operate with as little information regarding its success or failure as do nearly all of our [crime] prevention and control programs. It is almost possible to count on the fingers of one hand the number of true experiments in which alternative techniques are compared; the number of systematic, though non-experimental evaluations is not a great deal larger. We spend millions of dollars a year in preventive and corrective efforts, with little other than guesswork to tell us whether we are getting the desired effects.

Let us now describe the four major types of knowledge that are needed in order to solve the crime problem:

1. *Knowledge derived from basic research that is concerned not only with crime causation, but with human behavior in general.* Our ability to understand deviant behavior depends heavily upon our ability to understand its counterpart— "normal," conforming behavior.
2. *Statistical knowledge on crime trends and the effectiveness of the overall criminal justice system.* An adequate information system is needed.
3. *Knowledge about the nature and operation of the various segments of the criminal justice system—the police, prosecutors, courts, and corrections.* We need a much better understanding of the impact of the policies, practices, and decision-making of these segments on offenders and the public alike.
4. *Knowledge derived from experimental innovation.* Just as experimentation is very much a part of other areas of society, so it should be in the criminal justice system.

In connection with point 3., one of the most important things to be remembered is that the various elements of the criminal justice system, like those in society as a whole, are inextricably tied together. For example, if changes are made in police practices, they will be felt by judges and correctional agencies. Or if the Supreme Court places restrictions on the kinds of police techniques that will be tolerated, or on the kinds of evidence that can be used against juveniles, the impact will reverberate throughout the entire system. Careful attention must be paid to the system-wide impact of whatever reforms are tried.

What little research has been conducted has provided some promising leads. In the search for alternatives to incarceration, for example, a few controlled experiments have shown that community programs may work just as well as, if not better than, prisons with even serious and repeat offenders (cf. Palmer and Warren, 1967; Hood and Sparks, 1970:186ff; Empey and Lubeck, 1971; and Empey and Erickson, 1972). Moreover, the savings, both in personal costs to the offender and in terms of money to the taxpayer, might be considerable. In the Silverlake Experiment (Empey and Lubeck, 1971:308–309), cost data indicated that for every 1,000 delinquents treated in the community, a saving of $2 million could be realized—a saving that could be put to work improving correctional effectiveness rather than providing bricks and guards. Yet, not only do studies of this type fail to constitute panaceas, they are pitifully small in number.

In response to those, both from the left and the right, who would suggest that we must act now, that we cannot afford the time necessary to build a more rational system, it should be noted that the task of implementing new approaches can proceed simultaneously with, and be a part of, the knowledge-building task. Crime is not simply a problem of social control to be solved by police or court action; it must also involve a wide range of social scientists and practitioners from a variety of fields.

CONCLUSIONS

Two major ideas have been suggested in this article: (1) crime in America must be understood as a problem that stems from, and must be dealt with as, a society-wide phenomenon; and (2) the search for solutions to the crime problem must be conceived in long-range and dynamic terms. The circumstances in which we now find ourselves are a function not merely of what police, courts, and correctional agencies have done, but of what society as a whole has done. Society is characterized by value conflict, dissension, and change, and the criminal justice system reflects these things.

In seeking solutions, therefore, a long-range and comprehensive perspective is required. Not only must changes be made in the criminal justice system itself, but in the other major institutions of society as well. All must share in the burdens of reform. Moreover, since the necessary knowledge is not available, but must be acquired, society must adopt a stance that will encourage knowledge-building and experimentation, and that will permit and encourage a systematic and rational search for solutions.

BIBLIOGRAPHY

Abernathy, M. Glenn. *Civil Liberties and the Constitution.* New York: Dodd, Mead, 1968.

Abraham, Henry J. *The Judicial Process: An Introductory Analysis of the Courts of the United States, England and France.* 2nd ed. New York: Oxford University Press, 1968.

Abrams, Arnold, *et al.* "Psychological Aspects of Addiction," *American Journal of Public Health,* 58 (November 1968), 2147.

Akers, Ronald L. "Problems in the Sociology of Deviance: Social Definitions and Behavior," *Social Forces,* 46 (June 1968), 455–465.

Albini, Joseph L. *The American Mafia: Genesis of a Legend.* New York: Appleton-Century-Crofts, 1972.

Alex, Nicholas. *Black in Blue.* New York: Appleton-Century-Crofts, 1969.

Allen, Francis A. *The Borderland of Criminal Justice: Essays on Law and Criminology.* Chicago: University of Chicago Press, 1964.

Allen, Richard C., Elyce Zenoff Ferster, and Jesse G. Rubin (eds.). *Readings in Law and Psychiatry.* Baltimore: Johns Hopkins Press, 1968.

Allport, Gordon W. *Becoming: Basic Considerations for a Psychology of Personality.* New Haven: Yale University Press, 1955.

Alschuler, A. "The Prosecutor's Role in Plea Bargaining," *University of Chicago Law Review,* 36 (1968), 50–112.

Alsop, Kenneth. *The Bootleggers and Their Era.* Garden City, N.Y.: Doubleday, 1962.

Amir, Menachem. "Patterns of Forcible Rape," in Marshall B. Clinard and Richard Quinney (eds.), *Criminal Behavior Systems: A Typology.* New York: Holt, Rinehart & Winston, 1967, pp. 60–75.

Angell, Robert C. "The Ethical Problems of Applied Sociology," in Paul F. Lazarsfeld, William H. Sewell, and Harold L. Wilensky (eds.), *The Uses of Sociology.* New York: Basic Books, 1967.

Ardrey, Robert. *The Territorial Imperative.* New York: Atheneum, 1966.

Arens, R. *Make Mad the Guilty.* Springfield, Ill.: Charles C. Thomas, 1969.

———, **and Harold D. Lasswell.** *In Defense of Public Order: The Emerging Field of Sanction Law.* New York: Columbia University Press, 1961.

Asbury, Herbert. *The Gangs of New York.* New York: Knopf, 1928.

———. *The Barbary Coast.* New York: Garden City Publishing Company, 1933.

Aubert, Vilhelm. "White-Collar Crime and Social Structure," *American Journal of Sociology,* 58 (November 1952), 263–271.

Bachrach, Peter, and Morton S. Baratz. "Two Faces of Power," *American Political Science Review,* 61 (December 1962), 947–952.

Bagdikian, Ben H. *The Information Machine.* New York: Harper & Row, 1971.

Baker, Joseph. *The Law of Political Unfairness, Public Meetings and Private Armies.* H. J. Just, 1937.

Ball, Harry V., and Lawrence M. Freedman. "The Use of Criminal Sanctions in the Enforcement of Economic Legislation: A Sociological View," *Stanford Law Review*, 17 (January 1965), 197–223.

Ball, John C., and Carl C. Chambers (eds.). *The Epidemiology of Opiate Addiction in the United States.* Springfield, Ill.: Charles C. Thomas, 1971.

Baltzell, E. Digby. *The Protestant Establishment.* New York: Vintage Books, 1966.

Bandura, Albert. *Principles of Behavior Modification.* New York: Holt, Rinehart & Winston, 1969.

———, and Richard H. Walters. *Social Learning and Personality Development.* New York: Holt Rinehart & Winston, 1963.

Banton, Michael. *The Policeman in the Community.* New York: Basic Books, 1964.

Barck, Oscar T., Jr., and Hugh T. Leflar. *Colonial America.* New York: Macmillan, 1959.

Barlay, Stephen. *Bondage: The Slave Traffic in Women Today.* New York: Funk & Wagnalls, 1968.

Barnet, Richard. "The Game of Nations," *Harper's*, 243 (November 1971), 53–59.

Barron, Milton L. *The Juvenile in Delinquent Society.* New York: Knopf, 1954.

Barth, Alan. *Law Enforcement versus the Law.* New York: Collier, 1963.

Baskin, J. *et al. Race-related Civil Disorders, 1967–69.* Waltham, Mass.: Lemberg Center for the Study of Violence, 1972.

Bassin, Alexander. "Daytop Village," *Psychology Today*, 2 (December 1968).

———, and Joseph Shelly. "Daytop Lodge: Halfway House for Drug Addicts," *Federal Probation*, 28 (December 1964), 46–54.

———, and Joseph Shelly. "Daytop Lodge—A New Treatment Approach for Drug Addicts," *Corrective Psychiatry*, 2 (July 1965), 186–195.

Bayley, David H., and Harold Mendelsohn. *Minorities and the Police.* New York: Free Press, 1969.

Beard, Charles A., and Mary R. Beard. *The Rise of American Civilization, vol. II.* New York: Macmillan, 1927.

Becker, Harold K. *Law Enforcement: A Selected Bibliography.* Metuchen, N.J.: Scarecrow Press, 1968.

Becker, Howard S. *Systematic Sociology on the Basis of the Beziehungslehre and Gebildelehre of Leopold von Wiess.* New York: Wiley, 1932.

———. *Through Values to Social Interpretation.* Durham, N.C.: Duke University Press, 1950.

———. "Becoming a Marijuana User," *The American Journal of Sociology*, 59 (November 1953), 235–242.

———. *Outsiders: Studies in Sociological Deviance*. New York: Free Press, 1963.

———. "Whose Side Are We On?" *Social Problems*, 14 (Winter 1967), 239–247.

Bell, Daniel. "Crime as an American Way of Life," *Antioch Review*, 13 (Summer 1953), 131–154.

———. *The End of Ideology*. New York: Free Press, 1959.

Belli, Melvin. *Dallas Justice*. New York: David McKay, 1964.

Bendix, Reinhard, and Bennett Berger. "Images of Society and Problems of Concept Formation in Sociology," in Llewellyn Gross (ed.), *Symposium on Sociological Theory*. Evanston, Ill.: Row, Peterson, 1959.

Bensman, Joseph, and Israel Gerver. "Crime and Punishment in the Factory: The Function of Deviance in Maintaining the Social System," *American Sociological Review*, 28 (August 1963), 588–598.

Bensman, Joseph, and Arthur J. Vidich. *The New American Society: The Revolution of the Middle Class*. Chicago: Quadrangle, 1971.

Berger, Monroe. *Equality by Statute: The Revolution in Civil Rights*. Rev. ed. Garden City, N.Y.: Doubleday, 1967.

Berger, Peter. *Invitation to Sociology: A Humanistic Perspective*. Garden City, N.Y.: Doubleday, 1963.

———, **and Thomas Luckmann.** *The Social Construction of Reality*. Garden City, N.Y.: Doubleday, 1966.

Bernard, Jessie. *American Community Behavior*. New York: Dryden Press, 1949.

Bianchi, Hermanus. *Position and Subject Matter of Criminology: Inquiry Concerning Theoretical Criminology*. Amsterdam: North Holland, 1956.

Bierstadt, Robert. "An Analysis of Social Power," *American Sociological Review*, 15 (December 1950), 730–738.

———. "Nominal and Real Definitions in Sociological Theory," in Llewellyn Gross (ed.), *Symposium in Sociological Theory*. Evanston, Ill.: Row, Peterson, 1959, pp. 121–144.

Binger, Carl. *Revolutionary Doctor—Benjamin Rush, 1746–1813*. New York: Norton, 1966.

Bird, Otto A. *The Idea of Justice*. New York: Praeger, 1967.

Bittner, Egon. "The Police on Skid-Row: A Study of Peace Keeping," *American Sociological Review*, 32 (October 1967), 699–715.

———. *The Function of the Police in Modern Society*. Washington, D.C.: U.S. Government Printing Office, 1970.

Black, Algernon D. *The People and the Police*. New York: McGraw-Hill, 1968.

Black, Donald J., and Albert J. Reiss, Jr. "Police Control of Juveniles," *American Sociological Review*, 35 (February 1970), 63.

Blaisdell, Donald C. *American Democracy Under Pressure*. New York: Ronald Press, 1957.

Bloch, Herbert A., and Gilbert Geis. *Man, Crime and Society.* New York: Random House, 1970.

Block, Herbert A., and Arthur Niederhoffer. *The Gang.* New York: Philosophical Library, 1958.

Blotnick, Elihu. "How to Counterfeit Credit Cards and Get Away with It: The Confessions of a Plastic Man," *Scanlan's Monthly,* 1 (June 1970), 21–28.

Blum, Richard H. (ed.). *Police Selection.* Springfield, Ill.: Charles C. Thomas, 1964.

Blumberg, Abraham S. *Criminal Justice.* Chicago: Quadrangle, 1967.

———. "Sex, Law, and the Changing Society," *Medical Aspects of Human Sexuality* (October 1970), 103–107.

———, **and Arthur Niederhoffer,** "The Police in Social and Historical Perspective," in Arthur Niederhoffer and Abraham S. Blumberg (eds.), *The Ambivalent Force.* Boston: Ginn, 1970.

Bonger, W. A. *Criminality and the Economic Conditions.* Boston: Little, Brown, 1916.

Boorstin, Daniel J. *The Lost World of Thomas Jefferson.* Boston: Beacon Press, 1948.

Bordua, David J. *The Police: Six Sociological Essays.* New York: Wiley, 1967.

———. "Recent Trends: Deviant Behavior and Social Control," *Annals of the American Academy of Political and Social Science,* 369 (January 1967), 149–163.

———, **and Albert J. Reiss, Jr.** "Command, Control and Charisma: Reflections on Police Bureaucracy," *American Journal of Sociology,* 72 (July 1966), 68–76.

Boskin, Joseph. *Urban Racial Violence in the Twentieth Century.* Beverly Hills, Calif.: Glencoe Press, 1969.

Bowers, William J. *Student Dishonesty and Its Control in College.* New York: Columbia University Bureau of Applied Social Research, 1965.

Bowsky, William M. "The Medieval Commune and Internal Violence: Police Power and Public Safety in Siena, 1287–1355," *American Historical Review,* 73 (October 1967), 1–17.

Bridgman, Percy W. "Determinism in Modern Science," in Sidney Hook (ed.), *Determinism and Freedom in the Age of Modern Science.* New York: Collier, 1961, pp. 57–75.

Brill, Leon. "Drug Abuse Problems—Implications for Treatment," *Abstracts for Social Workers,* 7 (Fall 1971), 3–8.

———. "Some Comments on the Paper, 'Social Control in Therapeutic Communities,'" *The International Journal of the Addictions,* 6 (March 1971), 45–50.

Bromsted, Ernest J. *Dictatorship and Political Police.* London: Routledge and Kegan Paul, 1945.

Brown, Claude. *Manchild in the Promised Land.* New York: Macmillan, 1965.

Brown, Robert. *Explanation in Social Science.* Chicago: Aldine, 1963.

Browning, E. "From Rumble to Revolution: The Young Lords," *Ramparts* (September 1970).

Bryce, James. *Modern Democracies.* London: Macmillan, 1923.

Buckley, Walter. "A Methodological Note," in Thomas J. Scheff, *Being Mentally Ill.* Chicago: Aldine, 1966, pp. 201–205.

Bunge, Mario. *Causality: The Place of the Causal Principle in Modern Science.* Cleveland: World Publishing, 1963.

Bunyan, John. *The Pilgrim's Progress.* New York: Revell, 1903.

Burgess, Robert L., and Ronald L. Akers, "A Differential Association-Reinforcement Theory of Criminal Behavior," *Social Problems,* 14 (Fall 1966), 128–147.

Burns, Haywood. "Can a Black Man Get a Fair Trial in This Country?" *The New York Times Magazine,* July 12, 1970.

Caldwell, Robert G. "A Re-examination of the Concept of White-Collar Crime," *Federal Probation,* 22 (March 1958), 30–36.

Cameron, Mary O. *The Booster and the Snitch: Department Store Shoplifting.* New York: Free Press, 1964.

Campbell, A., and Howard Schuman. *Racial Attitudes in Fifteen American Cities.* Ann Arbor, Mich.: Studies for the National Advisory Commission on Civil Disorders, Institute for Social Research, 1968.

Cantor, Nathaniel. "The Search for Causes of Crime," *Journal of Criminal Law, Criminology and Police Science,* 22 (March-April 1932), 854–863.

———. "Crime—A Political Problem," *Ideas in Action,* 1 (1946), 51.

Cardozo, Benjamin. *The Nature of the Judicial Process.* New Haven: Yale University Press, 1931.

Carlin, Jerome E., Jan Howard, and Sheldon L. Messinger. *Civil Justice and the Poor: Issues for Sociological Research.* New York: Russell Sage Foundation, 1967.

Carney, Frank J., Hans W. Mattick, and John D. Callaway. *Action on the Streets: A Handbook for Inner City Youth Work.* New York: Association Press, 1969.

Carroll, Lewis. "Through the Looking Glass," in Martin Gardner (ed.), *The Annotated Alice.* New York: Bramhall House, 1960.

Carter, Robert M., and G. Thomas Gitchoff. "An Alternative to Youthful Mass Disorder," *The Police Chief,* 37 (July 1970), 52–56.

Cavan, Ruth Shonle. *Juvenile Delinquency: Development, Treatment, Control.* Philadelphia: Lippincott, 1969.

Cecil, Hugh H. R. *Conservatism.* London: Williams and Norgabe, 1912.

Chambers, Carl D. *An Assessment of Drug Use in the General Population.* New York: Narcotic Addiction Control Commission, 1971.

Chambliss, William J. "A Sociological Analysis of the Law of Vagrancy," *Social Problems,* 12 (Summer 1964), 66–77.

———. *Crime and the Legal Process.* New York: McGraw-Hill, 1969.

Chapman, Samuel G. *The Police Heritage in England and America.* East Lansing: Michigan State University Press, 1962.

Chein, I. "Narcotics Use Among Juveniles," *Social Work,* 7 (April 1956).

Chevigny, Paul. *Police Power: Police Abuses in New York City.* New York: Pantheon, 1969.

———. *Cops and Rebels.* New York: Pantheon, 1972.

Churchill, Allen. *The Incredible Ivar Krueger.* New York: Holt, Rinehart & Winston, 1957.

Cicourel, Aaron V. *The Social Organization of Juvenile Justice.* New York: Wiley, 1968.

Cipes, Robert M. *The Crime War: The Manufactured Crusade.* New York: New American Library, 1968.

Clark, Alexander L., and Jack P. Gibbs. "Social Control: A Reformulation," *Social Problems,* 12 (Spring 1965), 398–415.

Clark, John P. "Isolation of the Police: A Comparison of the British and American Situation," *Journal of Criminal Law, Criminology and Police Science,* 56 (September 1965), 307–319.

Clark, Ramsey. *Crime in America.* New York: Simon and Schuster, 1970.

Clinard, Marshall B. *The Black Market: A Study of White Collar Crime.* New York: Holt, Rinehart & Winston, 1952.

———. "Corruption Runs Far Deeper than Politics," *The New York Times Magazine,* August 10, 1952.

——— (ed.). *Anomie and Deviant Behavior: A Discussion and Critique.* New York: Free Press, 1964.

———. *Sociology of Deviant Behavior.* 3rd ed. New York: Holt, Rinehart & Winston, 1968.

———, **and Richard Quinney** (eds.). *Criminal Behavior Systems: A Typology.* New York: Holt, Rinehart & Winston, 1967.

Cloward, Richard A. *New Perspectives for Research on Juvenile Delinquency.* Washington, D.C.: U.S. Government Printing Office, 1956.

———. "Illegitimate Means, Anomie and Deviant Behavior," *American Sociological Review,* 24 (April 1959), 164–176.

———, **and Lloyd E. Ohlin.** *Delinquency and Opportunity: A Theory of Delinquent Gangs.* New York: Free Press, 1960.

Cohen, Albert K. *Delinquent Boys: The Culture of the Gang.* New York: Free Press, 1955.

———. *Deviance and Control.* Englewood Cliffs, N.J.: Prentice-Hall, 1966.

———, **and James F. Short.** "Research in Delinquent Subcultures," *Journal of Social Issues,* 14 (Summer 1958).

Cohen, Bernard. "The Delinquency of Gangs and Spontaneous Groups," in Thorsten Sellin and Marvin E. Wolfgang (eds.), *Delinquency: Selected Studies.* New York: Wiley, 1969.

Cohen, Morris R., and Ernest Nagel. *An Introduction to Logic and Scientific Method.* New York: Harcourt, Brace, 1934.

Commager, Henry Steele. "The Ambiguous American," *The New York Times Magazine,* May 3, 1964.

———. *The American Mind.* New Haven: Yale University Press, 1970.

Conklin, John E. *Robbery and the Criminal Justice System.* Philadelphia: Lippincott, 1972.

Connor, Walter D. "The Manufacture of Deviance: The Case of the Soviet Purge, 1936–38," *American Sociological Review,* 37 (August 1972), 403–413.

Conot, Robert. *Rivers of Blood, Years of Darkness.* New York: Bantam, 1967.

Conwell, Chic. *The Professional Thief.* Chicago: University of Chicago Press, 1937.

Cook, Fred J. *The FBI Nobody Knows.* New York: Macmillan, 1964.

———. *The Corrupted Land.* New York: Macmillan, 1966.

———. *The Secret Rulers.* New York: Duell, Sloan and Pearce, 1966.

Cook, Shirley J. "The Social Background of Narcotic Legislation," *Addictions,* 17 (Summer 1970), 14–29.

Cook, Thomas I. "The Political System: The Stubborn Search for a Science of Politics," *Journal of Philosophy,* 51 (February 1954), 128–137.

Coser, Lewis A. *The Functions of Social Conflict.* New York: Free Press, 1956.

———. "Social Conflict and the Theory of Social Change," *British Journal of Sociology,* 8 (September 1957), 197–207.

Cramer, James. *The World's Police.* London: Cassell, 1964.

Crawford, Paul L., Dan I. Malamud, and James R. Dumpson. *Working with Teen-Age Gangs.* New York: Welfare Council of New York City, 1950.

Cray, Ed. *The Big Blue Line: Police Power vs. Human Rights.* New York: Coward-McCann, 1967.

Cressey, Donald R. *White Collar Crime.* New York: Holt, Rinehart and Winston, 1961.

———. *Theft of a Nation: The Structure and Operations of Organized Crime in America.* New York: Harper & Row, 1969.

———, **and David A. Ward.** *Delinquency, Crime, and Social Progress.* New York: Harper & Row, 1969.

Crime in the United States: Uniform Crime Reports, 1971. Washington, D.C.: U.S. Government Printing Office, 1972.

Cumming, J., and F. Cumming. "Mental Health Education in a Canadian Community," in B. D. Paul and W. Miller (eds.), *Health, Culture and Community.* New York: Russell Sage Foundation, 1955.

Curran, William J. *Law and Medicine.* Boston: Little, Brown, 1960.

Currie, Elliot P. "Crimes Without Criminals: Witchcraft and Its Control in Renaissance Europe," *Law and Society Review*, 3 (August 1968), 7–32.

Dahrendorf, Rolf. "Out of Utopia: Toward a Reorientation in Sociological Analysis," *American Journal of Sociology*, 67 (September 1958), 115–127.

———. *Class and Class Conflict in Industrial Society*. Stanford, Calif.: Stanford University Press, 1959.

Daniels, Jonathan. *The Devil's Backbone*. New York: McGraw-Hill, 1962.

Dash, Samuel, Robert Knowlton, and Richard Schwartz. *The Eavesdroppers*. New Brunswick, N.J.: Rutgers University Press, 1959.

David, Austin. "What About 'Reaching Out': An Account of the Boston Youth Project," *Round Table*, 19 (1958).

Davis, David E. "The Phylogeny of Gangs," in E. L. Bliss (ed.), *Roots of Behavior*. New York: Harper & Row, 1962.

Davis, Kingsley. "Jealousy and Sexual Property," *Social Forces*, 14 (March 1936), 395–405.

———. "The Sociology of Prostitution." *American Sociological Review*, 2 (1937), 744–755.

———. "Illegitimacy and the Social Structure," *American Journal of Sociology*, 45 (September 1939), 215–233.

———. "The Myth of Functional Analysis as a Special Method in Sociology and Anthropology," *American Sociological Review*, 24 (December 1959), 758.

———. "Sexual Behavior," in Robert K. Merton and Robert A. Nisbet (eds.), *Contemporary Social Problems*. 2nd ed. New York: Harcourt, Brace & World, 1966.

DeFleur, Melvin, and Richard Quinney. "A Reformulation of Sutherland's Differential Association Theory and a Strategy for Empirical Verification," *Journal of Research in Crime and Delinquency*, 3 (January 1966), 1–22.

Deisher, Robert W. *et al.* "The Young Male Prostitute," *Pediatrics*, 43 (June 1969), 936–941.

DeRopp, Robert S. *Drugs and the Mind*. New York: Grove Press, 1961.

Dershowitz, Alan M. "Increasing Community Control Over Corporate Crime: A Problem in the Law of Sanctions," *Yale Law Journal*, 71 (September 1961), 289–306.

Deutsch, Albert. *The Trouble with Cops*. New York: Crown, 1955.

Devlin, Patrick. *The Enforcement of Morals*. New York: Oxford University Press, 1965.

Dickson, Donald T. "Bureaucracy and Morality: An Organizational Perspective on a Moral Crusade," *Social Problems*, 16 (Fall 1968), 143–156.

Dinitz, Simon, Russell R. Dynes, and Alfred C. Clarke. *Deviance: Studies in the Process of Stigmatization and Societal Reaction*. New York: Oxford University Press, 1969.

Djilas, Milovan. "On Alienation," *Encounter*, 36 (May 1971), 8–15.

Dock, William. "The Clinical Value of Alcohol," in S. P. Lucia (ed.), *Alcohol and Civilization*. New York: McGraw-Hill, 1963.

Dolci, Danilo. *The Man Who Plays Alone.* New York: Pantheon, 1968.

Dollard, John. *Caste and Class in a Southern Town.* Garden City, N.Y.: Doubleday, 1957.

Donnelly, Richard C. *et al. Criminal Law.* New York: Free Press, 1962.

Douglas, Michael. *Dealing.* New York: Knopf, 1971.

Dow, Thomas E., Jr. "The Role of Identification in Conditioning Public Attitude Toward the Offender," *Journal of Criminal Law, Criminology and Police Science*, 58 (March 1967), 75–79.

Drosnin, Michael. "Ripping Off: The New Life Style," *The New York Times Magazine*, August 8, 1971.

Durkheim, Emile. *The Division of Labor in Society.* New York: Free Press, 1964.

Duster, Troy. *The Legislation of Morality: Drugs and Moral Judgment.* New York: Free Press, 1970.

Duvall, Henrietta *et al.* "Followup Study of Narcotic Drug Addicts Five Years After Hospitalization," *Public Health Reports*, 78 (March 1963), 185–193.

Easton, David. *The Political System.* New York: Knopf, 1953.

Eddy, Nathan B. *et al.* "Drug Dependence: Its Significance and Characteristics," *Bulletin of the World Health Organization*, 32 (1965), 721–733.

Edelhertz, Herbert. *The Nature, Impact and Prosecution of White-Collar Crime.* Washington, D.C.: Law Enforcement Assistance Administration, U.S. Department of Justice, 1970.

Ehrmann, Henry W. (ed.). *Interest Groups on Four Continents.* Pittsburgh: University of Pittsburgh Press, 1958.

Eidelberg, Paul. *The Philosophy of the American Constitution: A Reinterpretation of the Intentions of the Founding Fathers.* New York: Free Press, 1968.

Eisner, Victor. *The Delinquency Label.* New York: Random House, 1968.

Eldefonso, Edward, Alan Caffey, and Richard C. Grace. *Principles of Law Enforcement.* New York: Wiley, 1968.

Ellingston, John R. *Protecting Our Children from Criminal Careers.* Englewood Cliffs, N.J.: Prentice-Hall, 1948.

Elliott, Mabel A. "Perspective on the American Crime Problem," *Social Problems*, 5 (Winter 1957–1958), 184–193.

Ellis, Albert, and Ralph Brancale. *The Psychology of Sex Offenders.* Springfield, Ill.: Charles C. Thomas, 1956.

Emerson, Robert M. *Judging Delinquents: Context and Process in Juvenile Court.* Chicago: Aldine, 1969.

Empey, LaMar T. *Alternatives to Incarceration.* Washington, D.C.: U.S. Government Printing Office, 1967.

———. "Contemporary Programs for Convicted Juvenile Offenders: Problems of

Theory, Practice, and Research," in *Crimes of Violence*. Washington, D.C.: National Commission on the Causes and Prevention of Violence.

———. "Delinquency Theory and Recent Research," *Journal of Research in Crime and Delinquency*, 3 (January 1967), 28–41.

———, and Maynard L. Erickson. *The Provo Experiment*. Lexington, Mass.: D. C. Heath, 1972.

———, and Steven G. Lubeck. *The Silverlake Experiment*. Chicago: Aldine-Atherton, 1971.

Engler, Robert. *The Politics of Oil*. New York: Macmillan, 1961.

Erikson, Kai T. "Notes on the Sociology of Deviance," *Social Problems*, 9 (Spring 1962), 307-314.

———. *Wayward Puritans: A Study in the Sociology of Deviance*. New York: Wiley, 1966.

Ernst, Morris L., and Alan U. Schwartz. *Privacy: The Right to Be Let Alone*. New York: Macmillan, 1962.

Esposito, John C. *The Vanishing Air*. New York: Grossman, 1970.

Esselstyn, T. C. "Prostitution in the United States," *Annals of the American Academy of Political and Social Science*, 376 (March 1968), 123–135.

Falk, Richard A. *Legal Order in a Violent World*. Princeton, N.J.: Princeton University Press, 1968.

Faralicq, René. *The French Police from Within*. London: Cassell, 1933.

Fasdick, Raymond. *European Police Systems*. New York: Century, 1915.

Fiddle, Seymour. *Portraits from a Shooting Gallery*. New York: Harper & Row, 1967.

Fingl, Edward, and Dixon M. Woodbury. "General Principles," in Louis S. Goodman and Alfred Gilman (eds.), *The Pharmacological Basis of Therapeutics*. 3rd. ed. New York: Macmillan, 1965.

Fink, Paul Jay *et al.* "Recent Trends in Substance Abuse: Morning Glory Seed Psychosis," *The International Journal of the Addictions*, 2 (Spring 1967), 150.

Ford, Clellan S., and Frank A. Beach. *Patterns of Sexual Behavior*. New York: Harper & Row, 1951.

Forster, Arnold. "Violence in the Fanatical Left and Right," *Annals of the American Academy of Political and Social Science* (March 1966), 143.

Fort, Joel. "A World View of Marijuana: Has the World Gone to Pot?," *Journal of Psychedelic Drugs*, 2 (Fall 1968), 1–14.

———. *The Pleasure Seekers*. Indianapolis: Bobbs-Merrill, 1969.

Frank, Jerome. *Courts on Trial: Myth and Reality in American Justice*. Princeton, N.J.: Princeton University Press, 1949.

Frankfurter, Felix. *The Case of Sacco and Vanzetti*. Boston: Little, Brown, 1927.

Freund, Paul A. *On Law and Justice*. Cambridge: Harvard University Press, 1968.

Friendly, Alfred, and Ronald Goldfarb. *Crime and Publicity: The Impact of News on the Administration of Justice.* New York: Twentieth Century Fund, 1967.

Fuller, Lon L. *The Morality of Law.* New Haven: Yale University Press, 1964.

Gable, Richard W. "Interest Groups as Policy Shapers," *Annals of the American Academy of Political and Social Science,* 319 (September 1958), 84–93.

Gagnon, John H., and William Simon. "Psychosexual Development," *Trans-action,* 6 (March 1969), 9–17.

Gandy, John M. "Preventive Work with Street Corner Groups," *Annals of the American Academy of Political and Social Science,* 323 (March 1959), 107–116.

Gannon, Thomas M. "Dimensions of Current Gang Delinquency," *Journal of Research in Crime and Delinquency,* 4 (January 1967).

Garceau, Oliver. *The Political Life of the American Medical Association.* Cambridge: Harvard University Press, 1941.

Gastil, Raymond D. "Homicide and a Regional Culture of Violence," *American Sociological Review,* 36 (June 1971), 412–427.

Gebhard, Paul H. *et al. Sex Offenders: An Analysis of Types.* New York: Harper & Row, 1965.

Geis, Gilbert. "Toward a Delineation of White-Collar Offenses," *Sociological Inquiry,* 32 (Spring 1962), 159–171.

———."The Heavy Electrical Equipment Antitrust Cases of 1961," in Marshall B. Clinard and Richard Quinney (eds.), *Criminal Behavior Systems: A Typology.* New York: Holt, Rinehart & Winston, 1967, pp. 139–151.

——— (ed.). *White-Collar Criminal: The Offender in Business and the Professions.* New York: Atherton, 1968.

Gellhorn, Walter. *Ombudsmen and Others: Citizen Protectors in Nine Countries.* Cambridge: Harvard University Press, 1966.

Germann, A. C., Frank D. Day, and Robert R. J. Gallati. *Introduction to Law Enforcement.* Springfield, Ill.: Charles C. Thomas, 1962.

Gerth, Hans, and C. Wright Mills. *Character and Social Structure.* New York: Harcourt, Brace, 1953.

Gibbs, Jack P. "Conceptions of Deviant Behavior: The Old and the New," *Pacific Sociological Review,* 9 (Spring 1966), 9–14.

Ging, Steven, and S. Steven Rosenfield. *The Quality of Justice in the Lower Criminal Courts in Metropolitan Boston.* Boston: Lawyers' Committee for Civil Rights Under Law, 1970.

Glaser, Daniel. *Adult Crime and Social Policy.* Englewood Cliffs, N.J.: Prentice-Hall, 1972.

Glueck, Sheldon, and Eleanor Glueck. *Unraveling Juvenile Delinquency.* New York: Commonwealth Fund, 1950.

Goffman, Erving. *Asylums: Essays on the Social Situation of Mental Patients and Other Inmates.* Garden City, N.Y.: Doubleday, 1961.

Goldberg, Theodore. "The Automobile: A Social Institution for Adolescents," *Environment and Behavior* (December 1969).

Goldfarb, Ronald. *Ransom.* New York: Harper & Row, 1965.

Goldman, Nathan. *The Differential Selection of Juvenile Offenders for Court Appearance.* New York: National Research and Information Center, National Council on Crime and Delinquency, 1963.

Goldstein, Abraham S. *The Insanity Defense.* New Haven: Yale University Press, 1967.

———. "Legal Control of the Dossier," in Stanton Wheeler (ed.), *On Record: Files and Dossiers in American Life.* New York: Russell Sage Foundation, 1969.

Goldstein, Herman. "Police Discretion: The Ideal versus the Real," *Public Administration Review,* 23 (September 1963), 140–148.

Goldstein, Joseph. "Police Discretion Not to Invoke the Criminal Process: Low-Visibility Decisions in the Administration of Criminal Justice," *Yale Law Journal,* 69 (March 1960), 543–594.

Goode, Erich. *The Marijuana Smokers.* New York: Basic Books, 1970.

Goodman, Paul. *Growing Up Absurd.* New York: Random House, 1960.

Gould, Leroy. "Changing Structure of Property Crime in an Affluent Society," *Social Problems,* 48 (September 1969), 50–60.

———. "Crime and the Addict—Beyond Common Sense," in James Inciardi and Carl Chambers (eds.), *Drugs and the Criminal Justice System.* London: Sage Publications, 1973.

———, et al. *Crime as a Profession.* Washington, D.C.: U.S. Department of Justice, 1966.

Gouldner, Alvin W. "The Sociologist as Partisan: Sociology and the Welfare State," *American Sociologist,* 3 (May 1968), 103–116.

———. *The Coming Crisis of Western Sociology.* New York: Basic Books, 1970.

Graham, Hugh Davis, and Ted Robert Gurr (eds.). *Violence in America: Historical and Comparative Perspectives.* New York: Bantam, 1969.

Greenberger, Martin (ed.). *Computers, Communications, and the Public Interest.* Baltimore: Johns Hopkins Press, 1971.

Greenwald, Harold. *The Call Girl.* New York: Ballantine, 1958.

———. *The Affluent Prostitute: A Social and Psychological Study.* New York: Walker, 1970.

Grinter, R. R., Sr. "Emerging Concepts of Mental Illness and Treatment: The Medical Point of View," *American Journal of Psychiatry,* 125 (January 1969), 865–869.

Gross, Bertram (ed.). *A Great Society?* New York: Basic Books, 1968.

Guyon, René. *The Ethics of Sexual Acts.* New York: Knopf, 1934.

Hacker, Andrew. "A Country Called Corporate America," *The New York Times Magazine,* July 3, 1966.

Hager, Don J. "This Delinquent Society," *Congress Weekly*, May 9, 1955, 12–13.

Hall, Jerome. *Theft Law and Society.* 2nd ed. Indianapolis: Bobbs-Merrill, 1952.

Halleck, Seymour L. *Psychiatry and the Dilemmas of Crime.* New York: Harper & Row, 1967.

Hanson, Norwood Russell. *Patterns of Discovery.* New York: Cambridge University Press, 1965.

Harden, Charles M. *The Politics of Agriculture: Soil Conservation and the Struggle for Power in Rural America.* New York: Free Press, 1962.

Harris, Richard. *Justice.* New York: Dutton, 1970.

Hart, H. L. A. *Law, Liberty, and Morality.* Stanford, Calif.: Stanford University Press, 1963.

———. *Punishment and Responsibility: Essays in the Philosophy of Law.* New York: Oxford University Press, 1967.

Hart, J. M. *The British Police.* London: Allen and Unwin, 1951.

Hartogs, Renatus, and Eric Artzt (eds.). *Violence: Causes and Solutions.* New York: Dell, 1970.

Hartung, Frank E. "White-Collar Offenses in the Wholesale Meat Industry in Detroit," *American Journal of Sociology*, 56 (July 1950), 25–34.

———. "Trends in the Use of Capital Punishment," *Annals of the American Academy of Political and Social Science*, 284 (November 1952), 8–19.

———. "White Collar Crime: Its Significance for Theory and Practice," *Federal Probation*, 17 (June 1953), 31–36.

Hayek, F. A. *The Counter-Revolution of Science.* New York: Free Press, 1964.

Heilbroner, Robert L. *et al.* *In the Name of Profit: Profiles in Corporate Irresponsibility.* Garden City, N.Y.: Doubleday, 1972.

Heisenberg, Werner. *Physics and Philosophy: The Revolution in Modern Science.* New York: Harper & Row, 1958.

Helpern, Milton, and Yong-Myun Rho. "Deaths from Narcotism in New York City," *The International Journal of the Addictions*, 2 (Spring 1967), 53–84.

Henry, Jules. *Culture Against Man.* New York: Random House, 1963.

Hernton, Calvin C. *Sex and Racism in America.* New York: Grove Press, 1966.

Hersey, John. *The Algiers Motel Incident.* New York: Knopf, 1968.

Hewitt, William H. *British Police Administration.* Springfield, Ill.: Charles C. Thomas, 1965.

———. *A Bibliography of Police Administration, Public Safety and Criminology.* Springfield, Ill.: Charles C. Thomas, 1967.

Heyman, Florence. "Methadone Maintenance as Law and Order," *Society*, 9 (June 1972), 15–25.

Hirschi, Travis, and Hanan C. Selvin. *Delinquency Research: An Appraisal of Analytic Methods.* New York: Free Press, 1967.

Hoffman, Abbie. *Steal This Book.* New York: Grove Press, 1971.

Hofstadter, Richard. *The Paranoid Style in American Politics.* New York: Knopf, 1965.

——, **and Michael Wallace** (eds.). *American Violence.* New York: Vintage Books, 1971.

Hollester, Leo *et al.* "Withdrawal Reactions from Chlordiazepoxide ('Librium')," *Psychopharmacologia,* 2 (1961), 63–68.

Hollingshead, August B. *Elmtown's Youth: The Impact of Social Classes on Adolescents.* New York: Wiley, 1949.

Homans, George Casper. "Contemporary Theory in Sociology," in Robert E. L. Faris (ed.), *Handbook of Modern Sociology.* Chicago: Rand McNally, 1964, pp. 951–977.

Honigmann, John J. "Value Conflict and Legislation," *Social Problems,* 7 (Summer 1959), 34–40.

Hood, Robert, and Richard Sparks. *Key Issues in Criminology.* New York: McGraw-Hill, 1970.

Hooton, Ernest A. *Crime and the Man.* Cambridge: Harvard University Press, 1939.

Horowitz, Irving Louis. "Consensus, Conflict and Cooperation: A Sociological Inventory," *Social Forces,* 41 (December 1962), 177–188.

——, **and Martin Liebowitz.** "Social Deviance and Political Marginality: Toward a Redefinition of the Relation Between Sociology and Politics," *Social Problems,* 15 (Winter 1968), 280–296.

Horton, Paul B., and Gerald R. Leslie. *The Sociology of Social Problems.* 4th ed. New York: Appleton-Century-Crofts, 1970.

Hughes, Patrick *et al.* "The Social Structure of a Heroin Copping Community," *American Journal of Psychiatry,* 128 (November 1971), 43–50.

Humphreys, Laud. *Tearoom Trade: Impersonal Sex in Public Places.* Chicago: Aldine, 1970.

Hunsberger, Bruce. *Railroad Street.* New York: Lyle Stuart, 1970.

Hunt, G. Halsey, and Maurice E. Odoroff. "Followup Study of Narcotic Drug Addicts," *Public Health Reports,* 77 (January 1962), 41–54.

Huxley, Aldous. *Ape and Essence.* New York: Bantam, 1962.

Huxley, Julian. *New Bottles for New Wines.* New York: Harper & Row, 1957.

Hynd, Alan. "The Original Cardiff Giant," *True,* 28 (1951), 71–78.

Hyneman, Charles S. *The Study of Politics.* Urbana: University of Illinois Press, 1959.

Inbau, Fred E., and John E. Reid. *Criminal Interrogation and Confessions.* Baltimore: Williams and Wilkens, 1962.

——, **and Claude R. Sowle.** *Criminal Justice: Cases and Comments.* 2nd ed. Brooklyn, N.Y.: The Foundation Press, 1964.

Inciardi, James, and Carl Chambers (eds.). *Drugs and the Criminal Justice System.* London: Sage Publications, 1973.

Inkeles, Alex. *What is Sociology?* Englewood Cliffs, N.J.: Prentice-Hall, 1964.

Institute of Public Administration. "Abuses in Crime Reporting," in Marvin E. Wolfgang, Leonard Savitz, and Norman Johnston (eds.), *The Sociology of Crime and Delinquency.* 2nd ed. New York: Wiley, 1970, pp. 114–116.

Isbell, Harris. "Medical Aspects of Opiate Addiction," in John O'Donnell and John C. Ball (eds.), *Narcotic Addiction.* New York: Harper & Row, 1962.

Jacobs, Paul. *Prelude to Riot.* New York: Random House, 1968.

Jackson, Bruce. *A Thief's Primer.* London: Collier-Macmillan, 1969.

Jaffe, Jerome H. *et al.* "Experience with the Use of Methadone in a Multi-Modality Program for the Treatment of Narcotics Users," *The International Journal of the Addictions,* 4 (September 1970), 481–490.

Janowitz, Morris. *Social Control of Escalated Riots.* Chicago: University of Chicago Center for Policy Study, 1968.

Jeffery, Clarence Ray. "The Structure of American Criminological Thinking," *Journal of Criminal Law, Criminology and Police Science,* 46 (January-February 1956), 423–435.

– – –. "The Development of Crime in Early England," *Journal of Criminal Law, Criminology and Police Science,* 47 (March-April 1957), 647–666.

– – –. "Criminal Behavior and Learning Theory," *Journal of Criminal Law, Criminology and Police Science,* 56 (September 1965), 294–300.

Jeffrey, Sir Charles. *The Colonial Police.* London: M. Parrish, 1952.

Jensen, Gary F. "'Crime Doesn't Pay': Correlate of a Shared Misunderstanding," *Social Problems,* 17 (Fall 1969), 189–201.

Johnson, Gerald W. *The Lunatic Fringe.* Philadelphia: Lippincott, 1957.

Johnson, Richard M. *The Dynamics of Compliance: Supreme Court Decision-Making from a New Perspective.* Evanston, Ill.: Northwestern University Press, 1968.

Johnson, Roswell D. "Medico-Social Aspects of Marijuana," *The Rhode Island Medical Journal,* 51 (March 1968), 171–187.

Johnston, William. *Cruising.* New York: Random House, 1970.

Jones, Harry W. (ed.). *Law and the Social Role of Science.* New York: Rockefeller University Press, 1967.

Joseph, Herman. "Heroin Addiction and Methadone Maintenance," *Probation and Parole,* 1 (Spring 1969), 18–40.

Kadish, Sanford H. "Some Observations on the Use of Criminal Sanctions in Enforcing Economic Regulations," *University of Chicago Law Review,* 30 (Spring 1963), 423–449.

– – –. "The Crisis of Overcriminalization," *Annals of the American Academy of Political and Social Science,* 374 (November 1967), 157–170.

Kafka, Franz. *The Trial.* New York: Vintage Books, 1969.

Kamisar, Yale. "How to Use, Abuse—and Fight Back with—Crime Statistics," *Oklahoma Law Review,* 25 (May 1972), 239–258.

———, **Fred Inbau, and Thurman Arnold.** *Criminal Justice in Our Time.* Charlottesville: University Press of Virginia, 1965.

Kaplan, Abraham. *The Conduct of Inquiry: Methodology for the Behavioral Sciences.* San Francisco: Chandler Publishing, 1964.

Kaplan, J., and J. R. Waltz. *The Trial of Jack Ruby.* New York: Macmillan, 1965.

Kaplan, John. *Marijuana: The New Prohibition.* Cleveland: World Publishing, 1970.

Karlen, Delmar. *Anglo-American Criminal Justice.* New York: Oxford University Press, 1967.

———. *The Supreme Court and Political Freedom.* New York: Free Press, 1968.

Katz, Harvey. "The White Collar Criminal," *Washingtonian Magazine,* 5 (May 1970), 65.

Kavaler, Florence *et al.* "A Commentary and Annotated Bibliography on the Relationship Between Narcotics Addiction and Criminality," *Municipal Reference Library Notes,* 42 (April 1968), 45-63.

Kefauver, Estes. *Crime in America.* New York: Doubleday, 1951.

Kennedy, Robert F. *The Pursuit of Justice.* New York: Harper & Row, 1964.

Kenney, John P., and Dan G. Pursuit. *Police Work with Juveniles.* 3rd ed. Springfield, Ill.: Charles C. Thomas, 1965.

Kephart, William M. *Racial Factors and Urban Law Enforcement.* Philadelphia: University of Pennsylvania Press, 1957.

Key, V. O., Jr. *Politics, Parties and Pressure Groups.* New York: Crowell, 1959.

Kinsey, Alfred C. *et al. Sexual Behavior in the Human Male.* Philadelphia: Saunders, 1948.

Kirchheimer, Otto. *Political Justice.* Princeton, N.J.: Princeton University Press, 1961.

Kirkwood, William, Jr. "Delinquent Gangs: A Selected Bibliography," *International Bibliography of Crime and Delinquency.* Washington, D.C.: U.S. Department of Health, Education, and Welfare, 1966.

Kitsuse, John I. "Societal Reactions to Deviant Behavior: Problems of Theory and Method," *Social Problems,* 9 (Winter 1962), 247–256.

Kittrie, Nicholas N. *The Right to Be Different: Deviance and Enforced Therapy.* Baltimore: Johns Hopkins Press, 1971.

Klein, J., and D. Phillips. "From Hard to Soft Drugs: Temporal and Substantive Changes in Drug-Usage Among Gangs in a Working Class Community," *Journal of Health and Social Behavior,* June 9, 1968.

Klein, Malcolm W. "Violence in American Juvenile Gangs," in Mulvihill and Tumin (eds.), *Crimes of Violence,* vol. 13. National Commission on Causes and Prevention of Violence, 1969.

———. *Street Gangs and Street Walkers.* Englewood Cliffs, N.J.: Prentice-Hall, 1971.

Klonoski, James R., and Robert I. Mendelsohn (eds.). *The Politics of Local Justice.* Boston: Little, Brown, 1970.

Kneesel, Stephan H. "Philadelphia's Fighting Gangs," *Youth Leaders' Digest,* 24 (1962), 5.

Knight, John. *The Story of My Psychoanalysis.* New York: McGraw-Hill, 1950.

Knopf, T. *Youth Patrols.* Waltham, Mass.: Lemberg Center for the Study of Violence, 1969.

Knowlton, Clark S. "Violence in New Mexico: A Sociological Perspective," *California Law Review,* 58 (October 1970), 1054–1084.

Kobrin, Solomon. "The Conflict of Values in Delinquency Areas," *American Sociological Review,* 16 (October 1951), 653–661.

———."The Chicago Area Project—A 25-Year Assessment," *The Annals of the American Academy of Political and Social Science,* 322 (March 1959), 19–29.

———."Sociological Aspects of the Development of a Street-Corner Group," *American Journal of Orthopsychiatry* (October 1961).

Kolb, Lawrence. *Drug Addiction: A Medical Problem.* Springfield, Ill.: Charles C. Thomas, 1962.

———, **and A. G. DuMez.** "The Prevalence and Trend of Drug Addiction in the United States and Factors Influencing It," *Public Health Reports,* 39 (May 1924), 1179–1204.

Kovel, Joel. *White Racism: A Psychohistory.* New York: Pantheon, 1970.

Krafft-Ebing, Richard von. *Psychopathia Sexualis* (original 1886). New York: Putnam, 1965.

Kretschmer, Ernst. *Physique and Character.* London: Kegan Paul, French, Trubner, 1936.

Krislov, Samuel. *The Supreme Court and Political Freedom.* New York: Free Press, 1968.

Kvaraceus, William C. "World-Wide Story," *The UNESCO Courier,* 12 (May 1964).

———*et al. Delinquent Behavior: Culture and the Individual.* Washington, D.C.: National Education Association, 1959.

Laertius, Diogenes. *Lives of Eminent Philosophers.* Translated by R. D. Hicks. Cambridge: Harvard University Press, 1959.

LaFave, Wayne R. *Arrest: The Decision to Take a Suspect into Custody.* Boston: Little, Brown, 1965.

Lane, Roger. *Policing the City: Boston, 1822–1885.* New York: Atheneum, 1971.

Larner, Jeremy, and Ralph Tefferteller (eds.). *The Addict on the Street.* New York: Grove Press, 1965.

Lasswell, Harold D. *Politics: Who Gets What, When, How.* New York: McGraw-Hill, 1936.

———. *Psychopathology and Politics.* New York, Viking Press, 1960.

———, **and Abraham Kaplan.** *Power and Society.* New Haven: Yale University Press, 1950.

Latham, Earl. *Group Basis of Politics.* Ithaca, N.Y.: Cornell University Press, 1952.

Lefkowitz, Louis J. "New York: Infiltration of the Securities Industry," *The Annals of the American Academy of Political and Social Science,* (May 1963), 53.

Lejins, Peter. "Pragmatic Etiology of Delinquent Behavior," *Social Forces,* 29 (March 1951), 317–321.

Lemert, Edwin M. *Social Pathology.* New York: McGraw-Hill, 1951.

———. "An Isolation and Closure Theory of Naive Check Forgery," *Journal of Criminal Law, Criminology and Police Science,* 44 (September 1953), 296–307.

———. "The Behavior of the Systematic Check Forger," *Social Problems,* 6 (Fall 1958), 141–148.

———. *Human Deviance, Social Problems, and Social Control.* Englewood Cliffs, N.J.: Prentice-Hall, 1967.

Lentz, William P. "Social Status and Attitudes Toward Delinquency Control," *Journal of Research in Crime and Delinquency,* 3 (July 1966), 147–154.

Lerner, Daniel (ed.). *The Human Meaning of the Social Sciences.* Cleveland: World Publishing, 1959.

Lerner, Max. *America as a Civilization.* New York: Simon and Schuster, 1957.

Lewis, Barbara. *The Sexual Power Of Marijuana.* New York: Wyden, 1970.

Lewis, C. S. *The Abolition of Man.* New York: Macmillan, 1947.

———. "The Humanitarian Theory of Punishment," *Res Judicatae,* 6 (June 1963), 224–237.

———. *The Screwtape Letters and Screwtape Proposes a Toast.* New York: Macmillan, 1967.

Lewis, Norman. *The Honored Society.* New York: Putnam, 1964.

Lewis, Sinclair. *Main Street.* New York: Harcourt, Brace, 1920.

———. *Babbitt.* New York: Harcourt, Brace, 1922.

Leys, Wayne A. R. "Ethics in American Business and Government: The Confused Issues," *Annals of the American Academy of Political and Social Science,* 378 (July 1968), 34–44.

Liebow, Elliot. *Tally's Corner.* Boston: Little, Brown, 1967.

Lindesmith, Alfred R. *The Addict and the Law.* Bloomington: Indiana University Press, 1965.

———. *Addiction and Opiates.* Chicago: Aldine, 1968.

———, **and John H. Gagnon.** "Anomie and Drug Addiction," in Marshall B. Clinard (ed.), *Anomie and Deviant Behavior: A Discussion and Critique.* New York: Free Press, 1964.

Lipset, Seymour M. *The First New Nation.* New York: Basic Books, 1963.

Lloyd, Henry D. *Wealth Against Commonwealth.* New York: Harper, 1894.

Lofland, John. *Deviance and Identity.* Englewood Cliffs, N.J.: Prentice-Hall, 1969.

Lofton, John. *Justice and the Press.* Boston: Beacon Press, 1966.

Logan, Andy. *Against the Evidence.* New York: McCall, 1970.

Lombroso, Cesare, and Guglielmo Ferrero. *The Female Offender.* New York: Appleton, 1903.

Lorber, Judith. "Deviance as Performance: The Case of Illness," *Social Problems,* 14 (Winter 1967), 302–310.

Lorber, Richard, and Ernest Fladell. "The Generation Gap," *Life,* May 7, 1969.

Louria, Donald B. "Medical Complications Associated with Heroin Use," *The International Journal of the Addictions,* 2 (Fall 1967), 241–251.

Lowenthal, Max. *The Federal Bureau of Investigation.* New York: Sloane, 1950.

Lundhert, George *et al.* (eds.). *Trends in American Sociology.* New York: Harper & Row, 1929.

Lunt, W. E. *History of England.* New York: Harper and Brothers, 1957.

Lynd, Robert S., and Helen M. Lynd. *Middletown in Transition.* New York: Harcourt, Brace, 1937.

Maas, Peter. *The Valachi Papers.* New York: Putnam 1968.

———. "A Classic Case of Corruption," *New York,* March 16, 1970.

Machiavelli, Niccolo. *History of Florence and the Affairs of Italy.* London: M. Walter Dunne, 1901.

MacIver, Robert. *Social Causation.* New York: Ginn, 1942.

Mack, Raymond W. "The Components of Social Conflict," *Social Problems,* 12 (Spring 1965), 388–397.

Magnuson, Warren G., and Jean Carper. *The Dark Side of the Marketplace.* Englewood Cliffs, N.J.: Prentice-Hall, 1968.

Mark, Max. "What Image of Man for Political Science?" *Western Political Quarterly,* 15 (December 1962), 593–604.

Marshall, Geoffrey. *Police and Government.* London: Methuen, 1965.

Marshall, James. *Intention in Law and Society.* New York: Funk & Wagnalls, 1968.

———. *Law and Psychology in Conflict.* Garden City, N.Y.: Doubleday, 1969.

Martin, John Bartlow. *Why Did They Kill?* New York: Ballantine, 1952.

Masters, R. E. L. *Prostitution and Morality.* New York: Julian Press, 1964.

Mathis, James L. "Sexual Aspects of Heroin Addiction," *Medical Aspects of Human Sexuality,* 4 (September 1970), 98–109.

Matson, Floyd W. *The Broken Image.* New York: Braziller, 1964.

Mattick, Hans W. "Form and Content of Recent Riots," *Midway,* 9 (Summer 1968), 3–32.

Matza, David. *Delinquency and Drift.* New York: Wiley, 1964.

———. *Becoming Deviant.* Englewood Cliffs, N.J.: Prentice-Hall, 1969.

———, **and Gresham M. Sykes.** "Juvenile Delinquency and Subterranean Values," *American Sociological Review,* 26 (October 1961), 712–719.

Maurer, David. *The Big Con: A Story of the Confidence Man and the Confidence Game.* New York: Pocket, 1949.

———. *Whiz Mob: A Correlation of the Technical Argot of Pickpockets with the Behavior Pattern.* New Haven, Conn.: College and University Press, 1964.

———. "The Argot of Check Forgery," *American Speech,* 16 (1964), 243–250.

McCague, James. *The Second Rebellion: The Story of the New York City Draft Riots of 1863.* New York: Dial Press, 1968.

McCarthy, James E., and Joseph S. Barbaro. "Re-directing Teen-age Gangs," in *Reaching the Unreached.* New York: New York City Youth Board, 1952.

McConnell, Grant. *Private Power and American Democracy.* New York: Knopf, 1966.

McCord, William M. "We Ask the Wrong Questions About Crime," *The New York Times Magazine,* May 3, 1964.

McEachern, A. W. et al. *Criminal Justice System Simulation Study: Some Preliminary Projections.* Los Angeles: University of Southern California, Public Systems Research Institute, 1970.

McGuire, Louise. "Social-Work Basis for Prevention and Treatment of Delinquency and Crime: Community Factors," *Proceedings of the National Conference of Social Work,* 1936, 579–589.

McIntyre, Jennie. "Public Attitudes Toward Crime and Law Enforcement," *Annals of the American Academy of Political and Social Science,* 374 (November 1967), 34–46.

Mead, Margaret. *Coming of Age in Samoa.* New York: Morrow, 1928.

———. *And Keep Your Powder Dry: An Anthropologist Looks at America.* New York: Morrow, 1943.

Medalie, Richard J. *From Escobedo to Miranda.* Washington, D.C.: Lerner Law Books, 1966.

Menninger, Karl A. *The Human Mind.* New York: Literary Guild of America, 1930.

———. *Man Against Himself.* New York: Harcourt, Brace, 1938.

———. *The Crime of Punishment.* New York: Viking, 1968.

Mercer, Jane R. "Social System Perspective and Clinical Perspective: Frames of Reference for Understanding Career Patterns of Persons Labelled as Mentally Retarded," *Social Problems,* 13 (Summer 1966), 18–34.

Merton, Robert K. "Social Structure and Anomie," *American Sociological Review,* 3 (October 1938), 672–682.

———. *Social Theory and Social Structure.* New York: Free Press, 1968.

———, **and M. F. Ashley Montagu.** "Crime and the Anthropologist," *American Anthropologist,* 42 (August 1940), 384–408.

Messik, Mark. *The Silent Syndicate.* New York: Macmillan, 1966.

Meyerhoffs, Howard L., and Barbara G. Meyerhoffs. "Field Observations of Middle Class Gangs," *Social Forces,* 42 (March 1964).

Michael, Jerome, and Mortimer Adler. *Crime, Law and Social Science.* New York: Harcourt, Brace, 1933.

Mikuriya, Tod H. "Marijuana in Medicine, Past, Present and Future," *California Medicine,* 110 (January 1969), 34–40.

Mill, J. S. *On Liberty.* Chicago: Regnery, 1955.

Miller, Arthur R. *The Assault on Privacy: Computers, Data Banks, and Dossiers.* Ann Arbor: University of Michigan Press, 1971.

———. "Federal Data Banks and the Bill of Rights," *Computers and Automation,* 20 (October 1971), 18.

Miller, David. *Scientific Sociology: Theory and Method.* Englewood Cliffs, N.J.: Prentice-Hall, 1967.

Miller, Walter B. "The Impact of a Community Group Work Program on Delinquent Corner Groups," *Social Science Review,* 31 (December 1957).

———. "Lower Class Culture as a Generating Milieu of Gang Delinquency," *Journal of Social Issues,* 14 (April 1958), 5–19.

———. "Generalized Theoretical Orientations to the Study of Gang Delinquency," *International Newsletter in Mental Health,* 1 (October 1959), 4.

———. "The Impact of a 'Total-Community' Delinquency Control Project," *Social Problems,* 1962.

———. "The Corner Gang Boys Get Married," *Trans-action,* 1 (November 1963), 10–12.

"Violent Crimes in City Gangs," *The Annals of the American Academy of Political and Social Science,* 364 (March 1966), 96–112.

———. "Theft Behavior in City Gangs," in Malcolm Klein (ed.), *Juvenile Gangs in Context: Theory, Research and Action.* Englewood Cliffs, N.J.: Prentice-Hall, 1967.

———. "Problems of Valid Information in Urban Unemployment Studies," *Proceedings of the Social Statistics Section of the American Statistical Association,* 1969.

———. "Subculture, Social Reform and the 'Culture of Poverty,'" *Human Organization,* 30 (Summer 1971), 114.

———. *City Gangs.* New York: Wiley, in preparation.

———, H. Geertz, and H. S. G. Cutter, "Aggression in a Boys' Street Corner Group," *Psychiatry,* 24 (1961).

Millis, Harry A., and Royal E. Montgomery. *Organized Labor.* New York: McGraw-Hill, 1945.

Mills, C. Wright. "A Diagnosis of Our Moral Uneasiness," *The New York Times Magazine,* November 23, 1952.

———. *The Power Elite.* New York: Oxford University Press, 1957.

———. *The Sociological Imagination.* New York: Oxford University Press, 1959.

Mitchell, William C. "Politics as the Allocation of Values: A Critique," *Ethics,* 71 (January 1961), 79–89.

Modlin, Herbert C., and Alberto Montes. "Narcotic Addiction in Physicians," *The American Journal of Psychiatry,* 121 (October 1964), 358–365.

Morris, Albert. *Criminology.* New York: Longmans, 1935.

Morris, Norval. "Impediments to Penal Reform," *University of Chicago Law Review,* (Summer 1966), 627–656.

———, **and Gordon Hawkins.** *The Honest Politician's Guide to Crime Control.* Chicago: University of Chicago Press, 1970.

Moynihan, Daniel P. "The Private Government of Crime," *The Reporter,* July 6, 1961.

Muller, Herbert J. *The Uses of the Past.* New York: Oxford University Press, 1952.

Myers, Gustavus. *History of the Great American Fortunes.* New York: Modern Library, 1936.

Mylonas, Anastassios, and Walter C. Reckless. "Prisoners' Attitudes Toward Law and Legal Institutions," *Journal of Criminal Law, Criminology and Police Science,* 54 (December 1963), 479–485.

Myrdal, Gunnar M. *An American Dilemma.* New York: Harper, 1944.

Nadel, S. F. *Foundations of Social Anthropology.* New York: Free Press, 1951.

———. "Social Control and Self-Regulation," *Social Forces,* 31 (March 1953), 265–273.

Nader, Ralph. *Unsafe at Any Speed.* New York: Grossman, 1965.

———. "Citizen's Guide to the American Economy," *The New York Review of Books,* September 2, 1971, 14–18.

Nagel, Stuart S. "Disparities in Sentencing Procedure," *UCLA Law Review,* 14 (August 1967), 1283.

National Commission on the Causes and Prevention of Violence. *To Establish Justice, to Insure Domestic Tranquility.* New York: Bantam, 1970.

National Commission on Reform of Federal Criminal Laws. *Study Draft of a New Criminal Code.* Washington, D.C.: U.S. Government Printing Office, 1970.

Navasky, Victor S. *Kennedy Justice.* New York: Atheneum, 1971.

Newman, Donald J. "White Collar Crime," *Law and Contemporary Problems,* 23 (Autumn 1958), 735–753.

———. *Conviction: The Determination of Guilt or Innocence Without Trial.* Boston: Little, Brown, 1966.

New York Academy of Medicine, Committee on Public Health, "Report on Drug Addiction, II," *Bulletin of the New York Academy of Medicine,* 39 (July 1963), 432.

Niederhoffer, Arthur. *Behind the Shield: The Police in Urban Society.* Garden City, N.Y.: Doubleday, 1967.

———, **and Abraham S. Blumberg** (eds.). *The Ambivalent Force.* Boston: Ginn, 1970.

———, **and Alexander B. Smith.** "Power and Personality in the Courtroom," *Connecticut Law Review,* 3 (Winter 1970–1971), 233–243.

Nisbet, Robert A. *The Sociological Tradition.* New York: Basic Books, 1966.

Nobile, Philip (ed.). *The Con III Controversy: The Critics Look at The Greening of America.* New York: Pocket, 1971.

Norris, Frank. *The Octopus.* New York: Doubleday and Page, 1901.

———. *The Pit.* New York: Doubleday and Page, 1903.

Oaks, Dallin H., and Warren Lehman. *A Criminal Justice System and the Indigent: A Study of Chicago and Cook County.* Chicago: University of Chicago Press, 1968.

O'Callaghan, Sean. *Damaged Baggage: The White Slave Traffic and Narcotics Trafficking in the Americas.* New York: Roy Publishers, 1969.

O'Donnell, John A. "A Follow-up of Narcotic Addicts," *American Journal of Orthopsychiatry,* 34 (October 1964), 948–954.

———. "The Relapse Rate in Narcotic Addiction: A Critique of Follow-up Studies," in Daniel M. Wilner and Gene G. Kassebaum (eds.), *Narcotics.* New York: McGraw-Hill, 1965, pp. 226-246.

———. "Narcotic Addiction and Crime," *Social Problems,* 13 (Spring 1966), 374–385.

Ohlin, Lloyd E. *A Situational Approach to Delinquency Prevention.* Washington, D.C.: U.S. Government Printing Office, 1970.

O'Kane, James M. "Ethnic Mobility and the Lower-Income Negro," *Social Problems* (Winter 1969), 302–311.

Ollendorf, Robert. *The Juvenile Homosexual Experience and Its Effect on Adult Sexuality.* New York: Julian Press, 1966.

Opler, Morris, "Living Patterns in the U.S.A.," in *Patterns for Modern Living.* Chicago: The Delphian Society, 1950, p. 567.

Overholser, Winfred. "Major Principles of Forensic Psychiatry," in S. Arieti et al. (eds.), *American Handbook of Psychiatry.* New York: Basic Books, 1959, 1887–1901.

Packer, Herbert L. *The Limits of the Criminal Sanction.* Stanford, Calif.: Stanford University Press, 1968.

Polier, Justine W. *The Rule of Law and the Role of Psychiatry.* Baltimore: Johns Hopkins Press, 1968.

Parker, Tony, and Robert Allerton. *The Courage of His Convictions.* New York: Norton, 1962.

Parsons, Talcott. *The Structure of Social Action.* New York: Free Press, 1949.

———. "The Distribution of Power in American Society," *World Politics,* 10 (October 1957), 123–143.

Pearlstein, Stanley. *Psychiatry, the Law and Mental Health.* Dobbs Ferry, N.Y.: Oceana Publications, 1967.

Pepper, Claude. *Marihuana: First Report by the Select Committee on Crime.* Washington, D.C: U.S. Government Printing Office, 1970.

Perrow, Charles, "The Sociological Perspective and Political Pluralism," *Social Research,* 31 (Winter 1964), 411–422.

Peterson, Virgil. "Fighting Nationally Organized Crime," *Vital Speeches,* October 15, 1958, 150.

Piliavin, Irving, and Scott Briar. "Police Encounters with Juveniles," *American Journal of Sociology,* 70 (September 1964), 206–214.

Ploscowe, Morris. *Sex and the Law.* Englewood Cliffs, N.J.: Prentice-Hall, 1951.

Polsky, Ned. *Hustlers, Beats and Others.* Garden City, N.Y.: Doubleday, 1969.

Poster, William. "'Twas a Dark Night in Brownsville," *Commentary,* 9 (May 1950), 464.

Poston, Richard W. *The Gang and the Establishment.* New York: Harper & Row, 1971.

Pound, Roscoe. *An Introduction to the Philosophy of Law.* New Haven: Yale University Press, 1922.

Powers, Thomas. "The Government Is Watching," *Atlantic Monthly,* 230 (October 1972), 51–63.

President's Commission on Law Enforcement and Administration of Justice. *The Challenge of Crime in a Free Society.* Washington, D.C.: U.S. Government Printing Office, 1967.

———. *Task Force Report: Assessment of Crime.* Washington, D.C.: U.S. Government Printing Office, 1967.

———. *Task Force Report: Corrections.* Washington, D.C.: U.S. Government Printing Office, 1967.

———. *Task Force Report: The Courts.* Washington, D.C.: U.S. Government Printing Office, 1967.

———. *Task Force Report: Crime and Its Impact—An Assessment.* Washington, D.C.: U.S. Government Printing Office, 1967.

———. *Task Force Report: Drunkenness.* Washington, D.C.: U.S. Government Printing Office, 1967.

———. *Task Force Report: Juvenile Delinquency and Youth Crime.* Washington, D.C.: U.S. Government Printing Office, 1967.

———. *Task Force Report: Narcotics and Drug Abuse.* Washington, D.C.: U.S. Government Printing Office, 1967.

———. *Task Force Report: Organized Crime.* Washington, D.C.: U.S. Government Printing Office, 1967.

———. *Task Force Report: The Police.* Washington, D.C.: U.S. Government Printing Office, 1967.

———. *Task Force Report: Science and Technology.* Washington, D.C.: U.S. Government Printing Office, 1967.

Puttkammer, Ernest W. *Administration of Criminal Law.* Chicago: University of Chicago Press, 1963.

Quinney, Richard. "Crime in Political Perspective," *American Behavioral Scientist,* 8 (December 1964), 19–22.

———. "The Study of White Collar Crime: Toward a Reorientation in Theory and Research," *Journal of Criminal Law, Criminology and Police Science,* 55 (June 1964), 208–214.

———. "A Conception of Man and Society for Criminology," *Sociological Quarterly,* 6 (Spring 1965), 119–127.

———. "Is Criminal Behavior Deviant Behavior?" *British Journal of Criminology,* 5 (April 1965), 132–142.

———, (ed.). *Crime and Justice in Society.* Boston: Little, Brown, 1969.

———. *The Problem of Crime.* New York: Dodd, Mead, 1970.

———. *The Social Reality of Crime.* Boston: Little, Brown, 1970.

Rabb, Selwyn. *Justice in the Back Room.* Cleveland: World Publishing, 1967.

Radzinowicz, Leon. *A History of English Criminal Law and Its Administration from 1750.* New York: Barnes & Noble, 1968.

Rainwater, Lee. "Post-1984 America," *Society,* 9 (February 1972), 18–27.

Ralph, C. H. (ed.). *The Police and the Public.* London: Heinemann, 1962.

Ray, Isaac. *A Treatise on the Medical Jurisprudence of Insanity.* Winfred Overholser (ed.). Cambridge: Harvard University Press, 1962.

Reckless, Walter C. *Criminal Behavior.* New York: McGraw-Hill, 1940.

Reevy, William R. "Child Sexuality," in Albert Ellis and Albert Abarbanel (eds.), *The Encyclopedia of Sexual Behavior.* Englewood Cliffs, N.J.: Hawthorn, 1961.

Reich, Charles A. *The Greening of America.* New York: Random House, 1970.

Reiss, Albert J., Jr. "The Marginal Status of the Adolescent," in John H. Gagnon and William Simon (eds.), *Sexual Deviance.* New York: Harper & Row, 1967.

———. *The Police and the Public.* New Haven: Yale University Press, 1971.

Reith, Charles. *A New Study of Police History.* London: Oliver and Boyd, 1956.

———. *The Blind Eye of History.* London: Faber and Faber, 1957.

Richards, Lourie, and Eleanor Carroll. "Illicit Drug Use and Addiction in the United States," *Public Health Reports,* 85 (December 1970), 1035–1041.

Richardson, James. *The New York Police: Colonial Times to 1901.* New York: Oxford University Press, 1970.

Ridgeway, James. *The Politics of Ecology.* New York: Dutton, 1970.

Riesman, David et al. *The Lonely Crowd.* New Haven: Yale University Press, 1950.

Rights in Conflict: A Report to the National Commission on the Causes and Prevention of Violence. New York: New American Library, 1968.

Rodell, Fred. "Our Unlovable Sex Laws," in John H. Gagnon and William Simon (eds.), *The Sexual Scene.* Chicago: Aldine, 1970.

Roebuck, Julian B., and Robert B. Hunter. "Medical Quackery as Deviant Behavior," *Criminology,* 8 (May 1970), 46–62.

Roeburt, John. *Al Capone.* New York: Pyramid, 1959.

Rogers, Everett M. *Diffusion of Innovations.* New York: Free Press, 1962.

Rooney, Elizabeth A., and Don C. Gibbons. "Social Reactions to 'Crimes Without Victims,' " *Social Problems,* 13 (Spring 1966), 400–410.

Roosevelt, Theodore. *The Roosevelt Policy,* vol. II. New York: Current Literature, 1908.

Rose, Arnold M. *Libel and Academic Freedom: A Lawsuit Against Political Extremists.* Minneapolis: University of Minnesota Press, 1968.

Rosenberg, Bernard, and Harry Silverstein. *The Varieties of Delinquent Experience.* Waltham, Mass.: Blaisdell, 1969.

Ross, Edward A. *Sin and Society.* Boston: Houghton Mifflin, 1907.

Roszak, Theodore. *The Making of A Counter Culture: Reflections on the Technocratic Society and Its Youthful Opposition.* Garden City, N.Y.: Doubleday, 1969.

Rourke, Francis B. "Law Enforcement Through Publicity," *University of Chicago Law Review,* 24 (Winter 1967), 225–255.

Rovere, Richard H. *Senator Joe McCarthy.* New York: World Publishing, 1960.

Royal Commission on the Police. *Final Report.* Cmnd. 1728. London: Her Majesty's Stationery Office, 1962.

Rubin, Jerry. *Do It! Scenarios of the Revolution.* New York: Simon and Schuster, 1970.

Rubin S. *Psychiatry and Criminal Law.* Dobbs Ferry, N.Y.: Oceana, 1965.

Rusche, George, and Otto Kirchheimer. *Punishment and Social Structure.* New York: University Press, 1939.

Rush, Benjamin. "Lecture on the Medical Jurisprudence of the Mind," in G. W. Corner (ed.), *The Autobiography of Benjamin Rush.* Princeton, N.J.: Princeton University Press, 1948.

———. *Medical Inquiries and Observations Upon the Diseases of the Mind.* New York: Hafner, 1962.

Russell, Donald Hayes. "Indecent Proposals and the Law," *Medical Aspects of Human Sexuality,* 4 (June 1970), 127–141.

Sachar, E. J. "Behavioral Science and the Criminal Law," *Scientific American,* 209 (November 1963), 39–45.

Sagarin, Edward. "Sex, Law, and the Changing Society," *Medical Aspects of Human Sexuality,* 4 (October 1970), 103–107.

———, and Donal E. J. MacNamara. "The Problem of Entrapment," *Crime and Delinquency*, 16 (October 1970), 363–378.

Salerno, Ralph, and Ralph Tompkins. *The Crime Confederation*. Garden City, N.Y.: Doubleday, 1969.

Salisbury, Harrison E. *900 Days: The Siege of Leningrad*. New York: Avon, 1969.

Salmes, Alwyn. *The English Policeman, 1871–1935*. London: George Allen and Unwin, 1935.

Schermerhorn, Richard A. "Man the Unfinished," *Sociological Quarterly*, 4 (Winter 1963), 5–17.

Schilling, Warner, Paul Y. Hammond, and Glenn H. Snyder. *Strategy Politics and Defense*. New York: Columbia University Press, 1962.

Schneir, Walter, and Miriam Schneir. *Invitation to an Inquest*. New York: Doubleday, 1965.

Schrag, Clarence. "Elements of Theoretical Analysis in Sociology," in Llewellyn Gross (ed.), *Sociological Theory: Inquiries and Paradigms*. New York: Harper & Row, 1967, pp. 242–244.

———. *Crime and Justice: American Style*. Washington, D.C.: National Institute of Mental Health, U.S. Government Printing Office, 1971.

Schuessler, Karl F., and Donald R. Cressey. "Personality Characteristics of Criminals," *American Journal of Sociology*, 55 (March 1950), 476–484.

Schur, Edwin M. "Sociological Analysis of Confidence Swindling," *Journal of Criminal Law, Criminology and Police Science*, 48 (September-October 1957), 296–304.

———. "Theory, Planning, and Pathology," *Social Problems*, 6 (Winter 1958-1959), 227.

———. *Crimes Without Victims: Deviant Behavior and Public Policy*. Englewood Cliffs, N.J.: Prentice-Hall, 1965.

———. *Law and Society: A Sociological View*. New York: Random House, 1968.

———. *Our Criminal Society: The Social and Legal Sources*. Englewood Cliffs, N.J.: Prentice-Hall, 1969.

———. *Labeling Deviant Behavior*. New York: Harper & Row, 1971.

Schutz, Alfred. *The Problem of Social Reality: Collected Papers, I*. The Hague: Martinus Nijhoff, 1962.

———. "Concept and Theory Formation in the Social Sciences," in Maurice Nathanson (ed.), *Philosophy of the Social Sciences*. New York: Random House, 1963.

Scott, Peter. "Gangs and Delinquent Groups in London," *British Journal of Delinquency*, 7 (July 1956).

Seeman, Melvin. "On the Meaning of Alienation," *American Sociological Review*, 24 (December 1959), 783–791.

Sellin, Thorsten. *Culture Conflict and Crime.* New York: Social Science Research Council, 1938.

———. "The Significance of Records of Crime," *Law Quarterly Review,* 67 (1951), 496–504.

———, (ed.). *Capital Punishment.* New York: Harper & Row, 1967.

Shaw, Clifford R. *Delinquency Areas.* Chicago: University of Chicago Press, 1929.

Shaw, George Bernard. "Preface," to Sidney Webb and Beatrice Webb, *English Prisons Under Local Government.* New York: Longmans, Green, 1922.

Sheldon, William H. *The Varieties of Delinquent Youth.* New York: Harper, 1949.

Shibutani, Tamotsu. *Society and Personality: An Interactionist Approach to Social Psychology.* Englewood Cliffs, N.J.: Prentice-Hall, 1961.

Shils, Edward A. "Social Inquiry and the Autonomy of the Individual," in Daniel Lerner (ed.), *The Human Meaning of the Social Sciences.* New York: World Publishing, 1959.

Shoolbred, Claude F. *The Administration of Criminal Justice in England and Wales.* New York: Pergamon, 1966.

Short, James, Jr. (ed.), *Gang Delinquency and Delinquent Subcultures.* New York: Harper & Row, 1968.

———, **and Frank L. Strodtbeck.** *Group Process and Gang Delinquency.* Chicago: University of Chicago Press, 1965.

Shulman, Harry M. "The Measurement of Crime in the United States," *Journal of Criminal Law, Criminology and Police Science,* 57 (December 1966), 483–492.

Sigfried, André. *America Comes of Age: French Analysis.* New York: Harcourt, Brace, 1927.

Silver, Isidore. *The Challenge of Crime in a Free Society.* New York: Avon Books, 1968.

Simmel, Georg. *The Sociology of Georg Simmel.* Translated by Kurt H. Wolff. New York: Free Press, 1950.

———. *Conflict.* Translated by Kurt H. Wolff. New York: Free Press, 1955.

Simon, Rita. *The Jury and the Plea of Insanity.* Boston: Little, Brown, 1966.

——— (ed.). *The Sociology of Law: Interdisciplinary Readings.* San Francisco: Chandler, 1968.

Sinclair, Andrew. *Era of Excess: A Social History of the Prohibition Movement.* New York: Harper & Row, 1964.

Sinclair, Upton. *The Jungle.* New York: Doubleday and Page, 1906.

Singer, Max. "The Vitality of Mythical Numbers," *The Public Interest,* 23 (Spring 1971), 3–9.

Skolnick, Jerome. *Justice Without Trial: Law Enforcement in Democratic Society.* New York: Wiley, 1966.

———. "Coercion to Virtue," *Southern California Law Review*, 41 (1968), 588–641.

Slater, Philip. *The Pursuit of Loneliness.* Boston: Beacon Press, 1970.

Sloan, Alfred P., and Boyden Sparks. *Adventures of a White-Collar Man.* New York: Doubleday, 1941.

Smith, Alexander B., and Arthur Niederhoffer. *Police-Community Relations Programs: A Study in Depth.* Washington, D.C.: U.S. Government Printing Office, 1970.

———, **and Harriet Pollack.** *Crime and Justice in a Mass Society.* Waltham, Mass.: Xerox Publishing Co., 1972.

Smith, Alson J. *Syndicate City.* Chicago: Regnery, 1954.

Smith, Bradford. *Why We Behave Like Americans.* Philadelphia: Lippincott, 1957.

Smith, Bruce. *The New York Police Survey.* New York: Institute of Public Administration, 1952.

———. *Police Systems in the United States.* 2nd rev. ed. New York: Harper & Row, 1960.

Smith, Ralph L. *The Tarnished Badge.* New York: Crowell, 1965.

Smith, Roger. "Status Politics and the Image of the Addict," *Issues in Criminology*, 2 (Fall 1966), 157–175.

———. "The World of the Haight Ashbury Speed Freak," *Journal of Psychedelic Drugs*, 2 (Winter 1968–1969), 185–186.

Sowle, Claude R. (ed.). *Police Power and Individual Freedom.* Chicago: Aldine, 1962.

Spiller, Bertram. "Delinquency and Middle-Class Goals," *Journal of Criminal Law, Criminology and Police Science*, 56 (December 1965), 463–478.

Spivak, Gordon B. "Antitrust Enforcement in the United States: A Primer," *Connecticut Bar Journal*, 37 (September 1963), 382.

Staude, John R., and Max Scheler. *An Intellectual Portrait.* New York: Free Press, 1967.

Stedman, Murray S. "Pressure Group and the American Tradition," *Annals of the American Academy of Political and Social Science*, 319 (September 1958), 123–219.

Steffens, Lincoln. *The Shame of the Cities.* New York: McClure, Phillips, 1904.

———. *The Autobiography of Lincoln Steffens.* New York: Harcourt, Brace, 1931.

Stern, Philip M. *The Great Treasury Raid.* New York: Random House, 1964.

Stevens, Shane. "The 'Rat Packs' of New York," *The New York Times Magazine*, November 28, 1971.

Stinchcombe, Arthur L. "Institutions of Privacy in the Determination of Police Administrative Practice," *American Journal of Sociology*, 69 (September 1963), 150–160.

St. John-Stevas, Norman. *Life, Death and the Law.* Bloomington: Indiana University Press, 1961.

Sturup, Georg K. *Treating the Untreatable: Chronic Criminals at Herstedvester.* Baltimore: Johns Hopkins Press, 1968.

Sudnow, David. "Normal Crimes: Sociological Features of the Penal Code in a Public Defender Office," *Social Problems,* 2 (Winter 1965), 255–276.

Sutherland, Edwin H. "White-Collar Criminality," *American Sociological Review,* 5 (February 1940), 1–12.

— — —. "Is 'White-Collar Crime' Crime?" *American Sociological Review,* 10 (April 1945), 132–139.

— — —. *White Collar Crime.* New York: Dryden, 1949.

— — —. "The Diffusion of Sexual Psychopath Laws," *American Journal of Sociology,* 56 (September 1950), 142–148.

— — —. "The Sexual Psychopath Law," *Journal of Criminal Law, Criminology and Police Science,* 40 (January-February 1950), 543–554.

— — —. "Crime of Corporations," in Albert Cohen, Alfred Lindesmith and Karl Schuessler (eds.), *The Sutherland Papers.* Bloomington: Indiana University Press, 1956, pp. 78–96.

Sutter, Alan G. "The World of the Righteous Dope Fiend," *Issues in Criminology,* 2 (Fall 1966), 194.

— — —. "Worlds of Drug Use on the Street Scene," in Donald R. Cressey and David A. Ward (eds.), *Delinquency, Crime and Social Process.* New York: Harper & Row, 1969.

Suttles, Gerald. *The Social Order of the Slum: Ethnicity and Territory in the Inner City.* Chicago: University of Chicago Press, 1968.

Sykes, Gresham, and Thomas E. Drabek. *Law and the Lawless.* New York: Random House, 1969.

— — —, **and David Matza.** "Techniques of Neutralization: A Theory of Delinquency," *American Sociological Review,* 22 (December 1957), 664–670.

Szasz, Thomas E. *The Myth of Mental Illness.* New York: Harper & Row, 1961.

— — —. *Law, Liberty and Psychiatry: An Inquiry into the Social Uses of Mental Health Practices.* New York: Macmillan, 1963.

— — —. *Psychiatric Justice.* New York: Macmillan, 1965.

— — —. "Justice in the Therapeutic State," *Indiana Legal Forum,* 3 (Fall 1969), 19–33.

— — —. *Ideology and Insanity.* Garden City, N.Y.: Doubleday, 1970.

Szulc, Tad. "George Jackson Radicalizes the Brothers in Soledad and San Quentin," *The New York Times Magazine,* August 1, 1971.

Taft, Donald R. *Criminology.* 3rd ed. New York: Macmillan, 1956.

Taft, Philip. "Violence in American Labor Disputes," *Annals of the American Academy of Political and Social Science* (March 1966), 127–140.

Tannenbaum, Frank. *Crime and the Community.* New York: Columbia University Press, 1938.

Tappan, Paul W. "Who is the Criminal?" *American Sociological Review,* 12 (February 1947), 96–102.

Tarbell, Ida M. *The History of the Standard Oil Company.* New York: Macmillan, 1904.

Tarde, Gabriel. *Penal Philosophy.* Boston: Little, Brown, 1912.

Tawney, R. H. *The Acquisitive Society.* New York: Harcourt, Brace, 1920.

Terry, Charles E., and Mildred Pellens. *The Opium Problem.* New York: Bureau of Social Hygiene, 1928.

Thompson, Craig. *The Police State.* New York: Dutton, 1950.

Thrasher, Frederick. *The Gang.* Chicago: University of Chicago Press, 1927.

Tiffany, Lawrence P., Donald M. McIntyre, Jr., and David L. Rotenberg. *Detection of Crime: Stopping and Questioning, Search and Seizure, Encouragement and Entrapment.* Boston: Little, Brown, 1967.

Tobias, John J. *Urban Crime in Victorian England.* New York: Schocken, 1972.

Tocqueville, Alexis de. *L'Ancien Régime.* Translated by M. W. Patterson. Oxford, England: Basil Blackwell, 1949.

———. *The Old Regime and the French Revolution.* Translated by Stuart Gilbert. Garden City, N.Y.: Doubleday, 1955.

Toffler, Alvin. *Future Shock.* New York: Random House, 1970.

Tompkins, Dorothy C. *Juvenile Gangs and Street Groups—A Bibliography.* Berkeley: Institute of Governmental Studies, University of California, 1966.

———. *White Collar Crime—A Bibliography.* Berkeley: Institute of Governmental Studies, University of California, 1967.

Traver, Robert. *Anatomy of a Murder.* New York: St. Martin's Press, 1958.

Trebach, Arnold S. *The Rationing of Justice.* New Brunswick, N.J.: Rutgers University Press, 1964.

Truman, David. *The Governmental Process.* New York: Knopf, 1951.

Tufts, James Hayden. *America's Social Morality.* New York: Holt, 1933.

Turk, Austin T. "Conflict and Criminality," *American Sociological Review,* 31 (June 1966), 338–352.

———. *Criminality and the Legal Order.* Chicago: Rand McNally, 1969.

———. *Legal Sanctioning and Social Control.* Washington, D.C.: National Institute of Mental Health, U.S. Government Printing Office, 1972.

Turkus, Burton, and Sid Feder. *Murder, Inc.* New York: Farrar, Straus, 1951.

Turner, Frederick Jackson. "The Significance of the Frontier in American History," in Henry Steele Commager (ed.), *Living Ideas in America.* New York: Harper, 1951, pp. 73–80.

Turner, Henry A. "How Pressure Groups Operate," *Annals of the American Academy of Political and Social Science,* 319 (September 1958), 63–72.

Turner, James S. *The Chemical Feast.* New York: Grossman, 1970.

Turner, William. *The Police Establishment.* New York: Putnam, 1968.

Tyler, Gus. (ed.). *Organized Crime in America: A Book of Readings.* Ann Arbor: University of Michigan Press, 1962.

— — —. "An Interdisciplinary Attack on Organized Crime," *Annals of the American Academy of Political and Social Science,* 349 (May 1963), 109–110.

United Nations, Department of Economic and Social Affairs. *Study of Traffic in Persons and Prostitution.* New York: 1959.

Vogel, Victor H. *et al.* "Present Status of Narcotic Addiction," *The Journal of the American Medical Association,* 138 (December 1948), 1019–1026.

Vold, George G. *Theoretical Criminology.* New York: Oxford University Press, 1958.

Volkman, Arthur P. "A Matched Group Personality Comparison of Delinquent and Nondelinquent Juveniles," *Social Problems,* 6 (Winter 1959), 238–245.

Vollmer, August. *The Police and Modern Society.* Berkeley: University of California Press, 1936.

Vorenberg, James. "The War on Crime: The First Five Years," *Atlantic Monthly,* May, 1972, 63–69.

Waldorf, Dan. "Social Control in Therapeutic Communities in the Treatment of Drug Addicts," *The International Journal of the Addictions,* 6 (March 1971), 29–43.

Walker, Daniel. *Rights in Conflict: A Report to the National Commission on the Causes and Prevention of Violence.* New York: New American Library, 1968.

Walker, Nigel. *Crime and Insanity in England.* Edinburgh, Scotland: Edinburgh University Press, 1968.

Wallerstein, James S., and Clement Wyle, "Our Law-Abiding Law-Breakers," *Probation* (April 1947), 107–112.

Ward, Lester F. *Applied Sociology.* Boston: Ginn, 1906.

Watson, Nelson A., and James W. Sterling. *Police and Their Opinions.* Washington, D.C.: International Association of Chiefs of Police, 1969.

Weber, Max. *From Max Weber: Essays in Sociology.* Translated by Hans H. Gerth and C. Wright Mills. New York: Oxford University Press, 1946.

— — —. *The Theory of Social and Economic Organization.* Translated by A. M. Henderson and Talcott Parsons. New York: Free Press, 1947.

Weihofen, Henry. *Insanity as a Defense in Criminal Law.* New York: Commonwealth Fund, 1963.

Weingarten, Gene. "East Bronx Story: Return of the Street Gangs," *New York,* March 27, 1972.

Westin, Alan F. *Privacy and Freedom.* New York: Atheneum, 1967.

— — —. "Civil Liberties and Computerized Data Systems," in Martin Greenberger (ed.), *Computers, Communications and the Public Interest.* Baltimore: Johns Hopkins Press, 1971.

———. *Information Technology in a Democracy.* Cambridge: Harvard University Press, 1971.

———, **and Michael A. Baker.** *Databanks in a Free Society.* New York: Quadrangle, 1972.

Westley, William A. "Violence and the Police," *American Journal of Sociology,* 59 (July 1953), 34–41.

———. *Violence and the Police.* Cambridge: The M.I.T. Press, 1970.

Wheeler, Stanton (ed.). *On Record: Files and Dossiers in American Life.* New York: Russell Sage Foundation, 1969.

———, **and Leonard S. Cottrell, Jr.** *Juvenile Delinquency: Its Prevention and Control.* New York: Russell Sage Foundation, 1966.

Whitaker, Ben. *The Police.* Middlesex, England: Penguin Books, 1964.

Whyte, William Foote. *Street Corner Society.* Chicago: University of Chicago Press, 1943.

Wigmore, John H. *Wigmore on Evidence.* 3rd ed. Boston: Little, Brown, 1940.

Wikler, Abraham. "Drug Addiction: Organic and Psychological Aspects," *International Encyclopedia of the Social Sciences.* New York: Macmillan, 1968.

Williams, Edward Bennett. *One Man's Freedom.* New York: Atheneum, 1962.

Williams, Robin M., Jr. *American Society: A Sociological Interpretation.* 3rd ed. New York: Knopf, 1970.

Willoughby, William R. *The St. Lawrence Waterway: A Study in Politics and Diplomacy.* Madison: University of Wisconsin Press, 1961.

Wilmer, D., R. Rosenfeld, et al. "Heroin Use and Street Gangs," *Journal of Criminal Law, Criminology and Police Science,* 48 (1957).

Wilson, James Q. *Varieties of Police Behavior: The Management of Law and Order in Eight Communities.* New York: Atheneum, 1971.

Wilson, O. W. *Police Administration.* 2nd ed. New York: McGraw-Hill, 1963.

Winick, Charles. "Physician Narcotic Addicts," *Social Problems,* 9 (Fall 1961), 174–186.

———. "Prostitutes' Clients' Perceptions of Prostitutes and of Themselves," *International Journal of Social Psychiatry,* 8 (1962), 289–297.

———, **and Paul M. Kinsie.** *The Lively Commerce: Prostitution in the United States.* Chicago: Quadrangle, 1971.

Wittner, Dale. "Log Jam in Our Courts," *Life,* 69 (August 1970), 18–26.

Wortzel, Robert K. "An Overview of Organized Crime," *The Annals of the American Academy of Political and Social Science,* 349 (May 1963), 5–6.

Wolfgang, Marvin E. "Violence, U.S.A.: Riots and Crime," *Crime and Delinquency,* 14 (October 1968), 289–305.

———, **and Frank Ferracuti.** *The Subculture of Violence: Towards an Integrated Theory in Criminology.* New York: Barnes & Noble, 1967.

———, **Leonard Savitz, and Norman Johnson** (eds.). *The Sociology of Crime and Delinquency.* 2nd ed. New York: Wiley, 1970.

Wood, Arthur Lewis. *Criminal Lawyer.* New Haven, Conn.: College and University Press, 1967.

Wrong, Dennis H. "The Oversocialized Conception of Man in Modern Sociology," *American Sociological Review,* 26 (April 1961), 183–193.

Yablonsky, Lewis. "The Delinquent Gang as a Near Group," *Social Problems,* 7 (Fall 1959).

———. *Synanon: The Tunnel Back.* Baltimore: Penguin, 1965.

———. *The Violent Gang.* New York: Macmillan, 1963.

Young, James H. *The Medical Messiahs.* Princeton, N.J.: Princeton University Press, 1967.

Znaniecki, Florian. *Social Actions.* New York: Farrar and Rinehart, 1936.

INDEX

A NOTE ON THE TYPE

The text of this book has been set in a computer typeface, equivalent to the linotype "Baskerville." The face is a facsimile reproduction of types cast from molds made for John Baskerville (1706-75) from his designs. The punches for the revived Linotype Baskerville were cut under the supervision of the English printer George W. Jones. John Baskerville's original face was one of the forerunners of the type-style known as "modern face" to printers—a "modern" of the period A.D. 1800.

Manufactured in the United States of America.

Composed by Volt Information Sciences, Inc.
Printed and bound by Halliday Lithograph Corp., West Hanover, Mass.